J. Ranade Workstation Series

BAMBARA/ALLEN • *PowerBuilder: A Guide for Developing Client / Server Applications,* 0-07-005413-4

CHAKRAVARTY • *Power RISC System / 6000: Concepts, Facilities, and Architecture,* 0-07-011047-6

CHAKRAVARTY, CANNON • *PowerPC: Concepts, Architecture, and Design,* 0-07-011192-8

DEROEST • *AIX for RS / 6000: System and Administration Guide,* 0-07-036439-7

GRAHAM • *Solaris 2.X: Internals & Architecture,* 0-07-911876-3

HENRY, GRAHAM • *Solaris 2.X System Administrator's Guide,* 0-07-029368-6

JOHNSTON • *OS / 2 Connectivity & Networking: A Guide to Communication Manager / 2,* 0-07-032696-7

JOHNSTON • *OS / 2 Productivity Tool Kit,* 0-07-912029-6

LAMB • *MicroFocus Workbench and Toolset Developer's Guide,* 0-07-036123-3

LEININGER • *AIX / 6000 Developer's Tool Kit,* 0-07-911992-1

LEININGER • *Solaris Developer's Tool Kit,* 0-07-911851-8

LEININGER • *UNIX Developer's Tool Kit,* 0-07-911646-9

LOCKHART • *OSF DCE: Guide to Developing Distributed Applications,* 0-07-911481-4

PETERSON • *DCE: A Guide to Developing Portable Applications,* 0-07-911801-1

RANADE, ZAMIR • *C++ Primer for C Programmers, Second Edition,* 0-07-051487-9

SANCHEZ, CANTON • *Graphics Programming Solutions,* 0-07-911464-4

SANCHEZ, CANTON • *High Resolution Video Graphics,* 0-07-911646-9

SANCHEZ, CANTON • *PC Programmer's Handbook, 2 / e,* 0-07-054948-6

WALKER, SCHWALLER • *CPI-C Programming in C: An Application Developer's Guide to APPC,* 0-07-911733-3

WIGGINS • *The Internet for Everyone: A Guide for Users and Providers,* 0-07-067019-8

CORBA

A Guide to the
Common Object Request Broker Architecture

Ron Ben-Natan

McGraw-Hill

New York   San Francisco   Washington, D.C.   Auckland   Bogotá
Caracas   Lisbon   London   Madrid   Mexico City   Milan
Montreal   New Delhi   San Juan   Singapore
Sydney   Tokyo   Toronto

Library of Congress Cataloging-in-Publication Data

Ben-Natan, Ron.
    CORBA : a guide to common object request broker architecture /
Ron Ben-Natan.
        p.   cm.
    Includes index.
    ISBN 0-07-005427-4 (pbk.)
    1. Object-oriented programming (Computer science)   2. Computer
architecture.   I. Title.
    QA76.64.B44   1995
    005.7—dc20   95-18634
                                                      CIP

McGraw-Hill

A Division of The McGraw·Hill Companies

    3 4 5 6 7 8 9 0   BKP/BKP   9 0 9 8 7 6

ISBN 0-07-005427-4

*The sponsoring editor for this book was Jerry Papke, the editing super-
visor was Caroline R. Levine, and the production supervisor was
Pamela A. Pelton. This book was set in Century Schoolbook by Priscilla
Beer of McGraw-Hill's Professional Book Group composition unit.
Printed and bound by Quebecor/Book Press.*

McGraw-Hill books are available at special quantity discounts to use
as premiums and sales promotions, or for use in corporate training programs. For more information, please write to the Director of Special
Sales, McGraw-Hill, Inc., 11 West 19th Street, New York, NY 10011. Or
contact your local bookstore.

 This book is printed on acid-free paper containing a minimum of
10% postconsumer waste.

Trademarks

Digital, Open VMS AXP, DECnet, VMS, VAX, ULTRIX, and ObjectBroker are trademarks of Digital Equipment Corporation.

Macintosh is a registered trademark and Apple is a trademark of Apple Computer, Inc.

IBM, OS/2, and AIX are registered trademarks and SOMObjects and System Object Model are trademarks of International Business Machines Corporation.

HP-UX is a registered trademark and Hewlett-Packard, HP Distributed Smalltalk, and HP are trademarks of Hewlett-Packard Company.

X/Open and the "X" symbol are trademarks of X/Open Company Limited.

Objective-C is a trademark of Stepstone.

Encina is a trademark and Transarc is a registered trademark of Transarc Corporation.

Sun, Sun Microsystems, NFS, and Solaris are registered trademarks and SunOS, SunSoft, ToolTalk, ONC, ONC+, and SPARCStation are trademarks of Sun Microsystems, Inc.

Microsoft, Visual Basic, MS, MS-DOS, and Windows NT are registered trademarks and Windows, Word, and Excel are trademarks of Microsoft Corporation.

System V is a registered trademark of UNIX Systems Laboratories.

UNIX is a registered trademark licensed exclusively through X/Open Company Ltd.

Open Software Foundation and DCE are trademarks and OSF, OSF/1, and Motif are registered trademarks of Open Software Foundation, Inc.

Novell is a registered trademark of Novell, Inc.

X Window System and XII are products of the Massachusetts Institute of Technology.

Postscript is a trademark of Adobe Systems.

Taligent is a registered trademark of Taligent, Inc.

ParcPlace and VisualWorks are registered trademarks and Objectworks\Smalltalk and Smalltalk-80 are trademarks of ParcPlace Systems, Inc.

HyperDesk is a registered trademark of HyperDesk Corporation.

ORB, Object Request Broker, OMG IDL, COSS, and CORBA are trademarks and OMG and Object Management are registered trademarks of the Object Management Group, Inc.

All other names of products and services mentioned may be trademarks or registered trademarks of their respective holders.

"…and all that Sarah saith onto thee, harken onto her voice…"
(Genesis 21)
To Rinat. My wife, my best friend, my guiding light.

Contents

Foreword

To fulfill the promise of truly distributed computing, interoperability must mean a world where *users* are free to make the choices—not the vendors. What is best-of-breed? Is it the set of software components you the software developer or user believe will best fit your business needs, regardless of who provides the component? Is it to be able to plug these components together and have them working together "out-of-the-box" as if they had come from a single source?

Some call this "plug-and-play." Some vendors have given us true plug-and-play within their own product environment (e.g., old Apple), or within a portion of the user environment (e.g., Windows). But true interoperability goes even a step further. Indeed, interoperability gives us the ability to replace and reconfigure the components at will. This is the reason for the existence of the Object Management Group, now the world's largest software consortium. The interoperation between software "parts" can be achieved only through wholesale agreements on the interfaces between them. CORBA, and Object Request Brokers in general, provide the model for this interaction and will become the implementation of client/server computing for years to come.

True interoperability is a tall order. And in a distributed environment it is even harder to pull off. It means developing an application with a "single" interface that is known and standardized throughout a network of physically disparate, heterogeneous computing platforms, operating systems, and communications transports. It must guarantee that an application written on machine A can converse and integrate with an application on machine B where both applications were independently developed. Can we expect our suppliers to hand it to us on a silver platter?

The world changed radically over the past 15 years, in large part due to the PC revolution. Here was the best example that may ever be known of an "open system"—a well-understood platform available from many different suppliers, and that nobody controlled (to IBM's later chagrin). It was an accident, but provided a ready market for tens of thousands of inexpensive shrink-wrapped applications.

This is the dirty little secret that gives the platform vendors nightmares: Everything in this industry is now driven downward by applications, not upward by the platform vendor (with a few notable exceptions, of course).

Add one more ingredient to the interoperability equation: If you're a platform vendor, your platform needs to be interoperable with the applications the customer uses or wants to buy—unless you have the market clout to define a new platform.

Let's face reality. No government, vendor, or really rich person can today mandate yet another data communications network as the "highway" of the future. Too many already exist. The same goes for systems management, operating systems, data management, and a slew of other commercially backed and government accredited standards. This book describes an architecture we believe will become the basis for the future of distributed computing systems. Who better than an actual "user" of the technology to describe the potential.

There is one area still available to get it right. We're working on it.

Christopher Stone
CEO, Object Management Group
Framingham, Massachusetts

Preface

This book is about CORBA and related OMG technologies. Since this scope is extremely wide, finding an appropriate name for the book that would fully describe the subjects covered yet be recognized by potential readers was difficult. This book was therefore given its present title because CORBA is the underlying technology base for most of the technologies discussed. It forms the framework within which the OMG works and creates technologies. However, the book is definitely not limited to a description of the Common Object Request Broker Architecture (CORBA). Rather, it describes a set of technologies that is being discussed and defined within the context of the OMG. These technologies encompass all issues relevant to software development; this is certainly a large scope.

This book is about distributed, object-oriented systems. It is becoming clearer and clearer as time goes on that these two technologies will form the basis for operating systems, development environments, databases, and so on in the future. Recognizing this as far back as 1989, the OMG has been diligently producing standards and specifications for the infrastructure required by applications being developed in an advanced, distributed, object-oriented manner. These definitions and specifications have become de facto standards in the software industry, and most of the leading vendors are already delivering (or will shortly be delivering) products which conform to these specifications.

This book is about standards. Although the OMG is not a formal standards body, it is producing specifications which almost immediately become de facto standards. This often follows from the fact that the OMG encompasses most of the leading software vendors throughout the world. These vendors are instrumental in defining the specifications and together produce technology which has a good chance of being accepted. Each technology that is defined by the OMG is by the most expert people in that field; therefore it comes as no surprise that the deliverables of the OMG are of such high quality.

This book is about industry agreement. Although not perfect, the

OMG is an excellent example of cooperation between direct competitors. Companies that are direct competitors in almost every arena work together toward a common understanding and agreement. Discussions are often at a very technical level and mostly maintain an almost academic level of integrity. It is exactly this kind of cooperation that guarantees both the quality of the specifications and their widespread acceptance. The OMG adoption process encourages this kind of cooperation. While it is common for several submissions to be proposed for every Request for Proposal (RFP), it is also common for the process to culminate with one final submission (and usually there are at most two) that is a joint proposal by several OMG members. While the submissions often delve into rather complex object-oriented models, the discussions and adoptions of the OMG remain extremely practical and concrete. The participants usually bring with them extensive prototypical (and often more than that) experience. Since the issues being addressed are usually the core of the vendors' products, which are often second or third generation, the discussion remains motivated by real systems and requirements. The OMG's bylaws themselves stress commercial availability, and a proposal can be formally accepted by the OMG only if the submitters address commercial availability.

This book is about users of OMG technologies. While the OMG has already produced many results and has influenced the direction of the software industry in an almost unparalleled way, it remains relatively unknown to the general community of software developers and users. Although many software professionals have by now heard of CORBA, it remains hard to find professionals who are knowledgeable about the vast developments of the OMG but are not directly involved with the OMG. It is almost impossible to find documentation of OMG technologies which is less detailed than the specifications themselves yet is detailed enough to actually describe the technologies (i.e., it is not a five-page collection of buzzwords). In this respect, this book tries to fill a void. It is not targeted to the professional ORB implementor. Rather, it is targeted to software developers and users, systems analysts and architects, and managers who require a detailed (yet not too detailed) presentation on the variety of issues and standards. The book tries to explain the various technologies in terms that can be comprehended by a large audience of software professionals. Its intention is that the important issues dealt with by the OMG be used and incorporated in software systems with or without vendors' products. Distributed object-oriented systems only come from a certain frame of mind; this book tries to introduce the reader to these concepts.

This book is about products. Since the inception of CORBA, many vendors have produced commercially available implementations.

These products offer not only ORB functionalities but also many other useful features in the form of object-oriented frameworks or support for distributed applications. Since the purpose of the book is to encourage the creation of distributed object-oriented applications, it does not just explain the technologies by describing the standards and specifications. It goes on to describe some of the leading commercially available implementations and how the concepts and specifications are implemented in real products. More than 25 percent of the book is devoted to generally available (GA) products.

This book covers the following topics:

- Chapter 1 provides an introduction to the OMG as an organization, its goal, and its procedures. It explains the technology adoption process carried out by the OMG. It also describes the Object Management Architecture (OMA) and the OMA Reference Model. This model provides a framework within which technology is adopted. Finally, a quick tour of the issues covered by the book is provided.

- Chapters 2 and 3 describe the Common Object Request Broker Architecture (CORBA). These chapters describe the different aspects and components of the architecture and how they are used to provide the CORBA functionality. Most of the discussion is dedicated to CORBA 1.1; however, Chapter 3 also discusses the improvements made by CORBA 1.2 and the topics being discussed within the framework of CORBA 2.0. Chapter 2 describes the CORBA Object Model, the CORBA IDL, stubs and skeletons, object adapters (OAs), the Dynamic Invocation Interface, client requests, different possible ORB implementations, and more. Chapter 3 describes the Interface Repository and the ORB and OA interfaces and then goes on to discuss CORBA 1.2 and CORBA 2.0.

- IDL is the language which is used for specifying interfaces, but it is not the language used by programmers when implementing objects or when implementing clients which make calls on CORBA objects. To use a programming language for these implementations, a mapping of CORBA IDL to the programming language is necessary. This is the topic of Chapter 4. Mappings are provided for C, C++, Smalltalk, and Objective-C.

- Chapter 5 begins the discussion of Object Services. These services are a critical layer in the success of the OMG. The chapter describes what Object Services are, how they are adopted (based on the Object Services Architecture and Object Services Roadmap documents), and the services defined in the first round by the Object Services Task Force (OSTF). These include the COSS 1 services—Naming, Event Notification, and Life Cycle—and the Persistent Storage Manager.

- Chapter 6 continues the discussion of Object Services. The Relationship, Externalization, and Transactions services (which are all part of Object Services RFP2) are described, as are the newly issued Object Services RFP3 and RFP4.

- Chapters 7 and 8 describe the Object Database Management Group (ODMG) and the ODMG-93 object database standard. Although not directly part of the OMG, this group maintains certain relationships with the OMG. Members of the ODMG also belong to the OMG, and the bodies influence each other. Since ODBMSs are a central component of object-oriented environments, and since the ODMG is the primary body producing ODBMS standards, it was felt that this book would be incomplete if it did not describe the work being done by the ODMG. Chapter 7 introduces the ODMG and its goal. It describes the ODMG Object Model and the architecture by which an ODMG-compliant ODBMS functions in an ORB-based environment. Chapter 8 goes on to describe the ODMG-93 specification, including the Object Definition Language, the Object Query Language, and mappings for C++ and Smalltalk.

- The rest of the book is devoted to commercially available products. Chapter 9 describes the HP Distributed Smalltalk product, Chapter 10 describes IBM's SOMObjects, and Chapter 11 describes DEC's ObjectBroker product and the link to Microsoft Object Linking and Embedding.

Finally, the book is about the future. As time goes on, the rate at which distributed object-oriented systems are being created is steadily increasing. It is no longer doubtful that tomorrow's systems will be based on these technologies. One only has to look at the vendors' own internal developments to be convinced. While this trend continues to affect the software industry, the OMG remains the primary supplier of distributed object-oriented standards in the industry. Not only will this remain true for the next couple of years, it will probably become more and more true because the OMG's momentum is continuously increasing. It should surprise no one if many more books are published in the next few years which attempt to introduce the reader to the complex world of the OMG; we hope this book is a beginning.

Ron Ben-Natan

List of Abbreviations

ACA	Application Control Architecture
ACID	Atomicity, Consistency, Integrity, Durability
AES	Application Environment Specification
API	Application Programming Interface
ASG	Abstract Syntax Graph
BOA	Basic Object Adapter
BOD	Board of Directors
BOSS	Binary Object Streaming Service
CDS	Cell Directory Service
CFA	Common Facilities Architecture
CFRM	Common Facilities Roadmap
CFTF	Common Facilities Task Force
CLSID	Class Identifier
COL	Context Object Language
COM	Component Object Model
CORBA	Common Object Request Broker Architecture
COS	Common Object Services
COSS	Common Object Services Specification
CRL	Class Repository Language
CRM	Communications Resource Manager
DAA	Distributed Application Architecture
DCE	Distributed Computing Environment
DCL	Data Control Language
DDE	Dynamic Data Exchange
DDL	Data Definition Language
DII	Dynamic Invocation Interface
DIR	Dynamic Implementation Routine
DME	Distributed Management Environment

DML	Data Manipulation Language
DNS	Domain Naming System
DOA	Database Object Adapter
DOE	Distributed Objects Everywhere
DSI	Dynamic Skeleton Interface
DSOM	Distributed SOM
DTP	Distributed Transaction Processing
HPDST	HP Distributed Smalltalk
IDL	Interface Definition Language
IML	Implementation Mapping Language
IOGF	I/O Group Format
IOV	Independent Object Vendor
IR	Interface Repository
ISV	Independent Software Vendor
JOSS	Joint Object Service Submission
LOA	Library Object Adapter
LOI	Letter of Intent
MML	Method Mapping Language
MVC	Model-View-Controller
NCS	Network Computing System
PO	Presentation Object
POF	Persistent Object Format
PORT	Portable Request Translator
OA	Object Adapter
OBB	ObjectBroker
ODMG	Object Database Management Group
ODBMS	Object Database Management System
ODL	Object Definition Language
ODP	Open Distributed Computing
OID	Object Identifier
OLE	Object Linking and Embedding
OM	Object Model
OMA	Object Management Architecture
OMG	Object Management Group
OMGTC	Object Management Group Technical Committee
OML	Object Manipulation Language
OMTF	Object Model Task Force
OQL	Object Query Language

ORB	Object Request Broker
ORB2TF	Object Request Broker 2.0 Task Force
OSA	Object Services Architecture
OSF	Open Software Foundation
OSRM	Object Services Roadmap
OSTF	Object Services Task Force
OT	Object Technology
PSM	Persistent Storage Manager
QOS	Quality of Service
RFC	Request for Comments
RFI	Request for Information
RFP	Request for Proposal
RPC	Remote Procedure Call
SIG	Special Interest Group
SO	Semantic Object
SOM	System Object Model
SQL	Structured Query Language
TF	Task Force
TTS	Trusted Time Service
UUID	Universally Unique Identifier
XTP	X/Open Distributed Transaction Processing

1

The Object
Management Group

The complexity of software development has produced a necessary revolution in systems development: object-oriented computing is steadily becoming more and more mainstream. Software vendors have already learned that to sell a product, they must advertise it as being object-oriented (whether this is true or not). The use of object orientation as a marketing tool is the result of growing recognition that the object-oriented paradigm is essential for constructing complex information systems in a timely manner. Corporations are steadily learning how to make use of this new technology and are beginning to build software that follows this new way of thinking. Some are more advanced and have been producing superior software by using object orientation for some years now. It is sufficient to look to the big software vendors themselves and see that their own internal development is steadily migrating toward object orientation; they have seen the advantages, are making the investment, and are reaping the benefits. The rest of the software industry is following closely. In a few years the large majority of software bought off the shelf will have been produced using object-oriented techniques.

The other major revolution which is occurring in the computer industry is the rise of distributed computing. Although the mainframe is still central in many corporations, it is steadily being replaced by networks of computers. Corporations have realized that the promise of tomorrow's information systems will not be delivered by these monolithic and expensive computers. The literature is full of such expressions as "downsizing" and "rightsizing." The large majority of vendors have already accepted this trend and are providing migration policies and services to enable their customers to make use of networks of distributed computing nodes. The future is clearly in distributed networks of computers working together and sharing resources to achieve common goals.

Although the trend toward distributed computing is taking longer than initially assumed, it is nevertheless real and unstoppable. The second generation of distributed systems is already taking the place of traditional information management systems and of first-generation *client/server* systems. The more expertise is available, the greater the momentum of this change will be.

The combination of these two trends is not new. Distributed systems were always discussed using objectlike terms (even if the formal vernacular was missing). Object orientation provides the most logical semantics for formalizing and describing distributed systems. In addition, the object-oriented revolution is coupled with the distributed computing era (as well as some other technologies). For example, object orientation is the base for graphical user interfaces (GUIs). The central role of GUI environments is directly correlated to the development of personal computers and workstations and the rise of networks of distributed computers (no one would dream of paying for mainframe resources to move a mouse on some user's desk). Networks of personal computers and workstations arose at approximately the same time that advanced graphical programming environments did. These environments were mostly object-oriented (e.g., the development of the Smalltalk environment at Xerox PARC was perhaps the first project to fully recognize the power of the personal graphical development environment). Each of these revolutions clearly complements and enables the other.

The two computing paradigms which are at the heart of the Object Management Group's (OMG's) work are object orientation and distributed computing. It is by now clear that these two paradigms will be the prevalent paradigms in the software industry in the future; the OMG has adopted these two and is laying the necessary foundations for building real systems based on these underlying concepts.

The future of software development therefore seems to be in the combination of distributed computing and object-oriented development. This was the underlying assumption that was made when the OMG was founded in 1989. Once this assumption (which was less obvious back in 1989 than it is today) was made, the OMG was formed to promote this revolution and to work toward its success. The OMG saw the opportunity provided by these technologies. However, success does not happen on its own (or at least it probably takes longer). The OMG therefore assumed the role of producing base designs that would ensure the success of these two paradigms, and it has since been busy promoting them and laying foundations that will ensure their success. It has learned much from previous mistakes made by the software industry and has structured its efforts appropriately. For example, the OMG is different from other vendor-based organizations in that it does not produce products. It produces only architectures and specifications, which are then implemented by software vendors. The major advantage is that this provides enough flexibility to allow different implementations to exist while ensuring portability and interoperability. Since the participating companies are presented with specifications which they themselves have been active in developing, they are more willing to adopt them.

The OMG is an international trade organization. Its members include information system vendors, users, and academic institutions. The OMG is a not-for-profit organization; each member pays yearly dues, and the OMG uses these dues to promote object technology and to lay down the framework and specifications which will promote portability, interoperability, and reusability.

This book describes the architectures, standards, and frameworks being defined by the OMG through the work done by its members. Through this standards adoption process, the foundation for tomorrow's object-oriented distributed software systems is being built today. As time goes by, it is becoming clearer and clearer that every major vendor will base its systems and software on the foundations which are being created by the members of the OMG.

1.1 Goals of the OMG

One of the OMG's goals is to promote object technology (OT). OT is seen by the OMG as the technology which will boost the software industry by increasing productivity, enhancing reusability, and allowing portability and interoperability. The OMG does not define its goals abstractly as promoting OT; it has defined a specific agenda for doing this. The OMG is dedicated to constructing a framework for distributed object-oriented systems (called the Object Management Architecture Reference Model) and populating this framework with detailed specifications leading to commercially available components that will make this vision a reality.

This framework stresses object orientation as the enabler of reusability, portability, and interoperability. The specifications of the individual components of the architecture define functionality in terms of object-oriented interfaces; they do not define implementations. Had implementation considerations been defined, the impact of the definitions would have been limited. Implementations always contain assumptions and tradeoff choices which may be appropriate for some environments but totally unacceptable for others. Instead, the

OMG's approach is to define functionality and interfaces only, thus allowing multiple implementations to be provided through conforming interfaces.

To ensure that its work does not remain "academic," the OMG stresses commercial availability. The OMG populates the Reference Model through a detailed adoption process which involves members of the OMG submitting proposals to the OMG. The OMG does not produce specifications in a vacuum. Rather, it plays the role of an open integrator, facilitating the industry leaders coming together to discuss these specifications. To ensure that the accepted specifications have direct industry impact, the OMG requires that proposed components be commercially available or be backed by a commitment to commercial availability. In fact, each proposal for adoption has to contain a "proof of concept" clause in which the submitters describe the work that has already been done to show the feasibility of the approach.

1.2 Members of the OMG

The OMG was created in April 1989 by Data General, Hewlett-Packard, Sun, Canon, American Airlines, Unisys, Philips, Prime, Gold Hill, SoftSwitch, and 3COM. Some of the important dates in the history of the OMG are shown in Fig. 1.1.

The OMG is constantly growing. From the modest 11 starting members, the OMG quickly grew to 80 members by 1991, 200 members by 1992, and 300 members by 1993. Today OMG membership includes over 400 organizations, as shown in Fig. 1.2 (this list is current as of July 1994). As the figure shows, there are four categories of members: corporate members, associate members, end-user members, and uni-

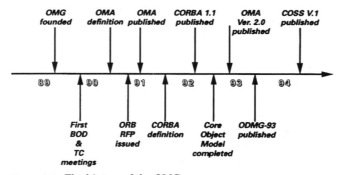

Figure 1.1 The history of the OMG.

3M
ABB Automation AB
ADV Technologies
ARCO
Abalon AB
Adv Cnpt/Martin Marietta
Aguas Munic. de Alicante
Alcatel Alsthom Recherche
Allen-Bradley
American Airlines
Ameritech
Apple Computer
Arinc Research
BBN
Bell Atlantic NSS
Bellcore
Boeing
Bouygues
Bull
CIL
CRIM
Cabletron Systems
Candle
Caterpillar
Center for Soft. Eng.
Chappell & Associates
Chorus Systems
City University
Cognos
Comp. Power Soft. Group
Conneticut Mutual
Corstar
DSG
Data General
Deere & Company
Digital Equipment Co.
Draper Lab
EDS
Easel

A.S.Veritas Research
ACT Financial
APIC Systems
ASCII
Abit Software

Alsys
American Express
Andersen Consulting
Arab Petroleum Investments
Arizona State University
BIS Banking Systems
Bell Northern Research
Berkeley Invst. Tech.
Booz, Allen & Hamilton
British Telecom
Bus. Class Cnsrt.
CITI
CSELT
Cadre Technologies
Canon
Cntr. Mfg. Compet.
Centre-File Ltd.
Charles Schwab
Cimage
Claris
Comp. Expert Sys. A.S.
Comp. Sciences Corp.
Cons. & Projects Group
DISA
DSTC
David Cittadini
Dialogic
Digitalk
Dun & Bradstreet
ELF
Ellemtel

A.C.S.E
ADB/Intellic International
APM
AT&T
Acxiom
Advanced Visual Systems
Air Force Inst. of Technology
Alcatel Network Systems
Amdahl
American Mngmnt. Systems
Antares Alliance Group
Arbor Intelligence Systems
ArtInAppleS
Baxter Diagnostics
BellSouth
Blanc & Otus
Borland
Brock Telecom
CBIS
CNA Insurance
CSK
Canadian Imperial Bank
Carnegie Melon University
Centerline
Cerri Logique
Chemical Bank
Citibank
Cogent Technology
Computer Associates
Compuware
Corelis
DMR Group
Data Access
De Montfort University
Digital Communications
Dr. Seufert Computer
E - Systems
EMS
Emeraude

Figure 1.2 OMG members (by category).

Enator	**Erasmus University**	Ericsson Info. Cons.
Ernest & Young	Expersoft	*FASTech Integration*
Federal Express	Fidelity Client/Server Sys.	Fidelity Investments
FileNet	*Flexiware Corp.*	Florida Power & Light
Fuji Electric	Fuji Xerox	Fujitsu America
Fujitsu Ltd.	*Fulcrum Technologies*	GEFM
GFAI	**GMD**	GPT Ltd.
GSI	GTE Laboratories	General Electric
General Research	Genesis	*Gensym*
Geomath	Gnopsis	*Gupta*
Harlequin	Hewlett-Packard	*Hitachi*
Household	Hughes Appl. Inf. Sys.	HyperDesk
IA	ICIM	**ICIS**
ICL	*IDC*	**IMA**
IOC	IST	Imagery
Implicit Software	Inference	InfoSource
Information Advantage	Information Builders	Inf. Mgmnt. Resources
Inf. Tech. Consortium	Informix	Ingenia
Ingres	**Inst. Prob. of Inf.**	Inst. for Defense Analytics
Integrated Objects	*Intel*	Intellicorp
Interactive Dev. Env.	IBM	Intersolv
Iona	*Isis Dist. Sys.*	*Itasca*
Justsystems	Jute	*iXOS*
KISS BV	**Kendall Square Research**	**KAPRE**
Knowledgeware	LBL	*Kennedy Carter*
Landmark Systems	*Linkvest*	LBMS
Los Alamos National Lab.	Lotus	*Lohara Software*
Lyon Consultants	*MCI*	*Lucid*
META	**MIT**	MCI Cons. Mrkts.
Marcam	*Mark V Systems*	MITRE
Matra Datavision	Matsushita	Mark Winter & Assoc.
Menai	Mentor Graphics	Mead Data Central
Meth. y Sys.	Micro Focus	Merrill Lynch
Microsoft	*Mitsubishi Electric*	*MicroTOOL*
Mobil	*Montran*	Mitsui
Mortice Kern Sys.	Motorola	Morrison Knudsen
NEC	*NIHS*	Mutual Life of Canada
NTT Data Comm. Sys.	*Nabnasset*	**NSA**
NIH	NeXT	National Comp. Board

Figure 1.2 *(Continued)*

NetLinks Technology
Nippon Steel
Nomura Research Inst.
Novadigm
O + O
OSG
Object Designers
Object-Oriented Pty. Ltd.
Objective Solutions
Oki
Ontos
OpenVision
PAR Tech. Corp.
POET Software
ParcPlace
Persistence Software
Philips
Price Waterhouse
Promis Systems
Qualix
RMC of Canada
Rascal Systems
Recognition International
Revelation Technologies
Roesch Consulting
SAP AG
SSA
Select Software Tools
Sequent Computer
Setpoint
Shell Development
Siemens Nixdorf
Sintef
Softeam
Software 2000
Sony Electronics
Star
Sterling Software
Suite Software

Net Labs
Network General
Nippon Tlgr. Tel. Co.
Norsk
Novell
O2 Technology
Oberon
Object International
Objective
Objective Systems
Olivetti
Open Engineering
Oracle
PFU
PTT Research
Patz. & Rasp GmbH
Petrotch. Open Soft.
PostModern
Prism
QDS
Quick
Raleigh
Rational
Research Centre Telekom
Reynolds and Reynolds
RogueWave
SES
Santa Cruz Operations
Semaphore
SerCon
Seybold
Sherpa Corp.
Sigma System
Smith New Court
Softlab, Inc.
Software AG
Southwestern Bell
starBase
Strategic Tech.
  Resources

Neuron Data
Nokia
Northern Telecom Inc.
Nurobase
OO Technologies
Object Design Inc.
Object Technology
Objective Comp. Sys.
Objectivity
Olivetti Inf. Tech.
OSF
Ordenadores
PIMB
Palladio Software
PeerLogic
Phi-Tech/SF
Powersoft
Progress
QUT
Quinary
Rand Information Systems
Realtime
Reuters
Ricoh
Royal Hong Kong Jockey Cl.
SPS
Santix Software GmbH
Schlumberg Technologies
Sematech
Servio
Shape Data
Siemens AG
Silicon Graphics
Sodalia
Softpro
Software Daten Service
Spacebel
Startext
Stratus

Figure 1.2 *(Continued)*

Sumitomo
Sveriges
Sybase
Symbiotics
System Wizards
Tandem
Tech. Univ. of Nova Scotia
Teradyne
Thoroughbred Software
Tractor
Trecom Bus. Sys. Inc.
USAA
Union Bank of Switzerland
Unisys
Univ. of Chicago
Univ. of Dublin
Univ. of Notre Dame
Univ. of Stuttgart
Univ. of Trondheim
VMARK Software
Visigenic
Whirlpool
X Consortium
Yokogawa Electric Corp.

Sun Microsystems
Swiss Fed. Inst. of Tech.
Sycomore
SynOptics
TASC
Taskon
Teknekron
Texas Instruments
Tivoli
TransTOOLS
Trinzic
UniSQL
Union Pacific
United Technologies
Univ. of Colorado
Univ. of Houston
Univ. of Paisley
Univ. of Tech. Vienna
Univ. of Ulster
Verilog
W.R. Grace
Wipro Infotech
X/Open
Zuken

Swiss PTT
Symantech
Sysdeco Mimer
Taligent
Tat Cons. Sevcs.
Telia Data
Thomson CSF
Toshiba
Transarc
UMIST
Unify
Uniplex
Univ. Nacional de la Plata
Univ. of Dortmund
Univ. of Michigan
Univ. of St. Thomas
Univ. of Tromso
Univ. of Wales
Versant Technology
Wang
WordPerfect
Xerox

Legend:
Corporate Member
End-User Member
Associate Member
University Member
Subscribing

Figure 1.2 *(Continued)*

versity members. Each member category has different responsibilities and rights. The major difference in responsibilities is the level in yearly dues. Corporate members typically pay higher yearly dues, whereas associate membership entails a much smaller investment. Since the OMG aims to encompass the whole industry, and academic institutions as well, it must be possible for extremely small organizations to participate. Therefore, dues for small organizations are scaled down; for example, associate membership dues can be as low as $1000 per year. This enables even extremely small organizations to participate in the OMG.

The OMG adoption process is strongly tied to corporate membership. Only corporate members may propose technology for OMG adoption. Submissions can be made by noncorporate members only through an endorsement by a corporate member.

1.3 Structure of the OMG

All decisions of the OMG are made by the OMG's board of directors (BOD). The BOD is not a technical body. Since the adoption process deals in complex technical specifications and issues, the BOD relies on the technical guidance of the Technical Committee (TC) and bases its decisions on the TC's recommendations. This consulting body is responsible for building the architecture adopted by the OMG. The TC bases its recommendations to the BOD on technologies proposed by task forces (TFs) and on the views of the TFs (since in some cases fine issues regarding proposals are best understood by the TF members). The policies and procedures of the TC, TFs, and other subgroups within the OMG are outlined in Soley (1994).

1.3.1 The board of directors

The BOD is the deciding body in the OMG. Any decision and adoption made by the OMG must be voted upon by the BOD. Decisions are based on both technical and business criteria. Thus the BOD may base its decisions on the state of the industry or the opinions of the end-user members (seen as representatives of the user community) as well as on the technical viewpoint.

1.3.2 The Technical Committee

The TC is composed of representatives of all members of the OMG. It is responsible for designing an abstract architecture for object-oriented applications upon which technology will be defined. This is called the *Object Management Architecture* (OMA), as described below. As the bylaws of the OMG state,

> the TC shall be responsible for developing, proposing and publicizing definitions, standards, extensions, and proposing resolution of issues relevant to the OMG Core Technology and its use in conjunction with both hardware and software.

The OMA Reference Model is to be used as an architectural reference for technology adoptions, which are presented to the committee as *items*. The TC (after a certain process) may recommend that the OMG BOD accept the item as part of the adopted architecture; if it is accepted, the item becomes a component populating one of the categories of the architecture.

The TC is appointed by the BOD and includes representatives of the OMG members. Its recommendations to the BOD are based on a TC vote. TC members representing corporate members have one vote per corporate member, and those representing end-user members have one vote combined (the end-user voter). The end-user voter is selected by the end-user special interest group (SIG). More than one TC member per company may participate in the TC process, but voting privileges are limited to one vote per company.

TC voting is based on a simple majority, the only exception being changes to policies and final recommendations to the BOD, which require a two-thirds majority. Only those companies that have been present at two of the last three TC meetings are allowed to vote at a TC meeting. This eliminates the possibility that a member that has not attended meetings or been a part of the process (and most likely is not knowledgeable about the proposals) will influence the vote. TC votes often take the form of a fax vote. The quorum for fax votes is less strict; it includes members who have been present at at least one of the last three TC meetings. Fax votes have a duration of between 6 and 10 weeks from their time of initiation to their termination and provide additional flexibility for making decisions outside the limited number of TC meetings.

1.3.3 Task forces, subcommittees, and special interest groups

Task forces, subcommittees, and special interest groups are types of working groups that may be formed by the TC. Each of them answers a different need. Subcommittees are formed to deal with procedural and definitional tasks, such as revisions in TC procedures, and are required to conform to the bylaws of the OMG. Task forces work on a particular technology adoption or issue, and special interest groups provide a forum for discussions of an area in which there is wide interest but that may not be of immediate interest to the TC. Any working group that has not met for a full year may be dissolved to eliminate phantom groups that may mislead external observers as to the work being done within the OMG.

A task force (TF) is made up of TC members and invited guests. TFs are formed to make recommendations to the TC regarding a specific issue or a particular problem and deal primarily with standards; their goals are directly defined by the TC. TFs will usually generate requests for information (RFIs) and requests for proposals (RFPs) to solicit technology proposals. Their structures and voting rules are more flexible, since they do not need to conform to the bylaws of the OMG. This allows TFs to have fewer "committee style problems" and to perform their work more rapidly. TFs generally meet more frequently than the TC.

TFs do not issue RFIs and RFPs directly; they recommend that the TC issue them. (Only TFs may make such recommendations to the TC.) These RFIs and RFPs are issued to the entire computer industry; they are not limited to members of the OMG and therefore allow the best possible technologies to be adopted. However, only corporate members may sponsor a technology to the TC. If a noncorporate member wishes to propose a technology to the OMG, it must go through a corporate member. This is necessary to ensure OMG control and promote OMG members' interests.

After the TC has issued requests, the TF typically reviews the proposals and makes recommendations to the TC. This process can be a lengthy one and involve several iterations and revisions. Recommendations to the TC are made only when the TF is satisfied with the results of the process.

Special interest groups (SIGs) are composed of TC members and invited guests and have a specific area of interest. This is usually more peripheral to the direct interests of the TC and often is broader and less focused than the area of interest of a TF. SIG goals are not defined by the TC, although the SIG itself is formed by the TC. SIGs promote technology explorations by generating discussion papers and suggestions; they are not directly involved in the formal adoption processes of the TC. However, SIGs are extremely important, since they provide a necessary validation track for the OMG.

1.4 Adoption of Technology

Technology adoption is done solely by the OMG BOD. Technology that is adopted must have an existing commercially available implementation; this ensures that adopted technology is not theoretical or abstract and that all issues that must be addressed when an actual implementation is developed have been considered. Every submission in response to an RFP must include a "proof of concept" statement which explains how the proposal has been tested toward an implementation. The requirements of the TC are less stringent; it may accept a submission that is being prototyped, whereas the BOD requires commercial availability. The actual determination of whether the technology sponsor plans to develop (or has developed) and commercialize the technology is made by the BOD.

The path to technology adoption starts from a TF, goes through the TC, and culminates within the BOD. RFIs and RFPs are proposed by the TF and formally issued by the TC. These requests solicit proposals from industry participants and start the adoption process. RFIs are issued first and are meant to collect information and opinions as to what are the most pressing issues within a technology category. After responses to RFIs have been collected and processed, an RFP is composed and issued by the TC (based upon the TF's recommendation). When an RFP is issued by the TC, every company that intends to respond to the RFP must submit a letter of intent (LOI) to the OMG. This is part of the detailed schedule for deliverables that is part of every RFP. This schedule is typically not shorter than 24 weeks and can even be longer than a year (e.g., the Object Services RFP3 has a 450-day schedule). The TF discusses the proposals and often requires a number of revisions. Proposals are often combined to create a small number of submissions (or even one single joint submission). The TF then makes its recommendations to the TC, which goes through a voting phase culminating with a recommendation to the BOD.

After a technology has been adopted by the OMG, it is continually monitored by the TC. This allows minor improvements and fixes as well as control over a revision and enhancement process. The revision process is usually handled either by a revision task force or directly by the relevant TF. Revision TFs are appointed by the TC at the time of the technology adoption to ensure a controlled maintenance process. The workgroups with the responsibility for revisions will typically include at least representatives of all submitters of the adopted technology.

The OMG defines an additional adoption path called the *fast track request for comments (RFC) procedure*. This allows a corporate member with a commercial implementation that has no competition to submit it as an RFC to the relevant TF for consideration. This is important for cases where the TC's interest is not great enough for it to start an adoption procedure, yet the technology is of importance to the member. A member may, for example, need to have the technology inspected and some standardization made as a result of user requirements; the RFC allows such a member to initiate the process.

1.5   The Object Management Architecture

The OMG technology process is driven by user requirements within the software industry. The members of the OMG see a user-driven approach as the best mechanism for producing systems that will be successful in the market. For example, many vendors in the past (and some even today) have opted for proprietary systems. This would tie their users to their offerings, and so a continuous flow of acquisitions could be guaranteed. However, the user community has been steadily moving away from proprietary systems, and most corporations today refuse to be tied too closely to one vendor. The OMG's primary goals are portability and interoperability. These goals provide enormous benefit to the end-user community. Even though the primary forces in the OMG are the major vendors, it has been recognized that tomorrow's technology must be open and that software consumers must be allowed to change the way their systems are developed and used.

The OMA is a general architecture, and a taxonomy of necessary components enabling the architecture is defined and detailed in the *Object Managment Architecture Guide*. The OMA outlines general technical guidelines that should be followed by every component within the OMA. These include the necessity for object-oriented interfaces, distribution transparency, a common object model forming a common base for all components, full support for all stages of the software's life cycle, a flexible and dynamic nature, high performance, robust implementations, and conformance with existing standards within the software industry.

1.6   The OMA Reference Model

The OMA Reference Model for the Object Management Architecture is shown in Fig. 1.3. The Reference Model provides the underlying framework which guides the OMG technology adoption process. It defines the categories of components necessary to realize the OMG's goals and vision. The Reference Model provides a direction sign for developing components that will realize the OMG's vision. Once this architecture has been defined, the OMG's work can be seen as providing detailed specifications for the components identified within the Reference Model.

As shown in Fig. 1.3, the model comprises four component categories: The Object Request Broker, Object Services, Common Facilities, and Application Objects. Application Objects represent the actual software being developed to solve domain-specific problems or provide off-the-shelf products. These objects make use of the other three categories, which provide a very rich development environment.

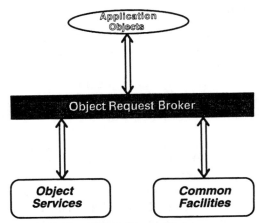

Figure 1.3 The OMA Reference Model.

Using the other three categories, application developers can rapidly create portable interoperable code which can later be reused by other application components. In this respect, the entire architecture is primarily aimed at providing the best possible environment for objects in this category.

The architecture's heart is the Object Request Broker, which provides the capabilities that allow objects to interact and work together to achieve a common goal. Object Services provide low-level system-type services which are necessary for developing applications such as object persistence, transaction capabilities, and security. Common Facilities provide higher-level services which are semantically closer to the application objects, such as mailing and printing facilities.

The collection of services provided by Object Services are necessary if an application is to be constructed at a reasonably high level without requiring the application developers to "reinvent the wheel" for every application (or, as many describe cases in which application programmers design software for which they do not have the right qualifications, "reinvent the flat tire"). Common Facilities provide an even higher level of functionalities that define general capabilities required in many applications. The difference between Object Services and Common Facilities might seem a little obscure; in reality, it is much clearer. Object Services have a "system orientation," whereas Common Facilities have an "application orientation." Another important difference is that while Object Services must be supported by all ORB environments on all platforms, support for Common Facilities is discretionary.

The OMA is composed of objects. Every component in the architecture is defined in terms of an object-oriented interface (although it does not necessarily have to have an object-oriented implementation). An object can request services from any other object by accessing these object-oriented interfaces. Any object can therefore provide services to any other object. The architecture thus transcends so-called client/server architectures, since every object is potentially both a client and a server. In fact, every request invocation defines a client and a server object in the context of the single invocation. The same object can therefore be required to service a request (making it a server) while the implementation invokes a request to get some information from another object (making it a client). Any object (including Application Objects, Object Services objects, and Common Facilities objects) will be involved in such relationships (both as clients and as servers). The taxonomy of which of the four categories an object belongs to is more a semantic definition based on domain and functionality.

Interaction is done using object-oriented interfaces. Any implementation, including non-object-oriented implementations and "legacy" software, can be made to provide object-oriented interfaces. These are often called *object-oriented wrappers* or *adapters* and are easily defined for the vast majority of software. In this way, the Object Management Architecture can provide an underlying model for all software components, including those which were previously developed or which are not necessarily object-oriented. In addition, since any nondistributed application is a special case of a distributed application (one which simply uses only one machine), the architecture can truly embed all software developments.

1.6.1 The Object Request Broker

The Object Request Broker (ORB) is the central component which allows the Reference Model to function. It provides the basic object interaction capabilities which are necessary for any of the components to communicate. It is therefore no wonder that this component was the first to be defined by the OMG (OMG, 1992b). It allows client objects to issue requests for objects to provide required services. These service requests are issued by the client in a location-, language-, and platform-independent way. The ORB is therefore the primary vehicle delivering interoperability and portability and enabling the building of true distributed applications.

Requests are issued by objects using an object-oriented interface as defined by the service provider. The client then constructs a request by specifying a reference to the object the request should be sent to, an operation name, and any other information that is necessary. This will typically include the parameters to be sent, but can also include such things as an environment context.

1.6.2   Object Services

The ORB provides the basic interaction capability, but this is insufficient for real applications to be developed. Applications need to assume that the underlying environment provides certain basic services and functionalities; this is the role played by the Object Services layer. For example, the ORB provides ways for requests to be delivered to service providers, but does not define how service providers are found. The Object Services layer may provide a "Trader Service" which provides functionality resembling the role played by the Yellow Pages in locating phone numbers for service providers; a client should therefore be allowed to query for objects that can provide certain functionalities.

The Object Services layer is of primary importance to the success of the OMG Reference Model. If this layer is not populated with enough functionality, the OMG's vision will not be realized. Even if the ORB is fully functional and usable, this will not enable applications to be built. Too much will have to be developed by the application itself, since the support provided by the ORB is at a very low level. Most application developers also lack the expertise to develop such functionalities on their own. A scenario in which each application needs to provide core services for itself is not feasible and is extremely wasteful.

Object Services are thus a primary component of the OMG Reference Model. In fact, once an initial ORB-based architecture was in place, the OMG (through the Object Services Task Force) began populating this layer with services such as a Naming Service, an Event Notification Service, a Relationship Service, and a Transaction Service.

Following the general concept of separation of interfaces from implementation, Object Services define only interfaces and a semantic specification of functionality. A service definition therefore supplies the developer with an API set and a description of the functional behavior that is provided. This does not place any limitations on implementations for the service. In fact, it is assumed that many implementations will be provided for each service. This is absolutely necessary. Services are generally complex. They may have different characteristics. Situations in which stressing one characteristic of the service leads to lesser support for another will be common. Since different users of the service will require different resolutions of such tradeoffs, different implementations will be necessary. This is formulated in the quality of service (QOS) notion introduced by the OMG, which allows different implementations stressing different attributes of the service to be provided.

1.6.3   Common Facilities

Common Facilities also provide services, but these services are typically at a higher level. They are closer to the application levels than are

Object Services. Examples of Common Facilities are compound document management, electronic mail, and help systems. Such capabilities can be used by many applications and can allow applications to be created faster in a portable and interoperable way. Like Object Services, they reduce the complexity of writing software within the OMG framework, thus helping to achieve the overall goal. In fact, since Common Facilities services are at a higher level, they will often cover more of the functionality that is necessary for the application than lower-level services. For example, a compound document framework would be preferable to a service supporting generic object graph relationships.

Common Facilities will often use services from the Object Services layer. They are therefore placed temporally after initial work on Object Services (just as those were started after the initial specification of the ORB). Ultimately they will probably be used extensively by application software, since they define higher-level behavior which may be closer to the application software requirements. At this time no specifications of Common Facilities have been defined; in fact, the first RFP for Common Facilities has only just been issued.

1.6.4   Common Facilities RFP1

Common Facilities RFP1 was first drafted in August 1994 and will be issued in the fall of 1994 (see Katin, 1994). The RFP solicits proposals for Compound Presentation Facilities and for Compound Storage Facilities. The RFP references the Common Facilities Architecture (CFA) document and the Common Facilities Roadmap (CFRM) as guiding documents for the process and goals of Common Facilities adoption. [These documents were not completed when the RFP was first drafted, yet the contents of these documents were informally discussed by the Common Facilities Task Force (CFTF).] The RFP calls for submissions to be completed by January 1995 and for a BOD vote in September 1995.

Compound Presentation Management refers to such issues as the management of multiple views which act as presentations of a single semantic object. This semantic object may be arbitrarily complex, and different presentations may provide different views stressing different semantic information. These views will typically be windows or other display objects, but may also have other roles (such as interfaces to other systems).

Compound Storage Management refers to the management of data objects in some storage constructs. Examples include the management of complex object graphs as a storage service. This facility is related to the repository issues, to the Portable Common Tools Environment (PCTE), and to a possible implementation using the Externalization, Relationship, and Life Cycle Object Services.

Since the Common Facilities adoption process is only in its earliest stages, we will not discuss Common Facilities in the remainder of the book.

1.7 The OMG Object Model

The OMG Object Model was defined by the Object Model Task Force (OMTF) and is the underlying object model for all OMG specifications and all OMG-compliant technologies. The OMG/OM is not part of the CORBA; it is more fundamental and is defined in the *Object Management Architecture Guide* (OMG, 1992a).

The OMG/OM provides common semantics that characterize objects in any OMG-based system. These semantics define the interfaces that are used to interact with object state and object behavior. The semantics define objects as instances of types and allow grouping of types into higher-order structures; type grouping occurs through the subtype/supertype relationship. The OMG/OM is implementation-independent. However, since it serves as the object model for object system implementation, it defines the semantics of type implementations as data structures for implementing the object state and a set of procedures for implementing the object behavior. However, since the OMG/OM must remain implementation-neutral, it does not restrict possible implementations. It only specifies the relationship between a type and its one or many implementations.

The OMG/OM as a model must underlie a very large technology base. Object orientation is a paradigm that can be (and is) manifested in many technology categories. For example, we talk about object-oriented programming languages, object-oriented distributed systems, object-oriented databases, and so on. Each of these sectors is unique in terms of the problems it is trying to solve and the tools that are being used. Each therefore requires a somewhat different model. Yet they all have a large commonality, since they all follow the object-oriented paradigm. The OMG/OM provides this common semantic core.

Since the OMG/OM must support this large variety of technologies, it needs to deal both with this commonality and with the differences. As is appropriate for any object-oriented solution, the OMG/OM does not attempt to provide a monolithic, all-encompassing definition. Instead, it is composed of a *Core Object Model, components*, and *profiles*. The Core Object Model is a set of definitions that must be supported in any OMG/OM-based system. This guarantees that even systems in different technology domains will be compatible. Components are extensions to the core that are not necessarily supported by all systems but that are required within some technology domain. Profiles group sets of components to define a model that is used by sets of sys-

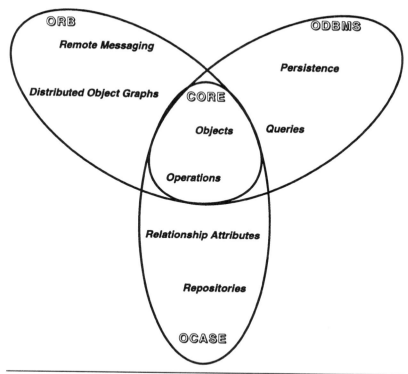

Figure 1.4   Profiles and components.

tems (usually a full technology domain). For example, Fig. 1.4 shows an object database profile that supports the core model but extends it with components such as persistence and queries.

Profiles are enhancements to the core model that are required for specific definitions and are therefore the mechanism by which the OMG/OM can be the base for such a variety of systems. Different profiles can share components. Profiles can also define similar components. This can happen because different domains may not agree on the importance or even the detailed semantics of particular notions. For example, distributed environments and ODBMS profiles may both support object relationships, but these may stress different properties. Although it is recommended that they share as much as possible, they remain a flexible way to provide different support while sharing a common base. This is especially important because profiles can also be sector-based. Thus profiles can be defined for the financial community or for the telecommunications community. These sector-based profiles have even more elaborate domain-specific semantics and thus cannot be hindered by inflexible structures.

1.7.1 Goals

The goal of defining a common object model is to facilitate interoperability between software components and to ensure portability of applications. Application portability means that software can be built in a way that guarantees that the construct used by the application will be available in different systems and as different vendor products. A common object model allows the application programmer to program to this model so that the software will be portable across all systems supporting it. Application portability is extremely important to application developers, but has yet to be fully realized. Such portability eliminates dependence on vendor companies and also eliminates unnecessary multiplicity and complexity in applications that need to work with many underlying models just because they have to access many software components.

Portability is usually divided into three types. In descending order, they are object code portability, source code portability, and design portability. Object code portability (also called binary portability) means that the executable can be run on different platforms. Source code portability means that the source code can be moved from one platform to the another, from which a new executable can be constructed (e.g., the source code compiled) to provide a version of the software on the new system. Design code portability means that there is an underlying set of assumptions and definitions from which the design is created in such a way that a transformation to another implementation set is straightforward.

The OMG/OM supports design portability. It defines a base semantics that ensures that application designs based upon this core will be portable across compliant systems. The OMG/OM is a model; it does not define a syntax. It therefore cannot support source code portability (and since it is an abstract definition, there certainly is no meaning to object code portability). Still, system designs are the fundamental architectural components in any system, and achieving design portability is a very big and necessary step toward other forms of portability. For example, there could be no source-level portability without design portability, since the architectural structures are required to be the same before source ports.

Interoperability means interaction between different software components and systems from different vendors running on different platforms. The Common Object Request Broker is the mechanism for achieving interoperability and provides the necessary transport mechanisms for allowing interoperability. This, however, is not enough, since object and operation semantics determine exactly what it is that is being sent over the transport layer; the OMG/OM is the core of this semantic definition.

Just as it is important to understand what the goal of the OMG/OM is, it is important to understand what it was not meant to be. It is not intended to be the ultimate and only object model. It was designed to be extensible, since inflexible and closed models always break. The OM was not built by trying to include everything, nor by trying to include only a least common denominator. It was designed to include the common constructs that are needed to support design portability and interoperability. Finally, it was not intended to serve as a meta-model, but rather as a specific object model which will be the base for compliance of object-based systems.

Compliance is meaningful only within the context of a particular profile (or possibly a number of profiles). However, part of profile compliance is a test for compliance with the Core Object Model. Compliance with a profile can mean two things. Full compliance means that the system fully supports any component within this profile. This means that all the profile functionality is fully supported. Partial compliance means that the system does not contradict any of the profile definitions. A system which is only partially compliant can support a subset of the profile's functionality.

The rest of this section provides an introduction to the OMG Core Object Model. This object model specifies what all OMG-compliant systems should support, and as such is the basic semantic definition for the rest of this book.

1.7.2   Objects and types

Any object model is based on a very small number of primitives; the OMG/OM is no exception. The basic concepts are objects, types, subtyping, and operations. Objects are used to represent entities. Objects have identities which cannot change over time (although the internals of the object may otherwise change) and encapsulate state and behavior. State captures object information, while behavior is implemented as operations that may be applied to the object. Operations may change the state of an object but not its identity; state provides information needed for operations.

Objects are instances of types. Types group objects which represent entities belonging to a group. A type provides a way of characterizing all instances of the type (objects belonging to this type); types may be related through a subtype/supertype relationship. A subtype specializes a supertype, meaning that any instance of the subtype may also be seen as an instance of the supertype (not in the instantiation sense, but in the usage sense).

Examples of objects are a bank account, a person, a security, and a bank. Types collectively group objects. Thus *Person* can be a type, and any person object will be an instance of this type. All bank account objects will be instances of the *BankAccount* type, which may have two subtypes, *CheckingAccount* and *SavingsAccount*. Any checking account object is also a bank account object. This relationship between types is often called the *IS-A* relationship. Each checking account has an identity, a state (the cash balance in the account), and operations that may be applied to this account object (e.g., to deposit money in the account). Operations may alter the state of the object (e.g., change the cash balance in the account). State also provides information for operations (e.g., a withdraw operation may first query the state to see whether the operation should be allowed).

Each object has an immutable identity. The Core Object Model defines an object identifier (OID) as a handle or a way to refer to the object. Operations may be invoked using the OID to reference the object. The model does not assume a comparison operation between OIDs and does not provide any requirements regarding the implementation of the OIDs. All OIDs belong to a set called *Obj*.

1.7.3 Objects and nonobjects

Objects are instances of a type. Objects of the Core Model do not change their identity. Profiles that require support for dynamic type changes (where the type of an object can change its type dynamically while the identity of the object does not) will require external layering to provide such capabilities. Types describe the operations that will be available for any object which is an instance of the type.

Types characterize the behavior of the objects within them when using operations. Each operation has a signature that includes a name, a set of parameters, and a set of results. The signatures defined within a type are collectively called the type's interface. Every object that is an instance of the type assumes the interface defined within the type. The interface of a type consists not only of the operation signatures defined within the type, but also of signatures that are inherited from supertypes.

Types are related through the subtype/supertype relationship. Together, they form a higher-order structure called a *type hierarchy*. This directed acyclic graph is rooted by the type named *Object*. The set of all object types is called *OTypes*.

Not all things are objects. The Core Model defines another set of entities called *nonobjects*; the set of all nonobjects is named *Nobj*.

Objects and nonobjects together form all *denotable values*; the set of all denotable values is named *DVal*. Every nonobject has a type called a *nonobject type*; the set of nonobject types is called *NTypes*. Nonobject types are not part of the Object type hierarchy, and the subtyping rules of the Core Model do not apply to them. The Core Model itself does not actually specify concrete nonobject types. This concept was included within the Core Model to be used by component and profile extensions because it was clear from inspection of concrete object models that such a concept would have to be supported. It was therefore felt important to incorporate at least the concept at the Core Model level.

The Core Model does not make any assumptions regarding objects, nonobjects, and denotable values. The actual profile or concrete model is therefore free to apply its concrete model as necessary. For example, C++ will map the C built-in types as nonobjects, and CORBA defines data types such as Short, Long, and Char as nonobjects. Smalltalk, on the other hand, defines all entities as objects; the sets of nonobjects and nonobject types in Smalltalk would therefore both be empty.

1.7.4 Operations

Operations implement requests. Requests specify what operation is to be performed and what parameters (if any) are to be passed to the operation invocation (these are sometimes called procedures or functions). Operations are defined by a signature that includes a name, a set of parameters, and a set of return values.

Operations are always associated with a *controlling parameter* which specifies the object for which the operation is invoked. The controlling type cannot be a nonobject type. This is similar to the use of *this* in C++, the use of *self* in Smalltalk, or the use of the first parameter in a function call as the controlling parameter in implementation of object models in C. The operation is required to be part of the controlling parameter type's interface. An operation is associated with only one type; the Core Model does not support object models that associate an operation with multiple controlling parameters (as there are in CLOS, for example) or operations not associated with any type. All operations within a type have different names. The Core Model does not support name overloading, as C++ does, for example.

Since the Core Model must be the basis for extremely diverse systems, the operation specification within it does not include many restrictive definitions. For example, the Core Model does not define a subcategory of operations that are side-effect-free (e.g., const member functions in C++). It does not address exception handling or atomic operations (which are absolutely essential for database systems), or concepts of private, public, or protected operations. Different profiles will therefore need to extend the base model to accommodate specific semantics required of operations.

1.7.5 Subtyping and inheritance

Subtyping and inheritance are two distinct concepts which are often collapsed into a single concept in many object models. The Core Model distinguishes between subtyping and inheritance and defines the interaction between these two concepts.

Subtyping is a relationship between types. It defines when objects of a type can be used by a construct expecting to receive objects of another type. For example, Liskov's substitution rules are shown in Fig. 1.5. The concept of specialization or refinement is also sometimes used to annotate subtyping. The Core Model supports multiple subtyping relationships. A type can therefore be a subtype of many types. The subtype/supertype relationship thus produces a directed acyclic graph.

1.8 A Tour of the Book

The OMG's architectures and specifications have a very good chance of becoming the underlying architecture and definitions for future computer systems. The participation and investment of most major vendors must be seen as a commitment to and belief in the approach of the OMG on the part of these companies. Recognizing this fact, this book tries to describe the OMG's world.

The OMG as an organization and the OMG's adoption process are very vendor-oriented. The specifications being created are very complex and extremely technical. This is necessary, since the functionali-

Liskov Substitution Principle (Strong Form)

T1 is a subtype of T2 if for each object O1 of type T1 there is an object O2 of type T2 such that for every program P defined in terms of T2 the behavior of P is unchanged when O1 is substituted for O2.

Liskov Substitution Principle (Weak Form)

T1 is a subtype of T2 if in any program P that expects objects of type T2 objects of type T1 can be substituted and the program will not fail, i.e., there will be no runtime errors.

Figure 1.5 Liskov's substitution rules

ties and interfaces being developed are to form the basis for implementations which will be provided by the different vendors. The vendors therefore have a very large stake in the process. This is compounded by the fact that for submissions to be considered, the submitters must already have made a start on implementations; this only increases the interest that the vendors have in making their submissions the accepted standard.

The result of this heavy involvement of vendors in the OMG process is that the specifications are necessarily very detailed and very technical (they have to be, since they define what a component does). On the other hand, since the deliverables of the OMG's working groups are not commercial products, documentation for these specifications that addresses the wider community of corporate developers and other software developers does not exist. This book intends to fill this void.

The OMG has already published (and will continue to publish) various of its specifications. Examples are the *Object Management Architecture Guide* (OMG, 1992a), the *Common Object Request Broker: Architecture and Specification* (OMG, 1992b), and the *Common Object Service Specification*, Vol. 1 (Siegel, 1994). These books are publications of the respective OMG specifications documents; they therefore are still detailed and complex and are primarily directed at implementors or advanced users of these components.

In addition to these books, the OMG maintains a very rich document repository which details all of the work being done within the OMG's scope. This repository is an invaluable source of information, and can be used to learn about every component within the OMA.

This book is not intended and cannot start to be a description of the OMG's work at the important and detailed level of the various OMG specifications. Although it is based on detailed information from the various OMG specifications and publications, it is directed toward a different audience. It is meant to be used by all software professionals (developers, analysts, managers, etc.) who are interested in the work being done by the OMG. The book thus takes the approach of explaining the specifications being produced but omitting many details which are irrelevant for anyone but implementors of the specifications. Annotations are provided that take the reader one step beyond the specification details and explain how the topic fits in with the rest of the architecture.

One of the problems this book faces is that the OMG's work is a moving target. One possible approach would be to wait until a technology is adopted before attempting a description. This is not the approach taken. Since this book is intended to explore the issues facing the OMG members and the approaches being taken to address them (not to fully describe the specification and interfaces), we can describe the technology and the approaches taken by submitters. In many cases it is better to observe the process and describe varying approaches since much can be learned from the discussions and evaluations internal to the OMG's work groups. This is the approach taken in the description of the CORBA C++ mapping, for example.

The topics addressed by this book are the primary issues of interest to the OMG. In some cases (e.g., Common Facilities), only a very brief discussion is possible (at this time), since so little has been defined. In other categories (e.g., Object Services RFP2 in Chap. 6), detailed work has been done, and although the adoption process has not yet been completed, it is possible to describe most of the issues, since a description of even a single submission will expose the reader to the problems and solutions. Wherever possible, we try to select a submission that has a reasonable chance of being accepted or at least contributing to the final accepted proposal. Since the discussion is not intended for component implementors, many differences between competing submissions are irrelevant. In cases where a serious divergence occurs (e.g., the approach to interoperability in CORBA 2.0), both approaches are generally described.

Some components have been specified and defined. In these cases, we outline the approach and definitions. Since we do not intend to fully describe any single component (but rather to give an overview of the plethora of issues addressed by the OMG), the reader is referred to the OMG publications for any elaborations and details that may be required. Although the text tries to remain as close as possible to the original OMG specifications, some allowances must be provided for omissions as a result of the limited space available for describing such a variety of topics. If a certain topic is of special interest to the reader, he or she should seek out the full OMG specifications.

The book also includes a description of the work being done by the Object Database Management Group (ODMG). This group is associated with the OMG but is not a task force, subcommittee, or special interest group. The ODMG is primarily interested in defining a standard for object-oriented database management systems and has recently published a book describing the ODMG-93 standard (Cattel, 1994); the description of the ODMG's work in this book is based on this specification. Since ODBMSs are a very important component in the OT world, we think it is important to include a description of the ODMG's work in this book. Together with the other OMG standards, this promises to be the basis for object-oriented standards which will guide a large (and growing) part of the software industry in the future. Once again, the description of the ODMG-93 standard is meant to be used by common software developers and not by ODBMS implementors. The description of this standard is probably more useful to such readers than the full specification, but anyone who requires a full description with complete specifications (including, for example, the grammatical definition for the definition language) must refer to the ODMG-93 publication.

Finally, since the book is addressed to users of these future technologies, the last three chapters are dedicated to a description of three commercially available implementations of OMG technology. There are by now quite a large number of CORBA implementations. The three implementations that were selected are products from three large vendors: IBM, DEC, and HP. Although these are not the only implementations available, they are certainly among the major ones. These implementations provide enough variety to expose the reader to the various alternatives available in the marketplace. Each provides a slightly different view and stresses certain characteristics. In addition, many corporate developers might prefer an implementation from one of these large system vendors to one from a smaller company.

The rest of this section provides a brief overview of the topics covered by this book. We hope the information provided in the book is useful and that it will promote the general interest in and usage of object technology in general and the OMG Object Management Architecture in particular.

1.8.1   CORBA

The Common Object Request Broker Architecture (CORBA) defines the architecture of ORB-based environments. This architecture is the basis of any OMG component and is the enabler of the OMG vision. It was the first component to receive a formal specification and is continuously being enhanced to support the technology emerging from the work of the OMG and its members.

CORBA has become one of the best-known buzzwords and is commonly used to refer to any of the components being defined by the OMG. This is often misleading, since the OMA defines various categories that must be populated, whereas CORBA deals in only one of these categories. Still, the ORB component is the most important component, and all the other categories are based upon the ORB, and so CORBA is used as a code word for the world of the OMG.

Chapters 2 to 4 of this book are dedicated to the ORB component of the OMA. The first two of these chapters describe CORBA in detail, while the third chapter discusses several programming language mappings of CORBA.

Chapter 2 introduces the reader to CORBA. The concepts and

issues leading to CORBA 1.1 are detailed, and the basic components are presented. The Interface Definition Language (IDL) and the way it is used for writing software consistent with the OMG's goal is described, and the heart of CORBA is revealed. Chapter 3 continues the description of CORBA 1.1 by detailing the pieces necessary for the architecture to work. The reader is introduced to the important roles played by the Interface Repository (IR) and the Object Adapter (OA) as well as the ways in which ORB architectures may be used for achieving specialized behavior.

CORBA 1.1 was available to the general public as early as 1992. This was an initial definition that would clearly be enhanced in the future. The OMG (and specifically the ORB 2.0 Task Force) has been busy defining the next generation of ORB architectures. Chapter 3 details many of the extensions to CORBA 1.1 that are being proposed. The next architecture which will be produced, known by the code name of CORBA 2.0, will be much more robust and functional than CORBA 1.1. The major issue which will be resolved in CORBA 2.0 is the issue of ORB interoperability, i.e., the capability of an object issuing a request to an object being managed by a different ORB (of a different vendor, on a different platform, in a different programming language, etc.). Most of the issues that will be addressed by CORBA 2.0 are extremely important for the success of the OMG and will be described in Chap. 3.

CORBA supports programming language independence. This means that objects that were written in one programming language can request services from objects that were written in another programming language. These programming languages need not necessarily even be object-oriented. CORBA supports this functionality by defining the Interface Definition Language (IDL). This is a language used for defining interfaces for objects that will participate in the ORB-based environment. IDL is a definition language only; implementation of the objects is still done using programming languages chosen by the developers. The IDL interfaces are mapped to programming language–specific stubs. These stubs are called by the client objects to request services. On the other side, the IDL skeletons will invoke the implementations, which may be in yet another programming language. To allow all this, mappings must be available from IDL to the respective programming languages. This is the subject of Chap. 4.

CORBA 1.1 defined a mapping for the C programming language. Using this mapping, most of the early CORBA implementations provided CORBA capabilities for programs written in C. However, to realize the potential of CORBA for providing interoperability between objects written in various programming languages, many such mappings must be formed. The C++ mapping, for example, was therefore an important task of the ORB 2.0 Task Force. Chapter 4 will describe the C mapping as defined in CORBA 1.1, the C++ mapping (including the various stages in the life of this binding), the Smalltalk bindings as defined in the HP Smalltalk-based CORBA product, and the Objective-C binding as proposed by NeXT Computer. It should be noted that although these mappings are at a relatively advanced stage, there are many other mappings on the table, and work on some of them has already begun. For example, a binding for COBOL has already been proposed and will be commercially available in the not so distant future.

1.8.2 Object Services

Object Services are the topic of Chaps. 5 and 6. Object Services provide the necessary functionalities to enable applications and other components to be written in ORB-based environments. The ORB itself provides the low-level connectivity capabilities that allow objects to relate to one another and require services. However, any object model will typically be complex and require additional support. Although such capabilities can potentially be packaged within the ORB, this is seen as the wrong way to provide these services.

The OMG approach is to keep components as simple and as modular as they can possibly be. This means that the ORB deals only with the issues it must deal with; other services should be defined as separate modular components above the ORB level. For example, object names should be supported, allowing objects to refer to other objects by name. Instead of making this an additional feature supported by the ORB, the OMG's approach is to define an Object Naming Service. This is part of the Common Object Services Specification Part 1 (COS-S1) and is described in Chap. 5.

Additional object services described in Chap. 5 are the Object Event Notification Service (allowing typed and untyped events to be delivered from one object to another in either a coupled or a decoupled way), the Object Life Cycle Service (defining how objects are created, destroyed, moved, or copied), and the Persistent Storage Manager (which provides a lightweight mechanism for object persistence which is upward-compatible with the ODMG-93 standard).

Chapter 5 also introduces the Object Services Architecture and the Object Services Roadmap as the guiding documents in Object Services adoption. This process is extremely important for the success of the OMG, and much work has gone into assessing how object services should be structured and what they should provide. The first three services which compose COSS1 (Naming, Event Notification, and Life

Cycle) are especially important, since they provide the initial Object Services Style which should be followed by the other services to come.

Chapter 6 continues the discussion of Object Services. Three additional services are described. The Relationship Service allows objects to be associated using semantically meaningful relationship objects. These are first-class objects which allow domain-specific structures to be directly modeled as CORBA objects. The Externalization Service allows objects to be transformed to a data stream that can be made external to an ORB. This representation can then be internalized by a potentially different ORB to reconstruct the object. The Transaction Service supports the notion of transactions allowing ACID properties (Atomicity, Consistency, Integrity, and Durability) in ORB-based environments. The Transaction Service is critical for any real-world application, as well as for other services. For example, the Relationship Service provides support for referential integrity only if a Transaction Service is made available (this is necessary to ensure that setting up the two links will be done as one atomic operation—i.e., it either completely succeeds or completely fails; without such a service, it is impossible to guard against the situation in which one reference is created while the creation of the other side of the link fails). Chapter 6 also outlines Object Services RFP2, RFP3, and RFP4 to provide the reader with the scope and direction to be taken by the OMG in terms of Object Services over the next couple of years.

1.8.3   The ODMG

Chapters 7 and 8 describe the Object Database Management Group and the ODMG-93 standard for Object Database Management Systems (ODBMSs). Databases are among the most important components of any system. ODBMS technology is therefore a very important part of OT. One of the major obstacles standing in the way of ODBMS acceptance is the divergence of the different ODBMS products. ODBMS products are very different from one another, and this poses a very big problem for software developers. The importance of an ODBMS standard has been recognized by the ODMG. This group includes over 80 percent of the ODBMS vendors today and is therefore in a very good position to produce such a standard, even though it is not a formal standards body. The ODMG-93 standard is the first very important step in standardizing ODBMSs and is intended to provide source code portability (over ODMG-compliant ODBMSs) for applications using such a product.

Chapter 7 describes the ODMG, its goals, and the process for defining an ODBMS standard. The ODMG has decided to provide an ODBMS standard within the context of the OMG, since this is assumed to be the prevalent object-oriented architecture. Chapter 7 includes a description of how ODMG-compliant ODBMSs will be integrated in ORB-based environments as well as how the ODMG Object Model extends the base OMG Object Model. (This is necessary because the ODMG constructs are database-related and include richer concepts than basic object invocations. For example, the ODMG Object Model defines relationships, properties, and database sessions.)

Chapter 8 describes the Object Definition Language (ODL), the Object Query Language (OQL), and the C++ and Smalltalk bindings defined by the ODMG-93 standard. The ODL allows the object schemas that are managed in ODMG-compliant products to be defined. The OQL allows these databases to be queried. The OQL is an object extension to SQL and is capable of supporting the much richer structures common to an object model over a relational model while maintaining similarity to SQL. One of the benefits of ODBMSs is that there are no two programming paradigms; the database interaction and the application coding are done using one consistent programming language and type system. To allow this to be possible, ODBMSs stress that the Object Manipulation Language (OML) of the database should be the programming language being used for application development. The ODMG supports this approach and provides bindings to C++ and to Smalltalk that allow database interaction from these programming languages. Chapter 8 provides an overview of these bindings and illustrates the approaches taken with examples.

1.8.4 Sample ORB products

Finally, the last three chapters of the book describe three of the most advanced commercially available implementations for CORBA and for some of the other components (e.g., most of the implementations include some Object Services). Chapter 9 describes HP's Distributed Smalltalk product, which is one of the two CORBA products produced by HP (HP also has a project called ORB + which is C++ based and is not commercially available at the time of writing of this book). Chapter 10 describes IBM's SOMObjects (SOM = System Object Model) or, as it is sometimes referred to, SOM/DSOM (DSOM = Distributed SOM). Chapter 11 describes DEC's Object Broker product. This chapter also describes the interfaces between the Object Broker product and the Common Object Model providing a link to Microsoft's Object Linking and Embedding 2.0 (OLE2.0) system.

Like any other publication, this book is limited and cannot cover all issues. The OMG is a very important organization, and it would be impossible to describe every topic relating to its work. The book tries to describe as much of the OMG's world as possible. Certain choices were required in order to limit the scope and focus on certain aspects. This is compounded by the fact that the OMG's work is a moving target and by the time the book is published many changes and developments will have occurred. Among the issues that this book does not address are many components whose role and structure have not yet been defined by the OMG. Apart from such issues, two main areas have been purposely limited because of resource limitations: additional product descriptions and relationships with other standards.

It should not be understood from this that these three products are the only available commercial products. In fact, there are tens of such products, some commercially available and some in advanced stages and soon to become commercially available. The purpose of this book in giving examples of products was not to provide a product guide but to expose the reader to various approaches taken by vendors in implementing the OMG's definitions. The goal is to demonstrate how the OMG's work comes into effect in the product market. The products chosen offer different strategies and demonstrate many issues described in the first eight chapters. The product chapters do not attempt to judge or compare the products and should not be used as an evaluation of them. Any development effort that requires an ORB should set up an evaluation structure. Other products may certainly be the preferred choice depending on project requirements.

The OMG does not exist in a vacuum. Many other organizations are working on issues which are very close to the OMG's work. For example, ISO's Open Distributed Processing initiative has many themes in common with the OMG. Since the OMG is a dominant organization in the object-oriented world, many such organizations have relationships with the OMG. For example, one of the primary contenders for the CORBA 2.0 interoperability capability is based in the Open Software Foundation's (OSF) Distributed Computing Environment (DCE) (this is described in Appendix A). In fact, OSF is one of the submitters of this proposal. Likewise, the Portable Common Tool Environment (PCTE) initiative is felt very strongly within the OMG on such issues as repositories, services, and facilities. Other relationships also exist. For example, the ODMG has formed a liaison with the ANSI SQL-3 committee, and the OMG is active in the ODP Trader initiative. All these relationships are of major importance, since they often shape the direction and decisions of the various groups. This sort of discussion, however, is a world of its own, and we have preferred to eliminate any of these descriptions wherever possible.

2

The Common Object Request Broker Architecture, Part 1

The OMG was founded to work within the software industry to provide an open architecture that would support multivendor, global heterogeneous networks of object-based software components. The *Object Management Architecture (OMA) Guide* (OMA, 1992a) was published as an architecture that would serve as the foundation for the development of detailed specifications and infrastructure for future object-based systems. The OMA defines many components that together enable the implementation of the OMG's vision. One of the primary elements (if not the primary element) defined in the OMA is the Object Request Broker (ORB). This component is the main mechanism which facilitates the workings of the OMA. The ORB is the facilitator for sending and receiving messages between different objects and components. The ORB environment was defined in the Common Object Request Broker Architecture and Specification (CORBA). The architecture was completed at the end of 1991 and published at the beginning of 1992 (version 1.1) (OMG, 1992b). It defines the architecture that enables the interoperation of the participants in the OMA. It is responsible for the seamless interaction of different and diverse object systems, and as such it is the central component in any OMA environment.

The Common Object Request Broker Architecture and Specification (Revision 1.1) was adopted from a joint proposal produced by Digital Equipment Corporation, Hewlett-Packard Company, Hyperdesk Corporation, NCR Corporation, Object Design, Inc., and SunSoft Inc. It was published as OMG Document Number 91.12.1 and as a book published by the OMG and X/Open (OMG, 1992b), and was the first widely available specification describing the adopted ORB technology. Chapter 2 and parts of Chaps. 3 and 4 describe the information in the CORBA 1.1 document. As much as possible, we try to follow the outline of this document. However, there may be cases where for reasons of clarity and lack of space, details of the specification are omitted. Section 2.1 describes the CORBA/OM as a concrete model for the OMG/OM abstract model. Section 2.2 gives an outline of the Common Object Request Broker Architecture (CORBA), and Sec. 2.3 details some of the components involved in an ORB architecture. Section 2.4 describes the Interface Definition Language (IDL). Section 2.5 gives an outline of the structure of a language mapping for CORBA. A mapping to a programming language provides interfaces to the CORBA concepts so that they can be used from the programming language the programmer is using. Since Chap. 4 in this book is completely dedicated to language mappings, we postpone the detailed discussion of the C language mapping and other mappings to that chapter. Finally, Sec. 2.6 details the Dynamic Invocation Interface in terms of the C language, and Sec. 2.7 provides an overview of such an interface in C++. Chapter 3 continues the description of CORBA 1.1 (including the Interface Repository, the ORB interface, and the Basic Object Adapter), and also provides details on CORBA 1.2 and the important extensions that will be provided by CORBA 2.0. Chapter 4 is dedicated to mappings of the CORBA specification to various programming languages.

2.1 The CORBA Object Model

The CORBA/OM is a concrete object model based on the OMG/OM described in the previous chapter. It therefore provides more detailed specifications regarding concepts defined in the OMG/OM, maps concrete constructs to abstract concepts, and defines model restrictions to build a model that can be implemented. The OMG/OM is an abstract object model that is the basic object model for many technologies. The CORBA/OM, on the other hand, provides the underlying definitions for a particular technology. Such an object model focuses on a particular set of constructs and on a certain view. CORBA in general is interested in providing mechanisms and interfaces that enable requesters of service (clients) to be separated from providers of service (servers). It is especially interested in the clients and the encapsulated interfaces that allow services to be provided. It is less interested in object implementations (apart from the notion of having servers provide services by activating implementations). The model is therefore focused on interactions between clients and servers, and especially on concepts meaningful to requesters of service.

2.1.1 Requests

Clients are entities that request service. A *request* associates a set of information with a particular point in time. The information includes the operation requested, the target object to which the request is made, the parameters of the request (in the form of values), and an optional context. An *object* is an encapsulation of services that may be requested by clients. A *value* is anything that may be a parameter in a request. Values can identify an object. An *object reference* is a name that identifies a certain object in a consistent way.

The result of a request is the provision of a certain service to the client. The client may or may not be returned a set of results. Requests may also cause the formation of exceptions to denote abnormal conditions. They may also provide additional information in the request context. The model supports the notion of a *request form* as a mechanism that can be used to issue requests. Request forms are either built within a certain programming language (using the programming language mapping) or dynamically created using the Dynamic Invocation Interface.

2.1.2 Operations

An *operation* denotes a service that may be requested. An operation is an entity that has a name and a signature. A *signature* defines the values that can be used for parameters and results in the operation request. An operation can be represented as

```
[oneway] <return result type> <operation name> (
    parameter1, ..., parameterN)
    [raises(exception1, ..., exceptionK)]
    [context(contextName1, ..., contextNameL)]
```

Each parameter has a mode and a type. The *mode* is one of *in*, *out*, or *inout*, according to whether the value is passed in from the client to the service provider, passed out from the service provider to the client, or both. The *type* defines what the set of allowed values for this parameter is. Each exception in the optional *raises* clause is an indication that this exception may be signaled to terminate the request. An *exception* usually means that the request was not completed successfully; it can be used to pass information back to the originator of the request. Each element in the optional context clause specifies a context that may be passed from the service requester to the service provider. A *context* can provide a service implementation with additional context information which may be required on an operation-specific basis.

The CORBA/OM defines two operation execution semantics. The default semantic is called *at-most-once*; this means that if the operation returned successfully, it was performed exactly once, and if an exception was raised, then the operation was executed either once or not at all. The optional *oneway* specifier indicates that the *best-effort* operation semantic should be used, meaning that the operation does not return any results and the requester does not wait for the provider to complete the operation.

2.1.3 Interfaces and attributes

An *interface* specifies a set of operations. The interface of an object describes the operations that may be used by clients to issue requests. Interfaces are defined using the Interface Definition Language described in Sec. 2.4. An interface may also have attributes. An *attribute* is modeled by a pair of accessor functions, one used to get the attribute's value and one used to set the attribute's value. An attribute may be specified to be *read-only*, in which case the setting function is omitted. Interfaces are related through the interface inheritance relationship. This mechanism allows objects to support multiple interfaces by supporting an interface that inherits from multiple interfaces.

2.1.4 Types

Types aggregate sets of values. A value may be a member of a type. The *extension of a type* (sometimes also called the type extent) is the set of values which are members of the type. An *object type* is a type whose member values are objects. Types are used to define what values may be injected into operation parameters. Figure 2.1 details the legal values in the CORBA/OM. Basic Value denotes values that are of basic types, whereas Constructed Value denotes types such as structures, unions, arrays, and variable-length arrays (sequence). Of special interest is the type *any*, which can represent any possible type.

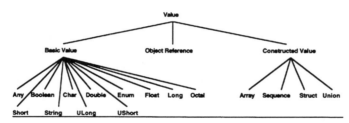

Figure 2.1 Values in the CORBA OM.

2.1.5 Implementations

Object *implementations* are the systems which actually perform the services requested by the clients. The implementations perform the behavior seen by the requester. The CORBA implementation model consists of an execution model which describes how services are performed and a construction model which describes how services are defined.

The execution model specifies that services are provided by executing code that operates on sets of data. The execution can deliver back a result, change the state of the system, or both. A *method* is a code segment that is executed upon getting a request.

The implementation model includes a construction model which specifies how object implementations are constructed. In particular, it needs to specify how methods are defined and how method dispatch is performed. The construction model must also specify how objects are created and destroyed.

2.2 The Common Object Request Broker Architecture

This section details the ORB-based architecture that supports portability and interoperability. Figure 2.2 illustrates a client making a request for a service to be provided by an object implementation. The client has an object reference for the object and activates operations for this object. This reference is opaque, and the client has no notion as to the location of the object implementation, the language used to implement it, or any other detail about the implementation. It has only a specification for an operation request which is part of the interface. The client issues the request, and the ORB is responsible for delivering the request to the object implementation in a format that the object implementation can respond to. It should be mentioned that the term *client* is specific to the particular request being issued. The client can itself be an object implementation that is being used by

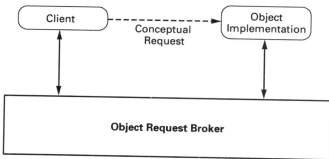

Figure 2.2 Client request and object implementation.

other clients. Thus there is no special annotation making an object a client object or an object providing service through the ORB.

Object interfaces are defined using the Interface Definition Language (IDL) that is part of CORBA and may be used in two ways. Interfaces are mapped to host programming languages as IDL stubs; the programmer may then use these stub routines to invoke requests. Interfaces are also stored in the Interface Repository, which provides information regarding interfaces and types at runtime. Thus clients can construct dynamic requests at runtime using the Dynamic Invocation Interface (DII). Clients interface with the ORB (both with IDL stubs and with the DII) in the natively used programming language. Therefore IDL stubs are mapped into the respective programming language and the DII services are provided from within the programming language. Since the DII is only one interface and the IDL stubs can be automatically generated from the IDL interface definitions, language mappings can be provided so that usage from within a programming language will be easily supported.

When the client has a handle to an object implementation and desires to issue a request, two possibilities are available. If the interface was defined in IDL and the client has a definition for the type of the object implementation, a static invocation can be issued. The request is made using an IDL stub specific to the interface of the target object. Otherwise, the DII can be used. This interface is independent of the interface of the target object and can therefore be used even without thorough knowledge regarding the target object's interface. The request is constructed at runtime and makes no use of IDL stubs. Instead the request is handled by the dynamic invocation module, which uses the information stored in the Interface Repository. Figure 2.3 illustrates the two possible request paths. Note that when

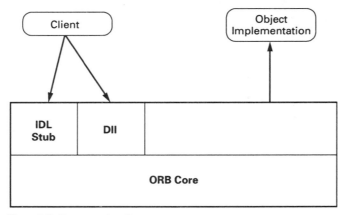

Figure 2.3 Two request paths.

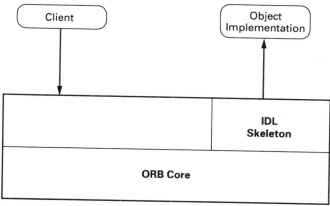

Figure 2.4 Request delivery to the object implementation.

the request is delivered to the object implementation by the ORB, that object is not aware and does not care which path was taken.

Figure 2.4 shows the delivery of the request to the object implementation. After the interface of an object has been defined using IDL, an IDL skeleton is generated. Requests are passed from the ORB through this skeleton. An IDL skeleton will be used regardless of whether the request was issued through an IDL stub or using the DII. The object implementation is made available using information stored in the Implementation Repository at installation time. Figure 2.5 summarizes the information used by clients and object implementations.

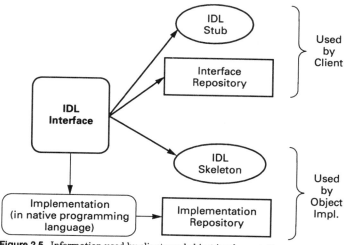

Figure 2.5 Information used by clients and object implementations.

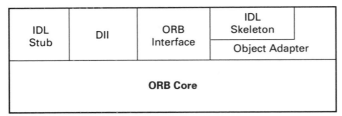

Figure 2.6   Conceptual ORB subcomponents.

CORBA defines a number of ORB subcomponents that interact to support this required functionality. Figure 2.6 illustrates a simple schematic view of these components. The schema does not mean to necessitate a particular decomposition of the ORB. In fact, CORBA does not make any assumptions or requirements regarding ORB implementations. It only defines the interfaces and services that must be provided by every ORB.

2.2.1 The ORB core

The ORB core provides the basic communication of requests to the various components. It can be seen as the underlying mechanism used as the transport layer. CORBA is meant to support multiple systems and thus was separated into modular components so that different implementations can be used. This both allows different ORB cores to be used by identical layers (while hiding the differences to external components) and allows different layered components to use the same core. The core provides basic object representation and communication of requests.

2.2.2 IDL stubs and skeletons

The Interface Definition Language is used to define interfaces, thus creating object types. The definition of the interfaces is the route by which a client is informed which services are supported by the object implementation. Each interface defined in IDL specifies the operation signatures through which requests are made. It should be noted that the IDL source code is necessary for allowing communication of requests, but the source is not necessary at runtime. The IDL definitions are used to create the stub and skeletons and are used to populate the Interface Repository. Only these are used when submitting a request.

Clients issue requests from within their host programming language. IDL is only a definition language; CORBA does not define a manipulation or invocation language. To allow interfaces written in IDL to be used from programming languages, mappings are provided.

A mapping will take an IDL definition and generate a stub for each interface within the native programming language. The stubs allow programmers to invoke operations defined as part of the target object's interface.

Implementation skeletons are generated for each interface within a programming language. They are the structures which actually invoke the methods implemented as part of the object implementation. They are called implementation skeletons because they are created from the IDL definitions yet include no implementation details. The developer of the object implementation must fill the skeleton with actual code that will be invoked when a request is received.

An IDL skeleton usually depends on the object adapter; there may be multiple skeletons for the same interface and the same language with different object adapters. It is even possible to provide object adapters that do not make use of IDL skeletons to invoke implementation methods, but rather create implementations "on the fly" when requests come in.

The Dynamic Invocation Interface allows the dynamic creation of requests. This allows a client to directly specify an object, an operation, and a set of parameters and invoke this request. The interface used is common to all objects and all operations, and does not make use of the stub routines generated for each operation in each interface. Information regarding the parameters and the operation itself is usually acquired from the Interface Repository.

2.2.3 Object adapters and the ORB interface

The object adapter provides an interface to ORB services which the object implementations can use. It also provides services needed when a request comes in from the ORB core and is delivered to the skeleton for method invocation. Since object implementations can be extremely diverse in terms of their characteristics, many object adapters are envisioned. This allows support for very diverse cases without changing the architecture.

Other services used by object implementations are provided directly through the ORB interface. This interface is identical for all ORB implementation and does not depend on the object adapter used by the object implementations. Naturally, this interface will still be mapped to the host programming language used by the object implementation. These operations are also available to the client objects.

2.2.4 Repositories

The Interface Repository (IR) maintains representations of the IDL definitions. These are persistent objects that are available at runtime.

The IDL information is therefore maintained as "live objects" to be used at runtime. For example, the DII will use the information maintained in the IR to allow programs to issue requests on interfaces that were unknown when the program was compiled. The IR service is also used by the ORB itself to perform requests. For example, the IR information is necessary for performing marshaling and unmarshaling of parameter values. The IR is also used as a persistent store for additional information pertinent to interfaces, such as annotations and debugging information.

The Implementation Repository maintains information needed by the ORB to locate and start up the object implementations necessary to fulfill a request. It is also used for additional information associated with object implementations, such as debugging information and security specifications. The Implementation Repository is specific to an operating environment, since it is used in the construction and activation of object implementations.

2.2.5   Object references

Requests are issued upon an object reference. An object reference is an opaque representation that is used to denote an object in the ORB-based environment. Both clients and object implementations use object references. Object references are uniform only within an ORB implementation; different ORB implementations can provide different representations. However, since both clients and object implementations use object references as opaque data values, different representations will not affect clients or object implementations. An ORB provides a mapping of object references to the programming language used. This mapping must not depend on the ORB representation of object references.

CORBA defines a distinguished object reference used to denote no object. This reference is guaranteed to be different from any other object reference. In some environments this maps to a reference of the null (or nil) object.

2.2.6   Example ORBs

CORBA defines an architecture for ORB-based environments. It does not place restrictions on ORB implementations. The CORBA specification itself provides a number of examples of ORB implementations, including a client, an implementation-resident ORB, a server-based ORB, and a system-based ORB. Figure 2.7 illustrates possible implementations (Unix terms are used for operating system concepts to make the description more concrete, but ORBs have no dependence on or relation with Unix).

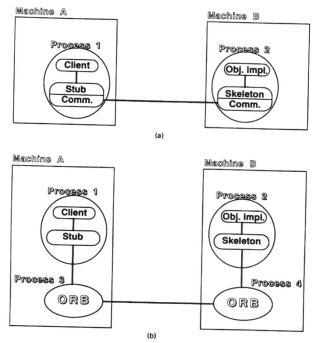

Figure 2.7 Possible ORB implementation strategies: (*a*) Client- and implementation-based ORB; (*b*) server-based ORB.

Clients and implementation-based ORBs implement the ORB as routines resident in the source and target sites which hold the client and the object implementation. Every client and every implementation process interacts with these routines, which collectively provide the ORB functionality. One may even think of an implementation where the stubs themselves are responsible for locating an implementation and use some interprocess communication mechanism to facilitate requests.

In a server-based ORB, interaction is done with servers who provide ORB functionalities. Thus clients interact with such servers to issue requests, and object implementations interact with these servers to provide service. The servers are responsible for the routing of the requests. In system-based ORBs, the ORB services are actually part of the services provided by the underlying operating system. This can increase robustness and security as well as provide increased performance using a variety of optimizations.

2.2.7 Foreign object systems

CORBA is the basis for interoperability between object-based systems. Since there are many object systems already available which are not designed to be CORBA-compliant, and since there may be object systems built in the future which will not be specifically managed by an ORB, CORBA suggests a variety of ways to integrate foreign object systems into an ORB-based environment. By allowing such integrations, CORBA ensures that interaction with all object-based systems is possible. This in turn allows CORBA to become the main component responsible for object interaction in any object-based environment.

The main goal of interfaces to foreign systems is to allow objects managed by foreign object-based systems to be accessible through the ORB and to allow such objects to issue requests on objects managed in the ORB-based environment. Since different object systems manage their objects differently and have different characteristics and constraints, CORBA describes a number of possible integration techniques. These are shown in Fig. 2.8.

Objects within a foreign system may be registered as object implementations of the Basic Object Adapter (BOA). For other foreign object systems, this will not be appropriate. If, for example, the foreign system will manage its own objects (for such reasons as perfor-

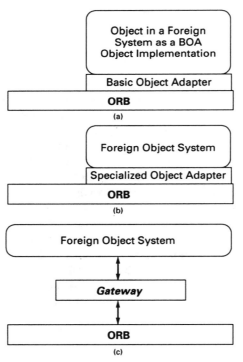

Figure 2.8 Possible integration of foreign object systems.

mance, specialized capabilities, etc.), then it will not present itself to the control of the BOA. In such cases, a specialized object adapter will be supplied. For example, the integration of object database systems conforming to the ODMG standard (this will be discussed in Chaps. 7 and 8) into an ORB-based environment is done through a specialized adapter called the Database Object Adapter. This adapter allows objects managed by the database to be registered with the ORB in a very efficient manner; more on this in Chap. 7. Finally, a foreign system may be integrated into an ORB-based environment using a gateway. This can allow the foreign system to behave as just another ORB in the environment.

2.3   Clients, Implementations, and Object Adapters

Clients issue requests that eventually end up invoking a method in the object implementation. Object adapters are the main interface through which object implementations access ORB services.

2.3.1   Clients

An object is a client in the context of a request (it is a client since it is requesting service from another object). The request is issued using an object reference, an operation name, and a set of parameters. Object references serve both as the handle on which the operation is requested and as possible values for parameters. In fact, the OMG/OM defined each operation to be associated with a controlling parameter; this is the object reference used for sending the operation in the CORBA/OM. Using the object reference for the target object and using object references as parameter values are no different.

A client makes a request from within the application code. The client code uses the IDL stubs as it would use library routines. This behaves similarly to a library function call. However, when the stub routine is called, the object reference for the target object is mapped to the object reference as represented by the ORB. The stub then calls the ORB, and the client request is managed by the ORB (see Fig. 2.9). The ORB is responsible for locating the object implementation and routing the request to that implementation, as well as delivering any results back to the client. If an error occurs during the method invocation or if the ORB cannot complete fulfilling the request for any of a variety of reasons, an exception may be delivered in the client's operating context.

If the client was compiled before the target object's interface was completed, it is possible that the stubs for the target object are not available. The client code therefore cannot access the interface for this object. In this case, the client can name the type of the object and operation to be invoked and use the DII. The client can then construct

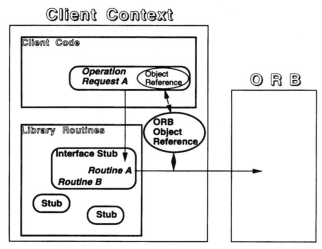

Figure 2.9 Client request using the ORB.

the call programmatically using a sequence of calls for building up the invocation and the parameters, and then starting the request.

A client uses object references to issue requests and as values for parameters. Clients normally receive object references as output parameters of past requests or from invocations that were sent to the client from other clients. (Recall that a client is one making a request; the object which is the client in a certain request may have been the object implementation in another call. In fact, an operation performed by an object implementation will often cause services to be requested by the object implementation in order to complete the original request; in these requests, the object implementation is the client.) Such object references can even be converted into a string format that can be made persistent by simply storing it to disk. This string can later be turned back into an object reference by the same ORB that converted the reference into a string.

2.3.2 Object implementations

Object implementations encapsulate the state and behavior of the object. These are internal to the object, but the behavior is used by the skeletons to provide services for the clients. CORBA defines only the necessary mechanisms for invoking operations. It does not define specifically how these objects are activated or stopped, how they are made to persist, how access control is handled, and so on. However, since these object implementations must function in a real environment, all these issues must be addressed. The implementation is free to make choices regarding these issues.

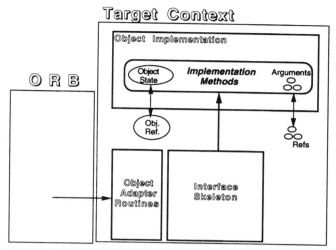

Figure 2.10 Delivery to the object implementation.

Figure 2.10 shows a typical use of an object implementation. The method is called from the interface skeleton and passed any object references that were sent as parameters. The object reference for which the call was made is used to identify the object state. The object implementation may interact with the ORB (primarily through the object adapter) to access services such as creating new objects and converting references to strings and back.

2.3.3 Object adapters

Object adapters are the primary ORB service providers to object implementations. The ORB itself also publishes an interface that may be used by the object implementation, but the object adapter provides most of the ORB-related services which will be commonly used by the object implementation. Object adapters publish a public interface that is used by the object implementation and a private interface that is used by the interface skeleton. The adapters themselves make use of the ORB-dependent interface. The following are examples of services provided by object adapters:

- Method invocation used in conjunction with the skeleton
- Object implementation activation and deactivation
- Mapping of object references to object implementations, generation of object references
- Registering object implementations so that they may be found when a request comes in

CORBA does not require all object adapters to support the same functionality or the same interface. Object adapters may be specialized, since they are a primary service provider for object implementations, as well as a major player in the request delivery mechanism (see Fig. 2.11). The CORBA specification itself defines only the Basic Object Adapter (BOA). Any CORBA-compliant implementation must provide a BOA; this will be discussed in the next chapter. However, the CORBA specification does not place any limitations on definitions of additional object adapters; in fact, the specification itself provides some examples of situations where additional object adapters will probably prove useful. Still, since object implementations rely on the object adapter interface, producing a very large number of object adapters is not recommended. This is not restrictive, since different object adapters should be used only when different services or a different quality of service is required. Thus each object adapter will typically be able to support a large set of object implementations.

An example presented in the CORBA specification is the Library Object Adapter (LOA). The BOA starts up a processing thread for each request, or even a separate process for each object invocation. This may be unacceptable for library implementations that may be shared by multiple clients. In addition, library objects may actually be running within the client's context, so that activation and authentication are not required, thus greatly improving performance. If these object implementations were supported through the BOA, these potential optimizations would not be possible. When the LOA is provided, the improved behavior can be attained.

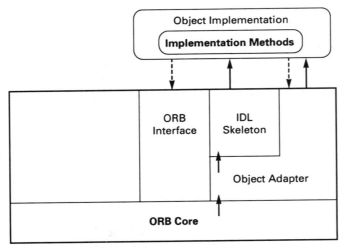

Figure 2.11 Object adapters.

2.4   The Interface Definition Language

The Interface Definition Language (IDL) is the language used to specify the interfaces that are used by clients to issue requests. Object implementations provide methods that provide the necessary services defined by the interfaces. Interfaces are defined in IDL and used by the client programs. IDL is not used for writing code, but only specifications. The client will therefore not be written in IDL; it will use the IDL interface specifications, but the actual call will be done in the native programming language. These calls will be a result of a mapping of the IDL interfaces to the programming language. The object implementations also are written not in IDL but in a (possibly different) programming language. The interface operations then map to the implementation methods.

IDL is used as a language-neutral way to define an interface. It is not a full programming language, but rather a definition or specification language. This section describes the IDL and gives examples of IDL constructs. The description will not provide a full grammar definition for that language; those who need a full grammar definition for IDL are referred to the CORBA specification, Chap. 4.

IDL is probably closest to the C++ programming language. It obeys the same lexical rules as C++, has similar syntax, and is expected to track changes made in C++ by the ANSI C++ committee. The IDL grammar is actually a subset of the C++ grammar with additions necessary for distributed invocations. IDL also provides full support for C++ preprocessing as well as a similar use of pragma definitions.

2.4.1   IDL specifications

An IDL file contains one or more specifications. Specifications are module definitions, constant definitions, type definitions, interface definitions, or exception definitions. Each of these specifications forms a naming scope where identifiers of types, constants, attributes, operations, and exceptions are scoped. Names follow conventional scoping semantics; a name can be used in an unqualified form within a particular scope. If it is not resolved within the scope, it is searched for in successively outer scopes. Qualified names can also use the form

<scope name>::<identifier>.

Names have global scope. Thus if an identifier by the name of identifier1 is defined in an enumeration definition named enumeration1, which is defined in an interface definition named interface1, which is defined in a module name-module1, then the global qualified name will be

::module1::interface1::enumeration1::identifier1.

```
module Accounts {

interface Account {
// Place here definitions for type, constants, attributes, account, etc.
};

interface CheckingAccount : Account {
// Place more definitions or override
};

interface SavingsAccount : Account {
// Ditto
};

interface PreferredCheckingAccount : CheckingAccount, SavingsAccount
{
        // Order of derivation is not significant; note that Account is
        // an indirect base interface through two inheritance paths.
        // If CheckingAccount and SavingsAccount have elements
        // with identical names then references to those must be
        // qualified.
};

};
```

Figure 2.12   Simple IDL specification.

Interfaces are composed of a header and a body. The header names the interface and specifies an optional inheritance structure. The interface body can contain declarations of constants, types, exceptions, attributes, and operations. The interface is therefore the main component in IDL specifications (hence the name *Interface* Definition Language).

Interfaces can be derived from zero or more interfaces. Derived interfaces inherit the declarations of the base interfaces and can include new declarations as well. Redefinitions of inherited declarations are also permitted in IDL. Multiple interface inheritance is supported in IDL, and therefore ambiguity resolution rules are supplied in IDL. Ambiguities must be resolved by qualifying identifiers.

Interfaces define the basic elements used by clients and object implementors. They serve as a grouping of operations and attributes. They also serve some more mechanical purposes, such as name scoping and organization of types, constants, and exceptions. Figure 2.12 gives an example of a simple IDL specification.

Note that contents, types, and exceptions are bound to an interface when it is defined, so that inheriting interfaces will not change the meaning of definitions. Thus if CheckingAccount defines a

```
const short AccountNameMaxLength 8;
void openAccount ( in char[AccountNameMaxLength] );
```

and `PreferredCheckingAccount` redefines `AccountName-MaxLength`, the signature for `openAccount` still accepts a character array of size 8.

Constructs for naming data types are available in IDL. These are similar (both in syntax and semantics) to C typedef declarations.

2.4.2 Data types

IDL supplies both basic data types and constructed data types. Basic data types available in IDL include long, short, unsigned long, unsigned short, float, double, char, boolean (can take only the values TRUE and FALSE), an octet type (an 8-bit quantity that will not undergo any conversions), and the type any. The any type can represent any value.

In addition to these basic types, IDL supports structures, unions, and enumerations. These are similar to C and C++ structs, unions, and enums. Other complex types include arrays and template types. Arrays are used for fixed-size multidimensional holders where each element is of a certain data type (similar to C arrays). The array size in each dimension is fixed at compile time. Template types include strings and sequences. A sequence is a one-dimensional array with a maximal size and a dynamically changing length. The length must not grow larger than the maximum length. Sequences may be either bounded or unbounded. Bounded sequences have a maximal size (which is specified at the time of declaration), whereas unbounded sequences do not have an explicit maximal size definition. Strings are similar to sequences of type char. Strings also have a bounded version as well as an unbounded version.

2.4.3 Operations

IDL operations have a declaration similar to C functions. Each IDL operation has a signature that consists of a name, a result type, and a parameters list. This list has zero or more parameter declarations. Each such declaration specifies a parameter name, a parameter type, and an attribute which determines in which direction the parameter is to be passed. An *in* attribute specifies that the parameter is passed from the client to the server, an *out* attribute means that the parameter is passed from the server to the client, and *inout* means both. For an inout parameter of type *string* or *sequence*, the outbound value may not be of a larger size than the inbound value.

Each operation has either standard semantics or *oneway* semantics. This is as defined in the OMG/OM; standard semantics are at-most-once semantics, whereas oneway semantics are best-effort semantics. This does not guarantee a delivery of the call. Operations with oneway semantics should not have out parameters, and the result type should be void.

Operation signatures also contain an optional *raises* clause. This specifies which exceptions may be raised from within an operation's invocation. If an exception is raised within an operation's invocation, the results of the out and the inout parameters are undefined. Operations using oneway semantics may not include a raises clause.

The operation signature can also include an optional context expression. This specifies a list of identifiers (which reference values) that are part of the client context and are passed as part of the operation invocations. These may then be used both by the ORB and by the object implementation for processing the request.

2.4.5 Attributes

Attributes of an interface are logically equivalent to a pair of accessor operations. Thus an attribute declaration of

```
attribute long cashBalance;
```

is equivalent to

```
long _get_cashBalance();
void _set_cashBalance(in long cb);
```

An attribute may be declared as *readonly*, in which case there will be only one function to retrieve the attribute value.

2.4.6 Exceptions

Exception declarations take the form of structures declarations. Exceptions have identifiers and member definitions. The value of the exception is associated with the exception using its members. Members are used to access the values when an exception is raised.

Standard exceptions corresponding to standard runtime errors are defined for the ORB. Table 2.1 lists the standard exceptions as defined in the CORBA specification. Standard exceptions may be raised by any operation in any interface without a need for an explicit raises clause. Each standard exception includes a `completion_status` which describes the relation between the operation invocation and the raising of the exception; this value will be one of:

Yes: The method in the object implementation completed before the exception was raised.

No: The method in the object implementation was never entered when the exception was raised.

Maybe: The method status is unclear.

TABLE 2.1 CORBA standard exceptions.

Exception Name	Exception Description
UNKNOWN	Unknown exception.
BAD_PARAM	Invalid parameter used.
NO_MEMORY	Memory allocation failure.
IMP_LIMIT	Implementation limit was violated.
COMM_FAILURE	Communication failure.
INV_OBJREF	Invalid object reference.
NO_PERMISSION	Attempted operation does not have permissions.
INTERNAL	ORB internal error.
MARSHAL	Error while marshaling a parameter or a result.
INITIALIZE	ORB initialization error.
NO_IMPLEMENT	Operation implementation is unavailable.
BAD_TYPECODE	Bad typecode.
BAD_OPERATION	Invalid operation.
NO_RESOURCES	Request has insufficient resources.
NO_RESPONSE	Request is not getting response.
PERSIST_STORE	Failure in persistent storage.
BAD_INV_ORDER	Invocation construct is out of order.
TRANSIENT	Temporary failure - reissue request and go on.
FREE_MEM	Can't free memory.
INV_IDENT	Invalid syntax for identifier.
INV_FLAG	Invalid flag used.
INTF_REPOS	Error while using interface repository.
CONTEXT	Error in context object.
OBJ_ADAPTER	Error detected by object adapter.
DATA_CONVERSION	Error in data conversion.

2.5   Programming Language Mappings

CORBA was designed to be language-neutral and to facilitate interoperability of clients and object implementations on different platforms, possibly implemented in different programming languages. The CORBA IDL is only a specification language; client implementations and object implementations are still done using programming languages. The functionalities supported by an ORB architecture must therefore be accessible from commonly used programming languages. Without such facilities, the CORBA architecture can not be used.

IDL is a specification language. In it, interfaces are defined. In addition, ORB and object adapter functionalities are commonly presented as interfaces (these are usually implemented as pseudo-objects—pseudo-objects have interfaces but may not actually be implemented by an object; they have the appearance of an object implementation with an interface just like any other, but the implementation may simply trap these operations from within the ORB and service them in the ORB). Clients will invoke procedures or functions from within the programming language being used. These are mapped to the IDL operations and cause a request to be started. On the other side, the object implementation is implemented in its native programming language (possibly different from the client's). When a request is delivered by the ORB and the object adapter, the IDL skeleton uses the programming language procedure to actually do the work. The method could potentially use the ORB or object adapter interfaces, or even become a client by issuing a request to another object.

CORBA defines how programming languages make use of the interfaces and services. CORBA actually provides two ways in which programming languages may invoke operations and access interfaces. One is using a programming language mapping, and one is using the Dynamic Invocation Interface (DII). Each programming language mapping will include both a static mapping of interfaces and a mapping of the dynamic interface. The static interface is basically a mapping of IDL specifications and CORBA-defined interfaces to the programming language. This enables the programmer to access invocations and services from the programming language. The assumption being made is that to issue a certain request, the IDL interface was written (put into the Interface Repository and other such mechanisms) and then translated into a programming language stub. This was then used by the programmer to issue the request. In most programming languages this means that the stub declaration was used by the programmer's code and compiled with it. This assumption is precisely what the DII avoids. The DII was designed to enable requests to be issued by programs that were created before the interfaces for the operations were defined. Since these interfaces were not ready, stubs could not have been prepared. Therefore, the static interface would not allow these operations to be used from the new code. The DII solves this problem by providing an interface that allows requests to be dynamically built. Instead of defining a specialized stub for each interface and a specialized procedure call for each operation, the DII provides a mechanism by which any operation can be invoked. It views all operations as common constructs that have a name, a list of parameters, and an object reference. By building the parameter list, any operation may be invoked.

The CORBA specification includes a mapping of IDL and of the DII to the C programming language. The DII mapping to C will be described in Sec. 2.6, and a brief overview of a possible DII mapping to C++ is described in Sec. 2.7. In this chapter we give only a brief explanation of what a mapping to a programming language must provide. We postpone the description of the C mapping to Chap. 4. Chapter 4 deals exclusively with mappings to programming languages. Four mappings will be described—one for the C programming language and one for each of the three most popular object-oriented programming languages (C++, Smalltalk, and Objective-C). Other

CORBA mappings (even to non-object-oriented programming languages, such as COBOL) are being thought of and will be available in the future as ORB-based architectures will become dominant in the industry.

2.5.1 Structure of a language mapping

Programming language mappings all have similar structures, since they must all provides access to the same set of features. All mappings provide means of expressing IDL data types, constants, object references, operations, attributes, and exceptions. The mappings also provide the interface to the ORB and to other related components, such as object adapters and the DII interfaces.

The basic DII implementation must provide a mapping for all IDL basic and constructed data types. Since most programming languages have similar (at least basic) data types, this mapping will be similar from one language to the next, yet differences will arise (e.g., the C mapping will map the boolean values TRUE and FALSE to 1 and 0, respectively, whereas a Smalltalk mapping will use the true and false objects, respectively). The language mapping for constructed data types will define what programming language constructs are used and how the programmer uses them.

Object references are used for invoking operations, for being passed as parameters to operations, and for performing ORB operations on; the mapping must define how each of these uses object references. Object references are usually represented as opaque types in programming language mappings. However, mapping for object-oriented programming languages may make use of programming language objects to represent CORBA objects.

IDL operation signatures must be mapped into an invocation structure. Operations have an underlying object reference, a parameter list, and a name. The mapping defines how the parameters are interpreted and used, and how the different modes (in, out, and inout) are implemented. The mapping must also define how invocations affect the flow of control, how exceptions interact with the programs, and different possible memory allocation policies involving parameters. Attributes are modeled as a pair of accessor operations.

Exceptions must be mapped. This includes how exceptions are defined, how they are raised, and how they are handled. Mappings of exception handling typically take one of two approaches. If the programming language has a built-in exception-handling mechanism (e.g., Smalltalk and now C++), then the mapping commonly makes use of the built-in mechanism, and the mapping is elegant and simple. Otherwise, exceptions must be mapped in a somewhat artificial manner, usually involving an additional environment object that is passed into every operation invocation and where exception conditions are stored for handling by the caller.

Finally, any mapping must provide access to ORB functionalities. Interfaces for using services supplied by the ORB and other components in the architecture must be provided to the programmer. Various mappings are possible, for example, a pseudo-object approach (described briefly above and in more detail in Chap. 4). Alternatively, an approach similar to an object library may be used. It is even possible to incorporate these operations as part of other interfaces which are inherited by other interfaces.

2.6 The Dynamic Invocation Interface

The Dynamic Invocation Interface (DII) allows requests to be built up and invoked dynamically by clients. The client need know interface-related information only at the invocation time; no prior knowledge (e.g., at compile time) is necessary. Although the structure and the process of performing requests are very different, the semantics of DII requests are identical to the semantics of requests issued using mapped IDL stubs. A DII request, like a static request, is composed of an operation name, an object reference, and a parameter list. Parameters are inserted into a name-value list, which is then used in the invocation. Since the DII always accepts a parameter list (as an object), it doesn't matter how many parameters there are; this allows the DII to support any invocation. These structures are built and used at runtime (these parameters may still be type-checked at runtime as well as compared to the information in the Interface Repository). It is analogous to the difference between sending a message to an object in Smalltalk (or in Objective-C) and using the *perform* mechanism—e.g., the difference between a static invocation

    aStringObject copyFrom: 10 to: 20

and the more dynamic form

    aString perform: #copyFrom:to: with: 10 with: 20

where the operation name (`#copyFrom:to:` as well as the two parameters (10 and 20) are passed into a fixed interface to cause the same invocation to occur.

The DII defined by CORBA allows such dynamic behavior, which is extremely important for any long-lived and critical system. It allows such systems to remain flexible and extensible. This section describes the CORBA DII and specifically the C mapping of the DII. The next section provides an overview of a possible mapping of the DII for C++.

```
struct  NamedValue {
        Identifier       name;
        any              argument;
        long             len;
        Flags            arg_modes;
};
```

Figure 2.13 The NamedValue structure.

2.6.1 DII structures

The basic structure which supports the DII is the *NamedValue* structure (shown in Fig. 2.13). This structure represents a single parameter. An *NVList* is used to hold all the parameters sent with an operation invocation. An instance of the NamedValue structure contains
the argument name, an argument value, the length of the argument,
and mode flags (which are similar to the mode specifiers in, out, and
inout in IDL and are called ARG_IN, ARG_OUT, and ARG_INOUT).
The value is inserted into a variable of type any which consists of a
type code and a pointer to the actual data.

2.6.2 Requests

A Request pseudo-object is used for the actual construction and invocation of requests. Recall that this means that a regular interface is
provided, although the actual implementation may not actually
involve an object implementation. The operations available in the
Request interface are

```
Interface Request {
        ORBStatus        add_arg(...);
        ORBStatus        invoke(...);
        ORBStatus        delete();
        ORBStatus        send(...);
        ORBStatus        get_response(...);
};
```

The DII separates the creation of requests from the actual invocation. Requests are first constructed and only then sent out. The first
step is actually creating a request. The call is made to the object
which will be invoked. The operation,

```
ORBStatus create_request (
        in       Context       ctx;
        in       Identifier    operation;
        in       NVList        arg_list; // The name-value list
        inout    NamedValue    result;
        out      Request       request;
```

```
                          in    Flags req_flags;
                    };
```

is not actually part of the Request interface, since it is performed on an arbitrary object. It is therefore part of the *Object* interface. Arguments are associated by either inserting an NVList object (that was prebuilt) or using successive calls of add_arg. Each call to add_arg specifies all the information required for that argument (its name, its data type, its value, its length, and flags). Only the value and length must be provided; other information that is provided is used for type checking and validation of argument order, names, and modes. This is checked by comparing it with the arguments that are expected for the operation. Instead of using add_arg, an NVList can be created using the following interface and passed directly into the request.

```
interface NVList {
    ORBStatus add_item(...);    // Used for adding a new item to the list
                                // in much the same way that add_arg adds one
                                // directly to the request; has identical
                                // arguments to add_arg.
    ORBStatus free();           // Frees the list structure and associated memory
    ORBStatus free_memory();    // Frees dynamically allocated memory; does not
                                // free the list.
    ORBStatus get_count(...);   // Returns the total number of items in the list.
};
    ORBStatus create_list(...); // This operation is not part of the NVList interface
                                // but rather a part of the Object interface. It is
                                // used to allocate a list and initialize the space.
```

The context information is passed to the object implementation that will service the request, and the result is returned by the result argument. The operation name itself is of a string type and conforms to IDL identifier rules.

After the request has been created and built, and all the necessary information (target object, operation name, and parameters) is embodied within the request, it can be invoked using the invoke operation. The DII also supplies facilities for issuing a group of requests simultaneously (without any guarantee on order). Finally, *delete* reclaims all resources taken up by the request once it has been completed.

2.6.3 The deferred synchronous model

Calling invoke through a request blocks the caller until the result comes back from the object implementation. This synchronous model is the standard model, but the DII supports a deferred synchronous model as well. If the send operation is used, the request is issued and the caller is not blocked. Control is returned immediately, and processing may continue. The caller can later use the get_response operation to determine whether the request has completed. This call determines whether the request has completed; if indeed the request has completed, the out parameters and return values of the request are returned. get_response will block until the request completes unless the RESP_NO_WAIT flag is used. If the request issued was defined using the oneway specifier or if a flag of INV_NO_RESPONSE was used while sending the request, get_response need not be used.

2.6.4 Context objects

Context objects are aggregations of 2-tuples, each one consisting of a name and a string value. These properties allow information to be passed from the client to the object implementations. Context properties are usually composed of information about the client's environment that the object implementation might find useful. Exactly what context information is to be passed to the server is the client's decision. Since all request invocations go through the ORB, the ORB may also use this contextual information.

Context property names are strings and are similar to a series of IDL identifiers separated by periods. Wildcarding may be used ("*") to specify any match. Such segments will match any identifier. In this way, context names can be matched in a very flexible manner that may be used by both servers and the ORB.

Context objects can be dynamically created or destroyed and may be chained together to provide environment context support. Each search for a context value will always start at the nearest context object, and so overriding in the usual sense can be used. In this way very elaborate context structures can be built by different applications. The operations included in the Context interface are

```
interface Context {
    ORBStatus set_one_value(...);    // Sets a single context property.
    ORBStatus set_values(...);       // Sets one or more context properties.
    ORBStatus get_values(...);       // Gets context property values. Can use wildcard
                                     // to match all properties with a name matching
                                     // the specified part and anything in the segments
                                     // which is a wildcard.
    ORBStatus delete_values(...);    // Deletes a property value from the context.
    ORBStatus create_child(...);     // Creates a child context object (chaining).
    ORBStatus delete(...);           // Deletes the context object.
```

```
};
ORBStatus get_default_context(...);  // This operation is not part of the Context
                                     // interface. It is part of the Object interface and
                                     // returns a reference to the default context object.
```

2.7   The DII Mapping to C++

This section presents a sample mapping of the DII to C++. We follow the general mapping of the Hyperdesk C++ mapping (see Chap. 4). Most C++ mappings of the DII are very similar. The differences usually pertain to the main mapping concept, not to the DII mapping specifically.

Mappings of the DII to C++ are very similar to the C mapping of the DII. The main differences involve the use of the C++ built-in facilities (such as encapsulation) to support the DII concepts in a more elegant way. The C++ mapping presented in this chapter provides three C++ classes. The CORBA::Request class is used to instantiate request objects. This class is analogous to the Request interface mapped to C. Objects of type CORBA::Arglist are used as the argument list of the request. This class is analogous to the NVList C construct. However, since the Hyperdesk mapping provides implicit memory management by each class, the management issues of NVLists are handled by the ArgList class. CORBA::Arg objects are used as components in CORBA::ArgLists and correspond to the C NamedValues.

2.7.1   CORBA::Request

The CORBA::Request class instantiates CORBA request objects to perform operations. The object specifies the reference to the target object, the operation identifier, and the operation arguments. In addition, the context and the environment used to return errors are encapsulated as well. The construction of request objects is done using one of the class's public constructors:

```
    Request(const Object& obj, const Identifier& oper, Environment&
env, ArgList& args);
    Request(const Object& obj, const Identifier& oper, Environment&
        env, const Context& ctx, ArgList& args);
    Request(const Object& obj, const Identifier& oper, Environment&
        env, const TypeCode& result_type, void* result_value);
    Request(const Object& obj, const Identifier& oper, Environment&
env, const Context& ctx,
        const TypeCode& result_type, void* result_value);
```

The class provides additional private constructors, an assignment operator, and a copy constructor. Note that if constructors that do not accept an `ArgList&` argument are used, then the argument list will be built using the *add_arg* method.

Two add_arg methods are provided; both associate an argument with the request. The two versions differ in that one includes the identifier of the argument, whereas the other does not (and simple ordering is used). Both methods have the TypeCode, the mode used for the argument, and a value pointer.

Once the request has been fully constructed (the argument list either has been provided in the constructor or has been built up using `add_arg` calls), the request may be issued by calling the `CORBA::Request::send()` method. The method does not block the caller; `poll_response` and `pend_response` may be used to determine whether the operation has completed. The `CORBA::Request ::send_oneway` method may be used for one-way requests where a response is not expected.

2.7.2   CORBA::ArgList and CORBA::Arg

Instances of `CORBA::ArgList` manage argument lists for the requests. Although argument lists can also be built up using the add_arg method of `CORBA::Request`, ArgList objects allow programmers to construct argument lists that may be reused from one invocation to the next, even for invocations of different operations (since even different operations may have similar signatures). The class uses syntactically convenient operators to construct the argument lists; for example,

```
Arg& operator++();       // Can be used to iterate over the argument list
Arg& operator[](ULong index);       // Can be used in the form aList[2] = obj
```

Each argument is represented by an instance of the class `CORBA::Arg`. Each such instance maintains a name, a TypeCode, and a pointer to the value. Accessor and management methods are supported by the `CORBA::Arg` class. Finally, a `CORBA::RequestGroup` class and an additional method in the `CORBA::Request` class are provided for issuing a group of requests simultaneously.

3

The Common Object Request Broker Architecture, Part 2

The previous chapter described the Common Object Request Broker Architecture (CORBA). The IDL was described, as well as how the programmer issues requests using either interface stubs or the DII. This chapter continues the exposition of CORBA 1.1 as defined by the OMG (OMG, 1992b). Three additional components of the CORBA architecture that are described in the CORBA 1.1 specification are presented: the Interface Repository, the ORB interface, and the Basic Object Adapter (corresponding to Chaps. 7 to 9 in CORBA 1.1). Section 3.4 describes the corrections made by the CORBA 1.2 specification. We then describe some of the issues that were not addressed in CORBA 1.1 and CORBA 1.2. These issues brought about the need for the next generation architecture, which will be manifested as CORBA 2.0. CORBA 2.0 is a major improvement over CORBA 1.1 and 1.2 and is much more complete. After describing some of the issues that were unresolved by CORBA 1.X, we give an example of a response to the ORB 2.0 RFI. We then give examples of the request for proposals (RFP) documents issued by the ORB 2.0 Task Force (ORB2.0 TF) and the OMG Technical Committee (OMG TC). Finally, we describe two proposals submitted as a response to these RFPs. In this way we can understand both the issues that are being considered in CORBA 2.0 and the process for deriving these widely accepted specifications.

3.1 The Interface Repository

The Interface Repository (IR) is, as its name suggests, a persistent repository for interface-related information. It is a central component of the operation of the ORB, as it is the central manager of the IDL definitions. This includes persistently storing this information, providing public access to it, distributing it, and managing it.

The two methods for creating and invoking requests are using IDL stub routines and using the DII. In both cases the interface definitions are a prerequisite, and in both cases the ORB itself is involved in the request fulfillment, and must know the structure of the request. This is necessary both for type checking reasons and for marshaling and unmarshaling operations. The ORB must therefore have access to the interface definitions; the IR provides these facilities.

The IR will also be a central component which will allow the interoperability of different ORB implementations (as will be seen in later sections). It is also an excellent source of information for other systems and environments, such as CASE tools (which may provide browsers and editors of type and interfaces) and IDL-to-programming languages compilers. The central role of the IR stems from the fact that it is the keeper of interface information, and interfaces are the most important components in an ORB-based environment (as in any object-based environment).

The IR maintains information as objects. This makes it very easy and natural for programs needing the information to get at it and use it. Interface definitions are represented as sets of objects that contain descriptions for the operations, exceptions, context objects, and parameter types. Constant values and typecodes (describing types as structures) are also maintained. Modules are used as grouping mechanisms; that is, objects such as constants, exceptions, type definitions, interfaces, and other modules may be grouped as a module in the IR. Navigation can then be performed using these groupings.

The IR provides an interface through which the objects are accessible. It provides operations for managing and accessing the objects maintained in the IR. Although these operations and the conceptual framework of the IR are those of an object representation of the interface information, the implementation of the IR is not restricted in any way, and an implementation may choose to provide a non-object-based implementation; the interface to the users of the IR remains object-oriented. For example, the information may be organized not as persistent objects but as some flat passive structure. However, when this information is accessed, appropriate objects are created for the use of the IR clients.

ORBs may access multiple IRs, and IRs may be accessed by multiple ORBs. Typecodes are central to ensuring consistency of different IRs, since the types are described in structural terms. Various systems may also provide IR interfaces if they desire to internally maintain type information yet collaborate in an ORB-based environment.

3.1.1   The structure of an Interface Repository

IR operations are defined for retrieving of information objects maintained in the IR. The specification, however, does not define what operations are available for inserting and creating the information objects maintained in the IR or for the IR administration operations. This was intentionally left unresolved to allow maximal flexibility for IR implementations, since such issues are extremely dependent on operating systems, development environments, and administration policies. The specification gives examples of different ways in which the IR can be populated, such as extraction from IDL definitions, using DII calls, or cloning of informational objects from another IR.

The CORBA specification does not place limitations on the implementation of the repository. Since different implementations may be radically different in many characteristics regarding distribution and replication, the IR definition in the CORBA specification does not provide additional specifications regarding the repository, the management and availability of the IR, or the repository characteristics. Important issues such as security-related topics (what is the security mechanism used, how does it relate to operating system security, what granularity is used for security, etc.) are not discussed in the CORBA specification. Only the retrieval interface is fully specified. This allows different implementations such as flat file structures and complex object database systems to be used. Such different implementation strategies will naturally have very different attributes, and will affect the way the IR can be used in different CORBA-compliant products. This is a good example of how different implementations of the CORBA specification can have very different characteristics and why it is very important to know the details of the different products when selecting a preferred environment; it is not enough to know that an environment is "CORBA-compliant."

The IR maintains information about interfaces. Each interface is represented by an interface object. The IR is therefore basically a collection of interface objects. Each object maintained in the IR can be one of the following types:

`AttributeDef`: An object representing an attribute.

`ParameterDef`: An object representing a parameter of an operation.

`ExceptionDef`: An object representing an exception that may be raised by an operation.

`OperationDef`: An object representing an operation.

`TypeDef`: An object representing a type definition (other than an interface).

`ConstantDef`: An object representing a constant.

`InterfaceDef`: An object representing an interface definition. This object will contain a collection of objects representing attributes, operations, types, constants, and exceptions.

`ModuleDef`: An object corresponding to a module definition. It may contain a collection of objects representing interfaces, types, constants, exceptions, and other ModuleDef objects.

`Repository`: A top-level organizational object that maintains a collection of definitional objects.

The possible containment relationships between these object types are illustrated in Fig. 3.1. In addition to these IDL-construct equivalent objects, the IR maintains information on types that are not interfaces. These types are maintained as *TypeCode* objects. A TypeCode is basically an association containing a "kind" field and a "parameter list:" field. TypeCode objects are used extensively by DII requests and when using the type any. They maintain enough information to completely define the structure of a type. For example, they are used to model IDL built-in types such as `sequence<long, 6>`.

The specification of the IR interface defines a minimal set of interfaces for using the IR. Additional operations will be defined by implementations of the IR to support capabilities such as

Interface browsers

Administrative operations

Versioning capabilities

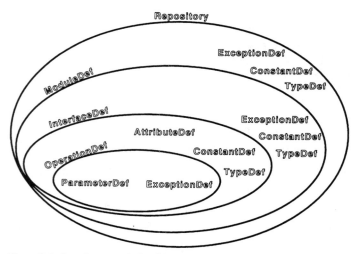

Figure 3.1 Containment relationships among IR object types.

Deletion of interfaces

IDL generation from IR information

Interfaces can be retrieved from the IR in three ways: An `InterfaceDef` object can be retrieved from the object reference, the IR objects and their enclosed collection of "XXXDef" objects can be traversed, or IR identifiers can be used. Getting the `InterfaceDef` using an object reference is done using the `get_interface()` operation, which is part of the ORB interface (as described in the next section). Traversing the IR structures is possible using the names of the individual substructures or using the IR identifiers.

3.1.2 IR containers

The IR interfaces include two base interfaces called *Container* and *Contained*. These interfaces are inherited from by all the XXXDef structures. The Contained interface is inherited by all the IR structures except the Repository interface—that is, by all types which may be contained in other objects. The Container interface is used by the `Repository`, `ModuleDef`, and `InterfaceDef`, that is, by all types which have collections of other objects. These interfaces mainly define navigational operations, which may be then used to locate objects within the IR. The Container and Contained interfaces are shown in Fig. 3.2.

The `Identifier` and the `RepositoryId` types are typedefed to be IDL strings. Identifiers name the constructs maintained in the IR and are not guaranteed to be unique within an IR; they are unique only within a module definition. These strings are used to conveniently name the IR objects in a way that is meaningful to the programmer. `RepositoryIds` are used by the ORB management system itself and are guaranteed to be unique within one IR. They are opaque structures, yet they may be used to retrieve IR objects as mentioned previously. `InterfaceName` is typedefed as an Identifier, and is thus also

```
Interface Container {                          Interface Contained {
   sequence<Contained>  contents(...);            attribute   Identifier     name;
   sequence<Contained>  lookup_name(...);         attribute   RepositoryId  id;
   struct Description {                            attribute   RepositoryId  defined_in;
      Contained  contained_object;                sequence<Container>  within();
      Identifier   name;                          struct Description {
       any           value;                          Identifier   name;
   };                                                 any        value;
   Description            describe();            };
};                                              sequence<Description>
                                                          describe_contents(...);
                                             };
```

Figure 3.2 The `Container` and `Contained` interfaces.

an IDL string. It is a description of the kind of structure represented by the IR object and assumes one of the following values (as a string):

```
ModuleDef
InterfaceDef
AttributeDef
OperationDef
ParameterDef
ExceptionDef
TypeDef
ConstantDef
```
all

The Container interface provides operations for locating objects that are contained within a particular object. The `contents` operation returns a list of such objects and can be used to recursively traverse the containment hierarchy starting from the Repository root object, proceeding through module and interface objects, and culminating with objects whose interfaces derive from the Contained interface. The operation can be used in various filtered modes. For example, the operation can return only contained objects of a certain type. The `lookup_name` operation accesses a named object within a containment subtree (i.e., the object the operation is invoked on and all objects contained by this object either directly or indirectly). Once more, various flags may be set to allow this operation to provide various filtering and search options. Finally, the `describe_inherited` operation returns a description for each of the object's contained objects.

All interfaces except the Repository interface inherit from the Contained interface. Attributes include a name, an id, and an id of the "enclosing" object. Each object meaningful to the programmer which is maintained in the IR has these three attributes. The id of the enclosing object may have two meanings. If the contained object is defined within the containing object (e.g., an operation is defined in an interface or a constant is defined in a module), then the enclosing object is the object in which it was defined. However, contained objects may be inherited. For example, an operation object may be defined in an interface named *interfaceA*, and another interface (*interfaceB*) may derive from interfaceA. The Contained object representing the operation in the interfaceB object will have the defined_in id of interfaceA. This represents the fact that the object is contained through inheritance and uses the semantic of identifying the object from which it was inherited. Note that this is consistent with the enclosing object identifier of the same object as contained in the interfaceA object. Although the meaning is different (it represents the object in which it was defined), it is still the same identifier.

The Contained interface defines two operations. The `within` operation returns a list of objects in which the object is contained. The `describe` operation returns a name and a structure of the object, as discussed in the next section.

3.1.3 The objects of an Interface Repository

Nine more interfaces are defined for the IR, each deriving from either the Container interface, the Contained interface, or both. The `Repository` interface inherits from the Container interface and provides global access to the IR. It instantiates the root object from which navigation of the IR objects begins. It inherits the operations defined in the Container interface and adds an additional `lookup_id` operation which may be used to retrieve an object in the IR using its unique RepositoryId.

The `ModuleDef` and `InterfaceDef` interfaces inherit from both the Container and the Contained interfaces. The `InterfaceDef` interface has an additional attribute

    attribute sequence<RepositoryId> base_interfaces;

which can be used to access all the interfaces which the interface object inherits from, and an additional `describe_interface` operation which returns a structure of the form

```
struct FullInterfaceDescription {
    Identifier                        name;
    RepositoryId                      id;
    RepositoryId                      defined_in;
    sequence<OperationDescription>    operation;
    sequence<AttributeDescription>    attribute;
};
```

which provides access to all attributes and operations of the interface.

Figures 3.3 and 3.4 show the interface definition and the description structure for `AttributeDef` and `OperationDef`, respectively. `AttributeDef` adds a type attribute which holds the TypeCode of

```
interface AttributeDef : Contained {
    enum AttributeMode {NORMAL, READONLY};

    attribute  TypeCode        type;
    attribute  AttributeMode   mode;
};
```

```
struct AttributeDescription {
    Identifier        name;
    RepositoryId      id;
    RepositoryId      defined_in;
    TypeCode      type;
    AttributeMode     mode;
};
```

Figure 3.3 The `AttributeDef` interface.

```
interface OperationDef : Contained {           struct OperationDescription {
  typedef Identifier       ContextIdentifier;    // name, id, and defined_in as usual
  enum  OperationMode {NORMAL, ONEWAY};          TypeCode          result;
                                                 OperationMode        mode;
  attribute TypeCode        result;              sequence<string>       context;
  attribute OperationMode    mode;               sequence<ParameterDescription>
                                                                   parameter;
  attribute sequence<ContextIdentifier>          sequence<ExceptionDescription>
                         context;                                    exception;
};                                             };
```

Figure 3.4 The OperationDef interface.

the attribute and a mode which determines whether the attribute is readonly or not. OperationDef adds an attribute for the TypeCode of the return result, an attribute specifying whether the operation should use the oneway semantic, and a list of context identifiers that apply to the operation. The operation description structure includes lists for the parameters and exceptions that may be raised from an exception invocation.

The ParameterDef interface inherits from the Contained interface and adds an attribute for describing the parameter mode (IN, OUT, or INOUT) as well as a TypeCode attribute. The TypeDef and ExceptionDef interfaces inherit from the Contained interface, adding a TypeCode attribute, and the ConstantDef interface inherits from the Contained interface, adding a TypeCode attribute and an attribute of type any for containing the value of the constant.

3.1.4 IR TypeCodes

TypeCode values are used to denote types of attributes and of arguments in operations. A TypeCode is an association of a kind with a parameter list and is used (as its name suggests) as a coding object for types which are part of many IDL declarations. For example, the IDL type sequence<long, 6> has a kind of tk_long and two parameters (long and 6). Table 3.1 lists TypeCode kinds and possible parameters.

3.2 The ORB Interface

Clients and especially object implementations may request services that are provided by the ORB-based environment. The interface to such services is provided by either the ORB interface or the Object Adapter interface. This section discusses the ORB interface. The operations provided by the ORB interface are those operations that are independent of the object implementation (and the object adapter it uses) and that can be used by both clients and object implementations (the Object Adapter interface is accessible only by the object implementation). The ORB interface must be supported by any ORB, no matter what its implementation strategy.

TABLE 3.1 IDL Typecodes

TypeCode Kind	TypeCode Parameter List
tk_null	
tk_void	
tk_short, tk_ushort	
tk_long, tk_long	
tk_float, tk_double	
tk_boolean	
tk_char	
tk_octet	
tk_any	
tk_typeCode	
tk_Principal	
tk_objref	interface id.
tk_struct	struct name, list of associations of member name and member TypeCode
tk_union	union name, TypeCode of discriminator, list of 3-tuples with label, member name, and member TypeCode
tk_enum	enum name, enum id
tk_string	maximum length
tk_sequence	sequence element TypeCode, maximum length
tk_array	array element TypeCode, length

The operations provided in the ORB interface are all implemented by the ORB. However, for model consistency, these operations can appear to be either ORB-implemented operations or operations on objects themselves. The ORB interface provides some additional operations, such as creating lists and retrieving the default context to be used by requests issued using the DII.

3.2.1 Object references and strings

Object references are opaque types. Therefore, they may not be readily exported from one ORB to another, and they are not a convenient persistent value representation. Except through direct ORB-based invocations, they cannot be passed from one application to another. To facilitate such communication of object references, the ORB interface provides operations for converting object references to strings and back. Strings may be conveniently stored and communicated. The two operations used for these conversions are defined as part of the ORB interface as

```
string  object_to_string ( in Object obj );
Object string_to_object ( in string str );
```

3.2.2 Operations on object references

The conversions of object references to strings and back are operations that can be applied to any object reference. The ORB interface supports additional operations that can be applied to any object reference. The operations described in this subsection have the additional characteristic that they seem to be services provided by the object references themselves; they are, however, implemented directly by the ORB and not by the object implementation referenced by the object reference. These operations are therefore defined in the Object interface. This should be identified as a pseudo-object, whereas the actual implementation is intercepted by the ORB. The operations provided by the Object interface include

```
boolean            is_nil();
Object             duplicate();
void               release();
InterfaceDef       get_interface();
ImplementationDef  get_implementation();
```

The `is_nil` operation tests an object reference for referencing no object (a value of `OBJECT_NIL`). The `duplicate` operation allows an additional object reference to the same object to be created. This operation is necessary, since object references are opaque and ORB-dependent. Neither clients nor object implementations can create object references. The `release` operation reclaims the storage used up by the object reference. Note that the object implementation is not involved in any of these operations and is totally unaware of their occurrence. Thus the object implementation can have no way to distinguish between requests delivered through an "original" object reference and those delivered through a duplicated object reference. The object implementation is also not affected by the release of an object reference (since it may be referenced by other clients).

The `get_interface` operation returns the Interface Repository object associated with this object and can be used to extract meta-information regarding the object type. The `get_implementation` operation returns an object that describes the object implementation from the Implementation Repository.

3.3 The Basic Object Adapter

The CORBA 1.1 specification defines the role of object adapters as the primary way in which object implementations access services provided by the ORB. This includes interfaces for generating object references, implementation registration, and request authentication. The object adapter also serves as a service layer between the IDL skeleton (above which the object implementation works) and the ORB core and is primarily responsible for activating the object implementations. CORBA 1.1 predicts that there will be not one but a number of object adapters, since the architecture will support a wide variety of objects with differing characteristics. Different granularities, lifetimes, policies, and usage will require various adapters that will be custom tailored to provide the necessary functionality for each group. A number of examples like the Library Object Adapter and the Database Object Adapter are envisioned.

CORBA 1.1 also provides a concrete and full definition of an object adapter called the Basic Object Adapter (BOA). This means that any CORBA-compliant ORB environment must provide an implementation of a Basic Object Adapter. The BOA is the most generic object adapter. This means that it can support any object implementation, but is therefore less suited for very specialized requirements. It does the job, but specialized adapters may do the job much more efficiently.

The Basic Object Adapter functionality can mostly be expressed in IDL and is packaged as the BOA interface. Functionalities that cannot be expressed in IDL are those that must map directly to the programming language of the object implementation (e.g., operations that bind the object implementation). The functionalities provided by the BOA are

Creation of object references

Translations of object references (in addition to the ORB functions to translate object references to strings and back)

Activation and deactivation of the object implementation

Activation and deactivation of other objects

Invocation of methods of the object implementation through the IDL skeleton

Authentication of the client making the request

The BOA uses a component called the Implementation Repository. When an object implementation is activated by the BOA, the BOA must use services from the underlying operating system. Using platform-specific information regarding the object implementation, the BOA can start up the object server. This nonportable information is maintained in the Implementation Repository and used by the BOA. The specific information structure of the Implementation Repository is not specified by CORBA, since it is platform-dependent. The binding mechanism between the actual object implementation program and the BOA is also not specified by CORBA, since it is both platform- and programming-language-dependent. The only assumption made by CORBA is that some facility is available for binding the actual method implementations with the skeleton. Once this is done, a two-way invocation scheme is set up, allowing the BOA to call the implementation methods and allowing the implementation to invoke BOA services.

A simple example helps us to more completely understand the function played by the BOA. We follow a very simplistic activation process involving the BOA, the object implementation, and the skeleton:

1. The BOA starts up an implementation using information maintained in the Implementation Repository and operating system services. This is typically called a server (or program).

2. The implementation will prepare itself for servicing requests. When it is finished with the initialization process, it informs the BOA that it is prepared to accept requests.

3. When a request comes in, the BOA informs the implementation, and the actual object that will provide the service will be started. If such an object has already been started (e.g., from a previous request or from an implicit startup stage), then this stage may be skipped.

4. The BOA passes the request through the skeleton to the object implementation methods corresponding to the request.

5. The BOA provides services that may be needed by the object implementations. The BOA interface may be used by the object implementation at any point.

3.3.1 The BOA interface

Figure 3.5 shows a part of the BOA interface as defined by CORBA 1.1. The interaction between an object implementation and the BOA can be separated into two parts. The first category is services provided by the BOA and used by the object implementation. These include creation and destruction of object references, and management opera-

```
interface InterfaceDef;            // As described in Section 3.1
interface ImplementationDef;       // Used by the ImplementationRepository
interface Object;                  // As described in Section 3.2

interface BOA {
    Object create ( .... , in InterfaceDef intf, in ImplementationDef impl );
    void dispose ( in Object obj );
    void change_implementation ( in Object obj, in ImplementationDef impl );
    void set_exception (
            in exception_type  major,  // None, user, or system exception
            in string          userid,
            in void*           param); // Pointer to data
    void impl_is_ready ( in ImplementationDef impl );
    void deactivate_impl ( in ImplementationDef impl );
    void obj_is_ready ( in Object obj, in ImplementationDef impl );
    void deactivate_obj ( in Object obj );
};
```

Figure 3.5 The BOA interface.

tions regarding object implementations and object references. The other category includes object implementation operations called by the BOA, usually using the skeleton. These include activation of the object implementation and calling an interface operation to service a client request.

The BOA makes use of both the Interface Repository and the Implementation Repository. The BOA interface assumes the existence of an InterfaceDef and an ImplementationDef IDL interface to access information maintained in these two repositories. The BOA does not make assumptions as to the implementation of these components, the integration in the ORB environment, and so on. By using these two IDL interfaces, it can access the functionalities it requires without limiting implementations.

There are two kinds of activations performed by the BOA. The first is called *implementation activation* and occurs when a request for a particular object comes in and a corresponding object implementation has not yet been set up. The second is called *object activation* and occurs when no instance of the object can presently handle the request, but the implementation has already been activated. An implementation may couple these two activations together if it is using a separate server for each object request. In general, however, these two are separate activations.

When a request first comes in and an implementation has not yet been activated, the BOA starts up the implementation using operating system facilities. The implementation initializes itself and calls the BOA operation `impl_is_ready` (or `obj_is_ready` if each implementation is coupled with one object). After the implementation is initialized, the BOA will start delivering requests through the skeleton mapping to the implementation methods.

CORBA 1.1 defines four activation policies that must be supported by any implementation of the BOA. The policies differ in the roles and interactions of the implementations, the objects, and the BOA.

The *shared server activation policy* is used when multiple active object implementations reside in one server (or program). The server is activated upon receipt of the first request to be serviced by any of the contained object implementations. After the server has been initialized and the BOA notified, each individual object within the server has to be activated before it can service requests. Therefore, before the first request is sent to an object, the object activation routine specific to that server is called; after that, the object is ready to service requests. Deactivations occur using the `deactivate_object` and `deactivate_impl` routines defined by the BOA interface. Figure 3.6 shows a schema of the shared server activation policy.

The *unshared server activation policy* is used when only one object implementation can be active in a server at any one time. Each object

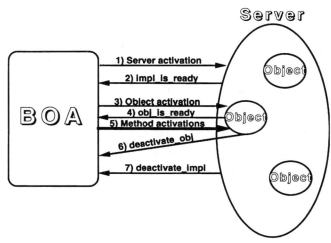

Figure 3.6 Shared server policy.

implementation therefore belongs to a different server and a server is activated for each object implementation. Figure 3.7 describes the interaction between the BOA and a server using this activation policy. The BOA is notified of the server initialization using the `obj_is_ready` operation (not `impl_is_ready`), and deactivation is done using `deactivate_obj`.

The *server-per-method policy* is shown in Fig. 3.8. Each invocation of a method is implemented by a separately started server. When the method completes, the server is deactivated. Several servers may be active at any point in time for the same object (if multiple methods

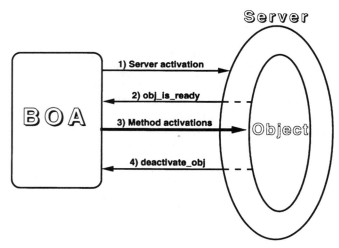

Figure 3.7 Server-per-object policy.

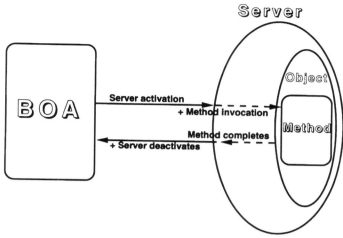

Figure 3.8 Server-per-method policy.

were invoked for that object). Different servers will even be started for multiple invocations of the same method.

The *persistent server policy* is used when the server is activated by an external component (not by the BOA) but still registers with the BOA and receives invocations. The server registers with the BOA using the `impl_is_ready` operation. The BOA will then treat the server as a shared server.

The BOA also provides certain operations supporting authentication and access control. Although the BOA does not enforce any specific style for security, it does guarantee that every method invocation will authenticate the "principal" (which can depend on the security environment used but usually means the originator of the request).

3.3.2 Object references

Object references are generated by the BOA using core ORB services. The operation provided by the BOA interface to create object references is `create`. The operation receives identification information chosen by the implementation (shown as the "..." in Fig. 3.5) as well as an Interface Repository object (corresponding to the interfaces implemented by the object) and an Implementation Repository object specifying the implementation to be used. The identifier information is typically used to distinguish between different objects, but even if two object references (to different objects) use the same identifying information, the two object references will not be the same.

The id value also contains a limited amount of storage that is usually used to locate a persistent representation of the object state if it is inactive. Since a client holding an object reference may use it at any time (even when the implementation is inactive), this storage may be used to find the information necessary to rebuild and restart the implementation.

The implementation associated with an object reference may be changed using the `change_implementation` operation defined in the BOA interface. The `dispose` operation is used to dispose of an object. This handles the destruction of the object only as far as the BOA and the ORB are concerned; the actual object must be destroyed and resources deallocated by the implementation. The `dispose` operation therefore has an invalidation type semantic and provides behavior that is consistent with a state where the object was never created.

3.3.3 C language mapping

The CORBA 1.1 specification provides a C language mapping; the BOA interaction must therefore also be mapped to the C programming language, since the object implementations make use of BOA services. One of the benefits of expressing the BOA as a pseudo-object is that the interface is expressed in IDL. IDL-to-language-specific mappings that are required for IDL stubs can therefore be used to create language mappings for the BOA operations. The same is true for the ORB interface described in Sec. 3.2. For example, the mapping of the `change_implementation` operation will have the following signature:

```
Object BOA_change_implementation (
    Object              boa_object,
    Environment*        env_object,
    ImplementationDef   impl_object);
```

When interacting with the BOA, implementation methods in C have signatures that are identical to the stubs created for the use of client code. The BOA makes use of these conventions when passing requests through the skeleton. When a method requires to terminate with an exception, it uses `BOA_set_exception` (which is the mapping of the `set_exception` operation from the BOA interface).

3.4 CORBA 1.2

The CORBA 1.2 specification (OMG, 1993) is a revision of CORBA 1.1 and contains various corrections and improvements. The changes remain within the scope of the CORBA 1.1 specification; they do not extend any of the definitions. It has been available from the OMG since December 1993 and was prepared by participants from Hyperdesk, SunSoft, DEC, and HP. It was completed by the ORB

Revision Task Force and contains three substantial changes as well as corrections of errors and typos, and improvements regarding clarity and style. The three major changes involve creating a CORBA module, mapping IDL types into C typedefs, and removing of anonymous declarations of sequence and array types.

The first major change was the creation of the CORBA module. All names defined in global scope are then moved to be internally defined within this module. This was done to eliminate the many name clashes with other software libraries that resulted. Other name changes include changing names such as ORBStatus to CORBA_Status and relocating some enumeration definitions to eliminate very long names (when globally scoped). The second major change was mapping the IDL types into C typedefs. This creates such types as CORBA_char, CORBA_boolean, and so on. This change was done to support portable code across different platforms and C compilers. The final major change is the removal of anonymous declarations such as

    sequence<short>   get_all_values();

within an interface; it now requires

    typedef   sequence<short>   seq_shrt;
    seq_shrt   get_all_values();

This change was made to simplify implementations of language mappings.

The changes made in CORBA 1.2 did not change the scope of the CORBA architecture and issues. Since much experience has been gained with CORBA 1.1 since its inception, many extensions and improvements were deemed necessary. CORBA 2.0 is the enhancement of CORBA 1.1 with many of these incredibly important issues addressed. The rest of this chapter will outline these issues and the proposed extensions.

3.5   CORBA 2.0

CORBA 1.2 replaced CORBA 1.1 as the most up-to-date accepted version of the ORB architecture at the Pittsburgh OMG meeting in June 1994. However, the improvements included in CORBA 1.2 were not much more than cosmetic corrections. From the time the CORBA 1.1 specification was published, it was clear that many issues had been left unspecified and that the architecture would have to be extended. Many of the omissions were actually purposely done, but it was clear that an extension and a major revision was needed. It was also clear that CORBA 1.2 was not going to be the next major version; that would be CORBA 2.0. Work on CORBA 2.0 started well before CORBA

1.2 was actually voted in. In fact, the Object Request Broker 2.0 Extensions Request For Information (ORB2.0 Extensions RFI) was published in December 1992 (Mischkinsky, 1992), meaning that the work of preparing the RFI had started even prior to that date. The due date for the responses to the RFI was set for April 26, 1993, and more than 18 responses were submitted! The ORB2.0 Task Force (ORB2.0 TF) has been very active in processing these responses, in creating RFPs, and in driving the formation of CORBA 2.0. It should not come as a surprise that there is such a wide degree of interest in this subject, or that so much work is being put into it. The ORB is the most central component of an OMG environment, and it is felt that CORBA 2.0 will be a much more complete architecture than CORBA 1.X.

This section will discuss the issues being addressed by CORBA 2.0. Although CORBA 2.0 has not been completely defined or accepted at the time this book is being written, much can already be learned about the proposed subjects and topics. The section will follow the CORBA 2.0 process by first describing the contents of the ORB 2.0 Extensions RFI. We then describe some of the suggestions made by various responses to the RFI, and the resulting RFPs issued by the ORB2.0 TF. Because of the volume of the details (especially of the responses) and the lack of space, the section provides only an overview of the major issues and suggestions. It is, however, sufficient for almost anybody except actual ORB implementors and members of the ORB2.0 Task Force.

3.5.1   The ORB 2.0 Extensions RFI

The purpose of the ORB 2.0 RFI (Mischkinsky, 1992) was to receive information and suggestions as to the future direction that should be taken to improve and extend CORBA. It listed areas which seemed to require such extensions, in the view of many industry participants. The RFI did not limit submitters to these issues but suggested that this framework be followed (unless the response submitter felt that it was inadequate). The responses to the RFI were then used to guide the creation of RFPs to extend CORBA.

The ORB is an extremely central component of CORBA; it is the communication mechanism allowing all other OMG-derived services. Therefore, it is extremely important that the ORB be as efficient and elegant as possible. This basically means that the ORB must be kept as simple as possible without compromising the functionalities that are required. The approach taken by the RFI was to guide submitters to provide services outside of the ORB (e.g., as Object Services or Common Facilities) wherever possible.

The RFI requested that any suggestions build on CORBA 1.1 (remember that CORBA 1.2 had not yet been accepted when the RFI was issued). Any issue raised by a submitter should be an extension or enhancement. These can be broadly classified into three types: extensions to CORBA that had been intentionally left incomplete (e.g., the Implementation Repository API), extensions to issues that were addressed in CORBA 1.1 (e.g., additional object adapters), and extensions to the ORB core that were not included in CORBA 1.1 (e.g., support for transactions).

Any submissions as a response to the RFI had to adhere to some guidelines. They all had to be based on the OMG Object Model and be upward-compatible with CORBA 1.1. In addition, the RFI included a detailed list of suggested response topics. These topics were deemed to be central candidates for required extensions, and although responses were not limited to these topics (or required to adress to all these subjects), they provided a framework for dealing with the extensions. The rest of this subsection follows the proposed topics outlined in the RFI.

Interoperation. Perhaps the most important topic on CORBA 2.0's agenda is the interoperability between different ORBs. One of the main objectives of CORBA is to support interoperability. However, CORBA 1.1 lacks any mention of how the ORBs themselves interoperate, so that the architecture does not fully address the interoperability issue. This is felt to be the biggest problem with CORBA by most of the technology users, since interoperation can be achieved only if all parts of the system use the same CORBA-based product; it is presently impossible to have one part of the application use HP's ORB and the other side use IBM's.

The RFI requested information regarding interoperability from both users and implementers. Users were asked to comment on the precise meaning of the required interoperability, what they expected, and what degree of interaction they required between different ORBs and between objects managed by different ORBs. Implementers were asked for opinions on interoperability approaches, mechanisms, and protocols.

Repositories. CORBA 1.1 defined both an Interface Repository and an Implementation Repository. However, many details regarding these central components are still missing. The IR specification defines only operations for retrieving the information; details as to how the IR is populated and managed were intentionally left unspecified. The Implementation Repository is even less well defined. It was actually defined only as a concept, and no details regarding its operations were provided. The RFI requested opinions and suggestions regarding both of these omissions and how the structure and operations for these two repositories should be addressed.

Object adapters.   CORBA 1.1 mentioned the necessity for different kind of adapters to service objects with different characteristics and even gave a number of examples (e.g., the Library Object Adapter and the Database Object Adapter). Still, only the Basic Object Adapter was actually specified and detailed. The RFI therefore asked for information regarding additional object adapters and issues related to such adapters.

Additional language bindings.   CORBA 1.1 provided a C language mapping. However, CORBA is meant to be programming-language-independent. Many more language mappings are therefore required to make this goal a reality. The C++ language binding was issued as a separate OMG initiative (although it is still discussed within the scope of the ORB2.0 TF), but the RFI requested information regarding what languages should be considered next for mapping as well as posing more specific questions, such as how object references should be mapped to the programming languages and whether built-in exception-handling mechanisms should be used for mapping of CORBA exceptions.

Compliance.   Many products claim to be "CORBA-compliant," since that is a very marketable property. However, no test suite has been defined to verify such claims. A verification and certification process is necessary for conformance issues. The RFI asked what the scope of such compliance should be and whether it is possible to be partially compliant. Other related issues included standard benchmarks for measuring implementation performance and IDL mappings. These issues were seen as central and important in view of the central role that ORB technology will play in the future.

Multimedia.   Multimedia is becoming an integral part of today's computer systems. Many applications and software systems make use of these information structures, and it is no longer uncommon to have multimedia functionalities in personal computers. In fact, support for multimedia is already becoming a standard requirement for any serious software development. Any basic architecture supporting today's and tomorrow's applications should therefore address the specific issues pertinent to multimedia.

Multimedia data types require special consideration, since the passing of these data types as data streams has unique characteristics. Such data streams may be classified into three main groups:

Static data streams needed to support images are typically much larger than classic data streams.

Sequential data streams needed to support animation sequences are potentially even more voluminous and require special handling, such as the propagation of deltas.

Isochronous data streams (meaning data streams that are continuous and received at a steady rate) needed to support speech or video transmissions are even more complex.

Any of these data streams require specialized considerations that were not dealt with by CORBA 1.1. The issues are not only issues of volume and synchronization of data streams, but also application-relevant issues such as how these data are controlled by an application and how an application interacts with multiple streams.

Transactions. Most real-world (and especially business type) applications require support for transactions and the ACID properties (atomicity, consistency, integrity, durability). CORBA 1.1 did not address this issue at all. The Object Services Task Force is addressing this issue (as we shall see in Chap. 6), but when the ORB2.0 RFI was issued, it was unclear how transactions would come into play. The RFI therefore requested opinions as to how transactions should be incorporated, whether the ORB itself should support such notions or whether some layering strategy should be used (and if so, what extensions to the core were necessary), and what attributes and functionalities regarding transactions should be supported.

Concurrency. Concurrency is central to distributed systems, yet it was not addressed by CORBA 1.1. The RFI asked whether it should be addressed by CORBA 2.0, and if so, how.

Asynchronous messaging. CORBA does not support a reliable asynchronous messaging model. Since many applications use this model, it should be possible to accommodate this model within CORBA. Opinions were to suggest approaches for incorporating this model.

Multiendpoint interaction and replication. Distributed application design is considerably more difficult than nondistributed application design. Many issues must be addressed by the designer. Even if the environment supports distribution transparency, performance-related issues often force the designer to inspect detailed distribution issues.

Even though such designs are more complex, distributed applications offer such tremendous benefits (such as fault tolerance, load balancing, and sharing of resources) that they are being used more and more. Very complex models such as different replication strategies, multicast-based distribution, and groupware-type applications are no longer scarce.

Such complex distribution models can naturally be implemented by the application builders using point-to-point primitives and handling many of the distribution issues from within the application. However, it would be much more convenient if some form of replication transparency could be provided for application developers to build upon. The RFI requested views regarding such issues (including whether they should actually be dealt with as part of CORBA 2.0).

Relation to standards. The OMG is not the only body working on object-based standards, and CORBA is not the only architecture achieving distributed interoperability support. The Trader architecture and the ODP effort in ISO is only one such example. The RFI asked submitters to address issues regarding what other standards are relevant to CORBA and what efforts should be made to ensure compatibilities and relationships with such standards.

3.5.2 RFI suggestions

Figure 3.9 lists companies that responded to the RFI. It is clear that because of the number of responses, it is impossible to describe the opinions and suggestions received as responses to the RFI. This section will therefore only present a summary of the main issues raised in several RFI responses as compiled by the ORB2.0 TF in preparation of the RFPs and detailed in Watson (1993b). The summary illustrates the issues that the responding companies believe to be the major issues to be tackled by CORBA 2.0.

The responses dealt with all the issues mentioned in the RFI and many more. The most important contribution of the responses was in providing information concerning the necessary functional requirements that CORBA 2.0 should provide. Many of the submitting companies already had commercial CORBA 1.1-based implementations and had accumulated a great deal of experience concerning how these environments are used and what they lack. Three functionality categories were identified as major areas that needed to be addressed by CORBA 2.0: federation of systems using multiple ORBs, dependabili-

Anderson Consulting	Bellcore	Bell Northern Research
British Telecom	Digital Analysis Corp.	Expersoft
Hypedesk	IBM (two submissions from	NeXT
ICL	two IBM laboratories)	Symbiotics
SEMATECH	Isis	TRW
Tandem	SunSoft	
Transarc	Tivoli	

Figure 3.9 Companies responding to the ORB2.0 RFI.

ty of ORB-based systems, and support for a variety of interaction models.

Federation issues include many requirements regarding the way that ORBs work together. The important ORB interoperability issue is the most critical functionality which must be addressed. Once environments using different ORBs can interoperate, a whole set of issues regarding system configuration and management arises. It should be possible to manage an ORB-based environment in a flexible and scalable way. This includes the ability to add a new ORB into an existing configuration, add new objects and adapters to a running ORB, and so on. Security in the ORB environment, as well as the interaction between different ORB environments which may be using different security models, must be addressed. Finally, an important issue is that of support for various sizes and characteristics of objects, especially support for small objects. Extensions to support these might be part of the ORB or part of object adapters, or there might be other possibilities.

Since the ORB is such a major component, many of the responses raised issues regarding the dependability of the ORB and different interaction models required by users to produce dependable applications. Such issues include management and monitoring facilities for the ORB, replication and workgroup models supported by an ORB, and a transaction model.

Interoperability.   CORBA 2.0 must address the issue of interoperability of ORBs from different vendors. This means that the architecture itself must be specific enough to ensure that compliant vendor products can achieve interoperability. Together with the definitions already included in CORBA, the promise of interoperability may finally be realized. Perhaps more than any of the other issues raised by the RFI and its responses, interoperability is likely to require that changes be made to the internal implementation of the ORB; it cannot be handled entirely by external interfaces and layers. Interoperability between ORBs primarily means dealing with the issues of inter-ORB requests and the passing of object references from one ORB to another. This may sound simple, but it is actually very complex. For example, when dealing with request interoperability, the following issues must be addressed:

Finding the destination ORB. Finding the ORB can involve many possible strategies. Requests can always be sent to the original location of the object; if the object migrates, it leaves some forwarding information to enable future requests to make their way to the right ORB. Alternatively, a strategy similar to the Internet gateway approach can be used, in which each ORB is aware of neighboring

ORBs and uses some redirection mechanism. The possible approaches range from simple local strategies to very complex global ORB registration techniques drawing from the Domain Naming System (DNS).

Network connections. For different ORBs to communicate with one another, the network protocols must be in synch. Standardizing of network protocols has never succeeded, and so some kind of gateway approach is probably necessary. However, the gateways must be well designed so as not to cause performance degradation.

Object references. CORBA specifies an opaque object reference type, allowing maximum flexibility in its implementation. Many of the new capabilities that might be supported by CORBA 2.0 may also affect object reference. A good example of this is security. It may be possible to package authentication information as part of the object reference to eliminate the overhead of the security mechanism. However, any such change to the object reference must weigh the benefits against the restrictions imposed by making the object reference more complex. Interoperability functionalities will also affect object references, at least as far as the format of object references used between ORBs goes. There should be a standard object reference format for inter-ORB requests. It should also be possible for ORBs to pass object references using some privately agreed-upon format (if that is more efficient).

Operation specification. Since the request involves an operation name, there must be an interoperable way to specify what operation was called. Some example solutions are the use of a string as the operation name and the use of identifiers in the Interface Repository (and ensuring coordination between the IRs).

Interface Repository. It should be possible to change the information kept in the IR and to add new interface definitions while the system is running. Operations should be added to the IR interface for writing and installing into the IR. All operations supported by the IR should be available at any time, even when the system is running. Thus it should be possible to change interface definitions, add new interfaces, remove interfaces, version interfaces, change interface inheritance structures, and so on.

Since the IR is the central repository for describing the interfaces and types in the system, it is central to many application domains. The IR could be extended to maintain additional information regarding interfaces. This would be a natural way to maintain interface-related information that could be accessed by any party interested in such information (e.g., CASE tools). To support this, the IR specification would have to be extended to provide capabilities for associating additional information with interfaces and for querying this information.

Implementation Repository. CORBA 2.0 should include a definition of the Implementation Repository. Since CORBA 1.1 did not actually specify anything about the Implementation Repository, even the basic architecture needs to be specified. Then basic management functions for building up the information maintained in the repository and accessing it are needed. Dynamic management of the Implementation Repository is also necessary, since object implementations tend to change much more frequently than interfaces do, and it must be possible to replace one implementation with another on the fly.

Initialization. CORBA 1.1 defines pseudo-objects such as the ORB and the BOA which are used by clients and (especially) object implementations for ORB-related services. No mention is made of how these objects are created and how the programmer accesses them. There are additional examples of initialization processes that are not completely defined by CORBA 1.1. CORBA 2.0 should define such initialization processes since without them each vendor will deliver a different approach to accessing these objects and it will be impossible to create portable applications.

Issues that should be addressed by initialization include providing an access interface to the ORB, the BOA, the IR, etc.; providing separate such interfaces for different object needs; and providing access to other object adapters. The initialization interfaces should not be platform-specific, should be mapped to multiple programming languages (initially to C and C++), and should not constrain implementations unnecessarily.

Object adapters. A set of object adapters must be defined as additions to the BOA to support objects that differ in terms of lifetime, granularities, implementation approaches, management, and so on. Although a variety of support mechanisms must be provided, it is suggested that there will not be a very large number of object adapters. To ensure that only a manageable number of adapters are formed (yet still support many object strategies), a more complete adapter architecture must be specified. Such an architecture should address

Abstraction issues. Multiple adapters providing specialized functionalities do not necessarily need specialized interfaces. Functions may be generalized and interfaces hide different behaviors; adapters should in general differ in implementations but not in interface (as much as possible).

Specialization issues. New adapters should be created as specializations of already defined adapters, and extension by deltas should be used.

Simplicity. If possible, functionalities should not be incorporated into the adapters, but rather packaged as external functionalities (e.g., using object services). This follows the general CORBA approach of keeping the ORB and the OA lean and simple.

After the overall architecture has been defined, many support styles could be offered. These include

Support for objects with varying characteristics

Support for different implementation styles (e.g., multithreaded) and locations

Support for resource balancing done by the adapter and resource management

Provision of management facilities

Other object-related issues include source code portability of object implementations across different adapters, effects that dynamic registration of adapters with ORBs may have on the interaction with other ORBs, the use of adapters for monitoring capabilities, and more.

The BOA itself must be able to support fine-grain objects. The present assumption of maintaining a large structure, including 1024-byte reference data and references to objects in the IR and in the Implementation Repository, does not allow support of many small objects. The repeated interaction between the BOA and the Implementation Repository also has its effect. All this overhead is unacceptable for objects the size of a cell in a spreadsheet. An upward-compatible extension to the BOA is necessary to support the creation and manipulation of small objects without incurring the present overhead.

Security.   Security has clearly been identified as a primary concern for any distributed environment. A long debate is in progress over whether security should be primarily handled by the ORB or primarily handled as an object service. It is clear that some combination is the best fit. In any case, the security mechanism should address many issues, for example:

Security and interoperability: What does this mean, and how is it handled?

How does the security mechanism look to the application programmer?

What security is coupled with interfaces as opposed to implementations?

How does security interrelate with other components and concepts?

Auditing.   Auditing is related to security and should probably be supported by the security mechanism. It should allow logging of security-related operations as well as other events. This could be extended to support transaction logging, ORB request logging, management operations logging, and so on.

Multimedia.   Since multimedia objects tend to be very large, it is impractical in terms of performance to require marshaling and unmarshaling of such data streams. CORBA 2.0 may allow direct data streams in such cases. Such functionalities must track the rapidly growing multimedia market and the standards being formed (especially regarding line protocols). Other support for multimedia includes isochronous data streams for the support of videoconferencing and the communication models required to support these modes. These issues are further complicated when taken in the interoperability context, where it is possible for communicating endpoints to reside on different ORB environments.

Transactions.   The general tendency was to support transactions as an object service; more on this in Chap. 6. However, it is very likely that such an object service will require support from the ORB component. For example, the transaction manager will be involved when messages that are part of a transaction are processed by the ORB (for example, to support the notion of a rollback). Transaction contexts may also be accessible using the environment object.

Relations to standards.   Many of the responses list industry standards that are relevant to CORBA. Since the ORB will play a major role in any distributed object-oriented environment, it should not be surprising that the number of such relevant standards is very large. Standards listed include ISO Open Distributed Computing (ODP) as the only real object-oriented distributed computing standard; OSF DCE and DME as major distributed systems and distributed system management standards; and the X/Open Distributed Transaction Processing (XTP), X/Open Communications Resource Manager (CRM), and ISO Transaction Processing protocol (ISO-TP) regarding distributed transaction-based systems. Other technologies which might not be formal standards but which are widely used are also relevant to the ORB architectures.

Management.   Management and monitoring facilities must be provided if the ORB is indeed to become the central component for object-oriented distributed environments. Performance data about the ORB as well as about other components must be captured and collected. The ORB might be used for capturing such data, as well as using such data for performance tuning. IDL interfaces should be produced to allow access to these collected data as well as to tune various performance-related concepts.

Dynamic reconfiguration.   The architecture must enable dynamic reconfiguration. It is unacceptable to require an initial monolithic setup stage, after which no changes can be made. It is necessary to provide an architecture that evolves as new ORBs are added, ORBs are removed, and other changes are made. Existing components must interact with newly created and added components. A supporting mechanism for such capabilities must be created and the appropriate interfaces defined. A mechanism must be devised for searching for components, locating available services, and so on. These must support dynamic reconfiguration and registration.

In addition, support should be provided for associating interfaces with implementations (in a dynamic and possibly changing way), and for defining relationships between interfaces.

Server DII.   As defined by CORBA 1.1, the DII is only available to clients for dynamically forming requests. It should be possible to support DII-type invocations on the object implementation side as well.

3.5.3   The ORB 2.0 RFPs

The primary purpose of CORBA 2.0 is to specify aspects that were missing in CORBA 1.1 and without which interoperability between ORBs and portability of applications cannot be attained. After accumulating enough suggestions from the responses to the RFI, the OMG issued two RFPs: the Object Request Broker 2.0 Interoperability and Initialization RFP (Watson, 1993a) and the Object Request Broker 2.0 Interface Repository RFP (Watson, 1993c). It was also specifically mentioned that additional RFPs might be issued regarding other ORB issues. Both RFPs were issued in May 1994, and voted upon by the Technical Committee in the fall of 1994.

The goal of the RFP on interoperability and initialization is to receive technology that will support interoperability between ORBs provided by different vendors and to extend CORBA to specify a portable way for clients to obtain initial object references. The goal of the Interface Repository RFP is to provide full IR services. This means that the base IR functionalities defined in CORBA 1.1 must be extended to specify how IDL definitions are loaded into the IR and how the IR service may be dynamically modified.

Interoperability and initialization.   The definition used by the RFP for interoperability (as defined in Watson, 1993a) is "the ability for a client on ORB A to invoke an IDL-defined operation on an object in ORB B, where ORB A and ORB B are independently developed" (p. 6). Criteria for evaluating responses include the ability to interoperate without prior agreement and knowledge regarding implementation decisions of each of the ORBs, how extensively all ORB functionalities are supported, and how information and semantics are maintained across ORBs. Interoperability between ORBs of different vendors is perhaps the single most important issue dealt with by CORBA 2.0.

Initialization refers to the fact that CORBA 1.1 failed to define how components such as the ORB and BOA pseudo-objects are accessed initially by the programmer. This deficiency eliminates the possibility of writing portable implementations and the construction of compliance tests. The RFP therefore requires responders to detail mechanisms for providing access to these and other initial object references. The RFP requires interfaces for C and C++ to be proposed as well as the language-independent concepts. This also includes dealing with such issues as how nonobject implementations access the BOA (e.g., how objects serving as object factories access the `object_creation` operation; object factories will be discussed in Chap. 5).

As in any OMG RFP, only requirements are defined, and submitters are free to use any approach they wish. It is interesting to note that this can lead to very different technologies. For example, two submissions to the interoperability RFP take almost opposite views regarding the implementation of interoperability. The IONA/SunSoft proposal uses the gateway approach. When an object in ORB B is used from an object in ORB A, the gateway serves as the object implementation in ORB A and as the client in ORB B (see Fig. 3.10). The proposal details the mechanisms and interfaces required to make the gateway approach work. One of the major advantages of the gateway approach it that it does not require any agreement regarding implementation issues or protocols for interoperability to be possible. Details regarding this proposal will be provided in Appendix B.

The approach taken by a second proposal differs from the gateway approach. The submitters view gateways and translation to be inferior to their proposal, which suggests interoperability based on a common low-level protocol. This second proposal is a joint submission by DEC, HP, HyperDesk, IBM, NEC, and the OSF. It is primarily based on agreement on low-level protocol between the interoperating ORBs. The submission asserts that the number of such low-level protocols will be small, making the approach feasible. The proposal does not preclude gateways, but is totally focused on "wire level interoperability." While defining a general approach to interoperability, the propos-

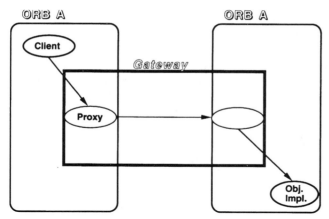

Figure 3.10 Use of a gateway for ORB interoperability.

al also fully defines one common protocol. This protocol is based on OSF's DCE and the DCE Application Environment Specification (AES) as the underlying protocol layer. The proposal then goes on to map CORBA constructs to DCE constructs and to use DCE functionalities where they fit what is required from an ORB environment (e.g., using the Kerberos authentication protocol until a full security service is defined by the OSTF). Appendix A provides a brief discussion of this proposal.

Interface Repository.   The Interface Repository RFP requires the IR to be extended with a mechanism allowing additions and modifications to and deletions from the IR. Update functions should be provided to allow tools to be created for dynamic management of the IR. In dealing with the complex IR issue, submitters must actually deal with a whole suite of issues from the domain of object-oriented programming language design and implementation, code management, and CASE tools, all within an environment meant to be the core of a distributed, all-encompassing, and prevalent architecture. Submitters must provide answers to questions such as

> What side effects on existing interfaces maintained in the IR may occur as a result of adding new interfaces or modifying existing ones? How do changes in inheritance relationships affect the IR?

> What happens when an interface is deleted from the IR? What happens to objects which implement or use this interface?

> Should versioning be supported? If so, what is the versioning model?

How do modifications, additions, and deletions affect running programs?

Should the IR allow extensions to maintain information which might be useful to other applications (e.g., maintaining creation dates and owners for code management and CASE tools)?

Is there a concurrency management model? What happens if two clients simultaneously modify the same set of interfaces? How can correctness be maintained?

How are multiple IRs used by a single ORB? How are relationships between interfaces residing in different ORBs handled?

What is the security model used by IRs?

4

Mappings of IDL
to Programming Languages

The previous chapter presented the Common Object Request Broker Architecture. The ORB was presented as the enabler of transparent and heterogeneous distributed applications. The ORB allows requests for an object's services to be made without regard to its implementation and location. For this to occur, the objects have to provide a specification of their supported services. This is done using the Interface Definition Language (IDL), as presented in the previous chapter. IDL is the language-neutral language defined as part of CORBA 1.1 to support interoperability between applications developed on different platforms using different programming languages. IDL is only a specification language in which types and interfaces are defined; applications are not coded in IDL. Therefore, in order to support language independence, IDL must be mapped into multiple programming languages. This will allow applications written in different programming languages to interoperate using CORBA.

As defined in the CORBA 1.1 specification (OMG, 1992b), any mapping of the IDL to a host programming language must include the following:

- *A mapping of all IDL data types, constants, and object references.* This includes providing a means of expressing basic data types, constructed data types, and constants in the target programming language. The mapping must also specify how an object is represented in the target programming language. Since the mapping must respect the semantics of the host programming language, the object representation is not dependent on the ORB's representation. The representation can use either an opaque handle to the ORB representation or a real programming language object. In the second case, the mapping must support identical object semantics of inheritance, operation signatures, and so on.

- *A mapping of operation signatures and invocations.* The mapping includes definitions for how input parameters are handled, how return values are handled, how operations map to the programming language procedures, and so on.

- *A mapping of the exception model.* If the target programming language's exception-handling mechanism (when such a mechanism exists) is being used, the mapping should describe how this mechanism is used for implementing IDL exceptions. Otherwise, the mapping should describe how operations are extended to support exceptions.

- *A mapping of IDL attributes.* Attributes are modeled by two accessor operations.

- *A mapping of the ORB interfaces.* This is necessary to allow programmers using the target programming language to access interfaces implemented by the ORB or one of the related components (the IR, the object adapter, DII, etc.). One approach might be to define these as a set of services packaged as a library. Another approach could involve pseudo-objects. A pseudo-object has an interface defined in IDL but is not implemented as an ORB managed object. Operations can only be invoked using the Static Invocation Interface (SII), and the ORB may intercept such calls and handle them. In this approach, the ORB interfaces would actually be defined as IDL interfaces. These interfaces would be part of a pseudo-object. The advantage is that the ORB interface can then be mapped into many programming languages. Since it is just another interface, it is handled by the mapping procedures, and ORB interfaces are no different from any other interface.

CORBA 1.1 defines a mapping of the IDL to the C programming language. Section 4.1 describes this mapping. Since IDL is intended to support interoperability between different programming languages, more mappings of the IDL to programming languages are required. The OMG is working toward the definition of additional mappings of IDL to various programming languages. This chapter is dedicated to language mappings of IDL. Mappings will be described for C, C++, Smalltalk, and Objective-C. It would be impossible to describe each of the host programming languages in the limited space of this chapter, so each section assumes a working knowledge of the programming language discussed. The Smalltalk mapping described is the mapping used in HP Distributed Smalltalk, and the Objective-C mapping described has been submitted to the OMG by NeXT Computer, Inc.

4.1   The C Mapping

The CORBA 1.1 specification includes a mapping of the IDL to the C programming language. This section describes this mapping and follows the general structure of Chap. 5 in the CORBA 1.1 specification (OMG, 1992b).

4.1.1   Name scoping and include file names

The C programming language does not have name space notions. Names for IDL constructs must therefore be appropriately scoped. Mapping an IDL global name to a C global name involves converting every ":" to "_" and eliminating leading underscores. For example, the IDL interface declaration

```
interface Client {
  enum status {regular, preferred};
  typedef string nameType;
};
```

would map into C global names of `Client_status` and `Client_nameType`. Note that such a mapping can be potentially ambiguous. For example, prepending the interface declaration of `Client` with the legal IDL typedef

```
typedef long Client_nameType;
```

would lead to an ambiguity in the C mapping. Underscores in the IDL declarations should therefore be used sparingly if one uses this proposed C mapping.

An interface definition of the file `<interface name>.idl` will by default create a C header file named `<interface name>.h`. This file contains all global names associated with the interface. Clients and implementations of this interface should include this header file.

4.1.2   Interfaces and operations, object references and implicit arguments, and inheritance

C does not provide support for functions that work on a certain object (like `this` in C++ or `self` in Smalltalk). Nor does it support inheritance. The C mapping uses standard C functions and pointers to simulate these. The object for which the operation is invoked is passed in as an additional pointer argument. Inheritance causes expansion of methods to all inheriting levels. The example interface

```
interface Account {
  void deposit ( in long dollars);
};
```

is mapped into C as

```
typedef Object Account;
extern void Account_deposit ( Account o, Environment *ev, long dol-
lars);
```

The first argument passed into the function is the account object. All interface references to an object are of type `Object`, which is really represented as a C pointer.

All interface operations therefore have implicit arguments preceding the operation's specific parameters. The first is always of type `Object` and represents the object receiving the request. The second is always an `Environment` * parameter that is used to return exception information from the function (more on this in a later subsection).

Inheritance is expanded into the inheriting interface. This has the effect of "flattening out" the inheritance graph. This is similar to expansions performed by early C++ "compilers," which were really preprocessors compiling the C++ code to produce C code. For example, an interface declaration

```
interface SavingAccount : Account {
  void accrueInterest ( in short numberOfDays );
};
```

is mapped into C as

```
typedef Object SavingsAccount;
extern void SavingsAccount_deposit (
  SavingsAccount o, Environment *ev, long dollars);
extern void SavingsAccount_accrueInterest (
  SavingsAccount o, Environment *ev, short numberOfDays);
```

4.1.3 Constants and attributes

IDL constants are mapped to C using the `#define` construct. IDL attributes are modeled as a pair of get and set operations. An attribute of the form

```
interface Account {
  attribute long cashBalance;
  readonly attribute long minimalBalance;
};
```

is mapped to C by naming the accessor functions as `_get_<attribute name>` and `_set_<attribute name>` and prepending the interface name to form the global name as described in Sec. 4.1.1. The C functions created for the above interface declaration would therefore be

extern long Account__get_cashBalance(Account o, Environment *ev);
extern void Account__set_cashBalance(Account o, Environment *ev, long cb);
extern long Account__get_minimalBalance(Account o, Environment *ev);

4.1.4 Mapping of data types

Table 4.1 shows the mapping of IDL basic data types to C built-in types. Enumeration values are mapped into `#define` constructs. IDL structured types are mapped to C structs. IDL union types are mapped to C unions packaged within a C struct. For example, the IDL union definition

```
union FrenchFranc switch (short) {
  case 1: short newFranc;
  case 2 : long oldFranc;
};
```

will be mapped to the C structure and access method

```
typedef struct {
  short _d;
  union {
  short newFranc;
```

TABLE 4.1 Mapping of IDL Basic Data Types to C Built-in Types

IDL Base Type	C Built-in Type
short, unsigned short, long, unsigned long	short, unsigned short, long, unsigned long
float, double	float, double
char	char
boolean	unsigned char
octet	unsigned char
enum	unsigned char
any	typedef struct any { TypeCode _type; void *_value; } any;

```
    long oldFranc;
    } _u;
} FrenchFranc;

#define newFrenchFranc 1
#define oldFrenchFranc 2
FrenchFranc *ff;
switch (ff → _d) {
  case newFrenchFranc: ....; break;
  case oldFrenchFranc: ....; break;
};
```

The IDL template type generator sequence<aType, aSize> is mapped to C as

```
#ifndef _IDL_SEQUENCE_aType_defined
#define _IDL_SEQUENCE_aType_defined
typedef struct {
  unsigned long _maximum;
  unsigned long _length;
  aType *_buffer;
} _IDL_SEQUENCE_aType;
#endif
```

The ifndef delimiter is necessary because multiple sequences with the same type but with different sizes will generate duplicate C definitions. When passing in a sequence object, the programmer is responsibile for setting the _buffer member to point to an array of the right size and type and for setting the _length member to the actual number of elements. When receiving a value from a function return, the programmer is responsible for freeing the allocated storage using ORBfree().

IDL strings are mapped to C null (\0) terminated character arrays. IDL arrays are directly mapped to C arrays.

4.1.5 Mapping of exceptions

Exception types are mapped to a C structure and an exception identifier. The IDL exception

```
exception balanceTooLow {
  long balance;
};
```

maps to the C declaration

```
typedef struct balanceTooLow {
  long balance;
} balanceTooLow;
#define ex_balanceTooLow <a unique id character string>
```

The id must uniquely identify the exception, since it is used as a handle in the exception-handling mechanism.

Recall that every C function generated from an IDL operation has an implicit environment type argument. The environment is passed back to the caller. One of the environment argument's purposes is to support exception handling. The `Environment` struct type in C has a member named `_major` of type `exception_type`. Upon return from an invocation, the `_major` field contains one of `NO_EXCEPTION`, `USER_EXCEPTION`, or `SYSTEM_EXCEPTION`. Once the caller determines that an exception has occurred, the `Environment` structure can be further queried using the following defined access functions:

```
extern char *exception_id(Environment *ev);       /* Returns a pointer to the
                                                      id char string */
extern void *exception_value(Environment *ev);    /* Returns a pointer to the
                                                      structure */
extern void exception_free(Environment *ev);      /* Returns storage allocated
                                                      for environment */
```

4.1.6   Argument passing and return values

Since C supports only call-by-value, if the mode of an argument is out or inout, the address of the variable must always be passed in (as is the common case in C functions). Arrays do not need to conform to this rule because of C's array/pointer semantics. The called function will dereference the parameter. For arguments of mode in, the parameter is passed in by value for basic data types, enumerations, and object references, and as addresses for structured data types.

A similar set of rules holds for results returned. Basic types, enumerations, and object references are returned by value. Strings and arrays are returned as a pointer to the first element in the C array. Structs, unions, sequences, and values of type any are returned as the value of the C struct representing the type.

4.1.7   The ORB pseudo-object

The ORB interface in the C mapping is provided as a pseudo-object. Requests are therefore made in the usual way, but the ORB may actually intercept the request and handle it directly. The definition of the ORB pseudo-object interface includes the following two IDL operations:

```
string    object_to_string( in Object obj);
Object    string_to_object( in string str);
```

These operations allow a C programmer to convert an object reference to its string form and back by calling

```
str = ORB_object_to_string( orbobj, &ev, obj);
obj = ORB_string_to_object( orbobj, &ev, str);
```

where `orbobj` is a reference to the ORB object and `ev` is of type Environment.

4.2 The C++ Mapping

The C++ mapping to IDL has had a strange and unfortunate history. After several submissions and iterations, the ORB Task Force (ORB TF) was left with two proposals. One proposal was submitted by IONA Technologies Ltd., NEC Corporations, and SunSoft Inc. (Lewis, 1993b). The second submission was by HyperDesk Corp. (Andreas, 1993b). Both were revised and submitted in November 1993. In December 1993 the ORB TF selected the HyperDesk proposal for the C++ binding. Shortly after that, HyperDesk (a relatively small company) went out of the ORB business. Since one of the RFP requirements was that each submitting company produce a commercially available implementation of the ORB, HyperDesk retracted the submission. This turn of events forced the ORB TF to reissue the RFP for a C++ binding in May 1994 (Watson, 1994).

Throughout the process, many industry leaders pointed out that the two proposals were not too different from each other and that a compromise could be found. Some also pointed out that both proposals had advantages and disadvantages, and that a joint proposal could fix many of the deficiencies of each of the two proposals. An example is Steve Vinoski's (of HP) paper (Vinoski, 1993).

When the ORB TF reissued the RFP, many of these industry leaders from such companies as HP, Novell, IONA, DEC, IBM, Expersoft, and SunSoft got together to attempt to come up with a joint submission. Their work was aided by Mark Linton and Doug Lea, two recognized C++ gurus who are politically neutral within the OMG. The submission is a combination of many of the ideas in the two original submissions as well as a lot of experience that the various participating companies have accumulated with C++ mappings. The submission (Vinoski, 1994) will probably be approved by the ORB TF and the OMG TC by the end of 1994.

Although the two original submissions (IONA/NEC/SunSoft, HyperDesk) will not be the final C++ mappings, most of the final mapping will be based on concepts from these two mappings. Since the purpose of this book is to educate the reader about the OMG concepts and not to provide a reference for ORB implementors, this section will review the two initial mappings as described in Lewis (1993b) and Andreas (1993b), as well as many of the ideas that led to the third combined submission. A great deal can be learned by contrasting the two initial mappings, since this is a good example of two concrete approaches to the abstract definitions in CORBA. In fact, more can be learned from such an exposition than from a dry statement of the IDL-to-C++ binding. The section will be organized as follows: At first we describe a possible C++ mapping to IDL. This mapping stresses the commonalty between the INS and the HyperDesk mappings. We then describe the two major issues on which the two mappings disagree and the reasoning behind each of the two mappings. Finally, we survey some of the unifying concepts that brought about the joint proposal. The discussion in this chapter is based on Lewis (1993b), Andreas (1993b), Vinoski (1993), Vinoski (1994), Andreas (1993c), Kessler (1993), Powell (1993), and Vanderbilt and Chen (1993). Because of the limited space of this chapter, many details have been omitted. The interested reader is refered to the above sources.

4.2.1 Name scoping

All names are scoped. The mechanism used is the namespace mechanism adopted by the ANSI C++ committee. IDL modules and interfaces provide a namespace. All definitions included in an IDL module are named by that namespace. These provide the name scoping necessary to avoid conflicts with other IDL components and other C++ libraries in general. If the namespace option is not yet available for a certain compiler, nested classes are used instead. The IDL code segment

```
module A {
    interface B {
        typedef char C;
    };
};
```

maps to C++ as follows (with namespace on the left and nested classes on the right):

```
namespace A {                                class A {
    class B {                                    public:
        public:                                      class B {
            typedef CORBA::char C;                       public:
        };                                                   typedef
    CORBA::char C;                                       };
        };                                           };
                                                 };
```

All components defined by the CORBA specification are used as if they were defined in a module by the name of CORBA. These map in C++ to the CORBA namespace (hence the use of CORBA::char in the example).

4.2.2 Interfaces, inheritance, and operations

Interfaces are mapped to C++ classes. These classes serve both for name scoping and for object references. Types, exceptions, and constants that are declared within an interface are mapped to the public part of the class. IDL inheritance is implemented by C++ public virtual inheritance. Operations are mapped to member methods.

4.2.3 Object references

The subject of object references is the major point on which the two submissions diverge. The Hyperdesk proposal uses stub classes to instantiate object references. All stub classes inherit (directly or indirectly) from the `CORBA::Object` base class. Instances of this class can represent any CORBA object. This class defines basic operators like constructors, a destructor, and an assignment operator as well as C conversion members and class-specific member functions. Object references may be widened and narrowed according to well-defined rules. The stub classes perform their own memory management, so the burden is taken off the programmer.

The INS mapping uses "Ref-based" semantics (sometimes also called "smart pointer" semantics). Each interface is mapped to a C++ class. This class, however, represents a pointer to a class that contains the members mapped from the IDL interface components. An object reference is an instance of this Ref class (to get the name of this class, append "Ref" to the interface name). The Ref class supports pointer semantics. In fact, one possible implementation for the Ref class is to use real C++ pointers by using a

```
typedef <class>* <class>Ref;
```

Another implementation could use real classes that overload `operator→`. The topic of object references will be further discussed in Sec. 4.2.8.

4.2.4 Constants and attributes

IDL constants map to C++ constants. For example,

```
const long myAccountNum = 1234567;
```

maps to

```
extern const CORBA::Long myAccountNum;
```

while a generated source file might include a line of the form

```
const CORBA::Long myAccountNum = 1234567;
```

Both mappings map an IDL attribute to two accessor functions. The mappings differ on the enclosing class (stub vs. Ref) and on memory management policies.

4.2.5 Mapping of data types

Basic IDL arithmetic types are mapped to built-in C++ types. The mapping creates a CORBA namespace to support these types. For example, the short IDL datatype will be represented in C++ by CORBA::Short, which is defined to be a C++ short. The boolean type is mapped to a C++ enumeration. The relevant definitions are

```
namespace CORBA {
    typedef short Short;
    typedef long Long;
    typedef unsigned short UShort;
    typedef unsigned long ULong;
    typedef char Char;
    typedef unsigned char Octet;
    typedef float Float;
    typedef double Double;

    enum Boolean {
      TRUE = 1,
      FALSE = 0
      };
};
```

IDL enumerations map into a C++ enumeration. The Hyperdesk mapping creates the enumeration as a "private" definition (this is not actually private in any sense, but it is not meant to be used directly; its name is not the name of the IDL enumeration but a mangled name instead). The mapping creates a class that represents the IDL enumeration. This class makes use of the created C++ enumeration. For example, a constructor with one enumeration typed parameter is created for the class. A long() conversion operator for the enumeration's value is defined, as are standard member functions. The INS mapping creates only a C++ enumeration that is meant to be used directly.

The IDL any type maps into a C++ class named CORBA::Any. An instance of the class CORBA::Any will always have a *typecode* (the actual member that returns the typecode differs between the two mappings, since object references are represented differently). If the typecode is not null or void, the instance also contains a value of the type specified by the typecode.

IDL structures map into C++ classes. The internal representation of the structure is hidden. Member functions provide access to the internals of the structure. Each member of the structure causes three accessor member functions to be created. For example, if a structure has an element of type short by the name of element, then the member functions that will be formed will be

CORBA::Short element() const;
CORBA::Short& element();
void element(CORBA::Short inputValue);

The INS mapping replaces the first of these functions with const CORBA::Short& element() const.

IDL union types map to C++ classes. Each class representing a union has discriminator accessor functions and union member accessor functions. Discriminator accessor functions allow the programmer to get and set the discriminator. Member accessor functions have semantics similar to those of structure members.

IDL sequences map to the C++ CORBA::Sequence template class. This class template is parameterized by the type of the contained elements. The template class provides constructors and a destructor, length accessor functions, and element index operators. Figure 4.1 shows the Sequence template class in the INS style mapping. The Hyperdesk mapping adds the element manipulator functions insert, append, and remove.

IDL strings are mapped to C++ character arrays in the INS mapping and to a CORBA::String class in the Hyperdesk mapping (this

```
namespace CORBA {
    template <class T>
    class Sequence {
        public:
            // Standard member functions
            Sequence ( const ULong maximum = 0 );
            Sequence ( const Sequence <T> &seq );
            Sequence ( Long maximum, Long length, T* buffer);
            ~Sequence();

            // Accessor member functions
            const Long& maximum() const;
            Long& maximum();
            void maximum ( const Long value );

            const Long& length() const;
            Long &length();
            void length(const Long value);

            const T*& buffer() const;
            T*& buffer();
            void buffer ( const T* value );

            // Index operators
            T& operator[] ( ULong index );
            const T& operator[] (ULong index ) const;
    };
};
```

Figure 4.1 Sequence template class in the INS style mapping.

```
namespace CORBA {
    template <ULong bound, class T>
    class Array {
        public:
            // Standard member functions
            Array();
            Array ( const Array <bound, T>& );
            Array <bound, T>& operator= ( const Array<bound, T>& );
            ~Array();

            //C conversion functions
            static Array<bound, T> _convert_from_c ( const void* c_value );
            void _convert_to_c ( void* c_value ) const;

            // Index operators
            const T& operator[] ( ULong index ) const;
            T& operator[] ( ULong index );
    };
};
```

Figure 4.2 Hyperdesk style mapping for arrays.

is necessary mainly because of memory management issues, as will be discussed in Sec. 4.2.9). IDL arrays are mapped to C++ template classes in much the same way as sequences are. Figure 4.2 shows the Hyperdesk style mapping for arrays.

4.2.6   Mapping of exceptions

IDL exceptions are mapped to C++ classes. Both proposals provide a mapping for exception handling for two cases: one where the C++ compiler includes support for C++ exception handling, and one where it does not. In the first case, the C++ mechanism is used for CORBA exception handling, whereas in the second, the CORBA environment is used to pass the exception information by the returning call.

IDL exceptions are mapped to C++ classes in much the same way structures are. Each member in the exception forms a set of accessor functions. Exception classes inherit from either the System Exception or the User Exception class. The exception hierarchy will therefore resemble that in Figure 4.3.

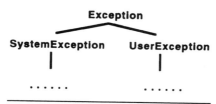

Figure 4.3 The exception hierarchy.

SystemException and UserException are noninstantiable classes. They merely aid in categorizing exception types. Any exception will be defined in one of these classes' subhierarchies. Exceptions are handled using the C++ exception-handling mechanism accepted by the ANSI C++ committee. The programmer defines a try/catch clause specifying the exception type to be handled. Any exception of that type or any subtype will be handled.

```
try {
    // The operation that might throw an exception
}
catch ( //The exception type to catch ) {
    // Error handling code
}
```

4.2.7 The ORB pseudo-object

The ORB interface is mapped to a C++ class of the form

```
namespace CORBA {
    class ORB {
        public:
            // Use ObjectRef instead of Object in the INS mapping
            Object string_to_object ( const String& str ) const;
            String object_to_string ( const Object& obj ) const;
            Context default_context () const;
    };
};
```

4.2.8 Different mappings of object references

The INS mapping maps object references to a Ref type. The Ref type acts as a pointer to the referenced class object. Many implementations can exist for this reference object. For example, a Ref class can be constructed. This class might overload the dereferencing operator and any other operator that will enable it to function as a reference. Another implementation could be a simple C++ pointer. A typedef statement might be used to define the Ref name as a pointer to the referenced class. The implementation decision is completely invisible to the client of the reference objects. For an interface named xxxxxx, the reference class is named xxxxxxRef. For a reference object named reference and an operation named operation with no arguments, the invocation structure is always reference→ operation().

The Hyperdesk mapping maps object references to stub classes. Each such class derives (directly or indirectly) from CORBA::Object. Each stub class provides standard functions, such as constructors and a destructor, an assignment operator, C conversion functions, and class-specific member functions. The Hyperdesk mapping does not use pointer semantics for object references. An invocation in this mapping would therefore look like `reference.operation()`. Pointers are not exposed to programmers, so there is less chance of misuse.

The INS proponents argue that pointer semantics have three main advantages: They provide a simple, elegant, and efficient mapping with little restriction; they provide easy interoperability with the C mapping of object references; and they pose no forward referencing problems. Others argue that these characteristics may seem to be true, but after closer scrutiny turn out to be misleading.

To support IDL inheritance semantics, public virtual inheritance must be used. This causes the memory layout of the classes to be complex and compiler-dependent. In addition, widening of a pointer to such a class actually changes the pointer (the bit pattern is actually changed). If object references use pointers, these characteristics will make it very hard to make pointer semantics work properly with the any type and with the DII. Since the Hyperdesk mapping uses objects as references to objects, virtual base classes are no longer necessary (for example, widening can be done using overloaded conversion operators).

Interoperability with the C mapping is also not as straightforward as it would seem. The C mapping uses pointers as object references, but all pointers have the same type (void*), wheras C++ pointers have distinct types. Since C++ pointers allow implicit widening by the compiler, and since such widening in the presence of virtual base classes will change the pointer values, it would be extremely difficult to exchange C and C++ pointers neatly. In fact, the only elegant solution would involve changing the C mapping to incorporate explicit widening functions.

4.2.9 Different mappings of memory management

The other major area of divergence between the two mappings is that of memory management. C++ does not force any particular style of memory management, but it provides many features that can help with consistent and "safe" memory management. The mappings differ in that the Hyperdesk mapping provides a memory management policy that is used by all classes, whereas the INS proponents stress that it is not the responsibility of the C++ mapping to enforce memory management policies.

In the Hyperdesk proposal, memory management for each object is that object's responsibility. Constructors, the destructor, the assignment operator, and so on help to encapsulate the management of dynamically allocated memory. When correct management is performed from within the classes, applications using these classes are freed from many concerns, and the usage of these classes becomes much simpler. Internally managed memory is of special importance

```
      CORBA::String corbaStr = str;
      anObject.operation(corbaStr);

                  (a)


try {
      CORBA::String corbaStr = str;
      anObject->operation(corbaStr);
      CORBA::string_free(corbaStr);
} catch (CORBA::Exception *exc) {
      CORBA::string_free(corbaStr);
}
                  (b)
```

Figure 4.4 Simple exception-handling code.

for programs using exception handling (as C++ programs and CORBA programs will). If memory management is done within the constructors and destructors, the memory will be freed by the destructors when the stack is unwound looking for a handling block. If explicit freeing is necessary, the exception-handling code becomes extremely complex and inelegant. Figure 4.4 shows an almost trivial example. The only reason the exception is caught in Fig. 4.4*b* is to free the memory; otherwise we would be creating a memory leak. Imagine what would happen when a complex object graph was being managed within multiple invocation levels and an exception occurred!

The INS submitters argue that the Hyperdesk advantage does no more than eliminate one call per value returned by a function. They claim that C and C++ programmers have always used pointers and have always been faced with memory allocation considerations. They claim that although the benefit is not great, the cost is. They argue that performance will be poor as a result of the memory management performed in the constructors, destructor, and assignment operator. They also claim that the C++ mapping will not be used extensively by programmers because higher-level tools will be available and memory management support can be layered on top of the INS mapping. The INS submitters believe that the differences between the two mappings stem from different views as to the mapping's purpose. They believe that the mapping should be focused on allowing interoperability while avoiding as far as possible making assumptions that may later limit the use of the mapping in any way. The mapping should therefore support as many usage patterns as possible, incur as low overhead as possible, and enforce as few directives as possible.

4.2.10 Toward the joint submission

After the Hyperdesk submission was withdrawn, the C++ binding was left in an incomplete state. As mentioned, a group of industry leaders decided to put together a joint submission that would learn from the mistakes of the original submissions and process and would form a complete and robust proposal that would be widely accepted. The joint proposal is based on the INS and the Hyperdesk submissions, and also on experience gained from initial prototypical and commercial C++ mappings. The proposal was delivered to the OMG on August 3, 1994, by Expersoft Corp., Digital Equipment Corp., Hewlett-Packard Company, IONA Technologies Ltd., International Business Machines Corp., Novell Inc., and SunSoft Inc. The proposal has both wide industry and OMG backing and will most likely be accepted.

The joint submission provides a very complete C++ mapping. In particular, it deals with the issue of how IDL interfaces are represented in C++ by recognizing that both the Hyperdesk and the INS representations have merit and that each will be required by different users on different occasions. The joint submission therefore provides *two* possible mappings for IDL interfaces. For each IDL interface I, two C++ classes are formed, called I_var and I_ptr (Iref is also defined to be an I_ptr for backward compatibility purposes). I_var has "variable" semantics, whereas I_ptr has "pointer" semantics. I_var objects therefore have built-in memory management functionality, and resources are automatically released by the class itself (as in the Hyperdesk submission). I_ptr has semantics similar to a C++ pointer (in fact, it will often be typedefed to be I*, as in the INS submission). Access to instances of both types is gained using " → " semantics.

The issue of memory management for parameters being passed to functions was resolved in a way that balances efficiency and simplicity for the programmer. The definition, however, is rather complex because of the necessity for supporting two basic strategies. Primitive data types are passed as normal C++ built-in data types. Object references of type I are passed as I_ptr. Dealing with aggregate types is more complex, since the issue of who allocated and who frees resources must be resolved. Parameters with an in mode are allocated by the caller, since the callee can only read these memory locations. Variable-length types of out and inout mode must be allocated by the callee. Fixed-length types of out and inout modes can be allocated by either caller or callee; the submission prefers that the caller allocate storage because then the stack may be used, resulting in higher performance. The submission also defines precise rules for the types that the parameters should take (typically I, I*, or I*&). These details are beyond the scope of this book; the interested reader is referred to Vinoski (1994).

4.3 HP Distributed Smalltalk's Binding to IDL

The OMG has issued an RFP for the Smalltalk language mapping. The goal is to standardize an IDL language mapping for Smalltalk. This

RFP came out at the end of 1993 (Watson, 1993d). The dates mentioned by this RFP include July 29, 1994, as the submissions due date, November 16, 1994, as the final submission deadline, and February 1995 as the TC vote. This means that the final IDL mapping for Smalltalk will not be available until sometime in 1995. Some initial proposals are already being proposed (see Mueller, 1994a and 1994b).

This seems to imply that discussing the Smalltalk mapping in this chapter is a bit premature. This is not true. In fact, a commercial product generally available since 1993 implements a full IDL mapping into Smalltalk-80. This section will therefore describe the mapping strategy used by this product as detailed in HP (1993a and 1993b). It is very conceivable that much of this mapping will find its way into the OMG mapping, since much experience and knowhow concerning this product's mapping is being accumulated.

The product's name is HP Distributed Smalltalk (HPDST), developed by Hewlett-Packard. HPDST will be described at length in Chap. 9. It is a CORBA-based environment for developing distributed applications. The native language of HPDST is Smalltalk. All applications are written in Smalltalk using the Smalltalk classes and the HPDST classes. The environment is, however, ORB-based, and interfaces are therefore also written in IDL. With the interfaces written in IDL and the mapping specified with the Smalltalk code (and the IDL specifications maintained in an Interface Repository part of the HPDST environment), the applications can remain CORBA-based. Interoperating with other platforms and programming languages therefore becomes feasible.

All code written in HPDST is standard Smalltalk code. To register an object as a CORBA object, one has to provide IDL declarations. HPDST maintains IDL code in its Interface Repository (IR). This is implemented within a Smalltalk class that is part of the HPDST environment (its name is DSTrepository). Methods of this class are actually written in IDL. HPDST also provides supporting tools that create an IDL skeleton from a Smalltalk class; more on this in Chap. 9.

The DSTrepository maintains the IDL specifications for the applications. These applications are completely written in Smalltalk. A request for an object or a service comes in through the ORB component. It must then be mapped into Smalltalk code. This mapping is performed by the HPDST class DSTMetaObject and its hierarchy as well as by the subclasses of the HPDST class ORBObject. These allow the IDL types, attributes, and operation signatures to be mapped into Smalltalk, so that the application developer need deal with nothing but Smalltalk. The mapping is used by the HPDST system to derive a Smalltalk message to send for every IDL operation that arrives through the object adapter. The mapping is responsible for mapping attributes, arguments, selectors, and so on. In addition,

HPDST implements the ORB environment in Smalltalk itself. It therefore inherently provides a mapping of the ORB and object adapter interface to Smalltalk.

4.3.1 Modules, interfaces, and operations

IDL modules are represented as Smalltalk methods of the class DSTrepository (HPDST's IR). Each such module contains declarations of interfaces, enumerations, types, constants, and exceptions. The IR is changed by updating these methods. HPDST provides Smalltalk methods of the ORBObject class for accessing a module's contents. These access methods allow the search to include or exclude inherited interfaces, define limits and levels, and so on. Figure 4.5 shows an example IDL module in the DSTrepository class.

The pragmas shown in Fig. 4.5 are important enablers of the mapping. The pragmas are implementation-dependent and are not part of IDL (together with a third pragma, CLASS, they are the only extensions to IDL made by HPDST). These pragmas can be ignored by an IDL compiler if the module or interface definitions are taken to another CORBA-compliant environment. When similar concepts are supported in a standard way in future releases of CORBA or in future Smalltalk bindings, they will also be replaced in HPDST.

The IDENTIFIER pragma helps HPDST to decide what Smalltalk class is implementing this interface. The SELECTOR pragma helps to map the operation to a Smalltalk method. Thus when an operation of an interface is requested, the mapping to a method selector in a certain class can be made. The interface declaration must contain these pragmas for the mapping to occur. Note that IDL supports multiple inheritance, whereas Smalltalk supports a single-inheritance model. The solution to the problem of mapping the multiple-inheritance model to the single-inheritance model also uses these two pragmas.

```
module  Account
'Each module must have a comment'
enum AccountKind { regular, preferred };
interface AccountPO: Presentation
        IDENTIFIER  =  '6473897aad3.06.01.11.ab.00.00.00'
'The IDENTIFIER pragma maps the interface to a Smalltalk class ...'
{
void deposit ( in float amountToDeposit)
        SELECTOR = deposit: ;
'The SELECTOR pragma maps the operation to a Smalltalk method ...'
. . . . . .
};
. . . . . .
}
```

Figure 4.5 Example IDL module in DSTrepository.

The IDENTIFIER pragma specifies the "most derived interface." This number uniquely identifies a class. The class may contain method implementations for operations that are defined in any of the (multiple) inherited interfaces. As long as the selectors are identical to the SELECTOR pragma specification and the IDENTIFIER pragma identifies where the method lookup should start, the correct method will be called. Chapter 9 will elaborate further on this subject.

HPDST provides supporting methods for accessing interface information. The Smalltalk method getInterface provides interface information about an object reference. This returns a first-class object that describes the interface (a meta-level object). Interfaces can themselves be sent messages; the InterfaceDef class provides many such services.

4.3.2 Operation parameters

IDL operations provide a more elaborate parameter model than Smalltalk. Smalltalk methods can have any number of input parameters but only one result object. Smalltalk is an untyped language, so it is not possible to place constraints on parameter values. IDL operations, on the other hand, can have any number of input parameters and any number of return values. Parameters in IDL have a mode and a type. The mode can be either in (i.e., passed into the operation only), out (i.e., a return value), or inout (i.e., both). The object to be passed in (or out) must be of the type specified by the parameter's type.

To perform the mapping, HPDST uses an array object as the single return value. All parameters with a mode of in or inout participate in the input parameters of the Smalltalk method. Parameters with a mode of out or inout will participate in the return value array object. The return value of the IDL operation also participates in the return array and is always the last element in the array. For example, the IDL operation

```
Account openAccount (
  in Person owner,
  in float firstDeposit,
  inout string preferredPID,
  out Person accountManager,
  in Branch branch
)
```

will be mapped to a selector of the form openAccountForOwner: firstDeposit:preferredPID:branch:, and the return value will be an Array with: aPID with: anAccountManager with: anAccountObject. For each in or inout parameter, the selector has an input argument, and for each out or inout parameter, the returned array has an entry. The last entry in the array is the actual object to be returned by the operation. Notice that the inout parameter is simulated by two parameters (one going in and one coming out) in the Smalltalk mapping. It is not the same object; they are two distinct objects. If it is necessary to have references to the input parameter reference the return value, the Smalltalk become: operator should be used.

HPDST does not attempt to type-check the Smalltalk methods mapped to the IDL operations. Not only is this difficult to do, it would cause the environment to behave differently from standard Smalltalk. Smalltalk is an inherently untyped language, and it was felt that the mapping must respect the programming language's semantics. If necessary, the implementer of the methods may do type checking when the method is invoked. In addition, HPDST provides a pragma specifier to allow programmers to specify the Smalltalk class of returned values. This can be done using a pragma definition of the form

CLASS = <Smalltalk class>

in the IDL operation definition.

HPDST maintains meta-information on operations in the form of instances of DSToperation. These objects respect the OperationDef interface as defined in the IR.

4.3.3 Attributes, constants, and exceptions

An IDL attribute definition maps into two Smalltalk methods. Every attribute declaration forms two accessor methods, one to get the value and one to set it. Attribute names are automatically converted from C conventions to Smalltalk conventions. For example, an attribute named account_number will be mapped to the accountNumber (to get) and the accountNumber: (to set) Smalltalk methods.

IDL constants are stored in a Smalltalk pool dictionary named ORBConstants. The dictionary key used is the constant's name (including the enclosing name). For example, the IDL constant declaration

```
interface Account {
  const maxNumberOfOwners = 10;
  ....
};
```

will create an entry in ORBConstants with key #'::Account::max NumberOfOwners' and a value of 10.

Smalltalk exception handling is very robust and fully supports the IDL exception model. The HPDST mapping uses the Smalltalk mechanism directly, so that exceptions can be raised by the error: invocations and caught by the handle:do: message. Exceptions can embed any structured value to be passed to the handling block. These values are marshaled by the ORB and passed over to the remote site which created the execution context. There the value is unmarshaled. This allows the same exception to be raised in the operation's client context.

The meta objects and the IDL interfaces for attributes, constants, and exceptions are DSTattribute and AttributeDef, DSTconstant and ConstantDef, and DSTexception and ExceptionDef, respectively.

4.3.4   Data types mapping

IDL is statically typed. Therefore any IDL operation declares the types of all its arguments. To map IDL into Smalltalk, all data types must be mapped. This will allow invocations of IDL operations and creation of correctly typed objects to be passed as arguments. HPDST devises a *type-to-class* mapping. This maps IDL types to Smalltalk classes. Every IDL type is provided a "representative" class. Smalltalk instances of these classes are passed as arguments into parameters that expect the corresponding type.

Base IDL types are mapped to classes within the Magnitude hierarchy. Table 4.2 outlines the base type mapping.

IDL template types include string and sequence. Instances of the Smalltalk class String are used to map IDL strings. Instances of subclasses of the Smalltalk Collection class are used to map IDL sequences. There is one major difference between IDL sequences and

TABLE 4.2 Smalltalk Mapping of IDL Base Types

IDL Type	Smalltalk Class
boolean	Boolean (true and false)
char	Character
float	Float
double	Double
integer	Integer
octet	Character or SmallInteger

Smalltalk collections: IDL sequences contain only elements of a certain type (or any of that type's subtypes), wherase Smalltalk collections can contain any aggregation of objects. HPDST does not enforce the correct use of collections to represent sequences; programmers should be aware of this IDL-imposed limitation when constructing collections that are to be passed as sequences. The inverse mapping uses instances of `OrderedCollection`. An IDL sequence value returned will therefore be instantiated as an ordered collection by default.

Smalltalk symbols represent IDL enumeration values. Each enumeration type maps into an array which holds the enumeration symbols in the order in which they were declared. This array can be accessed from the `ORBConstants` pool dictionary. For example, an enumeration in Account with two possible values (regular or preferred) will use the symbols `#regular` and `#preferred`, and create an `Array with: #regular with: #preferred` in the pool dictionary.

Structured IDL types created using the `struct` IDL construct map into two kinds of Smalltalk objects. Smalltalk collections can be used as structures, since a Smalltalk collection can contain elements of different types (classes). It is the programmer's responsibility to ensure that the objects in the collection have the corresponding types as defined in the IDL structure and that they are ordered correctly. If this is not so, the collection will not be correctly marshaled. Note that only Smalltalk collections that are sequenced can be used for structures. The default used by HPDST for return value structures is instances of `OrderedCollection`.

Other Smalltalk classes can be used to produce and accept structure values. The constraint on such a class is that it must provide a method selector with the field name for any field in the structure and that it must provide a method for setting all the fields. For example, the following structure

```
struct Complex {
  double real;
  double imaginary;
} CLASS = Complex;
```

can be represented by a Smalltalk class `Complex` as long as

The class has methods `real` and `imaginary`.

The class has a method `real:imaginary:`

The `CLASS` pragma is used.

IDL unions are mapped to instances of the `Association` Smalltalk class. The association's keys are the discriminator values, and the values are the union members. It is the programmer's responsibility to ensure that the values and keys are instances of classes matching the IDL types specified by the unions. For example, a union of the form

```
union UnionExample switch (Discriminator) {
  case Option1: string option1;
  case Option2: float option2;
  case Option3: Complex option3;
};
```

can be populated by any of the following Smalltalk objects:

```
#Option1 → 'Any string …'
#Option2 → 3.1415927
#Option3 → (Complex real: 2 imaginary: 1)
```

The IDL type any can be represented by any Smalltalk class which implements the typeObject method or by associations where the value holds the object and the key holds the type specifier. Any such class (and any such association object) can be used as a value for an input parameter of type any. Output parameters of type any become instances of the Association class, with the value being the object itself and the key being whatever the typeObject method of the object returns. By adding the value method to Object, HPDST provides access uniformity in both cases. Thus when an object representing a type any object is to be accessed, the value message should be sent. If this is an association object, the object in the value section will be returned. If it is an object of a different class, the object itself will be returned (because of the implementation of the value method in Object).

IDL allows typedef expressions for defining new types. The HPDST mapping for new types simply uses the CLASS pragma. Any typedef expression should therefore use a CLASS pragma to specify which Smalltalk class should be used in the mapping.

4.4 The Objective-C Mapping

The Objective-C mapping described in this section follows a mapping proposal submitted to the OMG by NeXT Computer, Inc (see NeXT, 1993). The goal of the mapping is to allow objects written in Objective-C to access objects whose interfaces are specified in IDL and to show how to create IDL interfaces for existing Objective-C objects. The mapping assumes that the Objective-C language is as described in [The Objective-C Language, NeXT] and as implemented in the NeXTSTEP environment.

The Objective-C language is defined as an extension to the C language. One of the design goals of Objective-C was to adhere as closely as possible to C and to add only a limited set of extensions. Accordingly, the Objective-C mapping is very similar to the C mapping. In fact, most of the mapping is exactly the same as the mapping described in Sec. 4.1 of this chapter. The differences are mainly on issues where Objective-C can provide direct support for IDL concepts, whereas the C mapping requires artificial constructs.

4.4.1   Name scoping and include file names

Objective-C classes provide the name scoping necessary for IDL naming contexts. No artificial name generation is therefore necessary (or possible, since the names are used in Objective-C classes and protocols). Only names for constants and exception names are global and derived as described in Sec. 4.1.1. Header files are generated as in the C mapping, and the Objective-C directive `#import` is used instead of `#include`. This eliminates the necessity for the `#ifndef/` `#define/#endif` construct used to avoid multiple inclusions of the same definition files.

4.4.2   Interfaces and operations, object references and implicit arguments, and inheritance

IDL object types can be represented in Objective-C either as objects of the generic type `id` or as instances of Objective-C classes that are created from the IDL definitions. IDL operations map into Objective-C methods. Method names are constructed from the IDL operation signatures. An IDL operation signature of the form

opName (arg1Type arg1, arg2Type arg2, ... , argnType argn)

is mapped to an Objective-C method with a selector of

- opName: (Environment *) ev : (arg1Type) arg1 ...   : (argnType) argn;

The number of colons in the selector is the number of arguments in the IDL signature plus one. The first colon (the one following the operation name) is used for the `Environment` variable.

IDL interface declarations are mapped to Objective-C protocol and class declarations. The use of Objective-C protocols is of utmost importance. Protocols are purely abstract constructs, and the class components in the mapping are defined to support a set of protocols. Since protocols are abstract constructs, they easily support the multiple interface inheritance of IDL. Using protocols for interface mapping also means that the Objective-C mapping preserves the abstract nature of IDL interfaces and that multiple implementations can be provided for a type. The IDL interfaces of

```
interface Account [
  long balance;
  void deposit ( in long dollars);
};
interface SavingAccount : Account [
  void accrueInterest ( in short numberOfDays );
};
```

will map to Objective-C as

```
@protocol Account <OMGObject>
- (void) deposit: (Environment *)ev : (long) dollars;
@end
@interface Account: OMGObject <Account> [
  long balance;
]
@end
@protocol SavingsAccount <Account>
- (void) accrueInterest: (Environment *) ev : (short) numberOfDays;
@end
interface SavingAccount <Account>
[ ]
@end
```

Note that all Objective-C objects that will be used in an ORB environment must inherit from the ORBObject Objective-C class. It would have been more natural had the mapping used the name Object instead. However, Objective-C already defines a root Object class.

4.4.3 Constants and attributes

Constants map to Objective-C constants exactly as described in the C mapping. Attributes map into get and set access methods as well as into an Objective-C class definition. For example, the IDL interface

```
interface Account [
  attribute double balance;
];
```

will map to

```
@protocol Account <OMGObject>
- (double)    _get_balance: (Environment *ev);
- (void)      _set_balance: (Environment *ev) : (double) b;
@end
@interface Account: OMGObject <Account> [
   double balance;
]
@end
```

4.4.4 Mapping of data types

All basic and constructed data types map to Objective-C types as described in the C mapping.

4.4.5 Mapping of exceptions

Mapping of exceptions is done as described in Sec. 4.1.5. Mapping of exception types to Objective-C types is similar to the C mapping. Exception handling is also similar.

4.4.6 Argument passing and return values

Arguments and return values follow the C mapping as described in Sec. 4.1.6.

4.4.7 The ORB pseudo-object

The ORB interface is mapped to an Objective-C protocol and class. The operations provided are identical to those provided as part of the C pseudo-object:

```
@protocol ORB <OMGObject>
- (string)   object_to_string: (Environment *) ev : (id) obj;
- (id)       string_to_object: (Environment *) ev : (string) str;
..........
@end
@interface ORB: OMGObject <ORB>
{ }
@end
```

5

Object Services, Part 1

ORBs provide the mechanism for making requests and performing operations in a platform-independent way; they are the fundamental component in any OMG-based technology. However, CORBA is only the foundation of a usable object-centric technology; it does not provide capabilities that will be required by application developers. CORBA provides the messaging facility that is the base of an object-oriented distributed environment; this is, however, not enough. Upon this foundation (including the IDL, which allows language-independent interfaces to be specified), the OMG Reference Model goes on to define other component categories that must be populated to ensure that the technology is usable for building applications. This includes Object Services, which are low-level support functions that are used by applications, and Common Facilities, which are higher-level functions such as I/O, mail, and workgroups. Like any other architecture, the OMG Reference Model takes a layered approach. First CORBA was defined. Once the underlying messaging facility was available, the low-level service functionalities could be defined. After that, the higher-level service functions can be defined. The most important category and the one in which most work has been done (outside of CORBA) within the OMG is the Object Services sector. Object Services is a collection of services that any software component may rely upon.

Object Services provide a set of functionalities that are available to application developers regardless of their platform or environment. Object Services therefore form (with CORBA) an architecture that allows the creation of portable object-based systems. As a set of basic functionalities available to all developers, Object Services must be available in a platform-, language-, and environment-independent way. Object Services must also be defined in a way that allows multiple implementations, each emphasizing different characteristics. The same service could be provided in multiple ways, each one being most suitable for a different set of applications. Object Services are thus typically specified as sets of interfaces; this allows them both to be independent of the environment and to allow multiple mappings to various implementations. These interfaces are expressed as IDL interfaces, thus making use of CORBA. Note that this does not imply anything about the implementation of the services; the implementation need not be object-oriented at all.

Object Services development is the responsibility of the Object Services Task Force (OSTF). This TF has been intensively working on providing a rich set of functionalities to application developers. Naturally, the TF prioritizes its work to first deal with services that are deemed to be fundamental to participating software components. The OSTF's work is in a way harder and more important than even the ORB TF's, since it deals with many issues. Each service may be used in very different ways, and the TF must therefore address every issue at multiple levels. The OSTF's work is critical, since applications will not be built in an ORB environment unless they can assume a certain base set of functionalities. Additional constraints include a desire for the different services to be consistent so that each one does not require detailed learning by clients and so that different services can be used together to achieve higher-level behaviors. In addition, Object Services are critical if interoperability is to be achieved (e.g., a security service will very much determine whether interoperability will be possible; no matter how "interoperable" the ORBs may be, if the security service does not address interoperability issues, applications will typically not be able to interoperate).

The purpose of this and the next chapter is to describe the work being done within the OSTF. The Object Services Architecture (OSA) and the Object Services Roadmap (OSRM) will be described in this chapter. The OSA specifies a base architecture to guide the Object Services adoption process, and the OSRM defines the ordering and the selection process for Object Services. This chapter also describes the object services included in Common Object Services Specification 1 (COSS 1) (based on the Joint Object Services Submission documents), which include the Naming Service, the Event Notification Service, the Life Cycle Service, and the Persistence Service. The next chapter describes the services which will be covered by COSS 2, including the Relationship Service, the Externalization Service, the Transaction Service, and the Concurrency Service. The next chapter also describes Object Services RFP3 (which solicits proposals for the Time Service and Security) and Object Services RFP4 (soliciting proposals for the Licensing Service, the Properties Service, and the

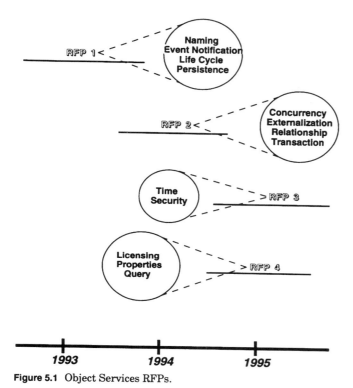

Figure 5.1 Object Services RFPs.

Query Service). Figure 5.1 illustrates the different RFPs, the services being defined, and approximate timetables.

5.1   The Object Services Architecture and the Object Services Roadmap

Object Services are a vital component of the OMG's goal of creating an architecture and framework for commercial object-oriented distributed environments. As described in the OMG Reference Model in Chap. 1, the ORB merely provides the low-level messaging functionality that is the base for any such environment. This is not enough for application developers. It would be similar to giving a nonexpert user a PC with only a skeleton of an operating system and no facilities such as a file system, a file manager, utilities, and so on. It is possible to use such a machine, but any company that tried to provide such configurations in today's market would quickly find itself out of business. The Reference Model therefore requires that two additional segments be populated: Object Services and Common Facilities. Recall that Object Services provide basic services and functionalities that will commonly be needed by every object (whether it is an application object or part of the Reference Model architecture). Common Facilities are services that have a higher-level semantic structure and are closer to functionalities assumed by users of applications.

The importance of Object Services is enormous. Object Services will often be the layer with which developers will interact the most. Most of the "computer science" functionalities (i.e., not business domain–specific) will be provided by components in this layer. The OSTF, as the workgroup responsible for populating this important layer, is therefore critical to the success of the OMG.

Since Object Services are a collection of services rather than one monolithic entity, the OSTF's work is composed of many subtasks. It was therefore necessary for a variety of reasons to detail some general architecture and rules for all services to follow. The most important of these reasons are:

- It was necessary to list the services that are most important for the architecture. An ordering among the services is necessary so that the most fundamental services can be provided before more specialized services.

- Since each service is autonomous (note that there may be dependencies between services; see next bullet), a common structure for RFPs and other parts of the adoption process is necessary. Also, since users of these services will use many separate services, a common style is necessary to ease the use of many services by a single developer.

- Services are often used in conjunction with one another. The architecture must enable a consistent use of them. In addition, one service may depend on another. It must be necessary to identify these dependencies and eliminate problems which they may cause.

- The architectural requirements of each service must be defined. The criteria by which service proposals will be adopted should be well known so that submitters may structure their responses accordingly.

To satisfy all these goals, the OSTF produced two documents: the Object Services Architecture (OSA) document (Thompson, 1992) and the Object Services Roadmap (OSRM) document (Lewis, 1992). These documents are the basis for the OSTF's work and provide an outline of the process, requirements, and priorities of Object Services adoption by the OMG. It should be stressed that although the documents were composed back in August 1992, they continually change to reflect the process of the OSTF.

The OSA details the goals of Object Services and the role they perform. It then goes on to list the architectural goals and the requirements from services. It outlines a set of conventions and guidelines that should be followed by services. The rest of the document provides detailed descriptions of services that will be necessary for the population of the Object Services layer in the Reference Model. The OSRM is a companion document to the OSA which provides additional details regarding the RFP process. It specifies the general structure required of the RFPs, the process which will be followed, and the criteria to be used for evaluation of proposals to the OSTF. The OSA and the OSRM define a framework that should be followed by all object services. This framework includes a specification of architectural requirements, policies, and guidelines, including:

Object Services should define functionality, not implementation. This allows multiple implementations to be provided for a service. The OSA uses a concept called "quality of service." Quality of service (QOS) is used to distinguish between different implementations for the same service. For example, a direct tradeoff may exist in some services between performance and flexibility. The same service can therefore be provided by an implementation which stresses performance at the cost of dynamic flexibility, while another implementation can stress flexibility at the cost of additional indirection levels (translating into reduced performance). These differing implementations of the same service are both justified; different applications may require the same functionalities but have different considerations, thus stressing different points. The design of Object Services must allow implementations supporting different QOSs. Supporting different implementations is possible only if Object Services are defined as interfaces (i.e., Object Services use a separation of interface and implementation as do other components in the OMA).

Services are defined by sets of interfaces. This is the Application Programming Interface (API) by which they are used. A specification of an Object Service is primarily the specification of the interfaces supporting it. Interfaces are provided in IDL and are object-oriented. This allows using the full architectural support of CORBA and other OMA components. Since Object Services will be used within the context of CORBA, this is a necessity.

Services contain multiple sets of interfaces. A service typically supplies three sets of interfaces: functional interfaces, management interfaces, and construction interfaces. Functional interfaces are used by application and facilities developers for accessing the service provided. Management interfaces provide administrative functionalities which might be needed for correct operation of the service, and construction interfaces are used by the service itself for internal management.

Although it may be possible that certain services might require extensions to CORBA (e.g., the Security Service), such extensions should be minimized. In cases where two specifications are possible, one extending CORBA and one not (perhaps leading to a slightly more complex specification), the proposal with no extension will most likely be preferred. Suggestions for CORBA extensions can be brought before the ORB TF. In any case, all submissions should clearly state any assumed extensions.

Services should provide a single and focused set of functionalities. Services should not be cohesive but rather modular. Users will then be able to use different services to achieve higher level functionalities. It is preferred that such dependencies and coupling be formed as a higher level while the services remain as independent and encapsulated as possible.

Services should have a consistent style. The approach taken by the OSTF is to have the first services (i.e., COSS 1) lay down a set of guidelines and style considerations which will then be adhered to by other services.

Object Services should be extensible within the service role (i.e., additional functionalities per this service may be added in the future) as well as extensible as a layer. It should be possible to add new object services that can interact with other services and are used by applications and facilities. Each service on its own is extensible by using various object-oriented principles such as inheritance.

Object Services will function as central providers of services for most applications. They must therefore provide functionality in a reliable, efficient, scalable, and portable way. Many of these issues are addressed by the separation of interface from implementation and by QOS, but service designers should be aware that their design is extremely important since it is used by so many consumers.

Inheritance and multiple inheritance are used extensively by the OSTF. Inheritance is the primary mechanism for allowing services to be extended, for allowing services to evolve (e.g., the interface continues to support applications that are using the service while the next generation interface is built by subtyping these interfaces and extending them), etc. Multiple inheritance is key to the modularity and self containment of interfaces as well as to using functionalities from multiple services to achieve a goal. Services define sets of self contained and well encapsulated interfaces. To get multiple sets of functionalities the application developers (or even other service designers) inherit from multiple interfaces. The use of multiple inheritance is very central to the approach taken by the OSTF; more so than in other areas of work within the OMG.

The OSA and the OSRM provide the framework for the work of the OSTF. This framework has been consistently used for deciding on service priorities, service requirements, and the construction of the OS RFPs.

5.2 Common Object Services 1

Common Object Services 1 include the Naming, Event Notification, Life Cycle, and Persistence Services and were part of the OSTF RFP1. Object Naming Services provide a way of associating a meaningful name with an object and resolving such a name within a naming context to retrieve the object. The Object Event Notification Service provides mechanisms for delivering events to objects.

Multiple delivery models are supported. Object Life Cycle Services provide operations to create, delete, move, or copy an object. Finally, the Object Persistence Service provides a mechanism for making an object persist beyond the scope of the program that created it.

The final specification for these services, the Common Object Services Specification (COSS) Volume 1 (Siegel, 1994), is the result of the Joint Object Services Submission (JOSS) 1 documents (1993a–1993e, 1994), which are the result of a lengthy process of revisions and improvements. Figure 5.2 lists the cosubmitting companies involved in the JOSS. It should be noted that all these companies plan to build implementations based upon the specifications defined in the JOSS.

Naming Services allow a name to be bound to an object within a certain naming context. This name can then be used to provide access to an object. This provides basic capabilities for name-based object management, which is extremely important in almost any object-based system. Naming contexts allow different namespace type scopes to be used. Naming contexts make up a graph of name spaces which can be managed in a distributed and scalable manner. The naming model itself is designed to be extremely generic and to be capable of supporting many implementation decisions and presently available naming facilities in object-based systems.

The Event Notification Service provides a distributed and scalable facility for delivering event information from event suppliers to event consumers. The service is designed as a collection of building blocks that can be combined in various ways to provide multiple behaviors (e.g., point-to-point or multicast, reliable or unreliable, synchronous or asynchronous, and various push or pull models). Different levels of support can be provided through the use of different building blocks and models that are part of the Event Notification Service. The provided interface may be subtyped by users requiring functionalities that are not provided in the base service.

AT&T/NCR
BNR Europe Limited
Digital Equipment Corporation
Groupe Bull
Hewlett-Packard Company
HyperDesk Corporation
ICL PLC
International Business Machines
  Corporation
Itasca Systems Inc.
Novell, Inc.
O2 Technology

Object Design, Inc.
Objectivity, Inc.
Ontos, Inc.
Oracle Corporation
Persistence Software, Inc.
Servio Corporation
SunSoft, Inc.
Teknekron Software Systems, Inc.
Tivoli Systems, Inc.
Versant Object Technology Corporation

Figure 5.2 Cosubmitters of JOSS 1.

Life Cycle Services include the creation, deletion, copying, and moving of objects. These are basic to any working object-based environment. CORBA defined how requests are issued to objects, but it never specified how objects are created (except that they could be returned from invocations). Different commercial implementations were therefore forced to come up with their own support for such issues. The Life Cycle Service fills this void with a design, a set of services, and a set of conventions for life-cycle operations in a distributed environment. The Life Cycle Service uses a concept called a *factory object*. These objects are used to create other objects. Factory objects are not special in any way; they are defined by an IDL interface and have no special characteristics. Many commercial implementations of first-generation ORBs had a similar concept.

The Persistence Service is implemented by the Persistent Storage Manager (PSM), which provides for the management of a CORBA object's persistent state. The service is often called the PSM since it is not accessed through the ORB, but rather uses a separate API. In this respect it is similar to a pseudo-object. This is done to facilitate efficient implementation, since the service will commonly be used to support many fine-grained objects. Apart from defining a separate API, the PSM uses a subset of IDL (the PSM DDL) to define persistent structures. The PSM interfaces theselves are mapped to different programming languages to provide access from various environments. The JOSS specification provides mappings to the C and C++ programming languages.

The PSM is a lightweight mechanism. It is not intended to replace ODBMSs. Actually, the PSM was designed to be consistent with the ODMG specifications so that an application using the PSM could later replace it with a full ODBMS. The PSM therefore does not handle such issues as concurrent access or multiuser transactions.

All services in COSS 1 were designed using a number of underlying principles. The effect of these principles is actually wider than just COSS 1. Since COSS 1 is the first set of services adopted by the OMG, these principles are the base for the object services' "style." These design principles are therefore of utmost importance to all object services.

5.2.1 COSS 1 and CORBA

Many of the COSS 1 design decisions build upon CORBA design decisions and the OMG Object Model. All the COSS 1 service specifications conform to the OMG/OM, and require no extensions to CORBA (e.g., no extensions to IDL are necessary). The PSM DDL is actually a subset of IDL, and name objects in the Naming Service are pseudo-objects defined using pseudo-IDL.

Specific design decisions adopted directly from CORBA include the separation of interface and implementation, the typing of object references using interface definitions, the exposure of clients to interfaces only, the use of interface inheritance as subtyping, and the use of multiple inheritance to allow packaging of responsibility and composing of multiple behaviors to specialized interfaces.

5.2.2 COSS 1 and other standards

COSS 1 conforms to such standards as the ODP Trader (topic 9.1 in ISO/IEC JTC1 SC21 WG7 N743), the ISO/IEC 10746 Basic Reference Model for Open Distributed Computing, and the CCITT Draft Recommendation X.900.

The Naming Service is consistent with such industry standards as DCE CDS, ONC NIS, and NIS+, as well as with X.500.

The PSM was designed to be compatible with the specifications of the ODMG (to be discussed in Chaps. 7 and 8). Part of the ODMG-93 standard defines language bindings to be used to access conforming object-oriented database management systems (ODBMSs). Since the PSM needs to provide programming language access to the persistent storage of objects, it was decided that the PSM interfaces would be a subset of the ODMG language bindings. This allows applications to be developed using the relatively simple and lightweight services provided by the PSM, yet be fully consistent with the ODMG-93 specification. The PSM mechanism can therefore be replaced at a later date by full ODBMS persistence mechanisms without unnecessary modifications to the application code. Application persistence mechanisms can then be enhanced to make use of the additional capabilities supported by ODBMSs.

5.2.3 COSS 1 service style

Each service in COSS 1 is specifically built to deliver a specific set of responsibilities. Each service is designed to be as simple as it possibly can while providing full support within a service topic. Each service is designed to be independent of other services (as much as possible). The services are modular and are designed as "building blocks" which can be composed to provide higher-level services.

All services share a consistent interface style. For example, callbacks are often used to register application-specific behavior while using a certain service. This style is often based on the CORBA interface style. For example, exceptions are used for all exceptional returns from operations, whereas return values are used for normal returns. Interface inheritance is used to share functionality and make services as modular as possible. By structuring all services as building blocks, reusability and polymorphism are enhanced.

The building block structure of services is used not only when interfaces are inherited, but also when different objects (even belonging to different services) collaborate in delivering functionality. This is true both within one service and across different services. Each service will typically be designed as a number of independent interfaces. To use a certain service, the application builder will typically use a number of these collaborating interfaces. This componentization allows the same plugability behavior to be used across services for providing higher-level behavior.

Services are designed to be used in a CORBA environment. They are designed to perform well in a distributed environment, and to allow scalable interoperable solutions. The services themselves are built as collections of CORBA objects defining IDL interfaces that can then be used by CORBA applications. All the support implicitly given to any CORBA object is therefore immediately available with all services. COSS 1 does not specify a particular solution for finding service objects; rather, this should be handled like any object-finding issue. It is not assumed that the Naming Service is used for locating service objects (although this is definitely a possibility). This allows any object location policy to be used with the object services.

5.3 The Naming Service

The Object Naming Service is defined in JOSS (1993a), which is the basis for the description in this section; it is also included in COSS (Siegel, 1994). The Object Naming Service provides a way of binding a name that is meaningful to humans to an arbitrary object. Names exist and are unique within a *Naming Context*. A Naming Context may have a name of its own (since it is an object) that exists within yet another Naming Context. In this way, a *Naming Graph* may be constructed to any depth and complexity. Names are bound and resolved within a Naming Context to produce object references. Since Naming Graphs are employed, the name to be resolved may be complex in that it specifies a path of Naming Contexts and a final name. This is similar to a path in a directory structure where each segment except the last specifies a directory and the last segment specifies a file name (or to a folder structure in a Macintosh environment, where each segment but the last is a folder name—e.g., Fig. 5.3). Names are not strings; they are structures. This structure includes the name specifier and a *kind* attribute. This allows names to be syntax-independent; for example, it is not necessary to encode semantic information in names (like having C source files be names with a ".c" extension).

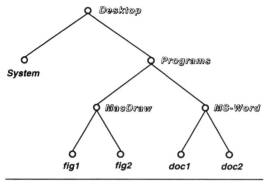

Figure 5.3 A Naming Graph.

The Naming Service employs name-value tuples where a name is bound to an object; this is called a *name binding*. Names provide a way to access object references. Names have no global bindings; they are meaningful only within a Naming Context and can be resolved only within the Naming Context in which they are defined. Names can be either *simple names* or *compound names*. A simple name represents a name binding within a direct name context (e.g., in Fig. 5.3, "fig2" is a simple name in the context of "MacDraw"). A compound name is a name having a number of components where each component but the last binds to a Naming Context (e.g., "Programs; MacDraw;fig2" is a compound name within the Naming Context of Desktop).

Names are not strings; rather, they are structures which have an *identifier* attribute and a *kind* attribute. This can be used to encode information in the kind attribute instead of encoding it in the identifier field, thus allowing for syntax-independent names. The Naming Service provides no interpretation facilities; names are simply a composition of identifier-kind structures. Semantics should be supplied by the users of the service.

5.3.1 The Naming Module

The Naming Service is primarily defined in the Naming Module. This module includes a number of definitions and two interfaces (the components significant to the discussion in this section are shown in Fig. 5.4).

The binding of a name to an object is done within a Naming Context. Names and objects are bound using the `bind` operation defined in the `NamingContext` interface, which accepts two parame-

```
module Naming {
    // Istring is used to support internationalization; it may be typedefed to string
    struct NameComponent {
        Istring id;
        Istring kind;
    };

    // Name is a sequence of NameComponent
    typedef sequence<NameComponent> Name;

    // BindingType is an enumeration which can denote an object or a naming context
    struct Binding {
        Name binding_name;
        BindingType binding_type;
    };

    interface NamingContext { .... };
    interface BindingIterator { .... };
};
```

Figure 5.4 The Naming Module.

ters: a name and an object. The name may be either a simple name or a compound name. Thus if ctxMacDraw is the Naming Context object corresponding to the MacDraw folder in Fig. 5.3, and ctxDesktop is the Naming Context object corresponding to the Desktop folder, then the following pseudocode segments have the identical effect:

```
ctxMacDraw → bind(<fig2>, fig2Obj); // Assume fig2Obj is the actual
                                    object reference
ctxDesktop→bind(<Programs; MacDraw; fig2>, fig2Obj);


(((ctxDesktop→resolve(<Programs>))→resolve(<MacDraw>))→bind
  (<fig2>, fig2Obj);
(ctxDesktop→resolve(<Programs;MacDraw>))→bind(<fig2>, fig2Obj);
```

The resolve operation provides the mechanism by which names are resolved within a context (as shown above). The NamingContext interface provides additional operations for rebinding and unbinding as well as a number of exceptions which are used to signal conditions relevant to improper naming structures or requests which cannot find correct bindings. Additional operations are provided for the creation of Naming Contexts (new_context and bind_new_context), for deleting a Naming Context (destroy), and for listing a Naming Context (List). The BindingIterator interface allows iteration over bindings using the next_one and next_n operations. A detailed discussion of these is beyond the scope of this book; the interested reader is referred to JOSS (1993a).

5.3.2 Names library

Names themselves are not directly manipulated by users. This allows the representation of names to change without breaking client code; to allow this, names must have interfaces. The optimal solution would have been to implement names as objects which have an interface which is accessed by users. Client code would then not break if internal representation changed as long as the interface remained fixed. The Naming Service defines names to be pseudo-objects and not objects. This is done so that names can be lightweight, since they will typically be used in many cases where they should pose no overhead. As pseudo-objects, they are still defined using an IDL interface (which is then mapped to respective programming languages), so that they are lightweight, yet hide representation details. The implementation of names as pseudo-objects is done using the *Names Library*, which supports the `LNameComponent` and `LName` pseudo-IDL interfaces. The term *names library* or *library name* used by the Naming Service might prove confusing to readers of the Naming Service specification. The term is used for the implementation of names as pseudo-objects; there is no "library" in the usual object-oriented sense.

5.4 The Event Service

The computer industry has been making the transition to client–server computing and network-based applications for a number of years now. The move toward true distributed applications is more recent but is rapidly growing. Any such migration involves the use of communication models between different components in the application. These models are extensively used by practically any software developer today.

Since these communication models are by now central to any software development, and since different applications have different needs, there are not one but many such communication models. Some examples of such models follow:

- One typical example is the use of Remote Procedure Calls (RPCs) (Fig. 5.5*a*) to send messaging information. RPCs are the distributed equivalent of a local function call where the invoking party is located on a different machine from the invoked procedure. Since such invocations typically include arguments, they can be used to deliver messages from one party to another. Although RPCs are in general a more powerful mechanism than simple message delivery, they are often used for such purposes. RPCs are central to many key technologies, such as the OSF's DCE and SunSoft's ONC.

- Many applications use one form or another of message queues (Fig. 5.5*b*). The concept involves some independent entity which manages queues on which different participants may place messages and from

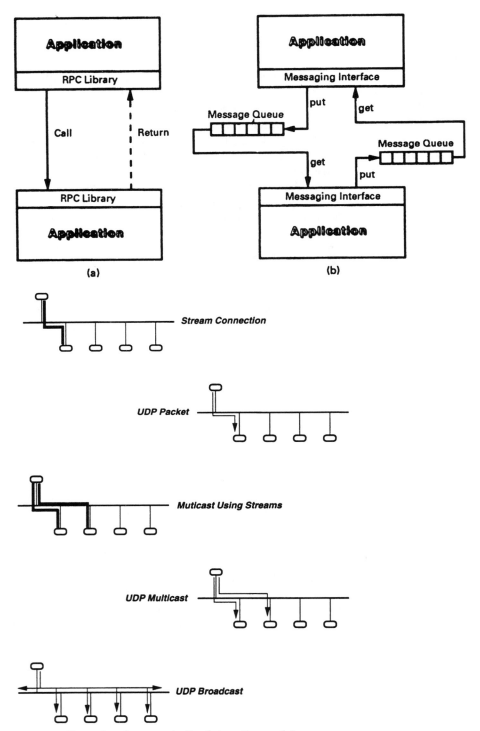

Figure 5.5 Examples of communication/interaction models.

which they may retrieve messages. The queues themselves may be implemented in a variety of ways; this is usually hidden from the users of the queues. The queues may support different functionalities, such as typing of messages, addressing of messages, and so on.

- Many applications have been and are being built using a variety of models built by the applications themselves on top of lower-level primitives. The most widespread of these is probably the use of Sockets in Unix-based applications. Using different socket types (e.g., TCP or UDP point-to-point, UDP broadcast), different communication models may be constructed. Figure 5.5c shows an example of reliable point-to-point, UDP point-to-point, reliable multicast, UDP multicast, and UDP broadcast.

- Finally, CORBA itself defines a very specific communication model. Requests are sent from the client to the object implementation. The invocation uses a synchronous model, meaning that the client waits for the reply from the object implementation (a deferred synchronous model is also defined). If the object implementation is not available at the time of the invocation, the request fails.

These examples do not begin to fully enumerate the possibilities for communication models that are being actively used. The different models have very different characteristics in various categories, such as synchronous versus asynchronous, point-to-point versus multicast, reliability, performance, fault tolerance, and support for distribution.

The Event Notification Service as defined by JOSS (1993d) and included in Siegel (1994) was designed to accommodate some of these communication requirements. It was especially designed for supporting communication between decoupled entities. It was designed to be flexible and to support various needs within such a category. The Event Notification Service does not presume to replace all communication mechanisms; it merely provides a very usable framework for designing and building communication entities that can be used by ORB-based applications.

The Object Event Notification Service was primarily designed to support decoupled messaging. For example, the parties involved do not have to know about each other, nor must they both be active for the event notification to occur. The service distinguishes between *event suppliers* and *event consumers*. In the simplest case, an event consumer and an event supplier are linked (each has a reference to the other), and events are passed from the supplier to the consumer. To allow decoupling of the supplier from the consumer, an *event channel* concept is defined as part of the service. Event suppliers still produce event information which is used by the event consumers; the event channel is used as the transmission medium between suppliers

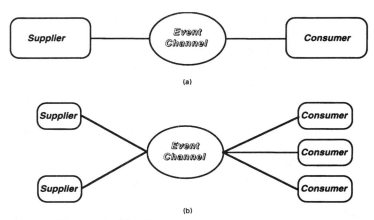

Figure 5.6 The event channel.

and consumers (see Fig. 5.6). This channel plays the role of the consumer as far as the suppliers are concerned, and plays the role of the supplier as far as the consumers are concerned. The suppliers are therefore completely decoupled from the consumers. In fact, the consumers may not be alive when the suppliers produce events and place them with the event channel. When the consumers are active, they can approach the event channel to retrieve the events.

The Event Notification Service supports two models by which consumers and suppliers work. In the *push model*, the supplier takes the initiative by "pushing" events to the consumer, whereas in the *pull model* the consumer "pulls" events from the supplier. Note that since the event channel plays the roles of both a consumer and a supplier, these two models are sufficient to fully describe an event notification scenario involving a supplier/event—channel/consumer combination. Figure 5.7 shows the four possible push/pull combinations for an event channel with a single supplier and a single consumer. Note that events *always* flow from supplier to consumer; the push/pull model specifies only the control of the delivery.

The Event Notification Service supports both typed events and generic events. The generic case means that the entire event is packaged as a single entity and delivered from the supplier to the consumer. Typed communication uses IDL operations for event delivery. The Object Event Notification Service specifies interfaces; it does not specify any implementation details. This is necessary to allow different implementations to provide different qualities of service (QOS). This is especially critical in the Event Service, since so many communication models and attributes must be supported.

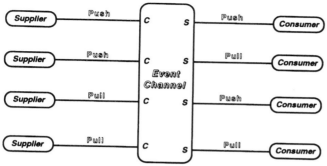

Figure 5.7 Possible push/pull model combinations for an event channel.

5.4.1 The EventComm module

Events flow from suppliers to consumers. Each consumer will hold a reference to the supplier object, and vice versa. The EventComm module defines four interfaces. The interfaces PushConsumer and PushSupplier are used when the push model is desired. This means that if two objects wish to communicate using the Event Notification Service push model, one must inherit the interface from Push Supplier and one must inherit the interface from PushConsumer. The actual passing of the event is done by using the push operation that is part of the PushConsumer interface. Thus the supplier object which is holding a reference to the consumer (which inherits the interface from PushConsumer) will invoke the push operation on the consumer object. Likewise, if the pull model is desired, the relevant interfaces will be PullSupplier and PullConsumer, and the actual event transfer will occur when the pull operation is invoked by the consumer on the reference to the supplier (which inherits the interface from PullSupplier). This is depicted in Fig. 5.8.

The PullSupplier interface actually has two operations that are used by the consumer: pull and try_pull. The pull operation blocks until an event is supplied or an exception is raised. try_pull is the nonblocking version which returns immediately if there is no event. In addition to these operations, each of the interfaces supplies an operation for disconnecting. The signature of these operations is

```
void disconnect_XXX_YYY ();
```

where XXX and YYY change from one interface to the other (e.g., in the PushSupplier interface, XXX is push and YYY is supplier).

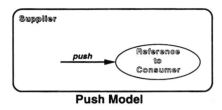

Push Model

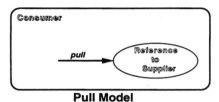

Pull Model

Figure 5.8 Consumer and supplier interaction in push and pull models.

5.4.2 Event channels

Event channels allow the decoupling of the consumer and the supplier. The event channel can best be seen as a consumer and a supplier
combined. It takes the role of the consumer as far as the original supplier is concerned. When an event is delivered to the channel from the
supplier, the channel then takes the role of a supplier when interacting with the original consumer. The original consumer and supplier
do not interact at any point in time; interaction is done only through
the event channel. The orginal consumer and supplier are therefore
completely decoupled.

Since the event channel is really both a supplier and a consumer,
there are four possible push/pull model combinations, as shown in
Fig. 5.7, when one supplier and one consumer are using the event
channel. An event channel may also be used for communication
between many suppliers and many consumers (thus, for example, a
multicast communication model is easily implementable using event
channels; there would be one supplier and multiple consumers
attached to the event channel). This case should be interpreted by
viewing the event channel as one consumer attached to all suppliers
and one supplier attached to all consumers (see Fig. 5.9). Any
push/pull model combination may be used for such many-to-many
communications (thus, if there are M consumers and N suppliers connected to the event channel, there will be $2^{(N+M)}$ possible push/pull
model combinations).

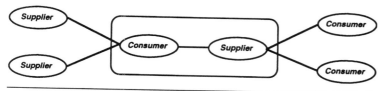

Figure 5.9 Using an event channel to implement multiconnections.

When an event channel is created, an object supporting the EventChannel interface is received. This interface has two operations of the form

```
ConsumerAdmin  for_consumers();
SupplierAdmin  for_suppliers();
```

Each of these operations returns an interface that is then used by consumers (suppliers). The for_consumers (for_suppliers) operation returns an object supporting the ConsumerAdmin (SupplierAdmin) interface. This object is then used by the consumers (suppliers) to add themselves to the event channel. Event channels must therefore be incrementally associated with consumers and suppliers. The operation to add a consumer (supplier) using the ConsumerAdmin (SupplierAdmin) interface returns a proxy supplier (consumer) object. This object inherits the supplier (consumer) interface and represents the event channel "emulation" of the role. Both push and pull models are supported in every case. For example, the SupplierAdmin interface is defined as

```
interface SupplierAdmin {
  ProxyPushConsumer obtain_push_consumer();
  ProxyPullConsumer obtain_pull_consumer();
};
```

5.4.3 The TypedEventComm module

Typed event communications support safer event communication (since the event is known to be acceptable by the consumer). The mechanism used for typed event communication is a bit more complex than that for generic event communication. In the typed case, the events are propagated using an agreed-upon interface. The additional complexity arises because this interface has to be agreed upon by both consumers and suppliers and has to be delivered to the supplier or the consumer, depending on whether the model used is a push or a pull model.

The typed push model involves an agreement between the supplier and the consumer upon an interface I. This must be an IDL interface where each operation has only parameters of mode in and no operation has a return value (this is necessary because events are not invocations; they do not support the notion of a response). The consumer then gets an object reference (representing the supplier) that supports the PushSupplier interface, and the supplier gets an object reference (representing the consumer) that supports the TypedPushConsumer interface (which is defined in the TypedEventComm module). The TypedPushConsumer interface provides a get_typed_consumer operation that is then used by the supplier to get an object reference supporting the interface I. This is then used to call operations defined by interface I on the consumer. Note that the consumer looks identical to the consumer in the generic communication; this is true because the push model is used, and so only the supplier needs to know the "typing information."

The typed pull model also involves an agreement on an interface; this time the consumer must be aware of this typing information, whereas the supplier can remain identical to the supplier in the generic event communication. In the typed pull model, the consumer and the supplier must again agree upon an interface. If, for example, the typed event interface to be used is defined by ScreenEvents, then the interface that would be agreed upon by the consumer and supplier under the typed pull model would be PullScreenEvents. This interface would have two operations for each operation in the ScreenEvents interface. For example, for an operation

    void   mouse_button_clicked (in ButtonID whichButton)

the following two operations would be defined in the PullScreenEvents interface:

    void   pull_mouse_button_clicked (out ButtonID whichButton)
    boolean   try_mouse_button_clicked (out ButtonID whichButton)

Both these functions are used by the consumer to pull an event of the specified type (in this case a mouse_button_clicked type event). The event data will be returned in the out mode parameters. The difference between the two operations is that the first blocks, whereas the second is nonblocking (the return value specifies whether an event of that type was available, in which case the event data are returned in the out mode parameters).

The setup in the typed pull model is similar to that in the typed push model: The supplier receives an object reference supporting the PullConsumer interface, and the consumer receives an object reference supporting the TypedPullConsumer interface (defined in the

`TypedEventComm` module). This interface then uses the `get_typed_supplier` operation to get the typed interface (in our example the `PullScreenEvents` interface). Operations from this interface are then used to get event data from the supplier.

5.4.4 Typed event channels

Typed event channels support typed event notification in the same way as generic event channels support generic event notification. Once more, typed event channels play the role of a typed consumer for typed suppliers, and the role of a typed supplier for typed consumers. Any combination of typed push/typed pull models can be used with typed event channels, and any number of typed suppliers or typed consumers can be attached to a typed event channel.

5.4.5 Composing event channels

Event channels can be composed. This means that an event channel can be a supplier (or a consumer) attached to a different event channel. This allows very complex event notification schemes to be built. This feature is also used to implement event notification with filtering. Thus one event channel could serve as a filter of events emanating from another event channel.

5.5 The Life Cycle Service

Commercial implementations of CORBA 1.1 quickly identified the fact that the important issue of object creation was left unspecified. The specification defined how objects interacted via requests, but there was no specific mention of how the life cycle of an object was controlled. Each implementation therefore had to define its own strategy for such important operations. Luckily, the concepts behind the Object Life Cycle Service were already mature, and since most of the companies delivering a commercial ORB implementation were part of the JOSS effort, many of the "proprietary" life-cycle implementations follow the JOSS Life Cycle submission.

The Life Cycle Service is defined by JOSS (1993e and 1994) and is included in Siegel (1994); these documents form the basis for this section. Object Life Cycle deals with the issue of how objects are created, deleted, moved, and copied in a distributed ORB-based environment. These issues are in some ways similar to issues of how object life cycle is handled in an object-oriented environment (like C++ or Smalltalk), but they are compounded by many complexities resulting from the distributed nature of the environment. Thus, for example, object creation must deal with issues such as initial values of the newly created object (an example of an issue that is dealt with by C++ constructors), how the location of the newly created object is determined, and what control over the implementation that is used for the object the client has (an example of issues that derive from the CORBA architecture).

Since objects can be arbitrarily complex, life-cycle issues need to be addressed for *object graphs*. This is not specific to a CORBA environment. Any object-oriented environment supports object references. Thus, when an object needs to be copied, the question of what to do with its references arises. This is addressed by all object-oriented environments. These environments usually distinguish between what is known as shallow copy and deep copy. In shallow copy, the object is copied but the objects it references are not; the new object will reference the same objects (see Fig. 5.10a). This is similar to copying a data structure with pointers in it. Deep copy means that the referenced objects themselves are copied as well (see Fig. 5.10b); this is usually done recursively (see Fig. 5.10c). Such policies may possibly be defined by the Life Cycle Service as well. This case is compounded by two major factors. The first is the distribution issue. Each object

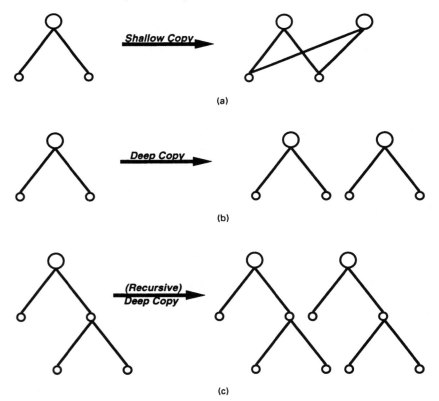

Figure 5.10 Deep and shallow copy.

```
module LifeCycle {
    // Key is typedefed to be a name of the Object Naming Service.
    // A Factory is an Object.
    // Factories is typedefed to be a list of Factory objects.
    interface FactoryFinder {
        Factories           find_factories ( in Key key) raises (...);
    };
    // Criteria is a list of name-value pairs.
    interface LifeCycleObject {
        LifeCycleObject     copy ( in FactoryFinder ff, in Criteria c) raises (...);
        void                move ( in FactoryFinder ff, in Criteria c) raises (...);
        void                remove () raises (...);
    };
    interface GenericFactory {
        boolean             supports ( in Key key);
        Object              create_object ( in Key key, in Criteria c) raises (...);
    };
};
```

Figure 5.11 The LifeCycle module.

may potentially reside in a separate environment, and the notions of copying and moving must be transparently supported. In addition, objects will typically be related using the language-independent Relationship Service (which will be part of COSS 2). The Life Cycle Service must therefore interact with the Relationship Service while dealing with issues pertaining to object graphs.

The Object Life Cycle Service defines the LifeCycle module. This module defines a number of types and exceptions as well as three interfaces. Figure 5.11 shows a partial listing of this module.

5.5.1 Object creation

The Life Cycle Service defines the notion of *factory* objects. Factory objects are objects that have operations which can be used by clients to create objects. Factory objects are not special objects. They are normal objects that publish an IDL interface that can be used by clients. The side effect of their operations will typically be the creation of a new object and the returning of a reference to that object. Just like any other object, factory objects may also have multiple implementations for a single interface. This allows the developer to provide various creation strategies for a single object type, thus allowing great flexibility. The fact that factory objects are no different from any other object can also be seen from the fact that there is no mention of factory-specific interfaces in the LifeCycle module.

The LifeCycle module does define the GenericFactory interface. This provides a creation service that is independent of the object type. This interface specifies a generic creation facility using the create_object operation. This operation has two parameters: a

Key, which is a name defined by the Naming Service that is used to identify the object type that is to be created, and a Criteria parameter, which is a list of name-value pairs. This allows a list of options to be passed to the generic factory object. This could be used for such specifications as resource requirements, initialization values, and preferences. The supports operation is also supported by the GenericFactory interface and tests whether the generic factory object can support the creation of the object as specified by the Key.

5.5.2 Object deletion

The remove operation defined in the LifeCycleObject interface is used for requesting that an object delete itself. Note that this means that to delete an object, the client must be holding a reference to the object supporting the LifeCycleObject interface.

5.5.3 Moving and copying objects

Moving and copying objects is done using the move and copy operations defined in the LifeCycleObject interface. This means that for an object to be moved or copied, it must support the LifeCycleObject interface. Each of these two operations has two parameters. The first is an object reference supporting the FactoryFinder interface, and the second is a Criteria name-value list.

The first argument of these two operations specifies where the object will be moved or copied to. If a move operation is requested, the object will be moved to the scope of the FactoryFinder. If the copy operation is requested, a copy of the object will be created in the scope of the FactoryFinder. When the object is copied, the new object is initialized with the values of the old object. The copy operation returns a reference to the new copy object. The Criteria parameter will typically be passed to the factory object that will be used for creating the object in the (new) location.

The FactoryFinder is used to specify the scope where the object should be moved or copied to. The target location is the scope where the FactoryFinder is defined. The reason for using a FactoryFinder to specify location is that these life-cycle operations will typically require a factory object for the particular object to be used. For example, the copy operation will involve the creation of a new object and an initialization of this new object with the values of the old object. The creation stage requires a factory object, which can be accessed using the FactoryFinder object.

The FactoryFinder interface supports the find_factories operation, which gets a Key argument that names the desired factory and returns a sequence of factory objects. Using the `FactoryFinder`, the life-cycle operations can therefore be completed.

5.5.4 Factories and `FactoryFinders`

Like any other CORBA-related component the Life Cycle Service separates interface and implementation. Thus the interface of factory objects is a simple IDL interface that is no different from any other interface. From a client's perspective, therefore, a factory object is no different from any other object. The factory object's implementation is written in a programming language just like any other object. The only difference in terms of the implementation is that the factory object creates *CORBA objects*. Apart from allocating resources as needed by the host programming language, additional resources are needed to introduce the new object into the ORB environment. For example, a BOA reference must be allocated to the new object if the object uses the BOA.

The life-cycle operations of move and copy are more complex than are apparent from the interface. Figure 5.12 shows a typical life-cycle process. The client object starts the procedure by invoking a life-cycle operation (1). The call includes a reference to a `FactoryFinder` object. The client is not aware of implementation details and resources that may be needed by the object for performing the operation (nor should it be, since this is private information of the object implementation). The object then uses the `FactoryFinder` to locate a factory object. The object can select among many possible factories one that is most appropriate (2). Once a factory object has been selected, the object communicates with the factory object using a private

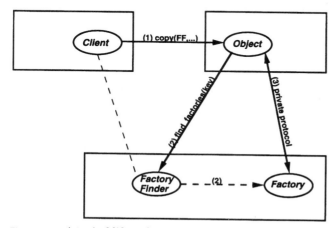

Figure 5.12 A typical life-cycle process.

and implementation-dependent protocol to complete the life-cycle operation.

5.5.5 Object graphs

The Life Cycle Service does not include specialized support for object graphs as part of the specification; however, an appendix to the specification specifically deals with such structures, since they are of major importance in any object-oriented environment. In fact, objects are almost always organized in such referential structures, and life-cycle operations will be invoked on object graphs in almost any scenario. The approach taken by the submitters of the JOSS to support distributed object graphs involves the Life Cycle Service, as well as the Relationship Service and the Externalization Service, which will be described in the next chapter (and are a part of COSS 2).

The Relationship Service allows objects to be associated using semantically meaningful relationships. Instead of using pairs of direct object references between the objects, another construct is used. This relationship construct may include semantically meaningful information that is helpful in handling the association. The relationship may also perform some support services like maintaining some form of relationship integrity.

Support for life-cycle operations for distributed object graphs is an excellent example of how Object Services are defined using a minimalistic and modular approach and then combined to define additional functionalities. The Life Cycle Service does not define life-cycle operations for these object graphs. Instead, a higher-level service is proposed which uses both the Life Cycle Service and the Relationship Service for supporting object graph life-cycle operations. This allows each individual service to remain fairly simple as well as to provide functionality for one focused issue. This approach is considered the correct object-oriented design approach; instead of monolithic APIs, focused sets of interfaces are produced which may then be combined or expanded to provide complete sets of functionalities.

A new service can be defined to support distributed object graphs. This is called the *Traversal Service*, and it is responsible for graph traversals. Such a traversal will be used when performing a life-cycle operation, since such an operation will typically involve multiple primitive life-cycle operations on each of the graph's objects. For example, if an object graph needs to be copied (which is normally the assumed behavior if a root of a tree is copied, for example), then the graph must be traversed, each object copied, and the relationships rebuilt in the new graph. The interaction between this service and the Life Cycle Service is fairly straightforward: When a life-cycle operation is issued for an object in an object graph, an object supporting the Traversal

Service interfaces is created. This object will iterate over the graph's components and issue a life-cycle operation on each of these. The details of the Traversal Service are beyond the scope of this chapter.

The discussion of the Traversal Service within the context of the Relationship Service must distinguish two important relationships that are probably the most commonly used: *reference* and *containment*. Containment is a one-to-many relationship in which the container object may be related to many contained objects. Reference is a many-to-many relationship. Although these relationships are no different from any other relationship, they are so common that the Life Cycle Service submitters define the behavior of life-cycle operations on object graphs connected using such relationships. In fact, specific interfaces were defined in the Traversal Service interfaces to handle these relationships. A definition of the propagation rules in these cases is also provided. Propagation rules define what semantic should be used for the life-cycle object (e.g., shallow or deep).

5.6   The Persistence Service

Making an object persistent typically means providing it with the capability of outliving the context in which it was created. This usually implies converting it into a representation which can exist after the program which created it (and in which it was originally represented) completes and that program's resources are reclaimed. Databases are the most common examples of persistence mechanisms, and object databases are examples of systems which provide (among other things) a persistent object service.

Object persistence is of major concern to every object-based application. Most applications must maintain some context between separate invocations. This typically means that some information has to be saved from one invocation of the application to the next. If the application is object-based, the functionality that is commonly required is the ability to make some of the application objects persistent.

Since object persistence is of such importance, it is not surprising to find that many vendors offer persistence mechanisms for the different object-oriented environments. The primary examples come from database vendors. Object database vendors offer object persistence and much more. Libraries for allowing object structures to be saved in a relational database are also available. Even platform-specific solutions can be found (e.g., using BOSS files in ParcPlace's Smalltalk offering). However, these approaches are vendor-specific and imply an implementation as well as a functional specification.

Following other Object Services, the Persistent Storage Manager (PSM) Specification defines a persistence service for ORB-based environments. As such, it is platform-independent and interoperable within CORBA. Like other specifications the PSM specification defines functionality and interfaces but does not define implementation. This allows users of the service to be supplied with different QOS offerings and even to upgrade from one implementation to another without application changes. In fact, the PSM is designed to allow upgrade to a full ODBMS and is specifically designed to be an upward-compatible subset of the ODMG standard, which will be discussed in Chaps. 7 and 8.

The PSM supports many functionalities that are assumed from a database; in this it is more comprehensive than simple persistency mechanisms. For example, it supports the notion of a single user transaction for allowing atomic updates where either every segment of the update is performed or none are. The PSM uses a data definition language (DDL) which is an attribute-based subset of IDL. This allows the PSM to be closely compatible with CORBA while benefiting from many of IDL's advantages, such as type safety and language independence.

While the PSM is an object service, it is structured a bit differently from other services in COSS 1. The PSM specification, like the specifications for the other services, includes interface definitions and language bindings (in this case to C and C++). In addition, the PSM specification also defines the PSM Data Definition Language (DDL), which is used to define persistent object state structures. It also defines a model (architecture) that provides the persistence functionalities. The PSM is described by JOSS (1993b).

5.6.1 The PSM DDL

The PSM DDL is used to define the data types maintained in a schema and representing the persistent state of application objects. The PSM DDL is an attribute-only subset of CORBA IDL. This means that all IDL constructs are supported except operations and exceptions; all IDL data types (except the any type) are supported by the PSM DDL. After the persistent object structures are defined in DDL, language mappings are used to access these from programs in much the same way as IDL is mapped to programming languages. This allows the PSM to be language- and platform-independent.

5.6.2 The PSM model

The PSM architecture has two components: the DDL Compiler and the PSM Library (see [OUVJ]). The DDL Compiler is used to convert DDL definitions making up a schema to a binding that can then be used at runtime. This process is called *schema generation*. The PSM Library is the runtime support component which allows the PSM to provide persistence capabilities using the schema binding (see Fig. 5.13).

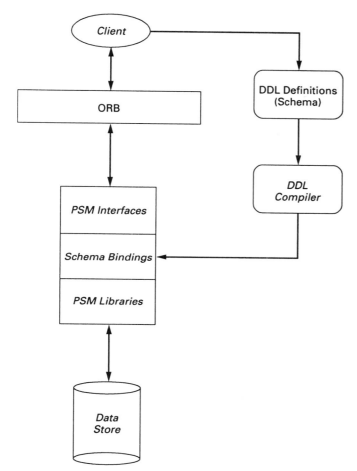

Figure 5.13 The PSM architecture.

Information is stored by the PSM as *data objects* which are instances of the DDL defined types. Each data object stores data of a certain type. These objects are designed to provide data encapsulation and are thus different from CORBA objects. Whereas CORBA objects emphasize behavior, data objects emphasize storage. For example, an attribute in a CORBA object does not necessarily imply a stored value, whereas in a data object it does.

DDL definitions define the types from which data objects are created. A set of DDL definitions makes up a *schema*. The schema is platform-independent and allows the definitions used by different PSMs to remain compatible and portable. The DDL compiler reads in such a schema specification and produces a *schema binding*, which is a platform-dependent definition used at runtime by the PSM.

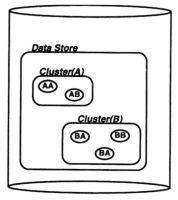

Schema A
    interface AA;
    interface AB;

Schema B
    interface BA;
    interface BB;

Figure 5.14 Data stores

Data objects are maintained by the PSM within *clusters*. A cluster is typed for each schema and can hold only data objects defined by that particular schema. This provides type safety and allows clusters to ensure that their users are using the correct schemas so that they will not inadvertently invalidate the data by using incorrect structures. Clusters make up *data stores*, which are the actual disk storage units (this is shown in Fig. 5.14). A data store may include one or more clusters. There are no limitations on the type or size of clusters a data store may contain (as long as the combined size of all clusters is not greater than the size of the data store). Cluster size may change dynamically during the lifetime of the data store. The size of the data store can also dynamically grow, for example to accommodate growing or additional clusters.

Clusters are the units for atomic updates, and each cluster can have only one sequence of updates. Each such update is called a *transaction*. All cluster updates (i.e., updates to the data objects within that cluster) that are performed within a transaction bracket (i.e., between a *begin* transaction and a *commit* transaction) are seen as one atomic unit. In the case where an *abort* ends the transaction, none of the updates take effect. Transactions may also involve updates to multiple clusters. The PSM also supports a Two-Phased Commit protocol.

5.6.3 PSM interfaces

The Persistence Service includes five main interfaces. The DataObject interface provides access to data object–related information. This includes operations needed for interaction with other parts of the PSM. The Cluster interface defines the interface to cluster functionalities, and the DataStore interface provides access to operations on data stores. The `Transaction` interface provides the operations necessary to administer transactions, and the `Library` interface provides an overall control interface to the PSM as a storage manager. These interfaces define the way in which users will access the functionalities provided by the Persistence Service. The typical way the PSM would be used would therefore be as follows:

For every CORBA object to be made persistent using the PSM, a DDL definition would be created. This can be derived fairly easily from the IDL definitions for the object.

These interfaces make up a schema, which is then used to create the schema binding using the DDL compiler. This is installed to be used by the PSM at runtime.

A data store is created to support the application, and a cluster typed with the particular schema is created within the data store.

When a CORBA object is created, a data object is created within the cluster to hold the object's persistent state.

Updates cause a transaction to be created to ensure atomicity.

The `DataObject` interface provides mainly testing and information operations, such as `_is_nil`, `_get_interface` (which returns an `InterfaceDef` object), and `_cluster` (which returns the cluster containing this data object). A `_mark_modified` operation can be used to mark which operations must be updated when a transaction commits. This operation may be used by certain implementations in order to maximize performance. In addition to this generic data object interface, a specific data object is created for each type defined in the schema. This additional interface inherits from the generic interface and provides an attribute slot for every attribute defined in the schema.

The `Cluster` interface is really composed of two interfaces. A generic `Cluster` interface is defined in the PSM name scope and provides management functions such as copying, deleting, and releasing clusters as well as access operations for retrieving the cluster's name and schema type. A schema-specific `Cluster` interface inherits from this generic interface and provides more detailed operations, including operations to manage data objects within this cluster. Since the managed objects are defined by the schema, this interface must be schema-specific.

The `DataStore` interface provides management and access operations such as `copy`, `destroy`, and `is_open`, as well as a `transaction_create` operation. This operation creates the transaction. Other operations on transactions are defined in the `Transaction` interface (including `abort` and `commit`, state access operations, and a prepare operation that is used when the transaction has to be coordinated with external events). In addition, a ClusterIterator interface is defined for allowing iteration over the clusters in a particular data store.

The Schema interface provides cluster management operations such as cluster_create, cluster_import, and cluster_open as well as initialization and release operations. Finally, the Library interface provides general PSM management operations to initialize and release a PSM Library, create data stores, open data stores, and so on. A TransactionIterator interface is provided for iterating over live transactions managed in the PSM Library.

Chapter

6

Object Services, Part 2

The previous chapter outlined the process taken by the OSTF in populating the Object Services segment of the OMG Reference Model. The OSA and the OSRM were described as the documents providing the framework and direction for Object Services adoption. The COSS 1 services were described, including the Object Naming Service, the Object Event Notification Service, and the Object Life Cycle Service; the Object Persistence Service (which was part of the JOSS documents) was also described.

This chapter continues the introduction of the reader to the world of Object Services. Since the adoption of the COSS 1 services (and even before that time), the OSTF has been issuing RFPs to continue to populate the Reference Model. At the time of this writing, three more RFPs have been issued. RFP 2 solicits proposals for the Relationship, Externalization, Concurrency Control, and Transaction Services, RFP 3 for Time and Security Services, and RFP 4 for Licencing, Properties, and Query Services.

RFP 3 and RFP 4 were issued in the middle of 1994 and are thus only at the early stages of their schedule. RFP 2 was issued at the beginning of 1993 and has been adopted. This chapter will outline the Object Services being requested in these three RFPs. Because of the status of each of these, details will be given only regarding the services making up RFP 2. Since at the time of writing this book COSS 2 had not been formed yet, and many of the services were still in the stages of revisions and formation of joint proposals, some of the sections in this chapter describe one approach or another. Since the description of the service is at a fairly high level, and since a first-phase revision has already been performed, this will not be very different from the final adopted service.

6.1 Object Services RFP 2

Object Services RFP 2 (Andreas, 1993a) requests submissions for (any subset of) the Relationship, Externalization, Concurrency, and Transaction Services. These services are of major importance to any real-world application and were therefore addressed immediately after COSS 1.

Relationships (often also called associations; see Rumbaugh et al., 1991) are constructs that are used for representing semantically meaningful relationships between objects. Object references are often used to represent such relationships when a first-class mechanism is not available. However, real relationship structures provide many added benefits. For example, the relationship itself can have attributes. The relationship itself may be responsible for ensuring referential integrity and the elimination of dangling pointers. In addition, the Relationship Service may cooperate with other services to provide higher-level functionalities (as was seen in the previous chapter regarding the cooperation of the Life Cycle Service and the Relationship Service for supporting distributed object graphs).

Externalization of an object means creating an external representation of the object's internal state. This representation can then be saved (possibly to disk). The Externalization Service implicitly suggests support for internalization; therefore, the representation that was the result of the externalization process could be used to reconstruct the internal state of the object. This combination can be used for a variety of life-cycle type and persistence type operations. For example, an externalization/internalization combination can be used to copy objects or to save an object's representation for later use.

Controlling concurrent access to objects is the goal of the Concurrency Control Service. Since everything in the OMA Reference Model will have an object-oriented interface, this service will provide the necessary mechanisms for building multiprogram and multiuser environments. Without such a service, any environment is extremely limited, since it may cause inconsistent behavior (for details on the importance of concurrency, see Ben-Natan, 1992). The Concurrency Service is not intended to enforce a certain concurrency model. There are a very large number of concurrency models, each used in certain scenarios. The goal is therefore to provide interfaces for such a service, yet allow multiple implementations which focus on different requirements. Since a concurrency control mechanism is relevant to any transaction-based environment, this service must also address requirements of the Transaction Service.

Any real-world information system of sizable responsibility requires transaction-based functionalities. This is the responsibility of the Transaction Service. Transactions provide ACID properties to applications:

- *Atomicity*. A transaction is a collection of operations that are performed as one atomic unit of work. This means that all these operations are completed or none of them are performed. When a transaction commits, we are therefore guaranteed that all of its operations have been performed. If a user aborts a transaction or if it is aborted for other system-related reasons (such as lack of resources), then the transaction is rolled back and none of its operations are performed.

- *Consistency*. Transactions guarantee that the application (if implemented correctly) and its data move from one consistent state to another. The consistency of a state is defined by a set of constraints and invariants which must be satisfied. The transactional property of consistency therefore allows an application that is implemented correctly to perform a set of operations that are guaranteed to create a new state satisfying these constraints.

- *Isolation*. Transactions typically run concurrently with other transactions. The isolation property guarantees that the result of completing a set of concurrent transactions is identical to the result of a serial execution of the transactions. This is necessary to ensure the consistency property of transactions. This requirement of the Transaction Service is the reason that the Transaction Service will have some form of dependency on the Concurrency Control Service.

- *Durability*. The operations of a transaction cause a new state to be formed. Once the transaction commits, this state is assured to be durable, i.e., persistent. The Transaction Service will therefore have some dependency on the Persistence Service.

The Transaction Service section of the RFP solicits proposals for the structuring of an Object Transaction Service within ORB environments. The service must describe how CORBA objects can make use of ACID properties and how these properties are interpreted in an ORB-based environment. Transaction Services need a way to handle concurrency; the description of the Transaction Service in this chapter therefore also includes issues pertinent to concurrency. The sections to follow will therefore describe the Relationship, Externalization, and Transaction Services. The Concurrency Control Service is at a less mature stage and therefore will not be discussed in this chapter.

6.2   The Object Relationship Service

Object orientation requires entities to be modeled as objects. Objects encapsulate data and behavior representing these entities. Objects serve as the basic unit of encapsulation and are, in this respect, "islands of their own." They are often considered "black boxes," since they publish a public interface and hide their internal representation and additional information. This allows both encapsulation and abstraction to be provided and is one of the primary features of object orientation.

However, objects are small constructs; they provide fine-grained modeling, yet they are insufficient to represent subsystems and applications. Objects interact and associate with other objects to provide functionality required by applications. An application will therefore be made up of many objects; in this respect, objects are not "islands." Entities in the real world participate in relationships. Since models represent the domain entities, they must also participate in relationships. Object relationships provide the construct that enables higher-order forms to be built in object-oriented systems. For an exposition of the subject of object relationships (often also called associations), see Rumbaugh et al. (1991).

Relationships between objects are derived from two main sources. The primary one is between entities in the application domain. They are often derived from semantic domain models [which may even be annotated as entity relationship diagrams (ERDs)]. However, object relationships are also derived from programming-level necessities. For example, one of the primary relationship types is the *containment* relationship. The notion of containment is represented by a relationship between two objects, one being the container object and the other(s) being the contained object(s). Thus a Portfolio object will be related with Investment objects through a containment relationship. An example of programming-level containment relationships is the use of collection classes (e.g., classes in the Smalltalk collection hierarchy). Each collection object contains objects; this can be used to construct domain containment relationships. Different collection types supply different containment policies. For example, Set objects do not contain duplicates, whereas SortedCollections maintain the contained objects sorted.

The containment relationship is only one example of the use of relationships as the object "glue" in object-oriented systems. Relationships are very common in such systems and provide many semantic notions in such applications. For example, an Account object would be *owned* by (possibly multiple) Person object(s). Each Person object can own any number of Account objects. An Employee object *manages* a Department object which is *managed* by the Employee object. Another example is the use of the dependency relationship in a Smalltalk environment. This relationship is used to notify dependent objects of changes made to an object. When an object should be a dependent of another object, it is added to the *dependents collection* of that object. This forms the relationship link. When the object changes, it will iterate over the dependents collection and send a message to every one of the dependents that it has changed; the dependent objects may then choose to take some action. This relationship is an example that might be considered a programming-level relationship. For some domains (e.g., the Smalltalk user interface), this may actually represent a domain-specific relationship.

Relationships are categorized by their degree and cardinality. The degree of a relationship specifies how many entities participate in the relationship. The examples of the previous paragraph are all binary relationships; i.e., they have a degree of two (e.g., Employee and Department). Most relationships are binary relationships (the reason might be related to the fact that most programming environments support only binary relationships), but relationships of higher degree are not uncommon. For example, Fig. 6.1 shows a ternary relationship (i.e., of degree three) between a Realtor, a Client, and a Realty. Note that the same object type can be used to represent multiple participants in a relationship. In the example in Fig. 6.1 we may decide to use the Person type for both the Client and the Realtor. This example could have been extended to show a four-way relationship had an Owner entity been added.

Relationship cardinality specifies the maximum number of objects that may participate in each of the relationship endpoints. Each such endpoint is usually given a cardinality of "one" or of "many." "One" means that at most one object may represent this endpoint of the relationship, whereas "many" means that more than one object may participate. The cardinality of a relationship sometimes refers to the maximal cardinality of its endpoints, and sometimes refers to the full cardinality information of all its endpoints. Thus, binary relationships may be one-to-one, one-to-many, or many-to-many. For example, the management relationship between Employee and Department may be defined as a one-to-one relationship in the case where a manager can manage a single department and each department is managed by one manager. The relationship between Investment and Portfolio, on the other hand, will be a one-to-many relationship, since a portfolio will typically contain many investments, while each investment object will belong to one portfolio. The relationship between Account and Person will be a many-to-many relationship, since an

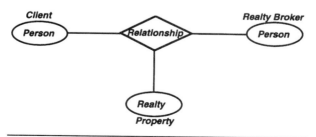

Figure 6.1 A ternary relationship.

account may have multiple owners and a person may own multiple accounts.

Relationships have additional characteristics apart from degree and cardinality. Relationships are often typed, so that the same entity may participate in many relationships, each being of a different type. Relationships may also impose typing restrictions on the participating objects. Thus the is_owned_by side of the Account/Person relationship can require that only objects of type Person are used at this endpoint. Such restrictions and other characteristics of the relationship endpoints are implemented using the notion of *roles* of the relationship. A relationship therefore defines the participating roles and then places restrictions as to which objects can be used for the relationship roles.

Relationships are also characterized by whether they themselves are first-class objects or not. Relationships may be implemented using supporting structures in the participating objects; in this case, the relationship itself is not a stand-alone object but resides as data structures in the participating objects. Another possibility is to make the relationship be an object itself. This would allow the relationship types using the normal object typing mechanisms, allow attributes, and operations to be attached to the relationship, and so on.

This section describes a revised submission to the Relationship Service and is based on the information included in this submission; see Chang et al. (1994). This is a Joint Object Service Submission (JOSS) presented by Groupe Bull, Hewlett-Packard Company, Ing. C. Olivetti & C. SpA, International Business Machines Corporation, Siemens Nixdorf Information Systeme AG, and SunSoft Inc. This is a revised submission which has a lot of backing within the OSTF; it will most probably be adopted (perhaps with minor changes). The proposal defines a relationship service for CORBA objects supporting relationships of arbitrary degree, cardinality, and type. The proposal also uses the notion of *roles* as representatives of the objects participating in the relationship. Both roles and relationships support interfaces through which attributes and operations may be added. Relationships and roles in the submission are first-class objects. The proposal also addresses issues pertinent to distributed object graphs which are linked by relationships, and discusses two relationship types which are the most commonly used (containment and reference).

6.2.1 Relationships

The support provided by the submission is primarily for the creation and navigation of relationships between two or more CORBA objects. The basic support is provided through interfaces for relationships and for roles.

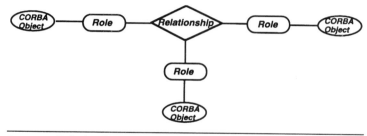

Figure 6.2 Relationship and role objects.

Relationship and role objects are first-class objects. Relationship objects are instances of relationship types. These types allow grouping of semantically similar relationships into higher-level constructs. A relationship object is used to associate CORBA objects. The actual interaction is done using role objects. These objects serve to connect the CORBA object to the relationship object. The degree of a relationship is defined as the number of role objects participating in the relationship (attached to the relationship object—see Fig. 6.2).

The submission defines interfaces for both relationships and roles. When a new relationship type is desired, it will inherit from the supplied interfaces. Most of the relationship support functionalities will be derived from these interfaces. Most of the supporting interfaces are defined in the `CosRelationships` module. In addition, the `CosObjectIdentity` module provides support for object identity (this is necessary because relationship objects in the proposal should have an identity, whereas CORBA objects do not).

Figure 6.3 describes the interfaces defined for the base relationship support. The `CosObjectIdentity` module includes an interface definition for `IdentifiableObject` which supports the notion of an object identity and provides the `is_identical` operation. This interface is used to provide relationship objects with an object identity. It

```
module  CosObjectIdentity {
        interface  IdentifiableObject { ... };
};

module  CosRelationships {
        interface  Relationship { ... };
        interface  Role { ... };
        interface  RelationshipFactory { ... };
        interface  RoleFactory { ... };
        interface  RelationshipIterator { ... };
};
```

Figure 6.3 Base relationship support interfaces.

was specifically created as a separate interface so that others that require the notion of object identity can use these definitions.

The CosRelationships module defines interfaces for relationships and roles, factory object interfaces for creating relationships and roles, and an iterator interface allowing iteration on the relationships a role is attached to. The Relationship interface provides access to the roles of a relationship and an operation to destroy a relationship. The relationship object is created using the create operation defined in the RelationshipFactory interface. This operation receives a sequence of role objects and returns a relationship between these roles. A RelationshipFactory object has attributes for relationship_type, degree, and named_role_types. When a relationship is created, these attributes must match the parameters of the creation operation; if they do not, one of various exceptions defined in the module is raised. For example, the number of roles received as parameters to the create operation must match the value of the degree attribute; otherwise the DegreeError exception is raised.

Role objects are created using the create_role operation in the RoleFactory interface. This operation accepts an object as an inbound parameter and creates the representing role object. The role object has attributes for role_type, max_cardinality, and min_cardinality. Although the cardinality is usually referred to as a characteristic of the relationship, it is actually an attribute of the role; the relationship cardinality is expressed as an aggregation of the role cardinalities. For example, when we say that a binary relationship is many-to-many, we mean that each of its two participating types has a many cardinality.

Once a role has been created, the Role interface provides operations for using the role. The Role interface provides navigation facilities so that the endpoints of the relationship (both the roles and the objects themselves) are accessible through the role. The navigation capability is provided by the get_other_role and get_other_related_object operations, which are part of the Role interface. These operations receive parameters specifying the relationship and the name of the target role. The relationship is needed as a parameter, since the role may be participating in multiple relationships. The get_relationships operation may be used to retrieve all the relationships in which the role participates. This operation returns an object supporting the RelationshipIterator interface, which can be used to iterate over the relationships using the next_one or next_n operation.

To illustrate the use of the interfaces defined in the CosRelations module, we explore the binary manages/is_managed_by relationship between the Employee and Department entities. The structure which will be constructed is shown in Fig. 6.4.

Figure 6.4 Structure of the binary `manages/is_managed_by` relation.

Figure 6.5 Creation of individual roles.

Figure 6.6 Creation of the links between relationships and roles.

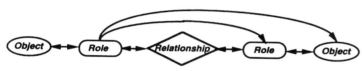

Figure 6.7 Traversing a relationship structure.

First, the individual roles are created using `RoleFactory::cre-ate_role` (Fig. 6.5). Each role is created to represent a different CORBA object; thus, different invocations of `create_role` will have different objects as parameters. The roles in this case will have different types, since the objects they represent have different types. Once the roles have been created, we are ready to create the relationship using the `RelationshipFactory::create` operations. This operation accepts a sequence of named roles and returns a relationship object. We pass in the sequence containing the roles that were previously created. The degree is verified against the number of roles in the sequence, and an exception is raised if they differ. The types of the role objects are also checked. The relationship creation operation uses the `Role::link` operation to create the necessary references between the roles and the relationship. This is shown in Fig. 6.6.

The relationship structure has now been created and is ready to be used. Using the role object interface, the `Role::get_other_role` or `Role::get_other_related_object` operation can be used to traverse the relationship (as shown in Fig. 6.7). For example, if the role object representing the manager is called `managerRole`, then the department object being managed can be fetched using the following (C++) pseudocode:

managerRole → get_other_related_object (theRelationshipObject, "Department");

(assuming that `theRelationshipObject` denotes the relationship and that the department role is named as `"Department"`). Finally, the relationship and role objects can be destroyed using the `Relationship::destroy` operation.

6.2.2   Object graphs

Relationships help to associate objects. These objects often form object graphs, where the edges of the graph represent the relationships. Common graph structures include directory structures, document/folder structures, class inheritance structures, and instance hierarchies in object-oriented systems. Since these structures are so common in object-oriented environments, the service submission specifically addresses the issue of object graphs.

The submission defines the `CosGraphs` module as shown in Fig. 6.8. Objects supporting the `Node` interface form the nodes of the service graph. A node maintains the related object and all of its role objects. The `Node` interface then supports operations for retrieving all of the object's roles or all roles of a certain type. Operations for adding and removing roles are also provided. Objects supporting the `Node` interface are created using the `NodeFactory::create_node` operation, which only requires the object participating in the relationship.

The major support that the submission provides for object graphs is the notion of a graph traversal. Object graphs maintain objects and relationships. Each individual relationship can be used and navigated as described in the previous subsection; the traversal notion allows the next higher level navigation capability.

Traversals of object graphs allow any subset of the edges and neighboring nodes to be traversed in any order. This capability is recursive; the traversal therefore provides an ordered directed traversal of the graph reachable from the originating node. Such traversals are provided using a traversal object. Such an object is created using the

```
module  CosGraphs {
    ...
    interface Node { ... };
    interface NodeFactory { ... };
    interface Traversal { ... };
    interface TraversalFactory { ... };
    interface TraversalCriteria { ... };
    interface Role { ... };              // Inherits from CosRelationships::Role
    interface EdgeIterator { ... };
};
```

Figure 6.8 The `CosGraphs` module.

`TraversalFactory::create_traversal_on` operation, which receives a handle to the starting node as well as a `TraversalCriteria` object and a traversal mode (e.g., Breadth First or Depth First; see Aho, Hopcroft, and Ullman, 1985).

The traversal object is then used to traverse the graph starting from the root node. The traversal object is similar to an iterator; it supports the `next_one` and `next_n` operations. The difference is that iterators normally iterate on very simple structures like sequences, whereas traversal objects iterate over (potentially) very complex graph structures. The criteria and mode guide the traversal as to the way the iteration should be performed. The TraversalCriteria object determines which edges will be included in the traversal, while the mode determines the ordering of the traversal.

The TraversalCriteria object is used to determine which edges and nodes will participate in the traversal. It supports an iterator-like interface and is used by the traversal object to iterate over edges and sequences of nodes. The actual traversal of the graph is performed by the traversal object. The traversal object makes continuous usage of the TraversalCriteria object. Whenever an edge is to be traversed, the TraversalCriteria object is consulted to determine which nodes should be visited and which edges emanating from the node should be added to the iteration. Note that the traversal object must maintain some memory of the traversal to eliminate infinite loops in case of cyclic graph structures.

To allow the traversal object to iterate over the edges of the graph, it must be possible to query a role object for its directed edges. To allow this, the submission defines a `CosGraphs::Role` interface which inherits from `CosRelationships::Role`. This interface adds the `get_edges` operation. The module also defines the `EdgeIterator` interface for constructing iterators over edges.

6.2.3 Containment and reference

The submission to the Relationship Service defines special interfaces for the *containment* and the *reference* relationships. Containment relationships are one-to-many, where the container may contain multiple objects and each contained object is contained in one container object. The reference relationship is a many-to-many relationship, where an object can reference many objects and be referenced by many objects. These relationships are no different from the general case; however, they are so commonly used that the submittors deemed it worthwhile to provide access to these relationships in a simpler way that would involve less work on the part of the application developer. These relationships provide no additional functionalities over general relationships. This can be seen in Fig. 6.9, where the

```
module  CosContainment  {
      interface  Relationship  :  CosRelationships::Relationship  {};
      interface  ContainsRole  :  CosGraphs::Role  {};
      interface  ContainedInRole  :  CosGraphs::Role  {};
};

module  CosReference  {
      interface  Relationship  :  CosRelationships::Relationship  {};
      interface  ReferenceRole  :  CosGraphs::Role  {};
      interface  ReferencedByRole  :  CosGraphs::Role  {};
};
```

Figure 6.9 The Reference and Containment relationships and interfaces.

specialized interfaces are shown to simply inherit the general interfaces and add no new definitions.

The reason for defining these interfaces even though they are empty is that they allow more specific semantics to be attached to the objects. For example, the semantics of CosContainment imply that the degree of the relationship must be two, that the roles must be of type CosContainment::ContainsRole and CosContainment:: ContainedInRole, that the cardinality of the container is any number, and that the cardinality of the contained object is 1. Similarly, the semantics implied by the use of the CosReference interfaces imply that the roles must be of type CosReference::ReferenceRole and CosReference::ReferencedByRole and that the degree of the relationship is 2. Any implementation of these interfaces *must* signal any other values as an exception. The user of these interfaces has therefore implicitly placed the above restrictions without having to explicitly fill in this information (as would have been the case had the general interfaces been used). The application programmer is therefore relieved of this tedium by the general use of these two relationships.

6.2.4 Relationships and object references

Object references are the primary mechanism used by CORBA to relate objects. When a client issues a request, it uses object references both for specifying which object the request should be sent to and for passing parameters with the request. Object references can therefore be used to form partial associations between objects. In the absence of a Relationship Service, such object references are indeed used to implement associations between CORBA objects.

The use of object references for implementing relationships is, however, lacking. The submission for the Relationship Service provides capabilities that are very hard to implement using object references; some examples are:

- Relationships are bidirectional; an implementation using object references would have to manage sets of references to allow two-way navigation over the relationship.

- Relationship can have attributes and operations. Most models require such capabilities and resort to artificial constructs if this support cannot be provided. Providing relationships which are first class objects allows the program to provide a better model that supports many relationship semantics.

- Roles are also first-class objects and can also have attributes and operations.

- Since roles and relationships are objects and have a well-defined IDL interface, they may be manipulated by objects which do not directly participate in the relationship. To provide such support when relationships are modeled by object references, the interfaces of the objects participating in the relationship would have to be changed.

- Relationships and roles may be typed.

- Assuming the availability of a Transaction Service, relationships can support referential integrity and eliminate the possibility of dangling references being formed.

6.3   The Object Externalization Service

Externalizing an object means extracting an external representation of that object and placing it on a data stream. Internalizing an object means reading in such a data stream holding the externalized object and rebuilding the object.

Externalization and internalization are not new concepts and were not invented for CORBA environments. Most developers who have been working with object-oriented environments for some time have come across this problem at one time or another (and in most cases sooner rather than later). The reason for this is that externalization is often used as the poor man's object persistence mechanism. Many development efforts have not used a persistence mechanism in the form of an ODBMS, and inexpensive persistence mechanisms are only starting to be widely available. Many object-oriented developers have also preferred not to use a relational persistence mechanism with an object layer for performance reasons. The object-oriented application developer is therefore often left with having to build a simple externalization mechanism for the use of the project. These mechanisms usually require each class to include externalization functions (how many developers have written save_youself type methods or overloaded the << operator in C++ for an application class?). Other environments provide built-in support for externalization. For example, the National Institute of Health Class Library has such a mechanism (see Gorlen, Orlow, and Plexico, 1990); ParcPlace Smalltalk has such a mechanism as well, called BOSS (Binary Object Streaming Service - see ParcPlace, 1992a).

All these mechanisms provide externalization used to implement object persistence. Externalization supports persistence by "converting" an object to a data stream. We want the object to exist even after the program exits. What we therefore do is convert the object to a (for example) byte stream that is kept on disk; when the program is started at a later time, we read in the byte stream from the disk and reconstruct the object. This last process is called internalization; externalization has no use without internalization, since we will always want to convert the stream back into an object.

The use of externalization facilities as a simple persistence mechanism is one of the uses of the Object Externalization Service requested by RFP2. Another use of the service would be copying an object between ORBs which have no link. Copying an object is normally done using life-cycle operations. However, life-cycle operations require that the ORB in which the object resides and the ORB to which the object should be copied be connected. Externalization does not require this. Thus the object can be externalized, the stream passed to the other ORB in some way (e.g., ftp, email, or even with a diskette), and then internalized on the other ORB. This approach can be used in general when different ORBs lack connectivity.

The Externalization Service is a part of Object Services RFP2. The main contender for the definition is the joint submission by IBM and SunSoft. This section will describe this proposal (see Martin, 1994). The goal of the submission is to provide the necessary interfaces and definitions to allow externalization and internalization of CORBA objects. For a CORBA object to be externalized, it must support the Streamable interface. Externalization streams are maintained by Stream objects, which are created by **StreamFactory** objects or FileStreamFactory objects. The proposal also provides interfaces that allow object graphs to be externalized and internalized. To allow this, the submission specializes the Node, Relationship, and Role interfaces of the Relationship Service. The important details of the Externalization Service interfaces are shown in Fig. 6.10.

6.3.1 Object externalization

Externalization can be performed only by objects supporting the Streamable interface. Once such an object is available and the client wants to externalize it, a stream object has to be created. This object

```
module  CosExternalization {
    ...
    interface  Stream:  CosLifeCycle::LifeCycleObject {
        void  externalize ( in CosStream::Streamable obj);
        CosStream::Streamable  internalize (in CosLifeCycle::FactoryFinder ff) ...;
        ...
    };
    interface  StreamFactory {...};
    interface  FileStreamFactory {...};
};

module  CosStream {
    ...
    interface  Streamable: CosObjectIdentity::IdentifiableObject {
        void  externalize_to_stream ( in StreamIO s);
        void  internalize_from_stream ( in StreamIO s, in FactoryFinder ff);
        ...
    };
    interface  StreamableFactory {...};
    interface  StreamIO {
        // write_* for all IDL basic data types, e.g.
        void  write_long ( in long l);
        void  write_string ( in String s);
        void  write_object ( in Streamable obj);
        // write_graph used for externalizing object graphs using relationships
        void  write_graph ( in CosCompoundExternalization::Node);
        // and now the corresponding read_* operations; the ... are for raises clauses
        long  read_long () ... ;
        string  read_string () ... ;
        Streamable  read_object () ... ;
        void  read_graph ( in CosCompoundExternalization::Node n, in FactoryFinder
ff) ... ;
        ...
    };

    module  CosCompoundExternalization {
        ...
        interface  Node: CosGraphs::Node, CosSTream::Streamable {
            void  externalize_node ( in CosStream::StreamIO s);
            void  internalize_node ( in CosSTream::StreamIO s,
                                     in CosLifeCycle::FactoryFinder ff,
                                     out sequence<Role> roles) ... ;
            ...
        };
        interface  Role: CosGraphs::Role {
            void  externalize_role ( in CosStream::StreamIO s);
            void  internalize_role ( in CosSTream::StreamIO s );
            ...
        };
        interface  Relationship: CosRelationships::Relationship {
            void  externalize_relationship( in CosStream::StreamIO s);
            void  internalize_relationship ( in CosStreamIO s,
CosGraphs::NamedRoles roles );
            ...
        };
        ...
    };
    module  CosExternalizationContainment  {...};
    module  CosExternalizationReference  {...};
```

Figure 6.10 The Externalization Service interfaces.

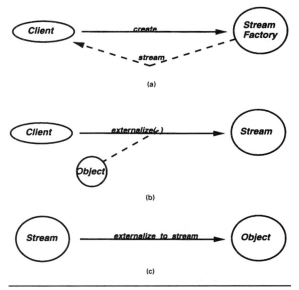

Figure 6.11 A simple externalization process.

is the handle to the actual data stream object. To create this object, the client calls the `create` operation for a factory object supporting the `StreamFactory` or `FileStreamFactory` interface (depending on whether or not a file will be used to contain the externalized representation of the object); this is shown in Fig. 6.11a.

Once the stream object has been created and the client has the reference to the object to be externalized, the `externalize` operation may be used for the stream object providing the object as a parameter (Fig. 6.11*b*). The externalized object may be a simple object or a complex object graph connected using relationships. The client is not required to distinguish between these cases; the service handles these issues internally. If the client wishes to externalize a collection of objects (not necessarily an object graph) using the Relationship Service, the `begin_context` and `end_context` operations must be used before and after the `externalize` calls; these operations are supported by the `Stream` interface.

The calls to begin and end a context are required when externalizing a collection of objects, since otherwise inappropriate behavior may result. Consider the structure shown in Fig. 6.12*a*, where every arrow is a simple object reference. If we are asked to externalize both objects *A* and *B* and we do so in a naive way, we will typically externalize object *C* twice: once as a result of calling `write_object` when externalizing object *A* and once as a result of calling `write_object`

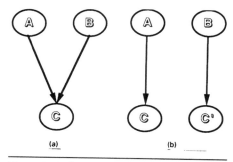

Figure 6.12 Issues regarding the externalization of a compound object.

when externalizing object B. When this stream would later be internalized, the resulting structure would be similar to Fig. 6.12b; this is
not the behavior we want. To solve this problem, some context management mechanism is required. (For example, many such mechanisms use a dictionary or have a table structure to track object references that have already been externalized. If the object has already
been externalized, it will not be externalized again, and a pointer will
be inserted instead. The table mapping the pointer values to the
object references is then also externalized. During the internalization
process, when an object is internalized, the table holds a pointer to
the newly reconstructed object. When an externalized pointer is read,
the table is used to find the new location of the object, and the object
reference is reconstructed correctly.) This is the purpose of the
`begin_context` and `end_context` operations. Note that
`Streamable` objects support the `is_identical` operation from
`CosObjectIdentity::IdentifiableObject`. This is necessary
precisely for the process of tracking which objects have previously
been externalized.

When the stream object receives the `externalize` request, it first
uses the reference to the object to be externalized to save information
specifying the factory and implementation information of this object.
This will later be used by the internalization process when reconstructing the object. It then invokes the `externalize_to_stream` operation
for the object, as Fig. 6.11c shows. At this point the object assumes control and is required to write its internal state out onto a StreamIO
object. The object uses the `write_*` operations defined in the
`StreamIO` interface for CORBA data types or the `write_object` operation for object references. The object iterates over its internal data
structures invoking such operations for the actual externalization.

If the object to be externalized is a node object in an object graph
connected using the Relationship Service, then the flow of events is

somewhat different. In such a case, the node object, upon receiving the `externalize_to_stream` request, would invoke the `write_graph` operation of the `Stream_IO` interface. This operation then assumes control and is responsible for the correct externalization of the object graph structure. This operation uses the extended `Node`, `Role`, and `Relationship` interfaces.

For each node, the `write_graph` operation calls `Node::externalize_node`. The node object is then responsible for externalizing its state as well as its roles (using the `externalize_role` operation in the extended `Role` interface). The relationships are externalized using the `externalize_relationship` operation in the extended `Relationship` interface called by the StreamIO object.

The externalization proposal therefore makes use of the Relationship Service for externalizing and internalizing object graphs. This is an example of how services which are defined to be focused on one set of functionalities collaborate to provide higher-level functionality while not taking away from the simplicity and modularity of each individual service. The externalization proposal also defines two additional modules: `CosExternalizationContainment` and `CosExternalizationReference`. These correspond to the two special relationship types defined by the Relationship Service joint proposal. Each of these modules defines three interfaces (a relationship interface and two role interfaces, one for each side of the relationship) corresponding to the definitions of these specialized relationships.

6.3.2 Object internalization

Once an object has been externalized to a data stream representation, we will want to internalize it and reconstruct the object (potentially at a later time and in a different place). The interfaces of Fig. 6.10 include operations for internalization; although the service is called the Externalization Service, it symmetrically supports full internalization. Internalization is the reverse of externalization, and the process taken by the participants (object, stream, etc.) is similar to the externalization process, but in reverse.

The internalization process begins when a stream object is sent the `internalize` operation. This operation takes a FactoryFinder object as a parameter; this will be used to locate the appropriate factory object needed for the object as well as to specify the location at which the object should be reconstructed (the FactoryFinder is therefore used to define the context for internalization much as it is used for the `move` and `copy` operations of the Life Cycle Service—this is an example of the general concept stated by the OSA that services must have a common style). The stream object proceeds to read the infor-

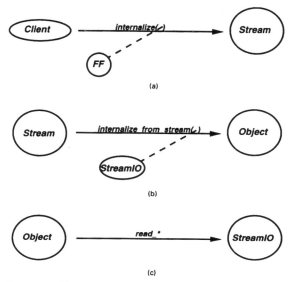

Figure 6.13 Internalization process.

mation that was stored specifying the externalized type and implementation. The FactoryFinder is then used to locate a factory object, which is used to create a corresponding object implementation. The stream then uses the `internalize_for_stream` operation provided by the created object, sending a reference to a StreamIO object (Fig. 6.13*b*). This object supplies the operations necessary for reconstructing the object. The object then uses the `read_*` operations provided by the `StreamIO` interface to perform the actual interpretation of the externalized information and to reconstruct its internal state (Fig. 6.13*c*).

Like the externalization process, the internalization process is slightly different for object graphs. When such a node is externalized, the relationship information was saved so that the internalization service could rebuild the object graph. In this case, the object being sent the `internalize_from_stream` request uses the `read_graph` operation of the `Stream_IO` interface. This is the parallel operation to the `write_graph` operation and has a similar role. The operation manages the internalization process and uses the `internalize_node` operation to read in the node. The node is responsible for reconstructing itself (using `read_*` operations) as well as for internalizing its role objects (using `internalize_role`). The rebuilding of the relationships themselves is the responsibility of the managing `read_graph` operation.

6.4 The Object Transaction Service

Transactional capabilities are of utmost importance to business domain applications. Many of today's systems rely on the concept of transactions as a fundamental capability, without which they could not deliver the functionalities they must. Since transactions are so central to the correct operation of many of today's mission-critical systems, it should come as no surprise that when RFP2 was issued, the number of responses to the Transaction Service was large. It should also not be very surprising that many of the submissions were similar in many respects, since transactional capabilities are fairly mature and are extensively used in the industry. Another reason for these similarities is the X/Open Distributed Transaction Processing (DTP) model, which provides a good base for transaction services.

After the numerous submissions were evaluated, the submitters all came to the conclusion that it would be extremely beneficial to the industry as a whole if a joint proposal could be formed that would be supported by all the major players in transaction services. After a fair amount of work, the members of the submitting companies produced a joint proposal. This was delivered in August 1994 by Groupe Bull, IBM, ICL, Iona, Novell, SunSoft, Tandem Computers, Tivoli Systems, and Transarc. This proposal is fully described in Houston (1994) and is the basis for the description in this section. Because of the complexity of transaction services in general and this proposal specifically, the description provided here will illustrate the main points but may omit some details or advanced features; the interested reader is referred to Houston.

Transactions are used to provide ACID properties to applications. ACID properties are atomicity, consistency, isolation, and durability and are necessary for the correct behavior of most applications in a distributed multiuser (or multiprocess) environment. The meaning of the ACID properties is commonly defined as follows:

- *Atomicity.* The actions performed as part of a transaction are considered to be one atomic action; this means that either they are all performed or none of them are. When a transaction commits, all the actions of that transaction are completed and cannot be interrupted or undone. When a transaction aborts (or is rolled back), all the operations are undone and the state will match that which existed before any of these operations were performed. Atomicity therefore allows a group of actions to be "uninterruptable"; either they are all performed or none are. This allows transactions to guarantee that the application moves from one consistent state to the next.

- *Consistency.* Transactions guarantee that the application (if implemented correctly) and its data move from one consistent state to another. The consistency of a state is defined by a set of constraints and invariants which must be satisfied. The transactional property of consistency therefore allows an application that is implemented correctly to perform a set of operations that are guaranteed to create a new state satisfying these constraints.

- *Isolation.* Transactions are mostly used in situations where multiple processing entities reference and change the same underlying resources and data. The isolation property means that transactions that are performed concurrently produce the same results as they would have had they been performed in a serial order. Serializability is used as criteria for correct operation in scenarios where shared data access and updates are performed. The isolation property guarantees the consistency of transactions in these concurrent scenarios.

- *Durability.* The durability property guarantees that the result set of a transaction that commits is durable (persistent) and will never be lost (except in the case of a catastrophe such as a destruction of the disk and all its backups). Durability is usually implemented using a persistent storage mechanism, but the definition of transactional durability does not specify how this is done or place limitations on what implementation is used; it only specifies that the result set of a completed transaction must be durable.

The Object Transaction Service provides transactional capabilities to components in a distributed ORB-based environment. It allows applications that are already making use of a distributed object-oriented CORBA environment to make use of transactional behavior, thus increasing reliability and robustness. It allows applications which must rely on transactional capabilities to be embedded in an ORB-based environment. The Transaction Service is also necessary to support the capabilities of other Object Services; for example, referential integrity can be supported within the Relationship Service only if transactional capabilities are made available. Without the notion of transactional atomicity, the Relationship Service cannot guarantee that both sides of the relationship will always be set to reference the participating objects as one atomic operation (i.e., that both references will be set or none will). Atomicity ensures that no dangling reference can occur (i.e., that the relationship is always maintained in a consistent state).

Transactional capabilities are by now widely known and extensively used. The Transaction Service that will be adopted by the OMG therefore cannot ignore related standards and must address the interaction with these transaction models. Since the submitting companies all provide transaction-related offerings in the marketplace, they are all aware of the standards and the models. The proposal for the Transaction Service is therefore directly related to the major standards, and the submission discusses the relationships with these standards both in terms of similar ideas and concepts and in terms of interoperating between the different models. The submission discusses relationships with such standards as X/Open TX, X/Open XA, OSI TP, LU6.2, and the ODMG standard. Interoperability and interaction with the X/Open DTP model is especially stressed throughout the submission (e.g., Houston, 1994, Section 4.10, Section 5.3, and Appendix B).

The Transaction Service as proposed in the submission has three module definitions: the Transactions module, the TSInteroperability module, and the TSPortability module. Some of the definitions in these modules are listed in Fig. 6.14 (for a complete IDL definition, see Appendix A of Houston, 1994). The Transactions module provides the major interface support required by users of the Transaction Service and will discussed in the following subsections. The TSInteroperation module provides the necessary definitions of context propagation structures required for Transaction Service interoperability, and the TSIdentification interface provides the necessary operations for interaction between the Transaction Service and the ORB. These and the TSPortability module allow service providers to support multiple components in different locations (using different ORBs), which potentially could be using different implementations of the Transaction Service while maintaining a common transactional context and ensuring consistent application behavior.

6.4.1 Service structure

The Transaction Service provides transactional support for applications in an ORB-based environment. The client application object typically starts a transaction using one of the operations in the Transactions module. This creates a transactional context that is associated with the client thread. The transactional context is then propagated to objects that the client sends requests to (either implicitly or explicitly). All such participating invocations then become a part of the client's transactional context. Operations may also be performed by the client outside of the transactional context—this is determined by the client. When the client decides to commit or roll back the transaction, it uses one of the operations in the Transactions module. The changes produced within all transactional objects within the transactional context would then also be committed (the same goes for a rollback).

The Transaction Service provides the operations necessary to allow clients and servers to share transactional contexts. It is used by all

```
module Transactions {
    // Vote for 2-phase commit protocol
    enum Vote {VoteCommit, VoteRollback, VoteReadOnly};

    // Multiple exception definitions: standard, ORB, heuristic, etc.

    interface Current {
        void         begin()           raises(...);
        void         rollback()    raises(...);
        void         commit(..)        raises(...);

        Status  get_status();
        string  get_transaction_name();
        Control    get_control();

        ...
    };

    interface Control {
        Terminator get_terminator()       raises(...);
        Coordinator get_coordinator()     raises(...);

        ...
    };

    interface Terminator {
        void         commit(...) raises(...);
        void         rollback();

        ...
    };

    interface Coordinator {
        Status  get_status();          // Plus get_parent_status and
get_top_level_status
        boolean    is_same_transaction(...);       // Plus
is_top_level_transaction etc.
        void        rollback_only() raises(...);
        string   get_transaction_name();
        RecoveryCoordinator    register_resource(...)     raises(...);
        Control    create_subtransaction()  raises(...);

        ...
    };

    interface Resource {
        Vote prepare();
        void commit()         raises(...);
        void rollback()       raises(...);

        ...
    };

    // The TransactionalObject interface is used to tag a transactional object.
Using
    // multiple inheritance eliminates the necessity of adding a flag to every
object (thus
    // requiring a change to previous definitions and wasting space); the
object type
    // that is to produce transactional objects simply inherits from this
interface.
    interface TransactionalObject {
    };
};

module TSInteroperation {
    ...
};

module TSPortability {
    ...
};
```

Figure 6.14 The Internalization process.

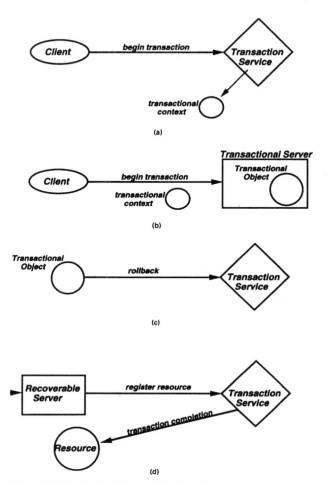

Figure 6.15 Using the Transaction Service.

components participating in the transaction. Figure 6.15*a* shows the first type of usage of the Transaction Service, where the client begins a transaction which causes the creation of the transaction context. The client would then issue requests that cause the transactional context to propagate to other transactional objects participating in the transaction. The propagation to a Transactional Server and a transactional object is shown in Fig. 6.15*b*. The transactional object can cause the transaction to be rolled back (Fig. 6.15*c*), but only the client may commit the transaction. Recoverable Servers managing resource objects also participate in the transaction as transactional objects. The Recoverable Server will register resources with the Transaction Service. Once a resource object has been registered, it will be informed when the transaction completes and given a chance to vote regarding the completion of the transaction (Fig. 6.15*d*).

Objects that participate in the transaction protocols are those that directly contain some state information that are part of the transactional context. The primary examples are databases that contain data that is part of the transactional context. These objects must participate in the commit and rollback process to ensure a consistent transaction state. These recoverable objects appear in Fig. 6.15 in the Recoverable Servers or as stand-alone transactional objects. Other transactional objects may exist that do not contain data that is part of the transaction changes but that might reference such data in other recoverable objects (where the client might have communicated with this intermediate transactional object). Since these objects do not contain data which is part of the transaction changes, they do not participate in the transaction completion protocols but are allowed to abort and roll back the transaction (e.g., in case of some fault).

The proposal to the Transaction Service supports two transaction models: the flat transaction model and the nested transaction model. The flat transaction model is similar to the X/Open DTP transaction model, whereas the nested transaction model allows transactions to have subtransactions (in multiple levels). The flat model is required by the proposal for a compliant implementation, whereas the nested model is not compulsory. Although the flat model is by far the more common model (explaining why it is required by the submission), more and more products are supporting the nested model as well (the flat model is a special case of the nested model where there is only a top-level transaction). For example, many ODBMS products already support nested transactions, providing finer control over concurrency, isolation, and recoverability. Support for nested transactions is required to allow long-lived transactions (transactions which may span days or even weeks), which are necessary in many domains, such as various engineering scenarios. This model is therefore fully specified by the proposal and will most likely be supported by at least some service implementations.

6.4.2 Transaction Service components

A transaction is started in one of two ways. Most application clients will use the *Current* pseudo-object defined by the `Current` interface in the `Transactions` module to start a transaction. Calling `Current::begin` will begin a transaction that will be associated with the client thread. The second way to create a transaction uses the `Factory` interface in the `Transactions` module. The returned object supports the `Control` interface. This interface will be discussed below. This method can provide more control over the transactional context, since it provides direct access to the separate components of the transaction (as will be described below), whereas using the Current pseudo-object, the transaction is viewed as one inseparable entity.

Once the transaction has been created, the client thread may issue requests. These requests may either be transactional requests (i.e., they involve transactional objects that maintain the transactional context) or not. If they are not transactional requests, they need no special consideration; if they are, then the transactional context is propagated to the service provider.

The Transaction Service core is composed of two objects: the *Coordinator* and the *Terminator*. The Coordinator is the enabler through which transactional objects participate in the transaction. The Terminator is used to commit or roll back the transaction. Access to these objects is through the `Control` interface (using `Control::get_coordinator` or `Control::get_terminator`). If a transaction was started using the Current pseudo-object, then the `Control::get_control` operation may be used to access the Control pseudo-object. A transactional object can also inquire about the current state of a transaction or cause it to be rolled back by directly using operations of the `Current` interface.

Recoverable objects are transactional objects that contain data or other resources that are part of the transactional context and must be managed by the transaction. The Coordinator is used by such recoverable objects to register resource objects within the transactional context (using `Coordinator::register_resource`). Once a resource object has been registered with the Coordinator, it will be managed by the transaction. When the transaction is to be committed, for example, it will participate in the two-phase commit protocol. The Coordinator will then use the `Resource::prepare` and `Resource::commit` (or `Resource::rollback`) operations. The prepare operation returns a vote of the resource relative to the prepare phase of the protocol.

6.4.3 The `Transactions` **module**

The `Transactions` module defines the types, exceptions, and interfaces required to support the proposed Transaction Service. Two enumeration definitions supply the values for the `Transactions::Vote` and `Transactions::Status` data types. Votes are used during the two-phase commit protocol, and Status specifies the transaction state. The module defines a large set of exceptions, which may be categorized into three groups: standard exceptions, heuristic exceptions, and miscellaneous exceptions. Standard exceptions may be raised by any request even if the exception is not declared in the operation's

TABLE 6.1 Interfaces of the `Transactions` Module

Interface	Usage
TransactionalObject	Used to tag an object as being transactional without the need for an explicit data element; multiple inheritance is used instead so that an object is a transactional object if it supports the *TransactionalObject* interface.
Factory	Used to create a new transaction.
Current	Provides the operation that will most commonly be used by applications to manage transactions.
Control	Provides access to the underlying objects managing the transaction; used when finer control over transaction management is necessary.
Coordinator	Used by the transaction participants (e.g. Recoverable Objects) for transaction coordination.
Terminator	Provides transaction termination operations used by the originating client or by a transactional object within the transactional context.
RecoveryCoordinator	Provides support for the recovery process that may be required by Recoverable Objects.
Resource	Provides the operations used by the Transaction Service for driving the two-phase commit protocol.
SubtransactionAwareResource	A specialization of the *Resource* interface used by Resource Objects supporting the nested transaction model.

signature. These exceptions are added by the proposal to the already defined set of standard exceptions of CORBA. Heuristic exceptions are raised when a heuristic decision was made that turns out to be a wrong decision (a heuristic decision is one that is made without full knowledge—e.g., a decision that is made by one of the transactional components as a result of a network failure).

The interfaces included in the `Transactions` module are shown in Table 6.1.

6.4.4   Relation to CORBA and other Object Services

The Transaction Service is a central component in any environment that is required to support robust applications. To support these functionalities, however, support must be attained from the underlying layers, including the ORB layer. The service therefore has some dependencies on the ORB component. In addition, the service relies on other Object Services and provides capabilities used by yet other Object Services. It is therefore not surprising that the Transaction Service has a relatively large number of relationships with other OMG components. These relationships can be divided into three main groups:

- Use of the Transaction Service by other components, such as the Relationship Service and Common Facilities

- Assumptions made by the Transaction Service about the ORB

- Dependencies of the Transaction Service on other Object Services

The Transaction Service will be used by components in the ORB-based environment that require ACID properties. One example that was already mentioned is the use of atomicity by the Relationship Service to support referential integrity. Common Facilities will also make use of features of the Transaction Service, since they have semantics which are closer to application domains and will require various ACID capabilities for such issues as compound information management.

The Transaction Service defines a number of additions to the ORB that should be discussed by the ORB2.0 TF if full transactional capabilities are to be achieved. These include such issues as the addition of a number of standard exceptions, ORB management of the transactional context and its propagation between participating components and threads, and especially issues regarding interoperability. To ensure that transactions may span multiple ORB implementations, the ORB2.0 TF must ensure correct support for transaction representation. For example, interoperating ORBs must be able to handle transactional context propagation across different ORBs and must be able to do translations of transaction representations so that operations such as `Coordinator::is_same_transaction` and `Coordinator::is_related_transaction` may be performed. These issues must be addressed by the ORB 2.0 submissions so that the ORB 2.0 selection process will ensure that CORBA 2.0 will support the Transaction Service.

In terms of dependencies on other services, the submission details dependencies on the Persistence Service, the Concurrency Control Service, the Recovery Service, the Logging Service, and the Backup and Restore Service. These services have not yet been defined, and most have not even been issued as RFPs; however, many of these services are implemented by commercially available products. Although they do not provide standard interfaces that will ensure portability and interoperability, and they are not targeted for an ORB-based environment, they can nevertheless be used by Transaction Service implementations.

The reason for the large number of dependencies on other services is that although the Transaction Service is meant to provide ACID capabilities to the ORB environment, it only plays the role of the transaction manager and does not provide all of the underlying tools and support necessary for implementing these capabilities. Other services will participate in providing many of these functionalities. For example, the Persistence Service will support durability, and the Concurrency Control Service will support isolation. This approach follows the general approach set by the OSA: Services should be modular and focus on one issue, and then collaborate to provide more complete functionalities.

6.5 Object Services RFP3

Object Services RFP3 (McCoy, 1994) requests proposals for Time Services and Security in OMA-compliant systems. Submissions need not necessarily respond to both issues; a submission can certainly include proposed specifications for only one of the two issues. The two services are coupled in one RFP because the Time Service is to provide a *Trusted Time Service (TTS)* for the security mechanisms. The RFP was issued in June 1994; proposals are due in February 1995, and the BOD vote is scheduled for September 1995.

Object Time Services are to provide capabilities for clock synchronization in a heterogeneous distributed environment. The services will provide a discrete clock synchronization for any component in the distributed environment using the service. The service should provide such capabilities as timers, alarms, definition of ordinal events (determining the order of event occurrence), and determining a value for an interval between the occurrence of two events. The capability must also provide a TTS that can be used by security mechanisms. TTS provides a time service with the additional characteristics of integrity, consistency, and reliability.

Security proposals are to provide mechanisms for allowing secure distributed environments based on the OMG Object Management Architecture. By security mechanisms a whole set of requirements is assumed. These include such things as cryptography and secure communications, identification and authentication, access control and security administration, and auditing capabilities. Security is somewhat different from other service types. It cannot be layered on top of present systems to provide additional capabilities; it must be designed to be part of the core system. This is the reason for many deliberations that took place prior to issuing this RFP concerning whether security could be solely defined as an object service or whether it should be part of the ORB2.0 RFP. Security is ultimately defined as an object service, but it will also be discussed in many other working groups of the OMG. Any proposal for security must be aware of such issues and must address portability and interoperability issues at the ORB level. Security proposals must also be aware that secure communications include such issues as integrity services, continuous services, and certification processes.

Security is a fundamental issue and is critical if ORB-based environments are to become used in the industry. Although security was addressed only in RFP3, this does not imply that the OMG and the participating companies think it less important than other issues handled by earlier RFPs. If anything, the reason for security's being addressed only in RFP3 is totally opposite: Security is not only very important, it is also a difficult issue to resolve and standardize. The OSTF and ORB TF therefore felt that preparatory work was necessary before security could be tackled directly. Some of this earlier work and issues raised in the process are described in Fairthorne (1994).

6.6   Object Services RFP4

Object Services RFP4 (Lewis, 1994c) was issued in May 1994. Submissions to the OSTF were due in September 1994, and the schedule requires a BOD adoption vote in June 1995. OS RFP4 solicits proposals for Licensing Services, Properties Services, and Query Services. Once more, submissions may address only a subset of these three.

Licensing Services include services supporting both licensing and usage metering and charging. The service must be structured to enable the support of multiple licensing strategies and usage gauging. The service must address many issues, such as what the granularity for licensing and usage monitoring is (naturally this must be flexible enough to support many usages), how the service is accessed and used, and management policies.

The Properties Service allows associating properties with objects. Properties have a name, a type, and a value. The Properties Service should allow the creation and manipulation of object properties. This can be useful in such examples as annotating document objects with a name, a creation date, and an author. Note that properties are associated with an object state but are external to its interface. For example, the interface of an object might have attributes; these are different from the properties associated with the object using the Properties Service.

The Query Service allows queries to be performed on collections of objects. Queries are defined in a nonprocedural declarative manner and involve a predicate defining the subcollection to be extracted from the base collection. Since SQL is by far the most common query language, the Query Service will necessarily have a language binding to SQL or to object extensions to SQL. The Query Service should define the relationship with the ODMG standard.

7

The Object Database
Management Group

The Object Database Management Group (ODMG) is a working group within the OMG. It was formed as a result of the lack of an ODBMS standard and frustration with the slow progress of standards bodies such as the ANSI X3H2 committee. The ODMG first met in the fall of 1991. It originally had five members (Object Design Inc., O2 Technology, Versant Object Technology, Objectivity Inc., and Ontos) and was organized by Rick Cattell (of SunSoft). Its purpose was to create an object database standard that can be used to ensure application portability between conforming ODBMS implementations. The ODMG has achieved much success in its mission, and continues to work towards the development of an ODBMS standard. It is affiliated with the OMG and addresses issues regarding ODBMSs within ORB environments.

The ODMG-93 standard was published by the ODMG as a book at the beginning of 1994 (see Cattell, 1994). It is the result of many years of work by the ODMG and by ODBMS vendors even before the formation of the ODMG. The ODMG-93 document is a work in progress document and will continue to dynamically reflect the advances made by the ODMG. It was published to promote the work done by the ODMG and to stimulate feedback from industry participants.

This chapter and the next chapter describe the ODMG's goals, its work, and the ODMG-93 specification. This chapter provides information about the ODMG as a group and the goals it is trying to achieve. It then gives an overview of the proposed architecture for incorporating an ODBMS into an ORB-based environment. The ODMG Object Model (ODMG/OM) is then described. This model defines the functionalities that are required by the ODMG from ODBMS implementations, and how these functionalities are used by application developers. The ODMG felt that it was important to publish an initial standards document even if it was not perfect. The ODMG-93 document itself contains annotations of deficiencies in the proposed standard and improvements to many of them. By getting the document out the door, the ODMG laid the foundation for further discussion and improvements. The last two sections of this chapter describe some of the functionalities omitted or deferred by the ODMG-93 specification.

The ODMG-93 specification itself is described in greater detail in the next chapter. The Object Definition Language (ODL) and the Object Query Language (OQL), as well as the C++ and Smalltalk bindings are described. Both this chapter and the next chapter are based mainly on Cattell (1994). Since the space allotted to these two chapters is not enough to fully describe the ODMG's work, readers requiring more detail than that presented by this book are refered to Cattell (1994).

7.1   History of the ODMG

The ODMG held its first meeting at SunSoft in the fall of 1991. It originally had five voting members and consistently tried to adopt rules that would promote quick progress. Members were added to the group as individuals and not as companies; this ensured a high level of devotion and expertise and allowed the work of the group to be intensive. The members were required to devote a week of every month to the group's work, to be senior technical experts, and to belong to a company that was shipping a commercial ODBMS. Other types of membership (e.g., reviewer membership) were defined to allow broader participation without slowing down the group's work.

The ODMG presently has many members. Figure 7.1 shows a partial listing of companies participating in the ODMG (companies on the left are voting members, and companies on the right are reviewers). The ODMG is affiliated with the OMG and is increasingly influ-

O2 Technology	ADB/Intellic
Object Design Inc.	Anderson Consulting
Objectivity	EDS
ONTOS	Hewlett-Packard
POET Software	Itasca Systems
Servio Corp.	MICRAM Object Technology
Versant Object Technology	Persistence Software
	Sybase
	Texas Instruments

Figure 7.1 Participants in the ODMG.

encing the OMG's work. It established liaisons with the ANSI X3H2 (SQL-3), the ANSI X3J16 (C++), and the ANSI X3J20 (Smalltalk) committees. It published the ODMG-93 standard as a book at the beginning of 1994 and continues to work on an ODBMS standard. It is collecting feedback and suggestions on how to improve the standard and the process. Submissions to the OMG and to ANSI will be made as appropriate. For example, the OMG's Persistence Service endorses the ODMG-93 standard for storing persistent object states.

The latest status of the ODMG's work can be obtained by sending mail to info@odmg.org. To get answers to questions, send mail to question@odmg.org or call + 1-612-953-7250.

7.2   Goals of the ODMG

Object-oriented databases have been commercially available since 1987. After many years of relative obscurity and a very small market, these products are becoming known and used. One of the major problems with ODBMS products is that they are very dissimilar from one another. Each product provides different functionalities and in different ways. Different products were designed using different approaches, and these differences are apparent even to the user. This poses a big problem for application developers, since it is hard to evaluate the technology, and once one product is chosen, the developers are pretty much locked into the choice they have made. Couple this with the fact that the ODBMS vendors are relatively small and young companies and some of the reasons for the reluctance of many corporate developers to use ODBMS become clear.

The ODMG's main goal is to address this problem. The success of RDBMS technology resulted very much from the standardization that it offered. SQL provides a very high level of portability as well as a simplification of what has to be learned and mastered. If ODBMSs are to become more readily used, there must be a common standard that will allow some level of portability.

Like the OMG with heterogeneous distributed object technology, the ODMG wanted to start building a standard for ODBMSs as soon as possible. Instead of waiting until the different ODBMS products are completely mature and then starting to work on resolving the differences and coming up with a standard (this being extremely difficult), the ODMG's goal is to provide an ODBMS standard early enough that it will be accepted by the vendors and influence the products as they evolve. Of course, the ODMG does not work in a vacuum. In fact, more than 80 percent of the ODBMS vendors participate in the ODMG and are heading the formation of the standard.

While the OMG focuses on design portability, the ODMG focuses on source code portability. The goal is to create a standard that will allow developers to write applications that may be ported across different ODBMS products. This implies that all the database languages must be standardized. To ensure portability, it must be possible to create a schema, manipulate entities defined by the schema, and query the information using standard languages. These do not relate to the product implementation. In fact, the vendors' products will still be very different, and even offer different functionalities. However, the standard will define a common object model and a common database language through which applications will use the products while maintaining a certain comfort level that portability provides.

7.3   The ODMG-93 Standard

The ODMG is not a formal standards body. It was formed by five members, each representing one of the major ODBMS product vendors. The original authors of the document were Tom Atwood (then with Object Design), Joshua Duhl (then with ONTOS), Guy Ferran (then with O2 Technology), Mary Loomis (then with Versant), and Drew Wade (then with Objectivity). The editors for the standard were Douglas Barry, Rick Cattell, Jeff Eastman, and David Jordan.

The ODMG-93 contains five main chapters. The first main chapter scopes the ODMG Object Model on which the standard is based in terms of functionality and semantics. The next two chapters describe the Object Definition Language and the Object Query Language, and the following two chapters provide bindings for C++ and Smalltalk.

The ODMG Object Model is described in Sec. 7.6. The ODMG/OM is a superset of the OMG Object Model and extends the model with characteristics specific to ODBMSs. The Object Definition Language (ODL) is described in Sec. 8.1. ODL is the language used to define the ODBMS schema. It is based on the IDL syntax and is semantically equivalent where the OMG/OM and the ODMG/OM match. The Object Query Language (OQL) is described in Sec. 8.2. OQL is a declarative language for querying ODBMSs. OQL is defined as an abstract syntax, and a concrete object-SQL-like syntax is also provided. The C++ and Smalltalk bindings are described in Secs. 8.3 and 8.4. These bindings map the ODL, the OQL, and especially the OML into the host programming languages.

7.4   ODBMSs and ORBs

The OMG's OMA defines a core model service. It then defines profiles that extend the core with additional functionalities. Two extensions are the ORB profile, which extends the model with distributed support, and the ODBMS profile, which adds such things as persistence and transactions (see Fig. 7.2). This, however, only defines certain

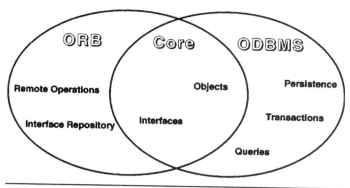

Figure 7.2 Extensions to the OMA added by the ORB and ODBMS profiles.

scopes of responsibility. It does not provide any guidance concerning the interaction of the different components and services in a dynamic environment.

The ORB plays the central role in the OMG environment. The distribution component will be used by all elements in the environment. The ORB provides elementary functionalities of object access, object creation, and interaction. Since any system will need communication between objects, the ORB plays the most central role in the OMG architecture. It is therefore appropriate for the ODMG to address the issue of how an ODBMS functions in an ORB environment.

Before we explain the ODMG model for ODBMSs in ORB environments, we must understand why ODBMSs are necessary in an ORB environment. As we have seen, the ORB allows objects (local or remote) to communicate, to provide services to each other, and to interact. Object Services described in previous chapters provide support for life-cycle operations, naming, relationships, and even persistence. Isn't it conceivable that ORB support is enough for managing and using persistent objects? Doesn't the ORB environment provide enough for ODBMSs to be redundant? The answer is theoretically yes, but pragmatically no. If the environment had infinite computing power and infinite bandwidth, then the ORB environment could be used for the same things as an ODBMS is. But in the real world, ORBs and ODBMSs are used for very different things.

The issue is that of granularity. The ORB deals with a relatively small number of objects. It deals in services and applications. The ORB model provides support for a coarse level of granularity. ODBMSs, on the other hand, are typically used by applications to support very fine granularity. Objects may be very small. It is not uncommon to find objects like cells in a spreadsheet application, code segments in a source management tool, and business model entities in a CASE tool. Cases in which millions of small objects are managed by the ODBMS are not uncommon.

It should be clear from the architecture of the ORB that support for such fine granularity is not practical. ODBMSs, on the other hand, have dedicated years of research to coming up with solutions to exactly these problems. The ODBMS vendors use different optimization techniques and architectures to support such object models. ODBMSs, however, could greatly benefit from the ORB environment.

ODBMSs provide support for defining, creating, manipulating, and querying persistent objects. They provide ACID properties (atomicity, consistency, integrity, and durability) that no real environment can do without. They have backup and recovery mechanisms and concurrency. Above all, they provide very high-performance object management. However, the focus of the ODBMS is within this one system. What the ORB adds to this is the infrastructure for accessing (and being accessed from) a distributed heterogeneous environment. The ORB can be used as the layer allowing access to multiple ODBMSs, and even allowing distribution between databases. A combination of ORB and ODBMS technologies would allow the utilization of optimized object management in a generic, portable, and distributed architecture.

Since the ODMG's goal was to design an ODBMS standard, and since the ORB standard was already defined by the OMG, it seemed proper for the ODMG to address the issue of how these two technologies interrelate. Since CORBA is the basis of any OMG architecture, it was necessary to fit ODBMSs into the ORB architecture. The way this is done is by defining an object database adapter (ODA) that maps sets of objects managed by the ODBMS to the ORB; these objects are not specifically registered with the ORB, since they are managed internally by the ODBMS. This architecture certainly conforms to CORBA; CORBA specifies that many object adapter types will be needed, and the ODA is just another of these.

7.4.1 The ODA architecture

Figure 7.3 illustrates the ODA architecture. In this architecture, the ODBMS interfaces with the ORB through an object database adapter. Objects managed by the ODBMS are either registered with the ORB or not. Most small objects will not be registered with the ORB, since the overhead for ORB management would be too large. These objects would be managed by the ODBMS. Since these objects will also need to be accessed by the ORB, some registration method is needed. This method must be efficient. For this, the architecture provides the ODA. The ODA allows the ODBMS to register sets of objects. The overhead will be low, since the ORB does not manage each of these objects separately. Instead, large sets of objects are seen as a single

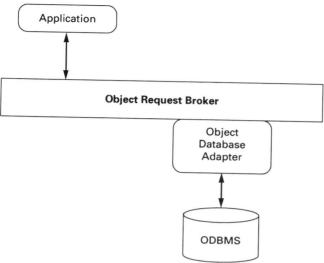

Figure 7.3 The ODA architecture.

object subspace. The ORB then uses the ODA to transfer control for interactions with these objects to the ODBMS.

The ODA architecture provides the best of all worlds. Since all objects are still reachable by the ORB (since the subspace is registered with the ORB), transparent heterogeneous distribution is still attained. In fact, the user's view of the world does not change. All objects are still accessible using the ORB semantics; only the management implementation changes. High performance in the management of many small objects is possible, since the real object management is done by the ODBMS. Since the ODBMS still acts as the object manager, techniques such as caching, indexing, and optimized accessed methods are extensively used. ODBMS products that have their own distribution layer can use their own internal mechanisms for managing the distributed database, potentially achieving higher performance than that achievable by going through the ORB. The interfacing with the ORB through the ODA can therefore be done at the logical (distributed) level and not necessarily at the physical database level (see Fig. 7.4).

The key to the architecture is the ODA. Every object adapter defined for the ORB architecture has very specialized attributes. The Basic Object Adapter (BOA) is the simplest OA; it maps as RPC to every operation invocation and is therefore the most general, but slowest. The Library Object Adapter (LOA) was defined to support

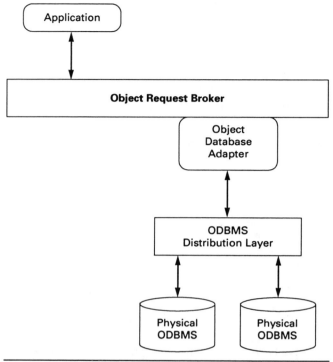

Figure 7.4 Interfacing with the ORB through the ODA at the logical level.

local invocations after the first RPC generation. The ODA has two special characteristics:

- It allows the ODBMS to register a subspace of objects with the ORB.
- It leaves the object management to the ODBMS.

The ODA supports containment semantics. The ODBMS serves as an object container; the internals of the container are opaque as far as the ORB is concerned. Once the subspace definition of the objects is registered, any request to an object included in this subspace is propagated to the container—that is, the ODBMS. The individual objects, the application, and the ODBMS have complete flexibility as to which objects will be directly registered with the ORB and which will use the containment semantics.

7.5 Overview of the ODMG Object Model

Before we delve into a detailed description of the ODMG/OM, it is appropriate to compare it to the OMG/OM. The OMG/OM is the base for all the OMG's work. Since the ODMG's goal is to come up with a standard for ODBMS within the OMG framework, it is necessary for the model used by the ODMG to be compatible with the OMG/OM. However, since the OMG/OM was designed to be extremely generic and all-encompassing, it is missing concepts which are compulsory for database management systems. It was therefore necessary for the ODMG to create a new object model that will be based on the OMG/OM where possible.

The ODMG/OM is an extension of the OMG/OM. It uses exactly the same definitions as the OMG/OM for the core components, and adds new constructs to support databases. As Fig. 7.5 shows, the ODMG/OM is a superset of the OMG/OM.

The base of the ODMG/OM is identical to the OMG/OM. A type is defined by an interface specification. A type defines state and behavior for objects. Objects are instances of types. An object has only one type, and this type persists throughout the object's lifetime. The OM does not define dynamic temporal type changes (this will probably be included in a future revision of the ODMG/OM). Types are related by a subtype/supertype relationship. A type (interface) may inherit from other types (interfaces). Multiple interface inheritance is supported. The behavior of an object is defined as a set of operations in the type. Operations have a signature (i.e., a name, argument types, and a return type). Operations cause method invocation in the object implementation.

Based on this model, the ODMG/OM adds new concepts. Types collectively define the database schema. Database schemas are dynamic, and many ODBMS vendors support schema evolution. Therefore, types in the ODMG/OM can themselves have attributes. Types are actually objects themselves. Two important properties that types have are an *extent* and a set of *keys*. An extent is the set of all instances of the type. It is used as a named handle into the database and is used

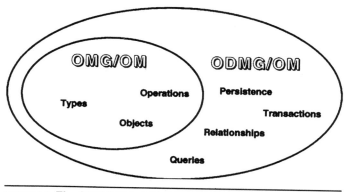

Figure 7.5 The ODMG Object Model.

for set-based queries. Extents are maintained by the system. Keys define a set of properties that uniquely identify an object within an extent. Keys are of major importance in performance-related issues when accessing, storing, or searching for objects within an extent.

The ODMG/OM also extends the instance model. Objects have additional features that are not defined in the OMG/OM:

The ODMG/OM supports relationships between objects. The ODMG/OM defines what a relationship is, how it is used, and how it is managed.

Collections are supported much like built-in types in the OMG/OM. The behavior and type hierarchy for collections are explicitly defined.

The ODMG/OM uses exception returns for operations.

Another way to see where the ODMG/OM extends the OMG/OM as far as objects are concerned is to view the two models' type hierarchies. Figure 7.6a shows the base type hierarchy of the OMG/OM, and Fig. 7.6b shows the base type hierarchy of the ODMG/OM. Note that in Fig. 7.6a the type DenotableValue is not specifically defined by the OMG/OM; however, the OMG/OM refers to "Dvals" as the set of all objects of type Object and Non_object. Note that the only difference in the two hierarchies is the names used. DenotableValue in the OMG/OM is called Denotable_Object in the ODMG/OM, and Non_Object in the OMG/OM is identical to Literal in the ODMG/OM.

As can be seen from Figs. 7.6a and b, the ODMG/OM is a richer model. It extends the OMG/OM hierarchy in three respects:

1. The ODMG/OM has a detailed subhierarchy under Object.

2. The ODMG/OM has a detailed subhierarchy under Literal.

3. The ODMG/OM has a rich property model, including relationships.

These extensions are necessary, since the ODMG/OM is to be the object model for ODBMSs. These systems provide a very rich functionality for managing objects of any size and characteristic. Since the ODMG/OM is specifically designed for ODBMSs, it was possible to extend the base model to accommodate them. This could be compared to the approach taken by the Object Services Task Force. Object Services include such services as persistence, transactions, and associations (relationships). These services, however, are to be provided within the ORB environment; therefore they must not extend the object model used by CORBA. ODBMSs, on the other hand, are object managers themselves. It is therefore possible to provide a richer

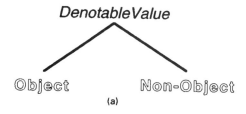

(a)

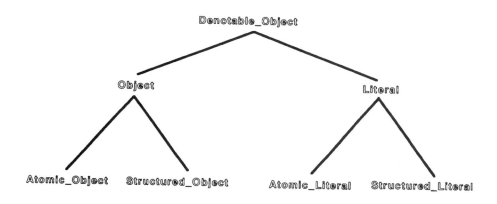

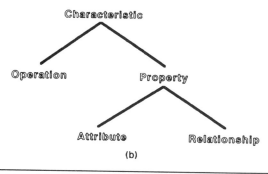

(b)

Figure 7.6 Base type hierarchies of the OMG and ODMG Object Models.

model. This is the approach taken by the ODMG. We now go on to inspect the ODMG/OM in greater detail.

7.6 The ODMG Object Model

The ODMG/OM extends the OMG/OM to model the support provided by ODBMSs. It is the object model to be used by all ODMG-compliant

ODBMS products. This section will describe the ODMG/OM as defined in the ODMG-93 specification; for completeness we mention parts of the model that are based on the OMG/OM as well.

7.6.1 Types

A type has an interface and implementations. A type can have more than one implementation conforming to the (single) interface. Interface specifications match those of the OMG/OM. The type definition includes information on the properties and operations supported by any instance of this type (i.e., any instantiation of one of the type's implementations). Each implementation consists of data structures supporting the properties of the type and methods (procedures or functions) that implement the operations defined by that type. Each type implementation provides exactly one method per operation declared in the type interface.

The concept of distinguishing between the type hierarchy and the implementation hierarchy and allowing multiple implementations per type is not new. Such ideas have been long debated in the object-oriented community, and several systems have been built around this concept [e.g., the language Portlandish (Porter, 1992)]. This concept is of major importance in the ODBMS world. It provides benefits from both the ODBMS vendor's and the user's point of view. For the ODBMS vendor, it provides a way to support a heterogeneous environment. For the user, it allows implementing the same concepts in ways which may differ in terms of performance, robustness, and so on. Because this support is provided from within the model, artificial constructs to do precisely these things are eliminated.

Types are objects themselves. Types have properties, such as extents and keys. Since types are objects, they are instances of a certain type. This is called the type Type, and its place in the type hierarchy is shown in Fig. 7.7. Since any type is an object and must therefore have a type, the type Type must also have a type (don't you just love models that allow the formation of such sentences?). To stop the infinite recursion of the type of a type, the type Type is not only a subtype of Atomic_Object but also an instance of Atomic_Object. This organization is very similar to the Smalltalk class library and the classes Object, Class, and MetaClass.

As a type, Type has an interface specification which details the properties and operations provided for each instance of this type. Properties include a name, an extent, and keys. Type also provides properties for implementing the type hierarchy, operations, and properties. The has_subtypes and has_supertypes properties provide for a set of subtypes, and a set of supertypes, respectively. has_properties maintains a set of properties; these are the properties that

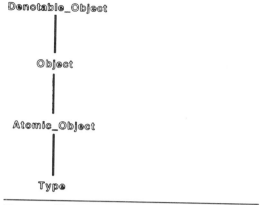

Figure 7.7 The Type type.

are defined for each instance of the type. has_operations is similarly defined for the operations. Type also defines operations. create_instance is provided for constructing instances. The operation signature makes it very similar to a constructor in C++. For example, to construct an instance of the type Account with an account number of 123456789 and an initial balance of $1000, use

Account.create_instance(accountNumber = 123456789, cashBalance = 1000);

The type hierarchy is constructed through type inheritance. A type can inherit from another type. All properties and operations are inherited from all supertypes. An instance of a subtype can therefore also be seen as an instance of all its type (direct or indirect) supertypes. Multiple type inheritance is supported by the model. Since inheritance is allowed but not forced, it is possible that a type will have any number of supertypes, including zero. The type organization is therefore not necessarily a hierarchy; it is in general a directed acyclic graph (DAG). The model uses redefinition specifications in cases of name clashes. For example, we may have a type Cowgirl that defines a draw operation and a Display type that defines a draw operation (obviously with totally different semantics). If we wish to create a subtype inheriting from both of these named CowgirlDisplay, we would have to redefine one of the operations using

drawGun redefines Cowgirl.draw;

7.6.2 Properties

A type can define a set of properties. Each property is instantiated in any instance of this type. Properties can be queried and manipulated.

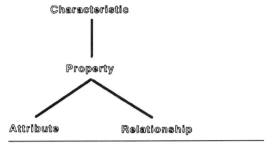

Figure 7.8 The property types.

Properties take the form of attributes and relationships. Attributes associate a value with every object of the type. Relationships are defined between two types and associate an object or a set of objects with every object of the type. The property types are shown in Fig. 7.8.

Attributes map a named value with instances of a type. Attributes are part of the type definition. Recall that a type will have one or more implementations. An attribute may be mapped to a data structure (field) in the implementation, but this is not necessarily true. An attribute may be of a derived (or calculated) nature, in which case there will be no storage allocation for the attribute. Attributes are not first-class objects and do not have identifiers, attributes, relationships, or operations. For each attribute, two accessor built-in operations are supplied. These operations are type operations. For example, the attribute accountNumber in the type Account will have the following two operations:

Integer get_accountNumber()   and   set_accountNumber(value: Integer)

Default initial values for attributes may be defined, as well as a specialized null value.

Relationships are defined between two types (the same type can actually serve both sides of the relationship). Only binary relationships are supported by the ODMG/OM; relationships may be one-to-one, one-to-many, or many-to-many. Relationships associate an object or a set of objects with a property in any instance of the type. A relationship definition also names the inverse side of the relationship. Relationships are guaranteed to maintain referential integrity. If an inverse specification is not included, the ODBMS may understand this to mean that the relationship can be implemented as an attribute. The operations defined for relationships are summarized in Table 7.1.

TABLE 7.1 Relationships Operations

1-to-1 Relationships	1-to-many Relationships	many-to-many Relationships
create, delete, traverse	create, delete, add_one_to_one, remove_one_to_one, traverse	create, delete, add_one_to_one, remove_one_to_one, add_one_to_many, remove_one_to_many, remove_all_from

7.6.3 Operations

Operations are part of the type definition and model the behavior of instances of the type. An operation has a signature which includes the operation name, the argument names and types, the return value type, and exceptions that might be raised by the operation. Operations defined within one type must have different names. Different types may have operations with identical names. Resolution of name overloading at runtime is done according to the first argument type.

The object model does not distinguish between side-effect-free operations and operations that may have side effects. Some ODBMS implementations and programming environments may want to provide a side-effect-free subcategory to allow query optimizations; this should be added only as a pragma so as not to compromise portability.

The Operation type (see Fig. 7.9) defines a number of built-in operations [invoke(), return(), return_abnormaly(Exception)]. In compiled languages these may not be directly invoked; instead, they are used by the compiler for every operation invocation. Some interpreted or dynamically compiled languages provide similar constructs, and in the mapping of the model to these languages, it is actually possible that these operations will be accessible to programmers. For example, Smalltalk allows any object to receive the perform: message where the argument is a method name. This is similar to the built-in invoke() operation.

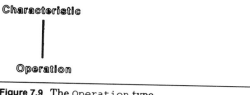

Figure 7.9 The Operation type.

7.6.4 Objects

Objects are encapsulations of state, identity, and behavior. Objects can be either mutable or immutable. Mutable objects have an identifier and may change their state throughout their lifetime. Immutable objects do not have a specific identifier; their state is their identity. They therefore may not change their state. Any apparent state change would mean that the object ceases to exist and a new object is being used.

Any object (mutable or immutable) is created with a certain lifetime. The ODMG/OM defines three object lifetimes:

```
coterminus_with_procedure

coterminus_with_process

coterminus_with_database
```

The three different lifetimes specify when the object will be destroyed and where space will be allocated for it. The first two lifetimes are commonly used within the programming language. The first lifetime is used for objects defined within a procedure. Space is usually allocated in the stack frame used by the procedure. When the procedure ends, the stack frame is released and the object no longer exists. The second lifetime allows an object to persist throughout an application session. Space is allocated on the heap or in static process storage. When the session ends, the object's storage is reclaimed. The third lifetime allows an object to exist in space allocated by the ODBMS and persist after process termination.

Figure 7.6*b* shows the base object hierarchy. The type `Object` is the root of the hierarchy for mutable objects, and the type `Literal` is the root for immutable objects. Since both mutable and immutable objects have an identity, the type `Denotable_Object` provides an `equal?` operation which returns true if the objects being compared have the same identity.

The type `Literal` has two subtypes (see Fig. 7.10). A literal object can be either atomic or structured. Atomic literals are such objects as integers, characters, and boolean values. Atomic literals do not need to be explicitly created. Structured literals are either immutable collections or immutable structures. Note that the types are explicitly named `Immutable_Collection` and `Immutable_Structure`; this is necessary to distinguish them from mutable collections and structure objects. A mutable collection object allows one to add elements, delete elements, and replace elements. An immutable collection, on the other hand, does not. For example, the immutable character string "ABCD" is a different object from the immutable character string "ABCE." A mutable collection of characters, on the other hand,

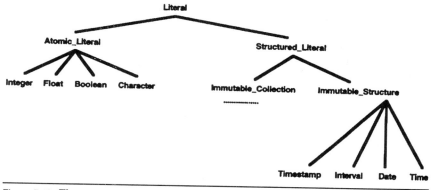

Figure 7.10 The `Literal` type and its subtypes.

would allow the user to replace the fourth character with "E" without causing any change in the object's identity. The definitions for the structures inheriting from `Immutable_Structure` in Fig. 7.10 are as in the ANSI SQL specification.

Immutable collections have a broad hierarchy which is parallel to the mutable collection hierarchy (for more details, see the next subsection). It includes immutable versions for arrays, sets, bags, lists, enumerations, and strings. Enumeration is used to define a closed set of instances as a type. Only the instances specifically defined in the enumeration may be objects of this type. The hierarchy is shown in Fig. 7.11.

The type `Object` provides instances of mutable objects. It provides an object identifier (OID) for its instances. Since these objects have an identity which is independent of their state, an object can also have a meaningful name. In fact, such an object may have many names. The `Object` type defines a property called `names` which denotes a set of character strings. An additional property maintains the type of the object. This is a property of type `Type`.

The type `Object` defines a set of operations. Any object instantiated from `Object` or any of its subclasses (direct or indirect) will therefore inherit these operations. These operations make it possible to

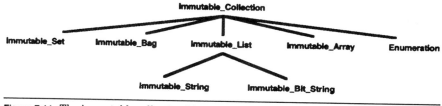

Figure 7.11 The immutable collection hierarchy.

compare objects using the OID (operation same_as?), to create object instances (operation create), and to delete objects (operation delete). Object creation allocates storage and assigns an OID. Initialization may also occur through some kind of constructor mechanism. Deletion deallocates the storage used by the object, thus removing it from the database. The object is removed from the type extent and from any relationships in which it participated.

7.6.5   Atomic_objects and structured_objects

The Object hierarchy is shown in Fig. 7.12. Atomic_Object has three subtypes: Type, Exception, and Iterator. Type was already discussed in a previous subsection. Iterator is a type generator for iteration types. It is defined as Iterator<T>. If T is replaced with a type name, a new type is instantiated. The new type provides instances for iterating over collections with elements of the named type. Iterators allow sequential access of elements in a collection. The operations supported by the Iterator<T> type generator (and therefore all of the iterator types) are reset(), first(), last(), more?(), and next(). The iterator maintains a current position within the collection. first(), last(), reset(), and next() alter the current position. Except for reset(), they all return the currently pointed to element. more?() is used to test whether all elements have been exhausted. New elements can be inserted into a collection that is being iterated on from within the iterator loop. The newly inserted elements will be returned in the iteration if the collection is unordered (set or bag), or if the collection is ordered and the insertion point is after the iterator pointer. The Iterator<T> type generator defines an iteration_order attribute allowing forward or backward iteration.

The Exception type supports the exception model in the ODMG/OM (which is very similar to the exception model in C++). Exception handlers are defined for a scope. If an exception is raised

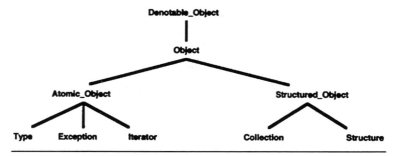

Figure 7.12 The Object hierarchy.

(or thrown) within that scope (and no exception handlers were defined in an inner scope), then the exception handler will catch the exception. The stack is unwound to the handler level, and object destructors are called if necessary. The handler may handle the exception or pass it on (or both).

An exception in the ODMG/OM is an object. Information pertinent to the reasons the exception occurred may be stored within the exception object. Since every object has a type, so do exception objects. The type of any exception object will be a subtype of the type `Exception`. Exception handlers define which type of exceptions they are willing to handle. A handler for a certain exception type will catch all exception objects that are of that type or any type that inherits from it. For example, if `DivideByZero` inherits from `MathError` and a handler for `MathError` exceptions is defined for a scope, then it will also catch `DivideByZero` exceptions that are raised. This is often used to provide multiple levels of exception handling.

Structured objects have two categories: collections and structures. Collections have a variable number of elements of one type hierarchy (i.e., they can hold elements of one type or any of that type's subtypes). Structures have a fixed number of slots. Each slot has a name, a value, and a specification of the type that the value must be of. The value can be any object of that type (or any of that type's subtypes). Each of the slots can have a different type specification.

The built-in type generator `Structure<el:Tl, ···, en:Tn>` allows the creation of structure types. This allows the type definer to specify the names and types of the slots. The main operations provided by the type generator are access functions to set and get values by name and life-cycle type functions for creating, deleting, and copying structures.

Mutable collections contain other objects. They can contain any number of objects of a certain type. The objects in the collection object may change over time (hence the mutability). Two collection objects that contain the same elements will still be different, since they are mutable; equivalence is based on the OID. The objects in the collection are not named. Each collection defines a containment semantic according to its type. Sets and bags are unordered collections, whereas lists and arrays are ordered. Ordered collections allow access by position. Among unordered collections, sets do not allow duplicates, whereas bags maintain the cardinality for every object put into the collection (i.e., for every object, it maintains how many insertions of the objects into the collection were made).

Collection types are derived from the type generators inheriting from the `Collection<T>` type generator. `Collection<T>` is an abstract type generator. It cannot be instantiated and merely forms the collection supertype generator for defining common properties

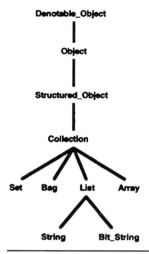

Figure 7.13 The Collection<T> hierarchy.

and operations for all collection type generators. Figure 7.13 shows the Collection<T> hierarchy.

Properties defined by the collection type generator include life-cycle type operations, insertion and removal, retrieval and testing, and an operation to create an iterator over the collection. The Set<T> and Bag<T> type generators add set operations such as union and intersection. List<T> and Array<T> add indexed operations. Table 7.2 summarizes most of the collection operations.

TABLE 7.2 Collection Operations

Type Generator	Operations
Collection<T>	create, delete, copy, insert_element, remove_element, replace_element, retrieve_element, select_element, select, exists?, contains_element?, create_iterator
Set<T>	union, intersection, difference, is_subset?, is_proper_subset?, is_superset?, is_proper_superset?
Bag<T>	union, intersection, difference
List<T>	insert_element_after, insert_element_before, insert_first_element, insert_last_element, remove_element_at, remove_first_element, remove_last_element, replace_element_at, retrieve_element_at, retrieve_first_element, retrieve_last_element
Array<T>	insert_element_at, remove_element_at, replace_element_at, retrieve_element_at, resize

7.6.6 The types `Database` and `Transaction`

Two more types are defined by the ODMG/OM; these are not "object model" types but rather "database" support types. The type `Database` allows a database to be represented as an object within the object model. Each database will be an instance of the type `Database`. The type supports operations for opening and closing the database and testing whether the database contains an object (using an OID), as well as implementation-dependent operations for database administration.

The `Transaction` type is the mechanism by which database transactions supporting necessary ACID (atomicity, consistency, integrity, and durability) capabilities are mapped into the ODMG/OM. An ODMG/OM transaction either occurs as a whole or does not occur at all. It moves the database from one consistent state to another consistent state. Once a transaction has been committed, the information cannot be lost and is persistent. The `Transaction` type supports the accepted operations of `begin()`, `commit()`, `abort()`, and `checkpoint()`.

ODMG/OM transactions support the nested transaction model, where a transaction can be nested within another. All transaction changes are visible only relative to the enclosing transaction. The nested transaction model is very important for distributed environments where many of the operations are remote (as is the case with ORB-based environments). If nested transactions are supported, then each remote operation can be invoked in the context of a separate nested transaction. If the operation fails, only the embedded transaction will be rolled back and not the enclosing transaction. While supporting nested transactions, the `Transaction` type supports the `abort_to_top_level()` operation as well. This will cause nested transactions to abort to the topmost level.

7.7 Extensions and Changes Needed

The ODMG-93 standard is a work in progress document. The ODMG is not a formal standards body, and the ODMG-93 is not a formal standard. However, the ODMG has a very large participation of ODBMS vendors, and the document is a very important step in the effort to define an object database standard. The ODMG decided to publish the document even though it was clear that it had some deficiencies. Even the published document has many "future direction" sections. It was felt that it was important to get the document out so that there would be some standard base. The ODMG also wanted to get feedback from a large community. By publishing the document, the ODMG hopes to eliminate the possibility that it will become anemic like many standards bodies, and to get feedback and suggestions for improvements from a large industry base. Since the publishing of the document, many industry leaders have commented on necessary extensions to the ODMG standard. This section gives a short overview of some of the proposed extensions. The next section gives an overview of some extensions proposed in the ODMG-93 document itself. To eliminate duplication, this section will not mention those extensions mentioned in the next section.

Relationship with the X3H2 Database Standards Committee. The goal of the ODMG is very similar to that of the X3H2 committee (the SQL-3 committee). The RDBMS vendors and some of the ODBMS vendors are working within the SQL-3 committee to provide an extended SQL. Most of the RDBMS vendors are already adding object management functionalities to their products and view an object-oriented database language as the post-relational database language. Since the ODMG includes most ODBMS vendors, and since the ODMG Object Query Language (OQL) is SQL-like, it is important that there be a high degree of interaction between the ODMG and the SQL-3 committee. It is important that eventually there be only one standard and not two. It would benefit both bodies if a high degree of cooperation could be achieved. The SQL-3 committee would benefit from the extensive work done by the ODMG, and the ODMG would benefit from functionalities proposed in SQL-3 that are missing in the ODMG specification.

Language bindings. The Smalltalk binding proposed in the ODMG-93 document is only a first proposal. Whereas the C++ binding is fairly mature, the Smalltalk binding is not complete. A more detailed mapping of all ODMG functionalities is necessary. In addition, a certification process for the C++ and Smalltalk language bindings should be supplied by the ODMG.

ODMG-93 compliance. Implementations of the ODMG-93 standard are promised in 1995, as many of the ODMG members are committed to implementing the ODMG-93 standard as part of their products within 18 months of the publishing of the document. It is not clear how many of the members will actually provide such implementations in this time frame, or what level of ODMG-93 support will be provided. A checklist process for assessing the degree of compliance would be of great benefit.

SQL syntax. The ODMG-93 OQL proposed a concrete syntax which is SQL-like. Some facilities that are supported by both OQL and SQL have different syntax. This unnecessarily confuses the user. Examples are the use of GROUP BY WITH in OQL instead of the more commonly used GROUP BY HAVING in SQL and SORT BY instead of ORDER BY.

View support. The ODMG-93 standard does not support views. Views are provided in all RDBMSs and allow users to view the database schema to be created. Views are used as a central mechanism for access authorization. It is felt by some industry leaders that views are not redundant in ODBMSs and that a mechanism should be added to support views as a type-like construct (just as a view in an RDBMS can be seen as a conceptual table).

Dynamic schema evolution. The ODMG-93 specification does not elaborate on dynamic life-cycle operations involving dynamic changes to types. Two important issues are not addressed: How do types change dynamically (e.g., adding attributes and operations, and what happens to the instances), and how are types added dynamically? It should be noted that some of the vendors participating in the ODMG have such capabilities.

Data control language. The DCL support provided in the ODMG specification is based around the `Database` and `Transaction` types. There are no access authorization constructs, triggers, or constraints. Although many of these issues are implementation-dependent (and that is the explanation for this omission given in the ODMG-93 document), it is possible to provide base functionalities to ensure portability of applications using basic control structures.

Meta data management at the type level. The ODMG-93 standard provides for meta data management at the object level. For example, names are attached to objects, lifetime is specified per object, etc. This can produce high overhead and complex problems of meta data management. It should also be possible to use a type as the level of access and control.

Extent semantics. The ODMG-93 standard should address the issue of how queries are associated with a type versus how they are associated with a type hierarchy. For example, an `Account` type may have many subtypes (checking accounts, savings accounts, money market accounts, etc.). When looking for all accounts opened before a certain date, then any instance in the type hierarchy under `Account` should be queried. Some queries, on the other hand, may be relevant only to a certain node in the hierarchy. Extents address only the first semantic notion; both should be addressed (see Fig. 7.14).

Set-based semantics. The ODMG allows operations, updates, insertions, and so on to be performed on individual objects. It should be possible to specify such activities on collections of objects.

Operation pragmas. The ODMG-93 standard states that operations can be invoked from within query expressions. Theoretically this is

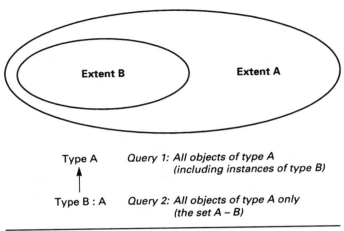

Type A   Query 1: All objects of type A
                    (including instances of type B)

Type B : A   Query 2: All objects of type A only
                    (the set A – B)

Figure 7.14 Extent semantics in a subtyping context.

simple, but practically there are many complex issues involved. Methods can reside on the client or the server, methods which are not side-effect-free do not allow query optimizations, and so on. These practical problems are extremely hard to solve and may become easier if the database languages address some of them at least as pragmas.

One should note that although many of these issues are not addressed by the ODMG-93 standard and have been brought forward by some industry participants as deficiencies of the ODMG-93 standard, it is exactly this kind of feedback that the ODMG meant to provoke by publishing the ODMG-93 document.

7.8 Future Extensions in the ODMG-93 Standard

As mentioned, the ODMG-93 standard includes many extensions that will be incorporated into later versions of the ODMG standard. These were not incorporated in ODMG-93 because it was considered more important to publish an initial base. This section details some of these extensions. Some extensions are based on the ODMG-93 standard (described fully in the next chapter).

The ODMG-93 document has many suggestions and extensions. Some of the extensions are well thought out and well organized. They are at a level such that they could almost have been incorporated directly into the document. They were intentionally left out in the interest of increasing the possibility that implementations of the standard could be delivered quickly. These extensions are described in the ODMG-93 document as "subsequent revisions." The extensions span the whole of the ODMG-93 scope, but most of the extensions are in the object model and in the C++ binding. We now describe some of these extensions.

Types and objects

Objects can be instances of more than one type.

Dynamic changes are supported: Objects may dynamically change their type and lifetime.

Since a type may have multiple implementations, the implementation may be chosen for each instance created.

Multiple types can use the same implementation (thus forming a many-to-many relationship between types and implementations).

Versions are supported both for types and for objects. Configurations define which versions of either objects or types may be supported.

Subextents may be defined using a predicate and used subsequently in expressions.

A fourth lifetime, `coterminus_with_thread`, may be used in multithreaded environments.

Attributes and relationships

Attributes and relationships may themselves have properties.

Better support for constraints and integrity management of attribute values is provided.

Attributes may be implicitly derived from participation in relationships.

Operations

Atomic operations are supported without requiring explicit transaction bracketing.

Remote operations with implicit nested transaction bracketing are supported.

Database, schema, and transactions

`Schema` and `Subschema` types will be introduced. Schemas and subschemas will provide better control over which types, versions, values, and so on are used. Subschemas will be used as the management level for security and access control.

`Interface` and `Implementation` types will be introduced to support meta data operations.

Support for long-lived transactions and nomadic computing will be introduced. Transactions will be able to persist after the process that created them terminates.

A transaction may include more than one process. Processes may dynamically join and leave a transaction. A transaction may access multiple databases.

C++ future binding.   The purpose of any language binding is to provide a mapping of the database functionalities into the programming language. There should be no difference between accessing database objects and accessing programming language objects. The recent C++ binding (described in the next chapter) achieves this goal to a very large extent, but there are a few constructs which differentiate between persistent and transient objects. The future binding remedies this and provides a truly transparent integration of ODBMS usage in C++.

There are two major differences that the future binding introduces. The first is in the handling of references. The present binding introduces a Ref<T> type generator. Access to persistent objects uses a smart pointer semantic using Ref<T>. Transient objects, on the other hand, use a normal C++ pointer and reference semantics. Although both allow dereferencing using the same operands, the distinction is still there. This will change in the future binding, and normal C++ pointers will also be used for persistent objects. Creating and deleting persistent objects will look identical to creating and deleting objects on the heap.

The second extension provided by the future binding is a complete integration of the Object Query Language into C++ grammar. SQL-like query expressions will no longer be issued as string expressions to be evaluated at runtime (similar to printf calls). Instead, a syntactic extension to C++ will be introduced and a preprocessor used to allow C++-like query expressions that can be (at least partially) optimized at compile time. The extension will take the form of

```
resultingCollection = collection [ predicate ];
resultingObject = collection [ predicate ];
```

where the predicate uses attributes, properties, nested access paths, operations, and more complex combinations of these.

8

The ODMG-93 Standard

In the previous chapter, the ODMG-93 standard for object databases as defined in Cattell (1994) was introduced. This chapter continues the description of this standard, specifically the database languages and bindings to these languages. Since a database maintains and manages information, it has three main languages used for information management. These are the definition language, the manipulation language, and the query language. The definition language allows one to define the structures that will be used to maintain the information in the database. The manipulation language provides constructs to access and use the information in a programmatic manner. The query language allows access to the information in a declarative, value-based manner. Since databases may be very complex software systems, they often have additional language components, such as a database management interface. This type of language is not related to the information management part and depends on the features supported by the database. It is a necessary component of complex systems which are critical to the operations of the environment, but it does not lend itself to standardization.

Since any database has a definition language, a manipulation language, and a query language, any database standard must define guidelines for the syntax and semantics of such languages. This is the subject of this chapter. The commonly used names for these three languages in non-object-oriented databases are data definition language (DDL), data manipulation language (DML), and query language (the standard in relational databases being the Structured Query Language, SQL). Since the ODMG standard is defined to work with objects, the word *data* should not have such a central focus. Instead, the languages defined in the standard are the Object Definition Language (ODL), the Object Manipulation Language (OML), and the Object Query Language (OQL). ODL is the language used to define the type interfaces; these are the ODMG schema constructs. The ODL is therefore used for defining schemas in ODMG-compliant databases. OQL is the language used to query ODMG-compliant databases. This includes both ad hoc querying and queries from within host programming languages. Finally, instead of defining a separate OML, the ODMG specification shows how to map the necessary manipulation structures into such object-oriented languages as C++ and Smalltalk.

This chapter first describes the ODL. The ODL is a programming language–independent DDL for objects. It allows the definition of object types that will be stored and used. Next, the Object Query Language (OQL) is introduced. The OQL is a query language that provides query functionalities for the complex ODMG data model. One of the purposes of object databases is to eliminate the necessity for two different programming languages in one application (one being the programming language and the other being the database manipulation language). The ODMG standard therefore does not define a programming language–independent OML; instead, the native programming language is used as the OML. The ODMG therefore gives sample bindings to the two main object-oriented languages, C++ and Smalltalk. These bindings include a mapping of the ODL, the OQL, and the necessary manipulation constructs. Of these two bindings, the Smalltalk binding is only a preliminary draft, whereas the C++ binding is extensive. This probably stems from the fact that the ODMG members' respective companies have many years of experience with C++ interfaces to ODBMS, but most of them are only starting to deliver Smalltalk interfaces. Of the 160 pages making up the ODMG standard, 64 pages describe the C++ binding, whereas only 13 pages discuss the Smalltalk binding. Section 8.3 describes the C++ binding to the ODL/OML, and Sec. 8.4 the Smalltalk binding.

8.1   The Object Definition Language (ODL)

Data definition languages provide a way to define data types and structures. The ODL provides a way to define object types and structures. Following the ODMG Object Model and the IDL, the ODL is a programming language–independent specification language that allows the definition of interfaces and object types. It allows the definition of attributes, relationships, typing information, and operational signatures.

The primary goal of the ODL is to ensure ODBMS portability of applications. An object schema defined in ODL should be portable across conforming ODBMS products. Since the ODL is also mapped into multiple programming languages, this would allow a schema defined in ODL to be portable across both programming environments and ODBMS products. Portability is already deemed extremely important in today's fragmented software world. Any standard for tomorrow's technology must stress portability. A language- and database-neutral definition language allows the application programmer to capture the semantic information without regard to the final deployment environment. This is especially important in database components, since they are often the central component in a software system. This is magnified by the fact that more and more applications need multiplatform support.

A complete specification of the ODL grammar is beyond the scope of this book. It is also not very useful for anyone except ODBMS implementors. The rest of this section will describe an example of an ODL schema for a securities account database. The example contains enough information to illustrate the ODL; note that the example may not be complete for lack of space.

The example schema (see Fig. 8.1) has four object types: `Person`, `Account`, `Security`, and `InvestmentConsultant`. Each account object is owned by a person and managed by an investment consultant. The `InvestmentConsultant` type is a subtype of a `Person`. An account can therefore be owned and managed by the same person (who is an instance of an investment consultant). Accounts contain securities. Each security instance can only be owned in one account at a time.

The ODL definition consists of schema definitions for all the types involved. Each type is defined with an interface specification clause. Each such clause defines the attributes, relationships, and operations of this type. Attributes have a name and a type (which can be any previously defined type). Relationships have a name, a type, and an inverse specification. The type can be either an object type or a collection type. Collection types are used for one-to-many and many-to-many relationships. The inverse specification specifies the name of the "other side" of the relationship. Operations have a signature which defines the name, the return value, and the argument types. Operations may also raise exceptions; that too is specified in the operation's signature.

We now give the interface definitions for the above schema. Note that there are many supporting structures (types) that are not provided for lack of space (e.g., `Address` would be an additional type).

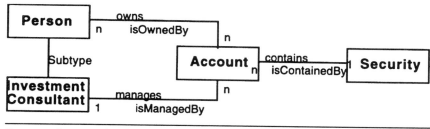

Figure 8.1 An example schema.

```
interface Person ( extent persons, key (socialSecurityNumber)) {

    attribute String socialSecurityNumber;
    attribute String name;
    attribute Address address;

    relationship Person spouse inverse Person::spouse;
    relationship Set<Account> owns inverse Account::isOwnedBy;

    Unsigned Short numberOfAccountsOwned();
    Boolean ownsAccount(in Account account);
    void addAccount(in Account account);
    void removeAccount(in Account account) raises (doesNotOwnAccount);
};
```

The ODL interface code segment for Person specifies that a person has three attributes: a social security number, a name, and an address. The social security number is the key to this type (it is assumed that the schema supports only people who have a social security number). A Person object participates in two relationships. One is with the same type, Person, and one with the type Account. A person can have a spouse. The spouse relationship supports this possibility. The inverse to this relationship is itself. If the person 11-11-1111 has the person 22-22-2222 as a spouse, then the person 22-22-2222 has the person 11-11-1111 as a spouse (see Fig. 8.2).

The second relationship is with the Account type. A person can own many accounts. Therefore the interface definition specifies that the owns relationship maintains a set of accounts. The relationship is therefore either a one-to-many or a many-to-many relationship. Since in the Account type definition the relationship specifier isOwnedBy specifies the use of a set, the relationship is many-to-many. The set construct is used because a person can't own the same account twice. If that were possible, a different collection template would have been used. For example, if an "awards" relationship is maintained for an investment consultant, a bag would be used (a bag is a collection that allows multiple entries of the same object). If an ordering within the collection was required, a list would have been used.

The next ODL segment defines the InvestmentConsultant type.

```
interface InvestmentConsultant: Person (extent investmentConsultants) {
attribute Enum Level [specialist, senior, junior] level;
relationship InvestmentConsultant reportsTo inverse
   InvestmentConsultant::directReports;
relationship Set<InvestmentConsultant> directReports
   inverse InvestmentConsultant::reportsTo;
relationship Set<Account> manages inverse Account::isManagedBy;
```

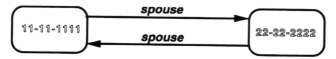

Figure 8.2 The spouse relationship.

```
  void manageAccount(in Account anAccount) raises
(managesTooManyAccounts);
  Unsigned Long salary();
};
```

The `InvestmentConsultant` type inherits from the `Person` type. The `InvestmentConsultant` interface therefore includes the `Person` interface as well. Investment consultants are organized in a hierarchical structure. This can be seen by the internal one-to-many relationship. Every investment consultant reports to one investment consultant (or zero); an investment consultant can have many direct reports. This is implemented by the `directReports/reportsTo` relationship. The `manages` relationship is a one-to-many relationship with the `Account` type. An investment consultant may be asked to manage an additional account. This is done by calling the `manageAccount` operation on the investment consultant with the account as the argument. Note that this operation may raise an exception named `managesTooManyAccounts`.

The `Account` interface and the `Security` interface have similar definitions:

```
interface Account (extent accounts, key (accountNumber)) {
  attribute Long accountNumber;
  attribute Long cashBalance;
  attribute Date openingDate;
  attribute Enum AccountStatus [normal, preferred];
  attribute Set<Service> services;
  relationship Set<Person> isOwnedBy inverse Person::owns;
  relationship InvestmentConsultant isManagedBy inverse
    InvestmentConsultant manages;
  relationship Bag<Security> contains inverse Security::isContainedBy;
  void deposit ( Dollars depositAmount);
  void withdraw ( Dollars withdrawAmount) raises (cantWithdraw);
  Boolean buySecurity (in SecurityId securityId, in Unsigned Short
    numberOfShares) raises (cantBuySecurities);
  void sellSecurities(in Set<Securities>) raises (cantSellSecurities);
};
interface Security ( extent securities, key (securityId)) {
  attribute SecurityId securityId;
  attribute String securityName;
  relationship Set<Account> inContainedBy inverse Account::contains;
};
```

The above example shows the use of a bag. An account can have 10 shares of a certain security. As defined, the schema implies that such an account would include 10 instances of the security. This cannot be done using a set; a bag is used instead. The set of services in the account defines what services the account provides to the owners (e.g., checking, credit cards, etc.).

To summarize, the ODL defines the database schema. A type is defined by specifying its interface in ODL. The definition includes such things as the type's characteristics, its attributes, its relationships, and operations that can be performed. Characteristics include information regarding inheritance, extents, and keys. Attributes, relationships, and operations specify the structure of the instances of that type and their interface.

Characteristics are information maintained at the type level, whereas attributes, relationships, and operations are instance-specific. The primary characteristic of a type defined in ODL is its location in the type hierarchy. A type (interface) can inherit from another type (interface). Multiple interface inheritance is also supported by ODL. Extents and keys are also type characteristics. An extent can be named for a type. The name will reference the set of all instances of the type. This is used as the primary entry point into the database, and is extensively used for set-based queries. Keys define a set of internal structures which ensure the uniqueness of an object within its extent. Keys are critical for performance-related issues in associative access.

Attributes, relationships, and operations are maintained at the instance level. If a type has an attribute of type String named status, then every object which is an instance of that type (or any subtype of this type) will have a separate attribute named status. Relationships are also maintained per instance. Two Account instances will have different isOwnedBy relationship sets with different instances of Person.

8.2   The Object Query Language (OQL)

OQL is a query language that supports the ODMG Object Model. It was designed to supply associative querying capabilities and value-based access. It is meant to be to ODBMSs what SQL is to RDBMSs. In this respect, the language was designed to be simple and intuitive. However, since it was built to support the richness of the ODMG object model, it is necessarily rich and complete.

OQL provides declarative access to objects defined using ODL following the ODMG Object Model. OQL was not designed in a vacuum. Many of the ODBMS vendors that participated in the ODMG work had their own query languages defined. Since SQL is a powerful querying language that is almost universally accepted in the RDBMS world, most of the query languages in the ODBMS products are SQL-like (one is called ObjectSQL, one is called OSQL, etc.). It should therefore come as no surprise that OQL has a syntax that is SQL-like. This is seen as a great strength of OQL, since it allows an easier migration process from SQL. OQL, however, is defined in such a way that other syntaxes may be defined for it. This allows the construction of an OQL mapping into a host language. It is therefore not necessary to invoke SQL-like calls from an application written in C++ or

Smalltalk (or another programming language). This is extremely important for maintaining a single programming paradigm for all parts of the application.

OQL, like SQL, can either be used as a stand-alone query language or be used in a host programming language. Like SQL, OQL is not computationally complete. This may seem to be a severe disadvantages of OQL. One of the ODBMS vendors' main arguments against RDBMSs has been that embedding the database language in a programming language causes two programming environments to be formed. This creates unnecessary complexity. Many problems then arise in supporting the two environments and the interface between them. It seems that since OQL is not computationally complete and is therefore used from within a host programming language, the same problems will persist with the use of OQL. This is not so.

When SQL is embedded in a host programming language, it maintains its own syntax and semantics. The programmer must therefore work with two syntax systems, two type systems, two semantic models, and so on. This causes the well-known impedance mismatch problem to occur. OQL is not embedded in a programming language. It defines an abstract syntax which is then mapped into a concrete syntax. One of these is a syntax similar to an extended SQL. Other concrete syntaxes are mappings of the abstract OQL syntax into programming languages. The programmer using C++, for example, will use a concrete syntax of OQL which respects the C++ syntax and semantics. There will be only one syntax, one type system, and one set of semantics. We shall see that the present C++ binding of the OQL does not fully achieve this goal. The ODMG is aware of this, and a future C++ binding will remedy the present binding's faults. It was felt that it was more important to get a standard, albeit imperfect, out the door rather than waiting too long to deliver a perfect binding that would be too late.

OQL is mapped into a host programming language in a way that makes it part of that language (or an extension to the language, much like using an external library of reusable components). OQL expressions are therefore part of the programming language's expressions. In addition, since types define operations which become callable methods, queries can include method invocations. The fact that the abstract definition of OQL is not computationally complete is therefore of no importance.

The rest of this section is devoted to describing OQL. Not every feature of OQL will be presented, and an informal description will be given rather than a dry syntactic grammar definition. For a more complete description, the ODMG specification should be consulted. The syntax used in this section is the concrete syntax which is SQL-like. Section 8.3, which describes the ODMG mapping for C++, also describes the mapping of OQL into C++. Section 8.4 does the same for Smalltalk. The schema defined in Sec. 8.1 is used in the remainder of this section for providing examples of OQL.

8.2.1 Extents and basic queries

Any query has to start out with a named handle into the database. These handles are either extents or named objects. Named objects are objects that have been explicitly named. As such, they provide an entry point into the database and can be used as a navigation root. Extents are a special case of named objects; they are set objects that have been explicitly named in the ODL interface declarations. Recall that the extent of a type is the set of instances of that type. For example, `accounts` was named as the extent for the type `Account`. This provides a handle into the database. Queries can start with this handle. The simplest type of query is simply

```
accounts
```

The result of this query would be to retrieve the set of all objects of type `Account`. More complex expressions involving select-from-where clauses can be formed using this handle. To retrieve all accounts having a cash balance greater than $1000, the following query would be issued:

```
select account
from account in accounts
where account.cashBalance > 1000.
```

To retrieve a collection of account numbers instead of the account objects themselves, use

```
select account.accountNumber
from account in accounts
where account.cashBalance > 1000.
```

The select clause may contain complex construction of objects. For example, to retrieve 2-tuples representing the account number and balance for preferred accounts, use

```
select struct(number: account.accountNumber, balance:
account.cashBalance)
from account in accounts
where account.status = preferred.
```

This example also demonstrates how objects are created. The construct `struct(…)` creates a value-based (immutable) object. To create identity-based objects, one uses similar constructs using the type name and inputting the necessary parameters. For example, to create a new account, the following constructor is used:

```
Account(accountNumber: 123456789, cashBalance: 500, _).
```

Retrieval expressions and object constructors may be freely intermixed:

```
select struct (manager: investmentConsultant.name
  totalCash: sum (select account.cashBalance
    from account in accounts
      where account.isManagedBy = investmentConsultant))
from investmentConsultant in investmentConsultants
```

This expression retrieves a set of structures. Each element is a 2-tuple containing a name of an investment consultant and the sum of the balances in all accounts managed by him or her. This query demonstrates a number of features of OQL:

- Attributes used in the expression may be inherited. The `name` attribute used for the investment consultant is really part of the `Person` interface definition.

- Queries and object constructors can be freely intermixed. Queries can be inserted into constructors, and constructors into queries.

- Collection expressions may be incorporated into queries. In the above example, the `sum` operation was applied to a set resulting from a query. Other expressions that may be applied to collection objects are `min`, `max`, `avg`, and `count`, as well as more complex operators such as a group-by operator, a sort-in operator, `for all` and `exists` operators, and more. Set-based collections objects also have additional expressions, such as `intersect`, `union`, and `except`. Indexed collection expressions include extraction of subcollections, concatenation, indexed access, and more. Some examples of collection expressions are given below.

```
min ( select account.cashBalance      /* select the minimal cash balance
  from account in accounts ).          in all accounts */

count ( accounts )     .               /* retrieve the number of accounts */

/* retrieve a set of 2-tuples. Each 2-tuple is an investment consultant
and the sum of the balances in the accounts managed by this consultant
(there is more than one way to skin a cat) */

group account in accounts
by (manager: account.isManagedBy)
with (totalCash: sum ( select acc.cashBalance from acc in partition)).
sort account is accounts by account.cashBalance /* sort by balance */

/* retrieve the strings for the important days (weekends) */
list ( "Monday", "Tuesday", "Wednesday", "Thursday", "Friday",
"Saturday", "Sunday")[6:7]
```

■ Relationships and operations may be freely intermixed in query expressions. Just as an attribute may be accessed as a part of an object, so can relationships and operations. This is the subject of the next subsection.

8.2.2   Attributes, relationships, and operators

Object-oriented models encapsulate state and behavior in one atomic unit. An object defines both data and operations. Operations and functions are as much part of the object as are its internal data structures. The OMG Object Model and the ODMG Object Model adhere to this principle. Operations in the ODMG Object Model are part of interface definitions, and the functions or methods invoked are part of the object implementations.

Like most object-oriented languages, OQL maintains a certain level of simplicity by treating all aspects of an object in a uniform way. To do this, OQL must treat relationship traversal and operation invocation in the same way that attribute access is treated.

If anObject is any object (an instance of a type, a collection, a structure, or the result of evaluating an expression) having an attribute named anAttribute, then the expression

anObject.anAttribute   and the expression   anObject → anAttribute

both retrieve the property's value in the object. Relationships and operations are handled in a similar way. Therefore if aRelationship is the name of a relationship in anObject, then

anObject.aRelationship   and   anObject → aRelationship

both traverse the relationship. Thus if the relationship is one-to-one, or many-to-one, then the expressions will yield the associated object. If the relationship is one-to-many or many-to-many, then the expressions will yield a set of objects. The same applies to operations. If anOperation is defined, then the expressions

anObject.anOperation(...)   and   anObject → anOperation(...)

will evaluate the method and return the result. If anOperation does not accept any arguments, then the more natural forms of anObject.anOperation and anObject → anOperation can be used.

In the ODL definition of the Account interface, cashBalance was defined as an attribute. An alternative schema definition could be to have the account maintain a collection of transactions and have the balance calculated by going over the transactions collection. In that case, the balance would no longer be an attribute. Instead, we would now have an operation of the form

```
Long cashBalance();
```

Although instead of an attribute retrieval, an operation is invoked, no query expression in OQL need change! If the signature included a date to be passed in (and the function was to calculate the balance for the end of the day based on the transaction collection), then queries would have embedded function call structures.

```
group account in accounts
by (manager: account.isManagedBy)
with (totalCash: sum ( select acc.cashBalance ( Date ("June 26,
1994"))
   from acc in partition)).
```

Since objects may be deleted, it is possible that a reference to a nil object will be used to get an attribute, traverse a relationship, or invoke an operation. If this happens, an exception is raised and an exception handler will receive control. Queries that are aware of such possibilities and wish to ensure that an exception is not raised can test for a nil reference. The expression anObject! = nil will evaluate to false if and only if anObject is a nil object at the time of the evaluation.

Expressions involving attribute extraction, relationship traversals, and operation invocation can be nested. Thus complex extraction paths can be easily defined. If, for example, the Address type has a zipCode attribute and "Daphne" denotes a named object of type Person, then Daphne.address.zipCode evaluates to this person's zip code. Note that the OQL definition does not specify how to perform the valuation; it only specifies what to evaluate. This declarative nature of OQL allows it to be optimized by query optimizers. The following queries show some more of OQL's functionality:

```
/* Starting with a named Person (Daphne), get the total balance in
all her accounts;  use the in operator for membership testing. */
sum ( select account.cashBalance
  from account in accounts
  where Daphne in account.isOwnedBy)
/* Retrieve the same result in a more elegant expression*/
sum ( select account.cashBalance
  from account in Daphne.owns)
```

Finally, suppose we needed a collection of all the securities owned by Daphne. We would want to use an expression of the form

```
select account.contains
from account in Daphne.owns
```

This expression is not what we need! This expression would retrieve a collection in which each element is a collection of securities. To solve problems of this nature, OQL defines the flatten expression. This expression converts a collection of collections of type T into a collection of type T. The query we desire is therefore

```
flatten ( select accounts.contains
          from account in Daphne.owns)
```

8.3   The C++ Binding to ODL/OML/OQL

The main goal of the C++ binding to the ODMG database language specifications is to allow the developer to use C++ for every aspect of the application and database interaction. Unlike with an RDBMS, interfacing with the database language must use the same language as the application language. A mismatch between these languages and type systems causes many problems. Providing a unified environment not only means that there is a consistent type system and a consistent programming paradigm, it also means that instances of the same type can be either transient or persistent. The transparency of object lifetime is therefore also of major importance. The binding is structured to change the host language as little as possible and to respect the C++ syntax and semantics. The binding's change set is therefore very small, and changes are packaged as a set of support classes much like other C++ libraries.

The C++ binding can be seen as two components. One is a set of guidelines or mappings that use C++ language features to implement ODL, OML, and OQL facilities. The purpose of such a set of guidelines is to remain as close to C++ syntax and semantics as possible. The C++ binding defined by the ODMG augments C++ with only one additional keyword: *inverse*. The inverse keyword is used in relationship specification. The second part is a small set of classes that provide most of the mapping of the OML. These classes can be divided into three sets. The first maps the ODMG/OM built-in types in a way that will ensure portability between ODMG-compliant ODBMSs. The second provides support for database functionality that is missing from a programming language like C++. The third is a set of classes supporting the implementation of the binding itself. The OQL is mapped using an oql function. This is a loose map of the OQL; it does not map the OQL directly into the language. Instead, it provides a function that accepts strings in the OQL concrete syntax described in the previous section. These strings are sent for evaluation at runtime.

8.3.1   Main design of the binding

The ODMG C++ binding is reference-based, making use of smart pointer concepts. The binding provides a template class Ref<T>. Any class that may have persistent instances will have a reference class using this template. For example, if the application will have persistent account objects, then the Ref<Account> class will be instantiated. Each persistent account object will then be referenced by a Ref<Account> object. All access to the real object will be done through the reference object. Since the Ref<T> template definition overloads dereferencing operators, dereferencing the Ref<T> object provides access to the persistent object. Thus an additional level of indirection is used to allow retrieval of the object from persistent storage to internal memory on demand (if it is not already there). This approach also allows pointer swizzling. By careful definition of the Ref<T> template class, these reference objects behave like C++ pointers. For example,

```
Ref<Account> acc;
Ref<Security> bond;
acc → depositSecurity(bond);
```

Any class that could have persistent instances inherits from Persistent_Object. A class that does not inherit (directly or indirectly) from Persistent_Object can have only transient objects. The ODMG binding does not actually require a conforming implementation to have a Persistent_Object class. As long as an inheritance specification identifies a persistence-capable class, the implementation of the binding remains compliant. For example, a preprocessor can be built to recognize the inheritance specification even without the presence of a Persistent_Object class.

The process of writing an application using the binding involves two stages. In the first stage (Fig. 8.3), the ODL files are used to generate C++ header files. The programmer writes ODL specifications. These specifications are used to create a C++ header file and possibly an implementation skeleton. The ODBMS schema is also created from the ODL file. The second stage (Fig. 8.4) involves creating the executable.

8.3.2 Objects, types, and operations

ODMG objects map directly into C++ objects, and ODMG types map into C++ classes. Every ODMG object is an instance of an ODMG type; every C++ object is an instance of a C++ class. Interface inheritance (ODMG subtyping) is mapped to public inheritance in C++. Both syntax and semantics are similar.

ODMG object attributes in an interface specifications map into data members in a C++ class. This is true both syntactically and semantically. An implementation can decide to make the data member private and provide accessor functions. For a data member called aData, the implementation would then provide the following two methods: getaData and setaData.

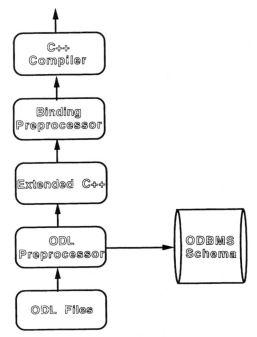

Figure 8.3 The first stage of writing an application: generating header files.

This type of implementation is important for planned extensions to the ODMG specification. In the present version of the ODMG standard, attributes can't be "first-class objects." For example, attributes cannot have properties. A future extension of the ODMG specification may include attribute properties. Another extension will allow a signal to be sent when an attribute value is accessed or changed. This is extremely useful and is used in many object-oriented environments. For example, Smalltalk-80 extensively uses the ValueHolder concept; this object encapsulates another object but allows the programmer to configure what happens when the encapsulated value is changed.

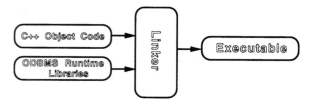

Figure 8.4 The second stage of writing an application: creating the executables.

Accessor methods to data members are a key component to provide a mapping to such future extensions.

Operations defined in an ODMG type map into C++ class methods. Since the ODMG ODL syntax and semantics are very close to C++, ODMG operation signatures are mapped directly to C++ method signatures. C++ method invocations therefore provide the implementation for OML calls. This allows operations to behave consistently across ODMG objects and C++ objects. The syntax and semantics of all invocations conform to the C++ object model whether the objects are transient or persistent.

ODMG structures map into the *struct* construct in C++. Since *struct* and *class* in C++ are interchangeable (with an appropriate private/public declaration), all ODMG types are mapped to classes in C++. The C++ class (or struct) is used for both mutable and immutable objects. Mutable objects have an object identifier and allow state changes. Immutable objects are objects that have no identifier. Their value is their identity; therefore their value cannot be changed. C++ classes and structs implement both mutable and immutable objects. An object defined as an internal data member in a class definition is used as an immutable object. A reference or a pointer should be used if a mutable object reference is necessary. The reasoning behind this mapping is that an embedded object is part of the enclosing object and cannot be seen as an independent entity. Users cannot get a reference to an embedded object. In fact, the memory layout of this object is a part of the enclosing object's memory segment, as in Fig. 8.5.

8.3.3 Object creation, deletion, and modification

Object creation, deletion, and modification are OML issues. Definition languages like ODL and IDL deal only with definitions. Creation, deletion, and manipulation are dealt with at the instance level during the runtime phase. The C++ binding implies that the C++ language is used as the OML. Therefore the C++ mechanisms for object creation, deletion, and modification are used.

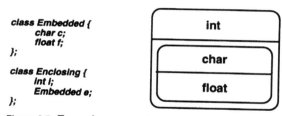

Figure 8.5 Example memory layout.

C++ objects are created either as automatic variables or using `operator new`. Since the C++ OML is based on smart pointers, the C++ OML binding uses `operator new` for the creation of objects. This operator is overloaded to accept specifications as to the object's storage placement. For backward compatibility, if no storage placement is entered, transient memory is assumed. An additional `operator new` allows the programmer to request that the created persistent object be clustered with a previously created persistent object. This allows the programmer to try to ensure that these objects are placed in neighboring locations to optimize related accesses. For example, if object A will always be referenced after object B, then object A will already be in the cache after object B is accessed so that no additional page fault will occur. The clustering request is seen only as a pragma; there is no guarantee that the ODBMS will cluster these objects together.

The ODMG C++ binding for C++ adds the following overloaded `operator new` forms:

```
void* operator new(size_t, const char* typename = 0);
void* operator new(size_t, const Ref<Persistent_Object> &clustering,
const char* typename = 0);
void* operator new(size_t, Database *database, const char* typename =
0);
```

The first of the three forms is used to create transient objects; the second and third forms are used to create persistent objects. The second form requests that the new object be clustered with the *clustering* object. The third form specifies the storage location for the newly created object. Examples of the usage of the operators follow (assume that *database* is of type `Database*` and correctly points to an ODMG database):

```
/* Create a transient object */
Ref<Account> transientAccount = new Account;
/*Create a persistent account in our database */
Ref<Account> persistentAccount = new(database) Account;
/* Create another persistent account in the same database; ask that
it be clustered with the  previous object */
Ref<Account> anotherPersistentAccount = new(persistentAccount)
Account;
```

Implementations of the ODMG C++ binding must provide these three forms of `operator new`. They may provide other implementations as well, but certain guidelines are stated in the ODMG C++ binding description for such additional operators. Any added parameter, for example, must have a default value defined. These guidelines are meant to ensure portability for applications that use only the base definitions.

C++ objects created with the new operator are deleted using the delete operator. This operator can only be called with the operand being a pointer (a void* type). Persistent objects in the C++ OML binding are of a Ref<T> type; they are not pointers. The delete operator therefore cannot be used to delete persistent objects. Persistent objects are deleted using the Ref<T>::delete_object member function, e.g.,

```
persistentAccount.delete_object();
```

Deletion of a persistent object is always subject to a transaction commit (as is the case with any change to be made to the database). Note that the C++ binding forces a syntactic difference in how transient and persistent objects are deleted. A future OML binding will use standard C++ pointers to reference persistent objects, and the delete operator will be used to delete persistent objects as well.

Persistent objects are modified by changing attribute values and relationship paths and invoking operations which change the object's state. No changes are visible outside the transaction boundaries until the transaction commits. To know which objects have to be written to disk upon a transaction commit, a mark dirty mechanism is used. When an object is modified, the call mark_modified() should be made. This informs the ODBMS that the object should be updated when a transaction commits. mark_modified() is a method in the Persistent_Object class. ODBMS vendors will most likely support automatic generation of mark_modified() calls to take the burden off the application programmer. This, however, will only be optional, since applications requiring very high performance will want to handle object marking themselves.

As mentioned, embedded objects are not independent; they are part of the enclosing object. A modification of an embedded object is therefore seen as a modification of the enclosing object. A mark_modified of the embedded object implicitly means a mark_modified of the enclosing object.

8.3.4 Collections and extents

Collections are very central to the ODMG object model. They are used for relationships, for extents, and for any object type that is not of a fixed size and structure. In fact, they are not specifically mapped into C++; they can only be supported by collections of objects. It is the user's responsibility to manage these collections. Management of these collections is done using collection operations as they are mapped into C++ collection class methods. The ODMG Object Model defines a standard set of built-in collection type generators:

```
Set<T>

Bag<T>

List<T>

Array<T>
```

These type generators are all subtypes of the abstract type generator Collection<T>.

The ODMG C++ binding relies on C++ templates for the implementation of collection type generators. There is a one-to-one mapping between ODMG/OM type generators and C++ templates:

```
template<class T> class Set: public Collection<T>

template<class T> class Bag: public Collection<T>

template<class T> class List: public Collection<T>

template<class T> class Varray: public Collection<T>
```

Types are created by instantiating a type generator with a class (or a built-in type). Thus List<int> creates a new type representing a list of integers. The type List<Ref<Account>> is the C++ mapping for a list of persistent accounts (i.e., this is the C++ implementation of the List<Account> defined in ODL). Instances of Ref<List<Ref <Account>>> will be the C++ representatives of ODMG lists of accounts.

Copy semantics of collections adhere to those of C++. If a collection object is assigned to another object of the same type, then the collection object is assigned to the new object and each of the elements is copied into the new collection object. The elements are copied using the copy constructors of the element's type (either user-defined or compiler-generated). This is also true when a collection object is embedded in another object; the embedded collection's copy semantics will be used from the enclosing copy constructors.

Of special interest are the copy semantics of the Ref<T> template. Since persistent objects are modeled using the Ref<T> type, copy semantics for persistent objects rely on the copy semantics of the Ref<T> type generator. Since Ref<T> models a reference to an object of type T, shallow copy semantics are used (i.e., pointer-based semantics). Thus if we have a list of persistent objects, each one being of type T, copying the list produces another list holding the same references. The Ref<T> objects are therefore copied, but the T objects are not. Figure 8.6a shows the object to be copied. Figure 8.6b shows the result after the assignment operation.

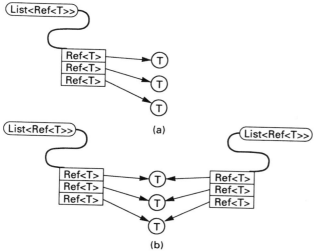

Figure 8.6 Copying Ref objects.

There is no Array template in the C++ binding; there is a Varray template. C++ has built-in support for arrays which are of constant size. Since the ODMG binding respects the host's language constructs, native C++ arrays are used whenever possible. The Varray template is added for cases where the size of the array may change after the array has been defined. The native C++ array and the Varray template fully cover the ODL Array type generator.

Any ODMG-compliant C++ mapping must support these four type generators (Set, List, Bag, and Varray). A C++ binding implementation can support additional collection type generators. Any such extension should conform to the copy semantics described above, and its behavior should be similar to that of the four generators defined in the ODMG binding.

A collection as defined in the ODMG specification holds only objects of one type. This does not preclude a collection of type Person having InvestmentConsultant objects, since this is a subtype of the type Person. Collection templates were meant to support any type. There are, however, certain requirements for a type T if it is to be used to form a Set<T>, Bag<T>, or Varray<T> type. The type T must have public default constructor, a destructor, and a copy constructor to support the copy semantic described above. It must have a public assignment operator and an equality test operator. If the type T will be used to form a List<T> type, it must also support an ordering operator. The ODMG C++ binding lists the following formal requirements as necessary for a type T to create a collection type:

```
class T {
public:
            T();
            T(const T&);
            ~T();
T&          operator = (const T&);
friend int operator == (const T&, const T&);
};

/* And for List<T> also */
friend int  operator<(const T&, const T&);
```

Note that many of these will be created by the C++ compiler if the user did not specify differently.

The C++ binding collection hierarchy mirrors the ODMG/OM collection type generator's type hierarchy:

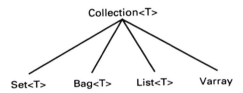

Collection<T>

Set<T>   Bag<T>   List<T>   Varray

Collection is an abstract class and cannot form instances. Many of the collection operations are defined in this class. These include constructors, destructors, assignment operators, equality test operators, collection attribute queries, insertion and deletion functions, retrieval functions, and more. In addition, an iterator creation function and OQL support functions are defined at the Collection level.

The OQL support functions defined in the Collection template class implement part of the OQL C++ binding (the second part is the oql function, which will be discussed later). The OQL functions defined in the Collection template class are

const T&   select_element(const char* OQL_predi-
                cate) const;

Iterator<T>   select(const char* OQL_predicate) const;

int   exists_element(const char* OQL_predi-
                cate) const;

int   query(Collection<T>&, const char*
                OQL_predicate) const;

select_element and exists_element allow the user to specify an OQL predicate and retrieve the object or test for its existence. select_element will raise an error if an object satisfying the OQL predicate does not exist or if there is more than one object satisfying the predicate. select returns an iterator on the collection of elements satisfying the OQL predicate. The `query` method returns the collection of elements satisfying the OQL predicate *in the first parameter*. The following call retrieves all accounts having a balance of over $10,000:

```
/* Note the use of the extent accounts */
Set<Ref<Account>> preferredAccounts;
accounts.query(preferredAccounts, "this.cashBalance < 10000");
```

The OQL predicate in all functions is a string with the syntax of an OQL `where` clause. Notice that "`this`" in the `where` clause is used to reference the tested element.

The `Set` class adds support for set union, intersection, and difference. Each operation is provided both in a functional syntax and as an operator. Each operation is also provided in several semantics regarding inbound operands and returning value (for example, should the result be returned as a change to one of the arguments, or should a new set be formed?). The class `Bag` provides similar support, but for bag semantics (i.e., an unordered collection that allows duplicates to be stored). The `List` class adds ordering functionalities, first and last access, addition, removal, and concatenation functionalities. `Varray` adds a resize method.

Elements in a collection are retrieved either through direct retrieval (e.g., methods like `retrieve_element_at` in the `Collection` class, `retrieve_first_element` in the `List` class, and `operator[]` defined in `Varray`) or by iteration. The `Collection` class includes the following method definition:

```
Iterator<T>    create_iterator() const;
```

This creates an Iterator object for iterating over the collection. This object is an instance of a type created from the `Iterator<T>` template class. This template class is part of the C++ binding. An iterator allows sequential iteration and retrieval of a collection's elements in a type safe manner. The main methods provided by the `Iterator` class are `reset()` for restarting the iteration, `not_done()` for testing whether all elements have been retrieved, `advance()` and `operator++()` for advancing to the next element, and `get_element()`. A `next()` method is provided that couples advancing accessing and testing. It is defined as

```
int    next(T& objRef);
```

and returns the same value that `not_done()` would while advancing the iterator and returning the next element. The following two code segments are therefore identical:

```
iter = accounts.create_iterator(); iter = accounts.create_iterator();
iter.reset();                       iter.reset();
while ( iter.not_done() ) [         while (iter.next(acc) ) [
  iter++;                                   /* do something withacc */
  acc = iter.get_element();         }
  /* do something with acc */
}
```

8.3.5 The oql functions

The oql functions are a set of overloaded functions providing OQL access to C++ programs. These functions allow expressions written in the OQL concrete syntax outlined in Sec. 8.2 to be evaluated in a C++ function call. The oql functions are procedural functions; they do not belong to any class. oql functions take a reference to a variable that is used to store the results, a string holding the OQL expression to be evaluated, and a variable list of arguments that are to be used as input operands in the OQL expression. This is similar to the structure of a printf() call in C. There are two major differences. Since an operand may be used in multiple places in the OQL expression, the expression references the operand by giving an ordinal number (printf can simply rely on the sequential ordering, since there is a one-to-one correspondence between the format string and the arguments). The second major difference is that the references in the OQL expressions also include typing information. A reference to an operand from within the OQL expression string takes the form of

$<ordinal number for the parameter><type of the C++ expression (coded)>

Type checking of the input operands is done at runtime. Any typing violation raises an error. The signatures for the oql functions are

```
/* The ... in all specifications is the variable-length argument list */
int oql(int&, const char* queryString, ...);
int oql(char&, const char* queryString, ...);
/* And similarly for all other built-in primitive types */
/* For Collection types; note that this is a parameterized function*/
template<class T> int oql(Collection<T>& aCollection, const char*
queryString, ...);
/* For the array type; recall that the native C++ array is used to map
cases of the Array ODMG/OM type; the query facility allocates the memory
for the array */
int oql(char*& anArray, const char* queryString, ...);
/* For objects */
template<class T> int oql(Ref<T>& anObject, const char* queryString, ...);
```

For example, the first oql function call retrieves the same collection of accounts as the collection query in the previous subsection; the second call retrieves those preferred accounts that were opened before 1994.

```
Set<Ref<Account>> preferredAccounts;
Set<Ref<Account>> oldPreferredAccounts;

/* A nonzero value is returned if the OQL expression is incorrect */
if (oql(preferredAccounts, "select acc from acc in accounts where
acc.cashBalance > 10000")) {
    /* error */
}

/* $1k means the first argument in the variable-sized argument list;
its type should be a Collection<T> subclass (k because c is used for
denoting a char) */
if (oql(oldPreferredAccounts, "select acc from acc in $1k where
acc.openingDate.year < 1994",
    preferredAccounts)) {
    /* error */
}
```

Although an SQL-like concrete syntax (described in Sec. 8.2) was provided by the ODMG, OQL is defined as an abstract syntax. The purpose of such a definition is to allow mappings of OQL into other languages which will be integrated with the host language. One should note that this was not done in the present C++ binding. In effect, the C++ binding of OQL is a number of functions allowing the input of C++ strings using OQL concrete syntax into the query engine. The query will be parsed and evaluated at runtime. In this approach, queries can be optimized at runtime only. The ODMG has already stated that a future binding will extend the C++ grammar, thus allowing a more integrated mapping of OQL into C++. This will allow queries to be optimized at compile time.

8.3.6 Relationships

A relationship defined in ODL is mapped into C++ using two members, one in each of the participating classes. Each member is an object reference if the relationship is one-to-one and a set specifier if the relationship is many-to-many (and one of each otherwise). Each set contains object references. The relationship member type will therefore be either Ref<T> or Set<Ref<T>> depending on the cardinality of the relationship. A concrete collection type generator will be used according to the characteristic of the relationship as defined in ODL. In addition, the inverse keyword is added. This is the first language extension that the C++ mapping forces and is the keyword that distinguishes relationships from ordinary data members. For example, the (extended) C++ class for Account will include the following relationship declarations:

```
class Account: public Persistent_Object {
    ...
    Set<Ref<Person>>         isOwnedBy   inverse  Person::owns;
    Ref<InvestmentConsultant> isManagedBy inverse  InvestmentConsultant;
```

```
Bag<Ref<Security>>              contains    inverse  Security::isContainedBy;
...
};
```

The `inverse` keyword identifies the relationship and implies that referential integrity of the relationship will be maintained. Referential integrity is the responsibility of the underlying ODBMS. An addition to the relationship by a C++ function will not automatically update the other side of the relationship. It is the ODBMS which is responsible for the side effect of the addition (or any other) operation.

The OML mapping provides C++ operations for using relationships. These include forming the relationships, building them up, traversing them, removing a segment, and deleting them. Table 8.1 shows relationship method categories and sample methods.

The following code segment gives an example for the `Account` relationship management:

```
Ref<Account> account1, account2;
Ref<InvestmentConsultant> bob;
Ref<Person> susan;
bob→manages.insert_element(account1);
/* The following line is equivalent to
bob→manages.insert_element(account2); */
account2→isManagedBy = bob;
account1→isOwnedBy.insert_element(bob);
/* Changed our mind; the real owner is Susan */
account1→isOwnedBy.clear();
account1→isOwnedBy.insert_element(susan);
```

TABLE 8.1 ODMG Relationship Method Categories and Sample Methods

Category	Sample Methods for 1-to-? Relationships	Sample Methods for many-to-? Relationships
Establishing relationship	set(...), operator=(...)	set(...), operator=(...), insert_element(...), replace_element_at(...)
Deleting relationship	clear(), delete_object()	remove_all(), remove_element(), remove_element_at(...)
traversing / retrieval	get(), operator Ref<...>(), operator->(), operator*()	get(), retrieve_element(...), operator[]()
Testing	operator==(), operator!=()	cardinality(), is_empty(), contains_element(..)

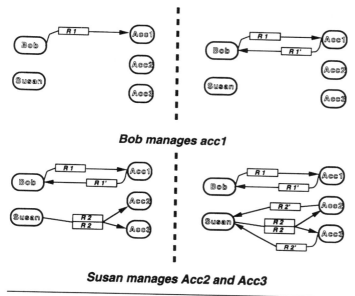

Bob manages acc1

Susan manages Acc2 and Acc3

Figure 8.7 Supporting relationship referential integrity.

Since the relationship is implemented using collection type genera-tors, full collection functionality is implicitly given. For example, iter-ator support is available for sequentially iterating over all elements of the relationship.

Figure 8.7 gives a detailed example of the internal references that are managed for the relationship. In the example, bob and susan are instances of Ref<InvestmentConsultant> and account1, account2, and account3 are instances of Ref<Account>. The left side of the figure shows the reference structures after C++ addition operations complete, and the right side shows the reference structure after the ODBMS completes the side effect necessary to ensure refer-ential integrity.

8.3.7 Support for ODMG/OM types

The ODMG object model defines a number of built-in types which are not part of the built-in C++ types. The C++ binding therefore provides class definitions for these support types. The classes provided are String, Date, Time, Timestamp, and Interval. The class defini-tions are meant to allow storage in ODMG-compliant ODBMSs and to ensure portability. Users of these classes are guaranteed source portability across conforming ODBMSs with a C++ binding. The classes were not designed to provide general-purpose library type support; their functionality may therefore be lacking as compared with similar classes in commercially available libraries. The following table summarizes the purpose of each of these support classes.

Class name	Description	Method categories
String	Used for string attributes	Constructors and destructors, assignment, copying, testing, and conversion to and from character strings
Date	Year/month/day	Constructors and destructors, assignment, arithmetic operators, comparison operators, testing, support for day of week and number of days in month, and conversion to and from operating system date types
Time	Denotes time; internally stored as GMT	Constructors and destructors, assignment, arithmetic operators, comparison operators, testing, component access, converting to and from operating system time types
Timestamp	Date and time	A union of date and time functionality
Interval	Used for time intervals	Constructors and destructors, component access, testing, arithmetic operators, comparison operators

8.3.8 Database support classes

The classes defined by the C++ binding were the result of mapping ODL, OML, and OQL structures to C++. This subsection describes classes that serve a very different purpose. Since the C++ binding must provide mappings of all operations needed to work with an ODBMS, support for database operations is necessary. The classes Database and Transaction provide a mapping of what is usually called the database control language. These classes allow the user to open a database, connect to it and start a session, and close it when the session is over. Transactions can be created using the Transaction class, and they can be committed or aborted. Database and Transaction objects cannot be made persistent. They are transient C++ objects. The model therefore cannot support the long transaction model.

The Database class provides a handle for the database connection. Using the open function, a database may be opened. A close call closes the database. The Database class also provides management facilities for creating named objects and adding additional names (aliases) to persistent objects, and a lookup facility allowing named lookup of objects. The following code example shows how a database is opened, an object is retrieved by name lookup, and an additional name is given. Note that for the changes to be recorded in the persistent store, they must be bracketed in a transaction using the Transaction class.

```
/* db is an instance of the database class; tr is an instance of the
Transaction class*/
db→open("BondMasterDatabase");
tr→begin();
Ref<Security> aBond = db→lookup_object("bond with sentimental
value");
db→set_object_name(aBond, "another name");
tr→commit();
db→close
```

The Transaction class allows bracketing of transactions. Any persistent change to the database must be bracketed in a transaction. Transactions do not affect transient objects. The methods defined for the Transaction class are summarized in the following table.

Method	Description
void begin()	Start a transaction
void commit()	Commit all modifications of the persistent store; all locks are released, and all changes are recorded
void abort()	Abort the transaction and roll back to previous consistent state
void checkpoint()	Record (commit) all changes without releasing the transaction context; locks are kept

The ODMG model supports nested transactions. A transaction bracket can be started within another transaction bracket. If the embedded transaction commits, the changes are seen only within the enclosing transaction bracket; they are not seen outside the enclosing transaction. If the enclosing transaction aborts, then the changes made by the embedded transaction are rolled back and aborted.

8.3.9 Classes supporting the binding implementation

Since the ODMG C++ binding is based on a smart pointer model, several support classes are necessary. Major support is provided by the template class Ref<T>. For any type T, Ref<T> provides a smart pointer type referencing objects. Ref<T> instances behave like C++ pointers, but they provide both type safety and smart pointer semantics guaranteeing some level of integrity. Ref<T> types can be used like C++ pointer types mainly because the Ref<T> template class overloads operator* and operator→. Dereferencing a Ref<T> instance will yield an instance of type T.

The class Ref_Any is defined to allow typeless smart pointer semantics. This class is used to convert between Ref<*> types with different type parameters. Any Ref<*> type can be converted to a Ref_Any and back, since the Ref<T> template class defines a constructor and assignment operator that take an argument of type Ref_Any. Ref_Any objects can be used to reference any type and are somewhat similar to the use of void* in C.

The Persistent_Object class is used to distinguish between transient objects and objects that may be persistent. Any class that requires persistent instances must inherit from Persistent_Object. The ODMG C++ binding specifies that a conformant implementation does not have to specifically implement a Persistent_Object class as long as the syntactical expression of a class inheriting from Persistent_Object (i.e., the form class .....:public Persistent_Object) distinguishes between classes that can only have transient instances and those that can have both transient and persistent objects. If an ODBMS implementation does not implement the Persistent_Object class, it still must implement the mark_modified function that is defined to be a member function of the Persistent_Object class and is used to inform the ODBMS runtime system of an object modification.

8.4   The Smalltalk Binding

The objective of the ODMG Smalltalk binding is to ensure that the programmer deals with one language only: Smalltalk. The ODBMS functionalities must be mapped into the Smalltalk language in a way that is fully consistent with the Smalltalk syntax and semantics. There should be one type system, and objects can transparently be transient or persistent. Smalltalk is a dynamically typed language. Every Smalltalk object is an instance of a Smalltalk class (which is itself an object). No type information is maintained about instance variables, arguments, and so on. When the source code is "compiled," no type checking can therefore occur. Instead, when a message is sent to an object at runtime, the system verifies that the object can receive such a message (i.e., that the object's class implements this method). If the object cannot handle this message, a "message not understood" error occurs. Since Smalltalk is dynamically typed, the type system cannot deal with the typing characteristics of the ODMG/OM and the OMG/OM. The binding therefore specifies that type checking will only be done by the ODBMS. This is not required from the ODBMS, but it is assumed that most vendors will perform type checking.

The Smalltalk class concept provides a very important component in the Smalltalk binding. The class object is a template from which objects are created. An instance is created by sending the "new" (or some similar) message to the class object. The class object maintains

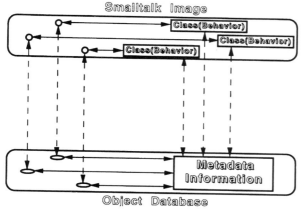

Figure 8.8 The Smalltalk `Behavior` class and schemas.

the method dictionary for the objects of this type; when a message is sent to the object, this dictionary (and the ancestors' dictionaries) is searched. The class object can also maintain additional data about the objects which are instances of this class; the class therefore maintains meta data, since it describes the structure of the individual objects. The class objects can therefore be used to represent the meta information maintained in the database. This allows the Smalltalk mapping to be very close to the ODBMS model. Issues like dynamic schema changes can be directly supported by the Smalltalk image; if an inheritance structure changes in the database (a schema change), it can be mirrored as a change in the subclasses and the superclass variables of the class `Behavior`; see Fig. 8.8

8.4.1 Objects, classes, operations, and attributes

Each object in the database maps to a Smalltalk object. Each ODMG object has a type; this type maps into a Smalltalk class (the Smalltalk object is an instance of this class). Although the ODMG model has a notion of immutability, this is not extended to the Smalltalk binding, since Smalltalk has no such notion. There are no constant or literal objects in Smalltalk, so both objects and literals in the ODMG/OM map into Smalltalk objects.

Smalltalk methods have syntax and semantics that are very different from those of ODL (and IDL) signatures. For one, ODL signatures are typed. The binding therefore defines how to construct the Smalltalk method definition from the ODL specification. For example, the ODL signature definition

void deposit (in Security aSecurity, in Date depositDate)

will be mapped into the following Smalltalk method in the `Account` class definition:

```
depositSecurity: aSecurity date: depositDate
```

This translation is similar to the result of reading in a C header file using ParcPlace's C Programming ObjectKit (CPOK). CPOK reads in a C header file. For each C function, a Smalltalk method with the same number of parameters is created. CPOK does not use the names of the arguments to form the Smalltalk method name. Smalltalk methods derived by CPOK therefore often have names like `with-draw:with:with:`. An implementation of the Smalltalk binding can use the argument names as defined in the ODL to create more meaningful names.

Attributes defined in the ODL definition will create two accessor methods in the Smalltalk class. Thus if an attribute named "security number" exists in the database schema of a `Security` type, then the `Security` class in Smalltalk will have the following two methods:

```
getSecurityNumber
setSecurityNumber: aNumber
```

An attribute in the ODL will usually be mapped to an instance variable in the Smalltalk class. This is not a requirement, since there may be derived attributes. Derived attributes (in the database sense of the word) are calculated from other attributes or function call values; they are not physically kept in the schema. For example, the schema describing a `Person` type can have an age attribute which is calculated by taking the difference between today and the person's birth date. There is no physical storage for a person's age; it uses the birth date attribute and calculates the result.

8.4.2 Relationships

Smalltalk does not provide a specific relationship construct. The mapping describes an implementation in Smalltalk for support for a relationship functionality. A relationship is mapped to an instance variable. If the relationship is one-to-one, then the variable will be an object reference. If it is many-to-many, it will be an instance of a `Collection` subclass (e.g., `Set`, `Bag`, etc.). The collection will hold multiple object references. If the relationship is one-to-many, then one side will be an object reference and the other a collection of object references. Access methods will automatically be generated in Smalltalk to support the relationship functionality. For example, a relationship definition of

relationship Set<Security> owns inverse Security::isOwnedBy

in the type `Account` will create the following Smalltalk methods in the `Account` class:

```
owns
addOwns: aSecurity
removeOwns: aSecurity
```

and possibly other utility methods. In addition, methods will be created (usually in the private category) to support the maintenance of referential integrity. Adding an object to the relationship set on one end of the relationship will automatically add the owning object to the relationship set on the other end of the relationship (if the relationship is many-to-many). For example,

```
addOwns: aSecurity
  "add the security object and call the utility method addToSelf"
  "In the Account class"
  aSecurity addToSelf: self.
  ^self owns add: aSecurity.

addToSelf: anAccount
  "a utility function to add the owning account"
  "In class Security"
  ^self isOwnedBy add: anAccount.
```

8.4.3 Extents

Smalltalk does not directly support the notion of extents. It is, however, extremely simple to implement extent support. One implementation would include a collection object in the class object. Any call to create a new object (the call being sent to the class object) will add the newly created object to the collection instance variable. Another implementation uses the `allInstances` method (defined in the `Behavior` class). Sending an `allInstances` message to a class object returns a collection object which includes all the instances of this class.

8.4.4 Sessions, locking, and transactions

Apart from the mapping of similar concepts from the ODMG world to the Smalltalk world, some extensions are required. Since the ODMG deals with database issues as well as object-oriented programming language issues, additions to the Smalltalk environment are required. This is done by adding new classes to the Smalltalk environment to support these database interfaces.

The primary example of such an addition is the `Session` class. This class allows the user to start up a database session, login, acquire locks, and bracket transactions. Some simple examples of the use of a Session object are

"Create a new session object and login to the database"
aSession : = Session new login: 'bondMasterDatabase'.

"Start a transaction"
aSession beginTransaction.

"Acquire a read only lock"
aSession acquireLock: #readOnly on: bondFord97.
...

"Commit the transaction; all changes will be committed to the database"
aSession commitTransaction.

8.4.5   Mapping the OQL to Smalltalk

Access to ODBMSs usually stresses the pointer navigation type of access. ODBMSs allow users to traverse object references directly. This point is stressed because it is the main deficiency of relational DBMSs. However, not all object accesses are easily based on pointers. Applications often require associative access (or what is also sometimes called value-based access). The OQL supports this type of access and is mapped directly into Smalltalk collection operations.

Smalltalk already has all the language constructs needed to support the OQL in a very intuitive manner. Using extents as the collections upon which the queries are defined (the examples here assume an extent implementation using the allInstances method), the select: method can be used for queries:

```
"Select all bond deals valued over $10M"
BondDeals allInstances select: [:aBondDeal | aBondDeal value >
10000000].
```

Since the built-in Smalltalk looping methods are used, queries can be simplified by moving some of the details from the where clause into the looping mechanism. Thus, using the detect: method, we can retrieve the first element only. Using reject: collect: and inject: into: can similarly simplify the query.

Operation	Description
select:	Test for a condition; return all elements in the collection that evaluate to true
detect:	Same as above, but return only the first element to evaluate to true
reject:	Same as select, but return only those elements that evaluate to false
inject:into:	Used to iterate over a collection performing some cumulative operation; an example is summation

All the above operations return a collection object that is the result of the query. Specific collection types can also be used to provide additional query support. For example, the `Set` class can be used to support `select  distinct` queries, since a `Set` object will not hold duplicates (as opposed to a `Bag` object, for example).

9

HP Distributed Smalltalk

HP Distributed Smalltalk (HPDST) is a CORBA-compliant development environment supporting the creation of distributed applications. HPDST is a collection of Smalltalk classes built using ParcPlace Systems' VisualWorks environment (which is based on Smalltalk-80). HPDST extends the base VisualWorks capabilities by providing classes and tools that enable the development of distributed applications. HPDST provides a very extensive set of services and capabilities that make the possibility of building distributed applications based on the OMG's work a reality. This chapter describes the HP Distributed Smalltalk product (see Hewlett-Packard, 1993a and 1993b).

HPDST is CORBA 1.1-compliant. Interfaces are declared in IDL. IDL operations are mapped to Smalltalk method selectors that provide the implementation model. An interface repository maintains the interfaces and modules. Any remote invocation starts out as Smalltalk code, goes through the ORB as IDL operations, and gets mapped back to a Smalltalk message. By consulting the ORB for the IDL specification and marshaling and unmarshaling arguments, HPDST is designed to be capable of communicating with objects implemented in other programming languages (e.g., C++).

HPDST implements both the CORBA Static Invocation Interface (SII) and the Dynamic Invocation Interface (DII). The support for the DII is provided only to remain fully compliant. Since Smalltalk already provides full dynamic binding, the DII will almost certainly never be used in HPDST. The SII will be more efficient and easier to use, and Smalltalk programmers will prefer to use Smalltalk for dynamic binding.

HPDST implements a substantial part of the Object Services, such as event notification, life cycle, and naming. These allow HPDST to fully support distributed application development while still remaining conformant to standards. HPDST supports CORBA 1.1, the

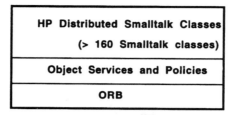

Figure 9.1 HP Distributed Smalltalk organization.

Common Object Services proposal from HP and Sunsoft, HP's Distributed Application Architecture (DAA), and NCS RPCs. The general organization within HPDST is shown in Fig. 9.1.

The Distributed Application Architecture (DAA) specified by HP is a set of policies, guidelines, and protocols that allow efficient interaction between fine-grained objects. The focus of the DAA is small objects typically used and managed by applications. The DAA is an HP proprietary extension of the Common Object Services that defines interfaces required for cooperative applications in distributed object-oriented systems.

NCS is HP/Apollo's Network Computing System. NCS Remote Procedure Calls (RPCs) version 2.0 have been adopted by the Open Software Foundation (OSF) as the standard RPC mechanism for the Distributed Computing Environment (DCE).

HPDST is itself developed using the VisualWorks Smalltalk environment. VisualWorks is also the development environment used to develop applications using HPDST. These become distributed applications by using and building atop the HPDST classes. Apart from being a very powerful development environment, VisualWorks allows HPDST to be available on many platforms. The VisualWorks environment (ParcPlace, 1992a and 1992b) is available on all major Unix platforms (SunOS, Solaris, HP-UX, AIX, etc.), on Microsoft Windows and Windows-NT, on OS/2, on the Apple Macintosh, and more. Any application built using the VisualWorks classes is guaranteed to be portable. In fact, the application does not even have to be recompiled. Once the image is moved to the new platform, it may be started up immediately. Only a small layer called the Smalltalk virtual machine is machine-dependent and is supplied for the various platforms by ParcPlace (in fact, the same platform may have multiple virtual machine versions, e.g., SPARC 5 versus SPARC 2). Since HPDST is built on top of this layer and uses only the portable VisualWorks classes (see Fig. 9.2), it is automatically portable across all platforms supported by VisualWorks.

HPDST also comes with an extensive user interface and an object management metaphor. This metaphor is used by the HPDST user interface to define buildings, offices, folder, file cabinets, and other

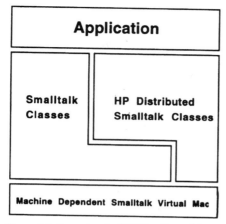

Figure 9.2 Layering in HP Distributed Smalltalk.

objects. Users may use this interface but are not required to. The containment metaphor is also only a guideline, but the developer can save a lot of work by using it and by reusing classes and methods from HPDST. The HPDST classes include many example applications. These applications may be used as code examples, but may actually be used as part of a larger application.

9.1 Designing Distributed Applications in HPDST

HPDST was built to be used to develop distributed applications. A correct distributed design will provide the maximum benefit from HPDST. A poor design will allow HPDST to provide only very limited benefit. HPDST therefore provides guidelines and policies for distributed application design. The main vehicle for this is the presentation/semantic split, which will be discussed at length in following sections.

However, guidelines are not enough. Distributed application design is relatively new, and it is not an easy thing. It has quite different design patterns from those known to most computing professionals and is a state of mind more than anything else. It is even different from the so-called client/server or RPC-based designs. The main difference is that a truly distributed application must look like a local application to anyone but the application designer. Location should be as transparent as possible.

Although the distribution issue is transparent to the user and to some of the application programmers, it is not transparent at all to the designer. In fact, the main responsibility of the designer is to address the distribution issues. It is the designer's task to use the HPDST capabilities to allow the users and programmers to be ignorant of these problems.

Performance is one of the main factors in a distributed application. Remote invocations behave differently from local ones. Remote requests go over a network; network traffic and performance therefore become critical to the application. The design must be built so as to eliminate (or reduce) as many of these bottlenecks as possible. Different presentation/semantic designs will have different characteristics.

Other design decisions have to address such issues as resource sharing and image autonomy (each image is autonomous and cannot be controlled from an external site; a design of an application may include some form of control relationships). Site autonomy tends to be more robust and scalable than a master-slave architecture and is therefore encouraged.

Object collaboration is also a critical issue. Many supporting services will need to be available if remote objects are to communicate. Naming services, object creation and destruction, policies for finding objects, event channels, links, and other such services are all required. HPDST supports a very extensive set of such object services to be used by distributed applications. A full section will be devoted to these services.

Finally, heterogeneity must be addressed in a system that attempts to support distributed environments. HPDST fully supports portability and interoperability between different platforms and operating systems by making use of the extreme portability of the ParcPlace Smalltalk implementation and by using CORBA. The IDL is used to provide a language-neutral interface language and to allow other programming languages to be used in the environment in the future. HPDST also supports and uses NCS RPC, including the UUID conventions.

9.2   An Example Application

In this section we build a very simple application. We will go through all the stages of building the application, registering it with the Interface Repository and the Factory Finder, and running it from a remote site. The application will use the presentation/semantic split paradigm of HPDST.

The application we will be building is a Smalltalk evaluator that can be activated from a remote site. The evaluator will receive any Smalltalk expression as a string and will evaluate the expression, sending the result string back as a reply. Since a Smalltalk expression can send any message to any object, and since such message invocations can trigger a large amount of work, this may be thought of as a batch processing engine for Smalltalk. One may imagine a scenario in which a server (or a number of servers) is waiting for clients to send it work using such Smalltalk expressions.

When such a server receives an expression to evaluate, it spawns a thread to actually do the work. The server creates as many threads as it receives expressions to be evaluated and remains available to be sent more expressions from remote sites. The local site can also send requests; distribution is to be handled transparently, meaning that the local submitter and the remote submitter look identical. The server maintains a status list on the evaluation threads. Every time a request arrives and a thread is spawned, a line of the form

Request submitted <expression>

is added to the list, where <expression> is the string that was sent over for evaluation. When the thread completes, a line of the form

Request completed <expression>

and the result string are returned to the submitter.

This description of the application is the "old-style" way of viewing things. It describes a client/server architecture, and this is actually not the way real object distribution should be explained. The application should really be described as an application where the distribution is transparent. The application is therefore really just an evaluator. You can give it a Smalltalk expression and this expression will be evaluated. Whether the evaluator is local or remote is unimportant and is transparent to the user of the evaluator. The remote evaluator will look identical to the local one (except perhaps in terms of performance). Once we have come to accept this way of viewing the application, we are ready to start building it.

9.2.1 Presentation/semantic split

We will build the application using the presentation/semantic split paradigm. This paradigm is promoted in HPDST, and most of the example applications provided with HPDST are built this way. (A part of the HPDST hierarchy showing presentation object classes and semantic object classes is shown in Fig. 9.3. Figure 9.3 also shows where our example classes are in terms of the presentation/semantic hierarchy.) The architecture helps in designing distributed applications in a structured and efficient manner. It separates a (local) presentation of the object from a shared semantic object which maintains the state and other central information. The presentation object is mostly responsible for implementing and managing the user interaction and communicates with the semantic object only when it is required to do so. The presentation object knows about its semantic object and sends it messages when needed. Many presentation objects (possibly on multiple machines) can be connected to the same semantic object. The semantic object knows about all the presentation

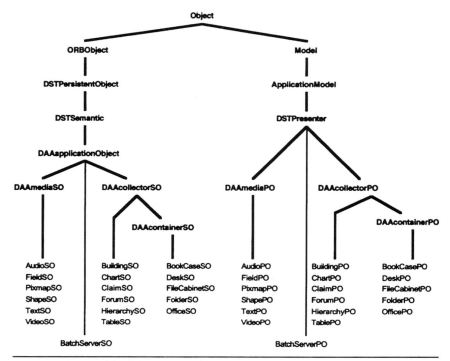

Figure 9.3 A part of the HP Distributed Smalltalk class hierarchy.

objects that it is connected to. When a state changes in the semantic object, it is propagated to all the connected presentation objects.

In our application, the semantic object will be the evaluator back end. The object will maintain a status list and will have a method for accepting a new evaluation. When this message is sent, the list will be updated with a "submit" line and a thread will be spawned. When the evaluation completes, the "completed" line is added to the list and the result is sent back to the submitting presentation object. Whenever the list changes (i.e., when an expression is submitted or completed), the new line is also broadcast to all the presentation objects. These presentation objects maintain a list, which is displayed in a list widget. The presentation objects therefore display the status list and are updated as evaluations start and finish. Each presentation object also has an interface for entering expressions and sending them to be evaluated, as well as a field in which the result is displayed. Figure 9.4 shows what a presentation object looks like.

9.2.2 Surrogates

Each presentation object maintains a reference to the semantic object, and each semantic object maintains a collection of references to the presentation objects. Since the semantic object may be on a dif-

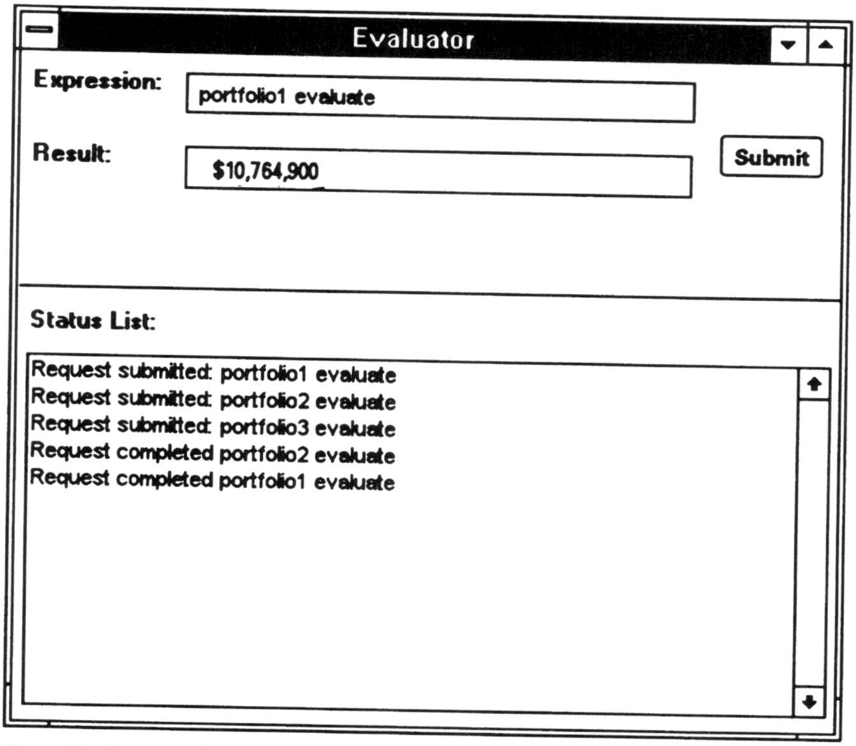

Figure 9.4 An example presentation object.

ferent image or a different machine from the presentation object, surrogates (sometimes called proxies) are used (Fig. 9.5). Objects can be
referenced only if they are on the same image. Therefore, if the presentation object is connected to the (remote) semantic object, the reference is actually to a surrogate object that is "standing in" for the
semantic object. The same is true for the presentation object references held by the semantic object. The creation and management of
the surrogates is done transparently without programmer intervention; it is this support which allows one to ignore the distribution
aspects of the application.

Let us look at an example scenario with presenter and semantic
objects. If a message is sent to the presenter object that changes only
the local state (for example, a change in a user interface variable,
such as the font of the display), the object handles the message locally. If a message that should change the shared state is sent to the presenter, it cannot be handled locally. The semantic object is not running locally, so Smalltalk cannot handle the invocation. However, a
surrogate is running locally. The message is forwarded to the surrogate. The surrogate sends the message to the semantic object via the
ORB. The semantic object gets the request from the ORB and per-

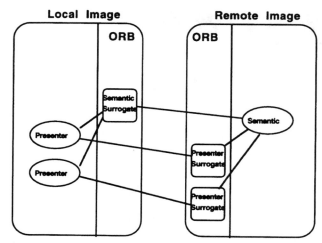

Figure 9.5 Use of proxies (surrogates) in HP Distributed
Smalltalk.

forms the state change. It then informs all the presenters of the state
change. Once again, the presenter objects are not running locally with
the semantic object, but the surrogates are. The message is sent
through the surrogates and through the ORB to the presenter objects.
In all the interactions the user does not know about the surrogates,
and even the programmer does not need to write supporting code.

9.2.3 The BatchServer code

Now let's write the application code. We keep the code as simple as
possible for this demonstration; a real application will naturally be
more elaborate. We first write the code for the semantic object. The
class for the semantic object will be `BatchServerSO`, and as a
semantic object it will inherit from `DAAapplicationObject`. The
`BatchServer` class will have a number of methods that are required
if the server is to work as an HPDST semantic object; these will be
covered shortly. It also has one method which actually does all the
work. This method is shown in Fig. 9.6.

The "client" objects are the presenters. The `BatchServerPO` class
inherits from the `DSTPresenter` class (which inherits from
VisualWorks' `ApplicationModel` class). As an `ApplicationModel`
subclass, the class has a number of methods that will be activated
from the user interface. The methods that are of interest are
`submitExpression`, `setResult`, and `addStatus`. The code for
these is given in Fig. 9.7. The `submitExpression` method is called
by the user interface to evaluate an expression. It is called when the
user clicks the Submit button in the user interface. The presenter

```
submit: aString by: aPO

"This method is called by the presenter objects to submit a job.
 Jobs submitted by sending a string with an expression.
 This string is evaluated using the Smalltalk compiler."

        | str |
        str := 'Request submitted: ', aString.
        "Add the status line to all presenters"
        self presenters do: [:po | po addStatus: str].

        "Now fork the job as a Smalltalk thread"
        [ | result |
          result := Compiler evaluate: aString.
          "Send the result only to the submitter"
          aPO setResult: result printString.
          str replaceElementsFrom: 9
                to: 17
                withCharacterArray: 'completed'
                startingAt: 1.
          "Now update presenters' status"
          self presenters do: [:po | po addStatus: str].
        ] fork.
```

Figure 9.6 The submit:by: implementation.

object merely sends the submit:by: message to the semantic object. As the code shows, the presenter object does not know or care that the semantic object may be at a remote site. The setResult and addStatus methods are called by the semantic object, as was explained in Fig. 9.6.

The key to the workings of the architecture is the surrogates. When the submitExpression message is called, the presenter must use the semantic object. The semantic message is not implemented in each presentation class. Instead, it is part of the support provided by inheriting from DSTSemantic. Since the semantic object is not local, the submit:by: message is actually sent to the surrogate object. The surrogate object cannot respond to this message, so it sends itself the doesNotUnderstand: messageSpecification message. This is trapped by the surrogate object and starts the remote invocation

```
submitExpression: aString
"Send the expression to the semantic object"
        self semantic submit: aString by: self

addStatus: aString
        self submissionList list addLast: aString

setResult: aString
        self result value: aString
```

Figure 9.7 submitExpression, setResult, and addStatus.

through the ORB. The methods for communicating from the semantic object to the presenter objects are similar.

9.2.4   Embedding in the ORB environment

Now that we have written the code, we must complete the integration of the application into the HPDST environment in general and into the ORB specifically. This involves three main issues: registering the different components in the Interface Repository (IR), registering the classes with the Factory Finder, and embedding the application in the containment model.

Since the surrogate will be sending the message to the semantic object through the ORB, the Interface Repository must contain the interface definitions that will be used. Interfaces must be written in CORBA IDL, and the mapping of these operations to the Smalltalk methods must be supplied. Since code is actually written only in Smalltalk, this is the logical place to start. Using our Smalltalk class (e.g., `BatchServerSO`), we can generate an IDL skeleton by invoking an HPDST-supplied method:

```
BatchServerSO asIDLDefinition
```

This generates a code segment similar to Fig. 9.8*a*. One can then edit this segment to provide the real information, as shown in Fig. 9.8*b*.

The IDL module should contain one interface declaration for each class that is to be distributed (this is not necessarily required but is good practice). Each message that is to be sent remotely should have an operation declaration which specifies what the signature is. All this is done in CORBA IDL. These then have to be mapped to the Smalltalk classes and methods. The mapping consists of two elements. Every class that is mirrored by an IDL interface has a unique number. This is implemented by the programmer as an instance method in the class by the name of `mostDerivedInterfaceID`. This method takes the form of

```
mostDerivedInterfaceID
  ^'59661bc23e02.02.0f.1c.68.13.00.00.00' asUUID
```

UUID is an NCS Universal Unique Identifier. Although the programmer implements this method, the task of coming up with the UUID is the ORB's. To get a UUID, the programmer performs `ORBObject newId` and then pastes the result in the method definition (to get a newId, the ORB must be running). When `asIDLDefinition` is called, the UUID is automatically copied from this method into the interface segment. The mapping of the class to the interface is therefore part of the automated process. The mapping of the IDL operations to the

```
module BatchServerSOModule
{
interface BatchServerSOInterface: ApplicationBase
        IDENTIFIER = '59661bc23e02.02.0f.1c.68.13.00.00.00'
{
'Please insert comment here'
SmalltalkObject submitBy(in SmalltalkObject aString, in
SmalltalkObject aPO)
    SELECTOR = submit:by: ;
.........
};
}
```

(a)

```
module BatchServerSOModule
{
interface BatchServerSOInterface: ApplicationBase
        IDENTIFIER = '59661bc23e02.02.0f.1c.68.13.00.00.00'
{
'Submit an expression to be evaluated'
void submitBy(in string aString, in BatchServerPOInterface aPO)
    SELECTOR = submit:by: ;
.........
};
}
```

(b)

Figure 9.8 IDL specification segments.

Smalltalk selectors is also automatically done, as can be seen in Fig. 9.8a. Remember that until version 3.0 of HPDST, each image maintains its own IR. Therefore the IRs of all images must be updated with every change or the remote invocations will not be completed.

After the IR is ready, the classes that will be remotely used must be registered with the Factory Finder. Registering the class with the Factory Finder is needed so that external clients will be able to instantiate it. Remember that these clients may be at remote sites on different images; they must have a way of instantiating the class.

The Factory Finder supports this by allowing the programmer to register a class. Each class must provide a UUID (this is the id by which it will be known). The UUID should be placed in the class's abstractClassId instance method. Once this is done, the Factory Finder must be initialized. This iterates and creates all the factory objects as well as registering with the Factory Finder. The Factory Finder is implemented by the class DSTFactoryFinder. This class maintains a dictionary associating class identifiers with class names. It can therefore perform the mapping as long as the class has been registered. There are three ways to do this. In the ORB or OA panel, one can pick the "Initialize Factories" option from the

"Configure" menu. Alternatively, one can execute the Smalltalk expression ORBObject initializeFactories or the expression

ORBObject factoryFinder contextBind: <a UUID> to: <a class>

to bind only the new class.

The final step is to provide a way for a presentation object to be created (locally) attached to a (remote) semantic object. This can be done in two ways. The easy way is to simply embed the semantic object within the HPDST containment paradigm. This is conceptually similar to placing it in a folder or a directory. The local image can have a link to this folder, and therefore the remote semantic object can be used. By clicking on the object, the HPDST environment will start up a remote session of the semantic object and a local session of the presentation object. These will be linked, and so the remote object seems to be running in the local image.

Although this approach is the simpler by far, it provides no insight into what is actually happening. Figure 9.9 provides a code segment for starting up such a session programmatically. The first line gets a handle to the ORB's Naming Service on the remote machine. Using the Naming Service, the Factory Finder is found on line 2. Line 3 uses the Factory Finder to create the remote object, and lines 4 and 5 create the attached presentation object and the user interface.

9.2.5 Sample run

The rest of this section will describe a sample run of the application. The scenario includes three client workstations and one powerful server. The server will be used to evaluate portfolios. Each client workstation can submit a portfolio to be evaluated. The presentation front end will be displayed on each client machine to monitor progress. Since all clients' jobs have the same priority and since dif-

```
| nameService factoryFinder so po |
"mosaic is the name of the remote machine; it should be in the hosts file"
1       nameService := ORBObject namingService: 'mosaic'.
2       factoryFinder := nameService contextResolve:
                        (DSTName onString: 'factoryFinder').
3       so := factoryFinder createObject: BatchServerSO getInstanceACL.
4       po := so createPresentation: nil
                types: #()
                  session: Session
                  access: #'read_write'
                  auto: true.
5       po attachWindow: Session
```

Figure 9.9 Programmatic startup of a remote session.

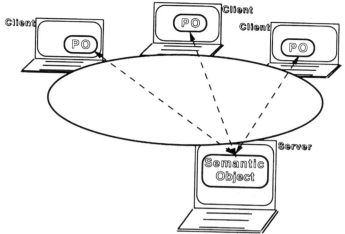

Figure 9.10 Example layout of presentation and semantic objects.

ferent portfolios may have different complexities, the completion order is not necessarily the submission order, nor is it affected by the client submitting it. Each evaluation is performed as a separate thread.

Figure 9.10 describes the layout of the machines. All workstations are running HPDST. All have access to the same evaluator server object. Since HPDST is used, the clients are not aware of the fact that the evaluator is remote; they simply submit the evaluations.

Each presenter object is running locally. The user perceives the complete evaluator as running locally. All the presenter objects are actually local front ends to one evaluator. This evaluator is running on a remote machine. The status list that will be displayed on each of the local machines will be identical for each presenter object (as long as the network and the machines remain functional). Figure 9.11 shows a job being submitted by one of the presenter objects. When the Submit button is pressed, the evaluation string is delivered to the remote semantic object. A thread starts processing the request, and the status list is updated in all presenter objects (including the one that submitted the job). Note that the example assumes that all the images are identical, or at least that the portfolio objects are known to both the presenter's image and the semantic's image.

Some time after this, a second presenter object (on a different machine) submits an evaluation request (see Fig. 9.12). Once again, the semantic object spawns a thread and updates the status lists of all presenter objects.

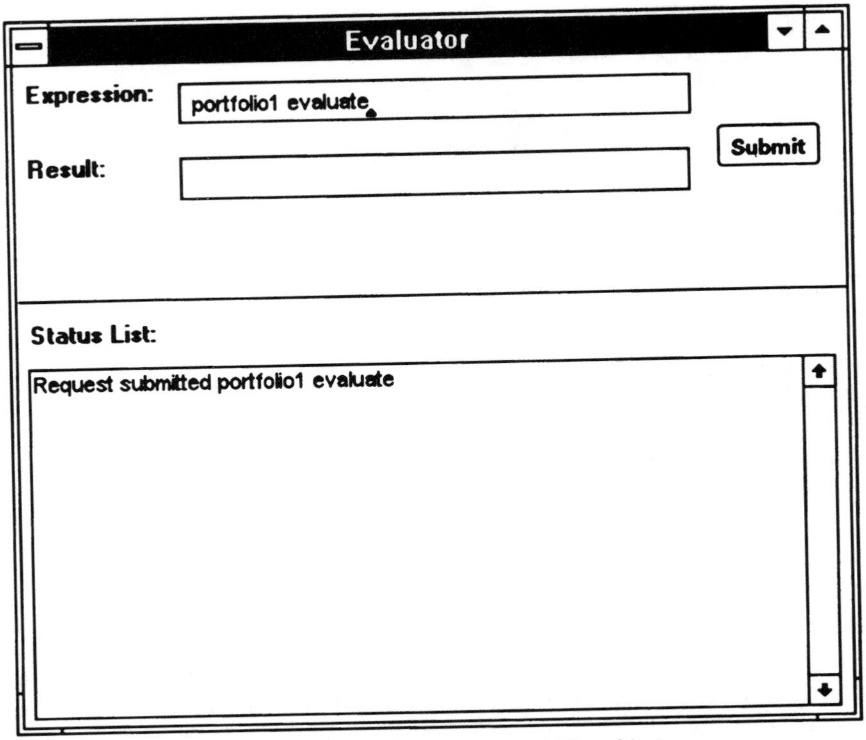

Figure 9.11 A job being submitted by one of the presentation objects.

Figure 9.13 shows the state at the second presenter object after a fairly long time. During this time, the third client machine submitted a third portfolio for evaluation. At that time there were three evaluation threads running in parallel. The first thread to complete was the evaluation of the second portfolio. At that time the status list was updated for all presenter objects, but only the second presenter object was sent the result of the evaluation.

After some more time, the first evaluation thread completes. All status lists are updated, and the result is sent to the first client. Note that at this time the third evaluation thread is still executing. This is shown in Fig. 9.14.

9.3 Developer Tools

Having built a very simple application, we can begin to appreciate the amount of support provided by HPDST—object surrogates, automatic presentation and semantic object connections, automatic IDL skeleton generation, an Interface Repository, Factory Finders, and so on. We should also realize by now that building a distributed application

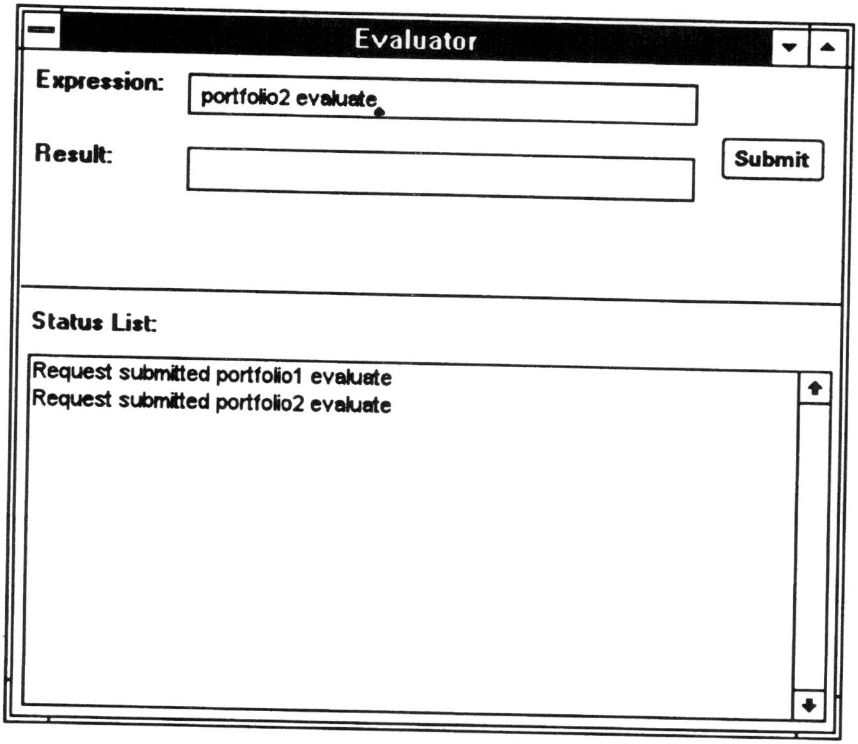

Figure 9.12 A job submitted by a second presentation object.

is an order of magnitude more difficult than building a local application. Building a distributed application is also quite different from
building what is usually (and sometime mistakenly) called a
client/server application. HPDST not only provides the internal support for distributed applications and guidelines for designing distributed applications, it also provides tools for the application developer.

The tools provided by HPDST can be roughly categorized into two
groups. The first set of tools are those provided with the ParcPlace
VisualWorks environment. These tools support local development,
browsing, and debugging. This is arguably the best development environment and tool suite available today. However, these tools have to
be augmented with tools that are specialized for distributed application development. These are provided as part of the HPDST environment. These tools are also built in Smalltalk using the underlying
development environment, but they are specifically designed to support distributed environments.

Most of the tools in HPDST are started from the HPDST control
panel. It provides access to the developer's tools. The tools are best

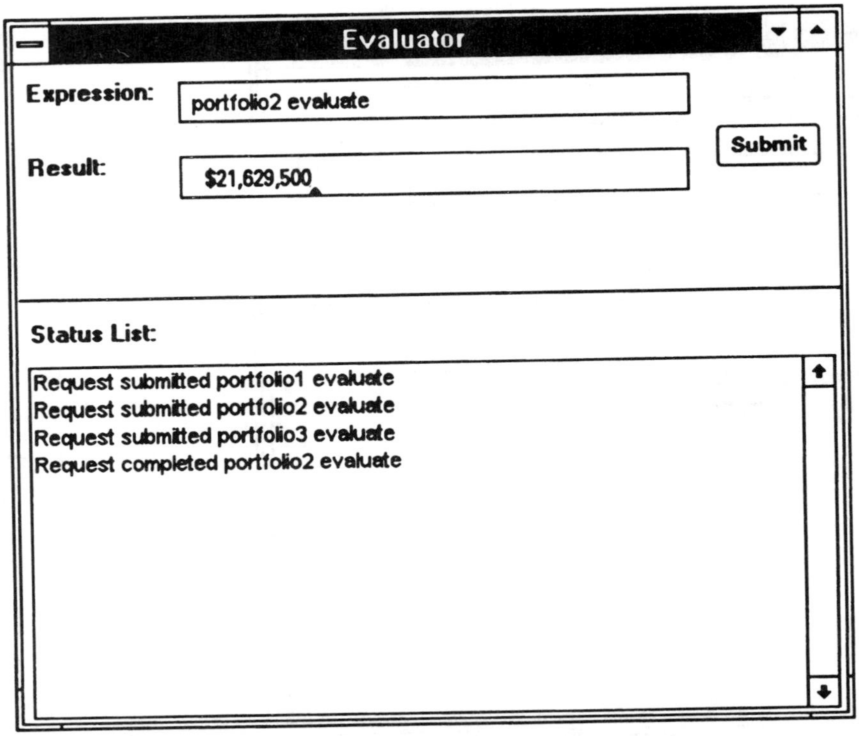

Figure 9.13 The state of the second presentation object after some time.

described by following the stages of developing a distributed application. The code is written using the Smalltalk browsers. Support from the HPDST environment includes such things as automated IDL skeleton generation, UUID generation, and factory registration. The code should first be tested locally. After the code is functional in the local environment, one has the option of using local *RPC testing*. This is a very important feature provided in HPDST. Testing and debugging a distributed application is much harder than testing and debugging the local version of that application. Issues like communications, race conditions, and ORB interfacing might obscure application errors and cause the developer many hours of frustration. HPDST therefore provides a track used for testing and debugging which "incrementally distributes" the application.

The first stage is to test the application locally. Both the presenter object and the semantic object are run locally. The next stage is to use the local RPC testing facility. This allows a local debugging session while still activating all components that will be used when the application is actually distributed. The local session will fully simulate the distributed support objects created in remote invocations. This

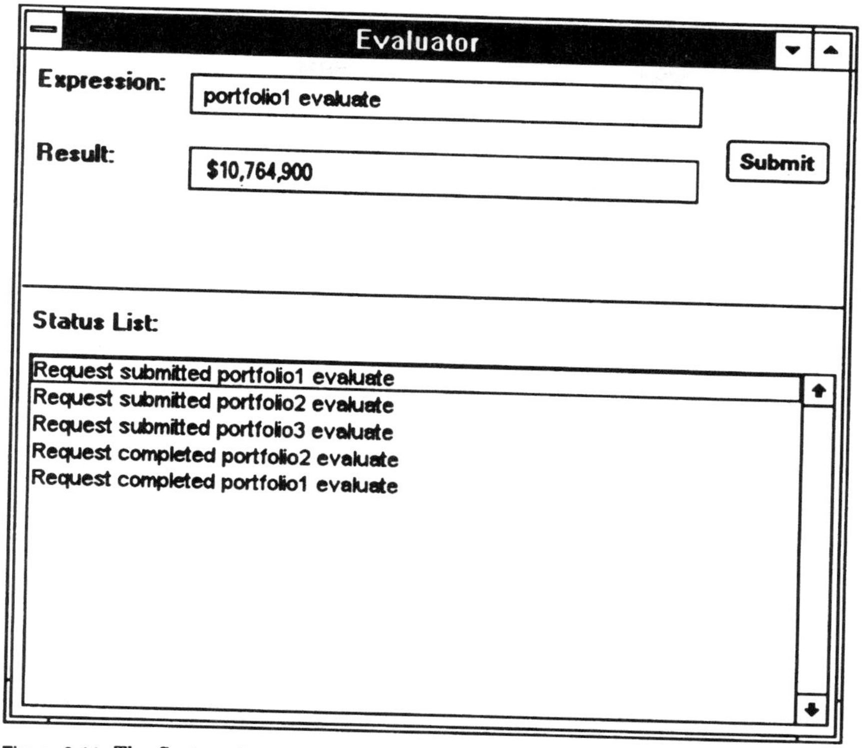

Figure 9.14 The first evaluation thread completes.

includes real surrogate creation, Interface Repository usage, Factory Finders, and so on.

Once the application works in the simulated distributed environment, we are ready to test it in the real remote environment. HPDST provides a debugger that is capable of handling a fully distributed execution stack, including errors that occurred on remote RPC threads. When an error occurs on a remote machine, a debugger similar to the Smalltalk debugger may be brought up. This is a read-only debugger of the remote execution context (it is read-only because changes made will really belong to the remote image and such changes cannot be made outside of that image). With such debuggers, as well as local debuggers, the developer is provided with full debugging capabilities at a level very close to that expected by a Smalltalk programmer (which is a very high level indeed).

The control panel also provides the developer with tools for performance profiles and a message logger that allows information about distributed RPCs to be viewed. The information provided includes the RPC type, status, target, and IDL interface used, and the message operation. The developer can control the detail level of the logger in

Exceptions only.
Request traffic only.
Request traffic and reply traffic.
Request traffic with parameters.
Request and reply traffic with parameters.
Request traffic including full protocol traffic.
Request and reply traffic including full protocol traffic.
All protocol traffic.

Figure 9.15 Different logging levels in HPDST.

terms of what messages are logged. The levels (in increasing order) allowed in HPDST are shown in Fig. 9.15.

Finally, HPDST provides a tool for browsing the Interface Repository. This tool allows the developer to navigate the IR, viewing the different components, such as modules, interfaces, operations, attributes, types, parameters, and exceptions. The IR browser provides both a textual and a graphic representation of these components. HPDST 3.0 provides very rich functionality in this tool, making it extremely useful for developers.

9.4   Object Services and Policies

Object services and policies provided in HPDST provide support for working with objects in a distributed environment. These services are based on a combination of HP's DAA and the OMG's Common Object Services. Since HPDST is a commercially available product that was implemented before the completion of the COS, it is based on the proposal for Object Services written jointly by HP and SunSoft. The services provided as part of HPDST are event notification, properties, naming, containment, links, associations, application objects, life cycle, presentation/semantic split, and dataviews policies. Event notification allows notification using asynchronous communication. Interaction is possible even if some component goes down temporarily. Properties provide policies for supporting external object attributes. The naming service provided in HPDST is the basis for identifying and locating objects. It is used extensively by many services, such as containment and links. The naming service provides a framework for names and also allows developers to define their own naming policies. Containment provides policies for objects in a hierarchical organization. Links support organization and association of objects. Links and associations provide a framework for implementing object relationships. Link support is more extensive than associations, and associations are therefore seldom used in HPDST. Application objects define policies for supporting clusters of objects that behave as one object. Life-cycle services provide mechanisms for creating, deleting, copying, moving, and externalizing and internalizing objects. HPDST extends CORBA life-cycle services with DAA life-cycle services to support complex container objects. The presentation/semantic split is a guideline for building distributed objects that can be remotely used. It is the basic metaphor by which distributed objects are used within HPDST. Dataviews provide a set of policies and protocols allowing semantic objects to interact and exchange information.

9.4.1 Event notification

The event notification service in HPDST is based on the event notification service proposal originally submitted to the OMG's Object Services Task Force by HP and SunSoft. It includes a number of predefined objects and a protocol for interaction. It can be used as a publish and subscribe model or as a simpler notification model as well.

The service provides three objects: the event supplier, the event consumer, and the event channel. Events are generated by suppliers and placed on an event channel. Consumers can either pull events or specify that events should be pushed from the channel. Event channels behave like consumers to the producer and like producers to the consumers.

An event channel is formed in stages. It is unconnected upon creation. The programmer creates an event channel by asking for the appropriate factory. The factory creates an object which supports the `EventChannel` interface. The `ConsumerAdmin` and `SupplierAdmin` interfaces are also supported by this object, since the `EventChannel` interface inherits from them (see Fig. 9.16). All these interfaces map to the `DSTEventChannel` Smalltalk class delivered as part of HPDST. For example, the operations defined in the `ConsumerAdmin` interface are implemented as Smalltalk methods in the Consumer-Admin category.

To understand the mapping implementation between the interface declarations and the Smalltalk implementations, the Interface Repository should be examined. Recall that the Interface Repository is implemented by the `DSTrepository` class. Figure 9.17 shows the relevant interface declarations. Note that `EventChannel` inherits from both `SupplierAdmin` and `ConsumerAdmin`. Each of these inter-

Figure 9.16 EventChannel inheritance structure.

module EventChannelAdmin module EventChannelAdmin {

    interface ConsumerAdmin
        IDENTIFIER = '5e1b8435476.87.0f.11.dd.33.00.00.00'
    {

        EventComm::EventConnection   add_push_consumer (in EventComm::Consumer c)
        SELECTOR = addPushConsumer: ;

        EventComm::Supplier   add_pull_consumer (in EventComm:EventConnection c)
        SELECTOR = addPullConsumer: ;
    };

    interface SupplierAdmin
        IDENTIFIER = '823748745.7a.aa.3b.00.00.00.00'
    {

        . . .

    }

    interface EventChannel : SupplierAdmin, ConsumerAdmin
        IDENTIFIER = '76435324534.7a.1b.1b.1b.00.00.00'
    {

        ConsumerAdmin   for_consumers()
        SELECTOR = forConsumers ;

        SuppliersAdmin   for_suppliers()
        SELECTOR = forSuppliers ;

        void   destroy()
        SELECTOR = destroy ;
    };
}

Figure 9.17 IDL specifications for EventChannel and inherited interfaces.

faces has a pragma specifying the UUID number for IDENTIFIER. Each operation has a SELECTOR pragma specifying the Smalltalk selector implementing the operation. The mapping is possible because of these two pragmas. The UUID in the EventChannel interface is that returned by the mostDerivedInterface method in the DSTEventChannel class. The name *mostDerivedInterface* actually explains how the mapping works. Note that some of the operations in the ConsumerAdmin and SupplierAdmin interfaces (having different interface UUIDs) are to be mapped to Smalltalk methods in the DSTEventChannel class. This is possible because the selector specification still maps the operation to a method name implemented in the DSTEventChannel class. When an operation is used, the UUID is used to determine which class has the implementation. The SELECTOR pragma determines which selector should be used. It does not matter what interface the operation actually belongs to in the IDL specification.

The HPDST implementation of the event notification service supports both the pull and the push models. The push model is used as a default. In this model, the supplier pushes the event to the consumer. A consumer may use the disconnect operation to ensure that no inter-

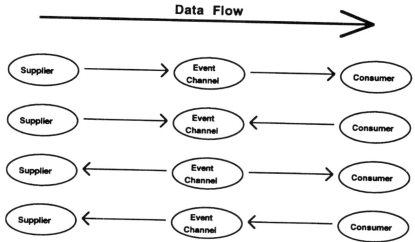

Figure 9.18 Four push/pull model combinations.

ruption occurs. In the pull model, the consumer requests events. A supplier may use the disconnect operation to eliminate interruptions. Since the event channel plays the role of the consumer for the supplier and the role of the supplier for the consumer, there are four push/pull model combinations possible, as shown in Fig. 9.18. When a consumer or supplier is added to the event channel, the communication mode (push or pull) is specified.

To understand Fig. 9.18, one should remember that the flow of information is always from the supplier to the consumer. The directional arrows in the four cases show the control information regarding who requests the information to be propagated. Therefore there are four cases; the possibilities are only determined by the modes that the supplier and consumer registered with the event channel.

Event types used in the push and pull operations are Any. This is the most generic and allows the event notification service to pass any object as an event. Other relevant interfaces are shown in Fig. 9.19. The EventConnection interface supports operations for the event channel. The disconnect operation is part of this interface. The Consumer interface provides the support for push-style consumers,

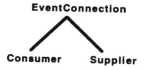

Figure 9.19 Additional interfaces for event notification.

Figure 9.20 HPDST implementation hierarchy for event notification.

and the Supplier interface provides the support for pull-style suppliers. The HPDST implementation hierarchy for the event notification service is shown in Fig. 9.20.

9.4.2 Properties

Properties in HPDST allow users to associate information with objects. For example, a document object may have properties associated with it for title, last date revised, owner, and so on. Properties can be used for holding information that will be used for object lookup. However, properties do not have to be unique. Properties can have permission sets associated with them. The property service is partly based on the OMG Object Services. It is extended with DAA property services by adding protected read-only properties. The IDL interfaces for the property service are shown in Fig. 9.21. The property set interfaces (PropertySet and ProtectedPropertySet) provide operations for defining and retrieving key-value pairs. Query operations are also provided. The reporting property set interfaces (ReportingPropertySet and ReportingProtectedPropertySet) support event notification for property sets by creating an event channel to a consumer. The HPDST classes used for the implementation of the property service are DSTproperty, DSTPropertySet, and DSTPropertyListIterator, which allows iteration over an instance of DSTPropertySet.

Figure 9.21 Interfaces for the property service.

9.4.3   Naming service

A name is an ordered sequence of components. Each segment is a context except the last one, which names an object. This is similar to path names in a hierarchical file system, where each segment names a directory and the last segment names a file, but is much more generic. The HPDST naming service supports binding an object to a unique name within a given context. Names can then be resolved to an object reference.

HPDST implicitly provides naming services for users of the containment policies. These built-in naming policies can be used if containment is desired. The framework can also be used as a stand-alone service. Interfaces supporting the naming service in HPDST are `NameContext` and `BindingIterator`. The Smalltalk classes implementing the naming service are shown in Fig. 9.22. `DSTName Component` instances serve as segments within a name (for contexts and object names). A `DSTName` instance is an ordered collection of `DSTNameComponent` objects. A `DSTNameContext` object contains a set of unique names and is used for nonleaf nodes in the naming graph. `DSTBindingIterator` objects allow iteration over a name.

9.4.4   Containment policies

The containment model implemented in HPDST is defined in HP's DAA to establish a hierarchy of objects that can be used and identi-

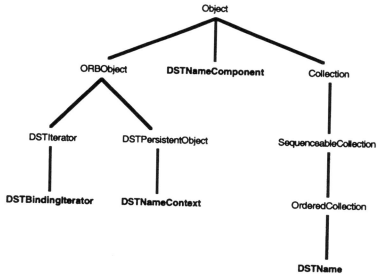

Figure 9.22 HPDST classes implementing the naming service.

fied according to their position within the hierarchy. The policy rules define a strict hierarchy that is composed of container objects. Each container can have zero or more elements. Containment relationships can occur only between objects in the same Smalltalk image. To provide more general support, links are used.

Links may be used to provide nonhierarchical relationships. Links do not break the hierarchy, since identification is done only through the containment relationship. Links are used only as a convenient pointer-based reference mechanism. Links are also used to associate objects in different images. In Fig. 9.23, containment relationships are shown by solid bold lines. Apart from the document objects, all objects in the figure are container objects. As discussed, the containment framework provides implicit naming services to the enclosed objects.

9.4.5 Link service

The link service is an implementation of the link service definitions in the DAA. It extends the containment model with an additional level of organizational flexibility and provides support for relationships. Links are HPDST's main facility for associating objects in different images. Links maintain a live connection. They remain active objects after they have been created (as opposed to file system links in most operating systems). Links can be used to propagate changes when they occur. They are first-class objects and have state and behavior.

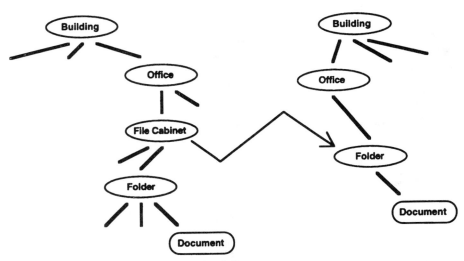

Figure 9.23 Links used for interimage associations.

A link always refers to the same object, even if that object's location changes. Therefore, life-cycle operations, such as moving, performed on an object do not disconnect the link. Links may be used for one-to-one, one-to-many, and many-to-many relationships. The containment relationship is an example of using the link service for implementing one-to-many relationships. The link service is implemented by the DAAlink class (which represents a link between application objects) and the DAAlinkInfo class (which provides read-only information about the link).

Links provide built-in support for referential integrity. Four levels of integrity support are provided. The levels differ in the binding level between both sides of the link. Links have two sides, called the head and the tail. The four support levels differentiate between the roles of the head and the tail. The four levels are listed in descending order of referential guarantee.

- *Containment* (see Fig. 9.24*a*). This mode supports the containment model. Every tail has one head; a head may have many tails. The existence of a tail ensures the existence of a head. The head maintains references to the tails and vice versa. After the link is established, it is not possible to delete the head without deleting the tails as well.

- *Reference* (see Fig. 9.24*b*). The head guarantees the existence of the tail object. The tail cannot be deleted without the head. The head maintains references to the tails and vice versa.

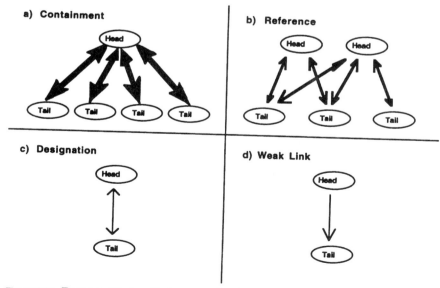

Figure 9.24 Four possible head/tail support levels

- *Designation* (see Fig. 9.24*c*). The head maintains references to the tails and vice versa, but there is no referential guarantee. The breaking party must notify the other party of the action.

- *Weak link* (see Fig. 9.24*d*). Only the head references the tails. A break can occur without notification.

9.4.6 Association service

The association service implements the COS association service. It is very similar to the link service, but it provides less functionality than links. It is therefore seldom used in HPDST and is provided only for completeness. The main difference from the link service is that associations are implemented as data structures managed by the objects involved in the relationship, whereas links are objects. For example, associations provide no support for referential integrity. Associations can be seen as lightweight implementations of links and may be useful in cases where performance and footprint are of utmost importance.

The association service includes two interfaces: one for initiating participation in an object graph, and one for the object graph's internal maintenance. The service supports path traversal within an object graph as well as operations on the object graph. The service is implemented by the Smalltalk classes DSTAssociate (used to create and maintain the connections of an object graph; each instance represents an object participating in the association) and DSTAssociate ConnectionIterator.

9.4.7 Application objects

Application objects allow the creation and support of aggregate objects. Large objects can be created to appear as single objects even though they are really complex aggregations of smaller objects. Compound documents, including text from a word processor, charts from a spreadsheet, and graphs, are among the best-known examples. From the user's perspective, an application object is a single object without any distinction, while from the programmer's perspective, the policy provides support for managing the complexity.

HPDST implements Application Assistant objects to serve as link managers. They are lightweight objects that stand in place of the application object and the underlying cluster and participate in most services and policies. The Smalltalk classes used are DAAapplicationObject for the cluster itself and DAAApplication Assistant.

9.4.8 Life-cycle services

Life-cycle services in HPDST provide methods for creating, deleting, copying, moving, externalizing, and internalizing objects. The life-cycle service is an implementation of DAA life-cycle services, which is a superset of the COS Life Cycle Service. HPDST life-cycle services support life-cycle operations for both simple objects (basic life-cycle) and application objects (compound life-cycle). An application object is a compound cluster of objects (some of which may recursively be application objects as well). Life-cycle operations on these are actually operations on object graphs. The life-cycle service supports the following operations on both simple and complex objects:

Creation. Factory Finders are used to activate creation.

Copy. Shallow-copy semantics are supported. Object references are copied, but the pointed-to objects are not; the new object will reference the same object as the old object.

Deep copy. As above, but the pointed-to object will be copied.

Move. This removes an object from one container, makes a copy, and renames it.

Delete. This removes an object if possible (some link semantics will not allow removal).

Throw away. This moves an object to the wastebasket object.

Externalize. This uses the marshaling facilities of the ORB to convert an object to a byte stream.

Internalize. This uses the unmarshaling facilities of the ORB to build an object from a byte stream.

The Smalltalk classes ORBObject, DSTtraversal, and DSTfactory Finder provide methods that collectively implement the life-cycle services.

9.4.9 Presentation/semantic split

The presentation/semantic split is defined as part of the DAA and is the main paradigm used by HPDST for implementing distributed objects. The policy supports multiple (possibly remote) presentation objects as views of one semantic object. Attributes and operations may be either part of the presentation object or part of the semantic object. The presentation object handles the bulk of the user interaction as well as processing which should be done locally. The semantic object maintains the shared persistent state and performs operations based on this state. The semantic object knows about its presentation objects and will send updates accordingly. Each presentation object knows about its semantic object and will communicate with it appropriately.

Since this is the main paradigm used by HPDST, the Smalltalk implementations of the presentation/semantic split are abundant. The DSTPresenter and DSTSemantic hierarchies are large and extensive (see Fig. 9.3).

9.4.10 Dataviews policies

Dataviews policies are rules that allow semantic objects in different images to communicate. They provide support for compound objects to share information. It is thus possible to have a price ticker object, a spreadsheet object, and a graph creator object all share common information.

Dataviews policies are implemented by the DAAport class, which provides an implementation of the dataviews protocol (part of the DAA). Semantic objects track their output port using these objects. The current support for dataviews in HPDST is extremely limited. Only the Smalltalk classes Number and TwoDList are tied into the dataviews protocol.

10

IBM SOMObjects

The SOMObjects toolkit is an IBM product that, among many other capabilities, provides a framework for developing distributed object-oriented applications based on a CORBA-compliant ORB. At the heart of SOMObjects is the System Object Model (SOM), which is the underlying technology targeted primarily at allowing the creation of *binary class libraries*. Binary class libraries are class libraries that were constructed using one object-oriented programming language and but that may be used from within another programming language. Binary class libraries allow the clients and the implementors of the classes be as decoupled as possible; the clients should not have to be recompiled if the implementation has changed internally. This type of sharing between different object-oriented development environments has been lacking, even though procedural libraries have been providing similar functionalities. SOM provides the necessary support to allow the creation of such object-oriented binary class libraries.

The basic enabler of such libraries is SOM IDL. SOM IDL is based on CORBA IDL and extends it in a number of ways necessary to support objects in the SOMObjects toolkit. The developer defines the interfaces of the objects to be included in the libraries using SOM IDL. These definitions are translated by the SOM compiler to the programming language of choice, where the methods are actually implemented. Since the interfaces are defined in SOM IDL, any programming language that has a binding for the IDL may be used for both the implementation and the invoking client. For clients, it must be possible to create and invoke requests, while for object implementations, the actual methods must be implemented. The client and the object implementation are totally decoupled; the interfaces are accessed in IDL, and so the client does not care (and does not know) what programming language was used for the object implementation.

The delivery of the requests from the client to the object implementation is done by the SOM runtime system (or the DSOM runtime system if the client and object are in different address spaces).

SOM stresses that libraries must be *binary* class libraries. This means that SOM provides an underlying runtime system that ensures binary usage of the libraries. Therefore, if an implementation change is performed that does not require a source code change to the client, no recompilation of the client is necessary. Changes to the object interface require client recompilation, since the access routines used by the client may have changed. These changes, however, are much less common; interfaces usually stabilize early in a development project's life, whereas implementations keep evolving. Changes that do not require recompilation in SOM include even such things as extending the class with more methods (actually changing the interface), adding superclasses (since SOM supports multiple inheritance), moving methods to superclasses, and even changing the size of the object. Most of these changes require client awareness in most all other object-oriented class libraries.

SOM ensures programming language neutrality through a series of design decisions. All interfaces are written in SOM IDL, and so clients can use any programming language that has a SOM IDL binding to access objects implemented in any programming language (that has a binding). This is sufficient for allowing programming language neutrality, but SOM goes a step further. SOM defines a common object model that is used by any application using SOMObjects. This object model is well defined yet is flexible enough to accommodate the object models of most object-oriented programming languages. For example, method resolution is flexibly controlled by the developer, and multiple dispatch strategies can be fitted to the appropriate programming environment or application. SOM defines a standard linkage convention allowing any programming language that can make external calls to activate the SOM runtime system and access SOM objects. This is not limited to object-oriented programming languages; in fact, the first programming language to have a SOM binding was the C programming language.

SOM includes a set of built-in libraries that make up the SOM runtime system. These classes provide the support required for the SOM object model, for method dispatching, for object reference management, and so on. The last component of the base SOM structure is the SOM compiler, which is used to translate the IDL specifications into a variety of implementation skeletons and client stubs.

SOMObjects provide much richer capabilities than are provided by SOM alone. While SOM remains the central technology of SOMObjects, and while all the added frameworks use SOM and the capabilities it provides, SOMObjects provides an extensive set of frameworks to be used by application programmers as a very rich infrastructure basis. These frameworks include

- *Collection and communication classes.* These provide support for standard data structures and socket communication wrappers as SOM objects that can be used by application programmers.
- *The Interface Repository framework.* This provides storage and retrieval capabilities for interface information and is used by SOM and other frameworks (e.g., Distributed SOM). It can also be used by application programmers who require access to meta information.
- *Distributed SOM (DSOM).* This is a CORBA-compliant ORB implementation that extends SOM with distribution transparency.
- *The Replication Framework.* This framework allows the construction of groupware applications where multiple users view the same semantic object and participate in the manipulation of this common view. The replication framework allows objects to be associated with one another as replicas of one semantic object. The framework then provides manipulation techniques that allow the synchronization of the replicas; if one replica will be changed, the change will be propagated to all of the other replicas. These replicas exist in separate address spaces and potentially on different machines. The replication framework does not use DSOM; rather, a specialized framework is provided for specifically supporting replicated objects.
- *The Event Management Framework.* This supports event management and callback dispatch, which is necessary in single-threaded environments but is often useful even in multithreaded environments that require certain integrity guarantees for event handling.
- *The Emitter Framework.* This allows programmers to quickly and easily create compilers that read IDL definitions and produce specialized output as defined by certain templates and algorithms. These are supplied by the programmer but are inserted into the framework in predefined procedures. This process is easy to perform, allowing multiple emitters to be created. This is useful for programming language binding creation but also for such things as producing automated documentation and information for CASE tools.
- *The Persistence Framework.* This provides SOM objects with persistence capabilities.

All of these frameworks provide an initial set of classes that can immediately be used by application programmers. These frameworks are all constructed in a modular and flexible way that allows the developer to extend any component by subclassing the default built-in class and implementing custom behavior. The frameworks are truly frameworks in the sense that multiple customizations are possible using simple replacement of different objects serving different purposes.

This chapter describes the SOMObjects Developer Toolkit, Version 2.0 as documented in IBM (1993a and 1993b). This version is supported on the AIX and OS/2 platforms and will be supported on other IBM and non-IBM operating systems including operating systems not used on personal computers or workstations (e.g., it will be supported on mainframe operating systems). The toolkit includes bindings for the C and the C++ programming languages; other programming language bindings will probably be available before this book is published. For example, the joint proposal for the Smalltalk-to-CORBA IDL binding (by HP and IBM—See Mueller, 1994a) is partly based on experience with binding SOM IDL to Smalltalk. Other programming language bindings for SOM will include non-object-oriented programming languages like COBOL.

10.1   The System Object Model (SOM)

The primary goal of SOM is to allow the production of programming language–neutral binary class libraries. SOM is the central component in the SOMObjects toolkit and provides capabilities used by all SOMObjects frameworks.

SOM separates interface specification and object implementation. Interfaces are created using the SOM IDL, while object implementations are done in programming languages which have SOM bindings. Interface definitions are also stored in the SOM Interface Repository and may be accessed as InterfaceDef objects to be used by application programs or by the SOMObjects components.

SOM is a very rich object model that can support most object models used today. It supports the notion of classes as first-class objects and metaclasses as objects describing the classes (or the classes' class, as in Smalltalk; see Goldberg and Robson, 1983). The SOM runtime system manages SOM at runtime. Class objects need to be created at runtime so that instances may be created. The class objects may then be accessed at runtime as objects, and methods can be performed for these objects. SOM supports class derivation and multiple inheritance. This allows it to support programming languages that require multiple inheritance as well as the various specifications coming out of the OMG. Many of the SOMObjects toolkit frameworks use multiple inheritance (e.g., see the use of multiple inheritance in the automatic generation of proxy classes in DSOM, discussed in Sec. 10.4).

Writing SOM applications involves the following:

- SOM IDL is used to define the interfaces and other definitions to be used.

- The SOM compiler is used to produce multiple translations of the interfaces. These will typically include header files to be used by the object's clients (implemented in one programming language), implementation skeleton files that will be used for the object implementation (which will be completed by the implementor of the object in a certain programming language), Interface Repository information, and more. The Emitter Framework (Sec. 10.7) describes how emitters can be constructed to produce additional translations of the IDL specifications.

- The client of the objects will then be developed. Include files generated by the SOM compiler will be used as if the SOM object were implemented in the client's programming language and running in the client's address space (modeled after local procedure calls). The client's program will include SOM runtime initialization code, since the management of SOM objects is done by a set of SOM components.

- The object implementation is completed based upon the skeleton produced by the SOM compiler.

- The client and implementation are compiled and linked, forming an executable. If the object implementation is changed at a later time with no changes to the interfaces, the client does not require recompilation. This is true even if the size of the object changes. When DSOM is used, the client and object implementation are not running in the same address space or necessarily on the same machine, so that the client may not even have to be halted for an object implementation to change.

10.1.1 SOM IDL

SOM IDL is based upon CORBA IDL and adheres to those definitions wherever possible. A number of extensions have been added to support SOM specific functionalities. All usages of these SOM specific IDL constructs should be delimited by

```
#ifdef
...
#endif
```

directives to allow easy location of non-CORBA-compliant constructs and automatic removal of them in later versions of SOM. For example, Implementation Statements (to be discussed below) are delimited by

```
#ifdef __SOMIDL__
...
#endif
```

directives, and private attributes or methods (not available in COBRA IDL) are delimited by

```
#ifdef __PRIVATE__
...
#endif
```

Since SOM IDL is almost identical to CORBA IDL, a full description of it is not provided here. Instead, a description of the major extensions included in SOM IDL is provided.

SOM IDL adds two type categories to CORBA IDL data types. For any SOM IDL type `T`, the type `unsigned T` is allowed in SOM IDL. CORBA IDL only allows `unsigned long` and `unsigned short`. Pointer types are also introduced by SOM IDL. For any SOM IDL type `T`, the type `T*` is allowed in SOM IDL.

The most important extension made by SOM IDL is the use of Implementation Statements. Implementation Statements specify implementation details and take the form of *instance variable declarations, passthru statements,* or *modifier statements.*

Instance variable declarations use syntax similar to that of ANSI-C to declare class instance variables having a SOM IDL type. These variables are private in the C++ sense; that is, they can be accessed only by the class's methods. These are different from the __PRIVATE__ directives, which are used for private IDL methods and attributes.

Passthru statements allow blocks of code to be passed unmodified to the output files generated by the SOM compiler. A passthru statement specifies what result file the block should be copied to as well as what the code block to be copied is. Passthru statements are provided primarily for backward compatibility with SOMObjects Version 1.0.

Modifier statements are used to provide additional information about IDL definitions. They provide information about interfaces, types, attributes, and methods. Table 10.1 details the most commonly used SOM modifier statements.

10.1.2   Inheritance in SOM

`SOMObject` is a class provided as part of the SOMObjects toolkit. This class defines behavior common to all SOM objects. Any class must therefore inherit (directly or indirectly) from `SOMObject`. SOM supports the notion of class inheritance, as is common in most object-oriented programming languages (e.g., in C++ as defined in Ellis and

TABLE 10.1   SOM Modifier Statements

Modifier	IDL Construct	Description
nodata	attribute	Specifies that an instance variable should not be created for the attribute. The get and set accessor methods are created for attribute access. This is used for attributes which are calculated and not stored
noset	attribute	Specifies that a set accessor methods should not be created by the SOM compiler; only a get accessor methods is created. Used for readonly (or const) attributes
persistent	attribute	Specifies that the attribute is part of the persistent representation of the type. This is used by the Persistence Framework.
callstyle=oidl	interface	Informs the SOM compiler to use old IDL style syntax.
classinit=<proc name>	interface	Informs the SOM compiler of the procedure to be used for initializing the class object. The SOM compiler will create a skeleton for the procedure implementation which will be completed by the class developer.
dllname=<filename>	interface	Specifies where the class implementation is loaded from (which library file).
functionprefix=<prefixstring>	interface	Used by the SOM compiler to prefix all methods in the class with the prefix string. This option is used to partially resolve name space conflicts.
majorversion= minorversion=	interface	Specifies the class's major and minor version numbers.
metaclass=<classname>	interface	Specifies the class's metaclass
method	method	Specifies that the method can be overridden.
procedure	method	Specifies that the method should not be overridden and informs the SOM compiler to use efficient direct dispatching for this method instead of requiring run time dispatching.
noooverride	method	Specifies that the method should not be overridden by subclasses but does not have the effect on the SOM compiler of changing the dispatching strategy.
override	method	Specifies that the method will be overridden by this class.
offset ; namelookup	method	Directs SOM as to the resolution method to be used for this method

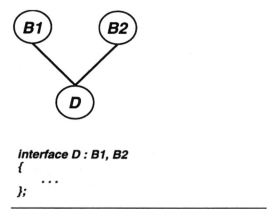

interface D : B1, B2
{
    . . .
};

Figure 10.1 A multiple inheritance example.

Stroustrup, 1990). Multiple inheritance is supported by SOM, and the class hierarchy is therefore a rooted directed acyclic graph.

Multiple inheritance introduces the possibility of potential conflicts when two superclasses define a method by the same name. SOM uses a *leftmost precedence rule*. This means that the method used will belong to the class that was leftmost in the inheritance specification. This rule is also known as the *first subclass rule*. Figure 10.1 presents an example in which the class D inherits from both B1 and B2. Both of these base classes define a method called f. In SOM, D would inherit f from B1, since it is the first subclass (left on the superclass list in the interface clause).

SOM provides two ways by which the default conflict resolution rule can be overridden. The simplest way is to override f in class D and manually call one or both of the f implementations in the base classes. The other possibility is to change the ambiguity resolution rule by using a metaclass method. The default SOM ambiguity resolution rule is defined in the SOM class SOMClass. The programmer can override this by defining a metaclass for class D (instead of using the default metaclass SOMClass) and overriding the procedure for constructing the class's method table.

10.1.3 Metaclasses in SOM

In SOM, every class is itself an object. The class object has methods and can be used like any other object at runtime. Since the class is itself a SOM object, it must have a class—this is the metaclass (a class of a class). The class is then said to be an instance of the metaclass. The metaclass defines the methods that can be performed by the class. This includes such methods as object constructors (i.e., instance creation and initialization methods of the class can be added to the metaclass), methods for changing the default class hierarchy management (e.g., the resolution of ambiguities resulting from multiple inheritance), and more.

A metaclass of a class is defined using the `metaclass` modifier (see Table 10.1). A metaclass does not have to be specifically defined for every class; it may be inherited. All metaclasses inherit (directly or indirectly) from `SOMClass` (which in turn inherits from `SOMObject`, so that the metaclass hierarchy is part of the SOM object hierarchy). If no specific metaclass is defined for a class, then the default `SOMClass` metaclass will be used.

Metaclasses have their own inheritance hierarchy structure, which may differ from the class inheritance hierarchy (as opposed to Smalltalk, for instance; see Goldberg and Robson, 1983). SOM provides a unique capability regarding metaclasses that is supported by only a few object-oriented development environments. While allowing a class to freely name its metaclass and its superclasses, SOM guarantees that no method resolution errors (errors of the type "message not understood") occur for subclasses. Figure 10.2 illustrates the problem that may occur with named metaclasses and class inheritance. The code is shown in Smalltalk syntax for concreteness. In this illustration, `Account` objects have an `addOwner:` method used for adding an owner to the account. This method checks for a maximum number of owners, which is a single value for all accounts and is therefore defined by the `Account` class object. This value is supplied by the `maxOwners` method defined in `AccountClass`. The code in `addOwner:` might look like

```
addOwner: aPerson
    | max |
    max : =  self class maxOwners.
    ....
```

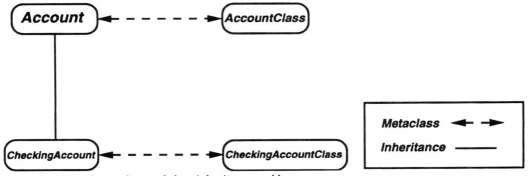

Figure 10.2 Named metaclass and class inheritance problem.

"self class maxOwners" invokes the maxOwners method on the metaclass object to retrieve the common value.

Suppose now that an instance of CheckingAccount (which names its own metaclass) were to invoke the maxOwners methods under the metaclass scenario shown by Fig. 10.2. A problem would occur, since the CheckingAccountClass metaclass does not implement the maxOwners method. When the self class maxOwners code was performed at runtime, a method resolution error would occur.

Smalltalk solves the above problem by not allowing metaclasses to be freely named by the programmer. The metaclass hierarchy matches the class hierarchy, and in our example, CheckingAccountClass would inherit from AccountClass. SOM provides a different and more flexible solution. SOM allows the metaclass to be freely named for each class. SOM will then automatically create a Derived Metaclass, as shown in Fig. 10.3. This automatic metaclass generation will guarantee correct ambiguity resolution, since the explicitly specified metaclass is first on the inheritance list. An explicit definition of the maxOwners method in our example will therefore always be used before an inherited implementation. Derived metaclasses are also used when multiple inheritance is involved. In this case the class has multiple superclasses, so that the metaclass must inherit from multiple sources.

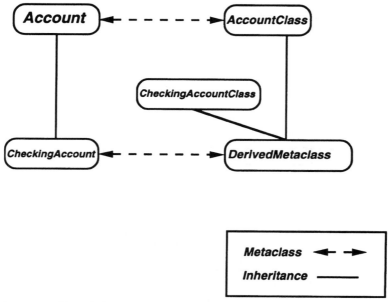

Figure 10.3 The solution: DerivedMetaclass.

10.1.4   Method resolution in SOM

SOM supports a very flexible notion of method resolution. In fact, three resolution strategies are supported:

- *Offset resolution*. This is the strategy used by C++ virtual functions. Polymorphism is implemented based upon the inheritance hierarchy and relying on static typing. To perform method resolution, a method token is retrieved from the class that first defined the method. This token is used as an index into the object's method table. Note that the names of the method and the class that first defined the method (in the superclass chain) must be known at compile time, since the method table access code is created at compile time.

- *Name-lookup resolution*. This is the strategy used by Smalltalk. Polymorphism is implemented using the object type and the methods it (or one of its superclasses) implements. Name lookup does not require the class name to be known at compile time. Instead, the search for the method is done at runtime. When an object receives a method invocation, the class object is used to determine which code will be executed.

- *Dispatch-function resolution*. This allows any dispatch strategy to be implemented by the object implementation. This strategy allows the class to provide any criteria for determining what code will be performed as a result of the method invocation. This strategy is similar to name lookup resolution in that the class object is consulted. However, the class is not restricted to a particular algorithm in terms of its response; it may use any lookup algorithm. Details of dispatch function resolution are beyond the scope of this chapter; the interested reader is referred to IBM (1993a).

The three method resolution strategies are ordered by decreasing performance and increasing flexibility. The default resolution strategy used in SOM in the programming language bindings available for SOM thus far (C and C++) is offset resolution.

10.1.5   SOM runtime objects

The SOM runtime environment includes a number of objects which are required for internal runtime support. These objects are automatically created when the environment is initialized:

```
SOMObject

SOMClass

SOMClassMgr

SOMClassMgrObject
```

The first three of these objects are class objects. SOMObject is the root class for all SOM classes and provides behavior common to all classes. It must be created to allow any class (and therefore any object) to be created. SOMClass plays the parallel role for metaclasses. Finally, SOMClassMgrObject is an instance of SOMClassMgr (and can therefore be created only after SOMClassMgr is). SOMClassMgrObject manages the classes used by the application and the environment, including the loading of the classes from the class libraries.

10.2   The Collection and Communication Classes

The SOMObjects toolkit provides a library of collection and iterator classes. These classes are similar to other commercially available library classes implementing various collections such as sets, lists, and dictionaries. The benefits for a SOMObjects user of using the SOMObjects collection classes over other such class libraries are twofold. First, these classes are already provided as part of the toolkit, relieving the user of the work (and the cost) required to integrate a new library into the environment. Second, the classes are SOM classes; multiple programming languages and environments may therefore make use of the collection classes. IDL definitions are provided for these classes to enable this language independence.

The collection classes are based on work done by Taligent (which is partly owned by IBM) and are primarily modeled as C++ collection classes. Figure 10.4 shows the hierarchy of the SOMObjects collection classes. An additional hierarchy provides classes for iterating over

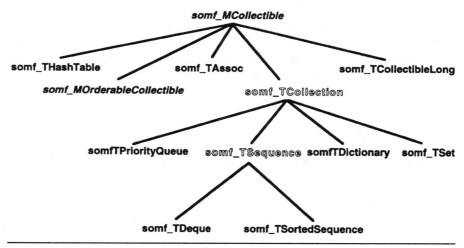

Figure 10.4 Hierarchy of SOMObjects collection classes.

collections. Like many collection class libraries, the SOMObjects collection classes are composed of abstract classes and concrete classes. The abstract classes in Fig. 10.4 (shown in outline) are `somf_TCollection` and `somf_TSequence`. The concrete classes provide data structures and operations implementing dictionaries, hash tables, linked lists, priority queues, queues, sets, sorted sequences, and stacks.

The `somf_MCollectible` and `somf_MOrderableCollectible` are *mixin* classes. These classes do not normally have semantics allowing them to be used by themselves; they are usually used in conjunction with other classes to produce new subclasses with specialized behavior (see Booch, 1991). The `somf_M` prefix is used in SOMObjects to denote mixin classes. The two mixin classes used in the collections hierarchy are used to provide operations necessary for containment in collections. This means that for an object to be contained in any of the collection classes' objects, its class must inherit from one of the collection mixin classes. By doing so, the object will supply necessary operations that will be used by the collection objects. For example, `somf_MCollectible` provides the `somfIsEqual` and `somfIsSame` operations, which are required for such collection operations as insertion, retrieval, and deletion (in most collection types).

In addition to the collection classes, the SOMObjects toolkit provides wrappers for socket functionality (Stevens, 1990). The `TCPIPSockets` class provides access to TCP/IP sockets, and the `IPXSockets` class provides access to Netware IPX/SPX sockets. The actual socket classes supplied with the SOMObjects toolkit support DSOM, the Replication Framework, and the Event Management Framework. Developers can create their own socket subclasses for their own specialized behavior. Note that the supplied classes provide the general framework for implementing such classes, but the concrete classes supplied which are used by DSOM, the Replication Framework, and the Event Management Framework should not be directly used by developers.

One of the advantages provided to a developer by these socket classes is that the socket interface is expressed in IDL (in the file `somssock.idl`) and can therefore be used in multiple programming languages and environments. Note that since most of the classes are intended to be used by internal frameworks of SOMObjects, only the IDL does not completely conform to CORBA IDL.

10.3 The Interface Repository Framework

The Interface Repository Framework is a set of classes providing programmatic access to the IR in SOMObjects. Applications may use these classes to access the definitions stored in the IR. These classes implement the IR application programming interface (API) as defined by CORBA. The framework, together with the actual SOM IR database, provides a CORBA-compliant implementation of the IR and the IR interfaces. The SOM IR extends the CORBA definitions by storing additional information such as SOM modifiers and providing operations to access this information.

The actual SOM IR database is a set of flat files. Each IR file is constructed by running the SOM compiler with the IR emitter over a specific `.idl` file. The file `som.ir` is provided with the toolkit and contains the IR information for the built-in SOM classes.

The API supported by the SOM Interface Repository Framework conforms to the CORBA definitions as presented in Chap. 3. The main operations provided by the classes in the framework are summarized in Table 10.2. The structure of the IR follows the CORBA definitions. The SOM IR maintains objects of type `ModuleDef`, `InterfaceDef`, `AttributeDef`, `OperationDef`, and so on. The `Repository` object is the container through which access is initiated and is accessed using the `SOM_InterfaceRepository` macro, using `SOMClassMgrObject`'s `somGetInterfaceRepository` operation, or using the `RepositoryNew()` method. The SOM IR also provides full TypeCode support.

TABLE 10.2   SOM IR Operations

Operation	In Type	Description
contents	Container	Return a sequence of the contained IR objects.
describe_contents	Container	Return a sequence of ContainerDescription structures for the contained objects.
lookup_name	Container	Return a sequence of objects matching a name. The lookup recursively returns all such objects in the containment hierarchy under the target container object.
describe	Contained, XXXDef classes	Return a Description structure containing the IDL definition information.
within	Contained, XXXDef classes	Return a sequence of container objects which contain the target object.

10.4 Distributed SOM (DSOM)

SOM uses a CORBA IDL as the language for defining interfaces. This allows applications using SOM to be language-independent; classes written using SOM can be used for any language for which a SOM IDL binding exists. However, SOM does not address distribution issues; this is handled by DSOM. DSOM extends SOM by allowing applications to use distributed objects in a location-transparent manner in addition to the implementation transparency provided by SOM. Objects in distributed networks or in other address spaces on the local machine may be accessed and used by programs in a transparent manner. In fact, the actual location of the object will usually be hidden from the program using the object. SOM IDL is used by DSOM to ensure that the program using the object does not depend on the object implementation. The client is therefore decoupled from the object implementation following the decoupling principle of CORBA. While using the base SOM functionality provides programming language independence within a machine, DSOM adds the distribution capabilities requested by CORBA. DSOM therefore extends SOM to supply an implementation for a CORBA 1.1-compliant ORB that is used by applications using SOMObjects.

SOM and DSOM were designed to be CORBA 1.1-compliant, adding only functionalities that are not fully defined in CORBA, yet must be addressed by any real ORB implementation. For example, life-cycle services were not yet defined when SOMObjects came out as a commercial product. Since any commercial ORB implementation must address how objects are created, moved, copied, and deleted, DSOM provides its own API for remote object creation. Another example is the issue of ORB initialization, which will be defined only in CORBA 2.0. SOMObjects will evolve over time to use the specifications accepted by the OMG so that the SOMObjects toolkit will remain as close to the OMG specifications (in terms of both ORB functionality and Object Services) as possible.

Apart from such extensions, SOM and DSOM follow the CORBA definitions closely. Some examples of DSOM's implementation of the CORBA 1.1 concepts are:

- The DSOM class SOMDObject implements the CORBA 1.1 Object interface. SOMDObject objects implement the CORBA object reference concepts as proxy objects. The proxy represents the actual object (which may be on any local or remote machine) in the client's address space and supports the delivery of requests from the client to the object implementation. The client can therefore maintain a view where the location of the object is irrelevant, since the local proxy serves as the object from the client's point of view. Proxies are created by DSOM whenever an object reference is passed; the client program need not be aware of this distribution issue. See Sec. 10.4.1 for more details.

- The implementation repository is used by DSOM as outlined in CORBA. `ImplementationDef` objects are used as defined by the CORBA `ImplementationDef` interface.

- The SOMOA DSOM class implements CORBA's BOA while providing a number of extensions. SOMOA uses the SOM compiler and the SOM runtime system to implement method dispatching. SOMOA also provides some of the ORB interfaces as defined by CORBA object adapters (e.g., `create`) as well as implementing the methods required for performing the mapping between object references and object implementation.

- DSOM supports the Context object as defined by CORBA.

- DSOM provides a full implementation of the CORBA DII.

10.4.1 DSOM proxies

`SOMDObject` objects implement CORBA 1.1 object references using proxy objects (see Fig. 10.5). When an object reference is passed to a client program, DSOM automatically creates the proxy object in the client's address space and makes the connection with the real object implementation using its own services. This automatic creation is done in a dynamic manner according to the object type. For example, if an object reference to an Account object is passed to a client program, DSOM will automatically build an `Account_Proxy` class that inherits from `Account` as well as from `SOMDClientProxy` (see Fig. 10.6).

`SOMDClientProxy` inherits from `SOMDObject` and provides the actual proxy support. In the construction of this new class (`Account_Proxy`), the SOM runtime system is used to dynamically create this class for use in the client's address space. `Account_Proxy` will include a method implementation for each `Account` method that

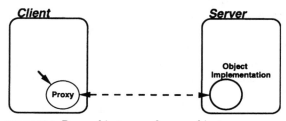

Figure 10.5 Proxy objects as reference objects.

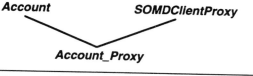

Figure 10.6 Automatic proxy class generation.

will simply delegate to the real object's method implementation using the DSOM remote invocation support.

10.4.2 DSOM client programming

DSOM client programming is similar to SOM client programming. Differences arise because the DSOM runtime environment must be used for remote life-cycle operations. These services are provided by the DSOM Object Manager SOMDObjectManager (derived from the ObjectMgr) class, which implements life-cycle operations, object location, and object activation operations. Developers may create their own specialized object manager by deriving a class from ObjectMgr and installing an instance of the new class as the object manager. SOMDObjectMgr provides basic life-cycle capabilities (creation and destruction), operations for locating servers implementing a certain type, and finding objects by id.

The steps taken by the client programmer in writing a DSOM client application are:

- *Initialization.* The DSOM runtime environment must be initialized (using SOMD_Init) before DSOM is actually used. All classes which will be used by the program must also be initialized by calling XXXNewClass (e.g., for the Account class, AccountNewClass would be called).

- Actual access of remote objects through the use of local proxies is then enabled. Objects are located or created using the DSOM runtime environment, as will be detailed below.

- Methods are invoked on remote objects through the local proxies. A proxy object appears to the client as the real object (in the local address space), and therefore requests to this actual remote object seem like no more than local SOM requests. This provides the DSOM distribution transparency.

- Object references passed as arguments and return values are automatically converted to proxies by the DSOM runtime environment completing the support for distribution transparency. Arguments and return values which are proxies are automatically converted to object references, so that when the object implementation receives the request, only standard object references appear.

- Objects that have already been created can be looked up by clients. Instead of creating a new object implementation whenever a service must be provided, the client may look for an already created object implementation.

- DSOM also supports externalization of proxy objects. It is possible to save references to remote objects by creating a string representation for any proxy and later using this external representation to reconstruct a usable proxy. The remote object must be identified and located. This is done by using the DSOM somdGetIdFrom Object and somdGetObjectFromId operations.

- When the remote object is not used by the client, it may be destroyed. Operations are provided to release only the proxy, only the object implementation, or both.

- Finally, the client program will finalize the DSOM runtime system by calling SOMD_Uninit and any other SOM finalization procedure.

10.4.3 Creating remote objects

DSOM provides various methods for creating objects. These differ as to whether the client cares about which server will actually create (and contain) the object implementation. The simplest operation is somdNewObject. In this case, the client does not care about the actual server where the object implementation will be instantiated, and SOMD_ObjectMgr is free to use any server that it deems appropriate. If the client wants the object implementation to be created in a specific server, other creation methods should be used. For example, somdFindServerByName can be used to access a specific server. This operation creates a proxy object for the remote server on which the somdCreateObj operation may be used to actually create the object implementation in that server. Servers may be selected by name, by id, or by whether the server supports a class specified by the client; this last option provides a simple and partial Trading Service. Figure 10.7 shows the two phases of creating the server proxy and creating the object proxy.

If the object is to be created using a specialized constructor, somdNewObject should not be used, since the default construction process, somNew, will be inappropriate. Instead, somdGetClassObj should be used to access the class object, which can then be used to invoke the specialized constructor.

10.4.4 DSOM server programming

Servers execute and manage object implementations in SOMObjects. The SOMDServer class provides instances of default server objects.

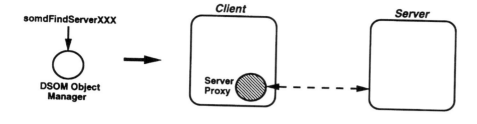

Phase 1 - Creating the Server Proxy

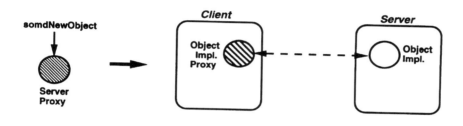

Phase 2 - Creating the Object Implementation Proxy

Figure 10.7 Creating the server proxy and the object proxy.

This class may be subclassed to provide specialized server behavior. The server object includes a SOMOA object—the SOM implementation for the Basic Object Adapter. Together these objects provide functionality for object activation, request dispatching, marshaling and unmarshaling, and so on.

For a server to be activated, its definition must be registered in the SOMObjects Implementation Repository as an ImplementationDef object. When a request to start a server is made through the somdd daemon (or during manual startup), the Implementation Repository is searched for this object. When it is found, the server may be started and the DSOM connection process continued; otherwise, service cannot be provided. The ImplementationDef object is maintained in the SOMD_ImplDefObject global variable and is used by the DSOM runtime system.

A server program usually includes the following steps:

- *Activation.* Server activation is done by the DSOM `somdd` daemon or by a manual process. The `somdd` daemon runs on every machine that provides DSOM support and is used as an "agreed-upon meeting place" for clients and servers. This is used by the DSOM runtime system to request service startup. Manual startup can be performed either by a command line request or by an application.

- *Initialization.* The server program must go through an initialization process that includes:

  1. DSOM runtime system initialization using `SOMD_Init`
  2. Initialization of the `ImplementationDef` object after retrieving it from the Implementation Repository
  3. Initialization of the object adapter using `SOMD_SOMOAObject = SOMOANew();`
  4. Application-specific initialization
  5. Invoking `_impl_is_ready` on the SOMOA object to inform the server that request processing may be initiated

- *Processing requests.* This is done either by passing control to a SOMOA loop (`_execute_request_loop`) or by maintaining control over the main loop within the application and calling `_execute_next_request` multiple times.

- *Exit.* By calling `_deactivate_impl` on the SOMOA object to finalize request processing and by calling finalization routines such as `SOMD_Uninit` and `SOM_UninitEnvironment`.

10.4.5 The DSOM management objects

Every server has a server object that functions as the server manager together with the object adapter. The default objects supplied by DSOM are the SOMDServer object and the SOMOA object.

The `SOMDServer` class provides methods for creating objects (`somdCreateObj`), deleting objects (`somdDeleteObj`), and finding class objects by id (`somdGetClassObj`). Methods are also provided for mapping between SOMObjects and SOMDObjects and for methods dispatch for SOM objects. These are used by SOMOA when mapping remote requests to local method invocations. When SOMOA is ready to dispatch the request, it calls `somdDispatchMethod` on the SOMDServer object, which will usually invoke `SOMObject::somDispatch`. The developer may override this default behavior.

If an object reference is required (for example, for a return value), SOMOA is used to create SOMDObject references using `create`, `create_construct`, or `create_SOM_ref`. Each of these has a slightly different implementation and representation; these details are beyond the scope of this chapter (see IBM, 1993a).

10.5 The Replication Framework

The SOMObjects Replication Framework facilitates the creation of applications where multiple users share a common view and interact with one another based on this common data. Such applications are sometimes called "groupware" applications. Applications of this type are becoming more common in the marketplace as time goes on, since they provide increased possibilities for cooperation and efficient use of information systems. In such applications, users that are geographically distributed can share the common view, which makes it appear as though they were sitting in one room and using a whiteboard. Groupware applications may involve a common board of a computer game, a military scenario and plan presented on a map, or a design of an electric circuit board, among others. The users interact by changing their views and having these changes propagated to the other users' views. For example, this would allow one user participating in a circuit design session to propose a change in the design by manipulating the graphical representation of the design. This would be propagated to the other participants, who would see the change appear in their views. They could then comment on the change by making other alterations to the design.

The SOMObjects Replication Framework provides the basis for such cooperative applications. The framework allows an object to be replicated in multiple address spaces in such a way that each replica is aware of the possible presence of other replicas. A change to the object is propagated to all the other replicas. Propagation is independent of the number of replicas. In fact, the application does not know the number or the locations of the replicas. The replicas may even dynamically change; i.e., a replicated object may dynamically leave or join the group of replicas.

The Replication Framework is based on the Model-View-Controller (MVC) paradigm of Smalltalk (Goldberg and Robson, 1983). The object state serves as the model, while the different replicas are manipulated by the application views. The views and the model communicate using an agreed-upon protocol. The Replication Framework provides the necessary support for managing the model. The interfaces for viewing the model are handled by the application. This is similar to the semantic/presentation split paradigm offered by HP Distributed Smalltalk (see Chap. 9).

To use the Replication Framework, the developer will inherit from the SOMRReplicbl class. For example, if an ElectronicCircuitDesign object is to be replicated, then a new class will be created by the

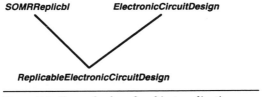

SOMRReplicbl   *ElectronicCircuitDesign*

ReplicableElectronicCircuitDesign

Figure 10.8 Example class for object replication.

developer, as shown in Fig. 10.8. By inheriting from SOMRReplicbl, the new class will support replication semantics. Support for the Replication Framework is also provided by the SOMR class. An instance of this class must therefore be created if the Replication Framework is used.

The Replication Framework uses socket type communication for propagating the changes between the different replicas. To do this, the framework must agree on the ports on which messages are sent. The Replication Framework uses a file, called the .scf file, specifying these attributes. This file is used only for the initialization process. Once the communication has been set up, the framework does not use any files, allowing it to provide good performance.

The Replication Framework uses a master-slave protocol. Among the replicas, one of the objects is the master. All propagations are actually done by that one object. This means that when any object desires to make a change, it will inform the master, and the master will then propagate the change. During the change, no other replica may ask for a change (this is similar to a lock being formed by the master). The number of messages for a single update for N replicas is therefore either $N - 1$ (if the master performed the update) or $N + 2$ (one message to effectively obtain the lock, one to send the update to the master, $N - 1$ messages for the update, and one to release the lock). The updates will always be serialized, since the master provides the "monitor segment." In addition, the master will always send the messages to the replicas in the same order, so that no matter which replica triggered the change, the order in which the replicas receive the change remains the same. The Replication Framework includes algorithms supporting fault tolerance that will elect a new master if the master replica should go down.

10.5.1 Operation and value propagation

The Replication Framework supports two propagation models. In operation propagation, the actual method which causes the change is propagated. If one of the replicas is modified as a result of invoking a method on it, then the method specification is propagated to the other replicas and invoked for all the other replicas. Note that for the replicas to achieve the same state, some limitations on the method must be observed. For example, if the method uses the physical machine's clock as a part of the state change computation, then the changes of the different replicas may differ. In value propagation, on the other hand, the actual state changes of the object are propagated to the replicas.

The two different propagation models differ in what is being propagated. Choosing the best propagation method is important for the application's performance. Each of the models involves a tradeoff between propagation time and the time for producing the state change. Each of the two models has characteristics making it more suitable in certain cases. As a rule of thumb, if the update methods are easily computed and cause large change sets, then operation propagation will be more efficient. If the change methods are computationally intensive (or otherwise resource intensive) but produce small change sets, then value propagation is preferable. In cases where the tradeoff is less clear, the selection should be based upon application benchmarks. Figure 10.9 shows the tradeoff space.

The actual decision on the propagation made is done by the method which updates the object. If operation propagation is used, then the _somrLockNlogOp and _somrReleaseNPropagate operations will be used to delimit the method which performs the update. If value propagation is used, then the _somrLock and _somrRelease PropagateUpdate calls delimit the updating method.

10.5.2 Directives

Since the objects participating in the Replication Framework are distributed on different machines, it is possible that events will affect

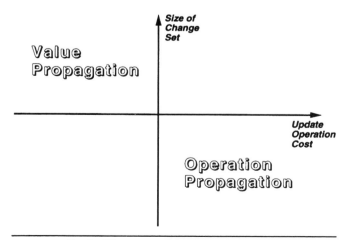

Figure 10.9 Tradeoff between value and operation propagation.

TABLE 10.3   SOM Replication Framework Events

Directive	Description
LOST_CONNECTION	Connection with other replicas has been lost but attempts to reestablish it are being made; no updates to the replica should be attempted.
CONNECTION_REESTABLISHE D	Connection to the other replicas has been reestablished.
BECOME_STAND_ALONE	The Replication Framework has given up trying to reconnect to the other replicas.
LOST_RECOVERABILITY	The .scf file cannot be updated.

the connectivity and availability of the different replicas. The actual propagation management is done by the Replication Framework classes, yet the participating objects must have a way of being informed of changes to the connection topology. This is accomplished through the use of directives. Directives are methods that are sent from the Replication Framework classes to the applications using the replicas and inform them of events such as network faults. Examples of such events are shown in Table 10.3. To accept directives and provide a response, the application should override the somrDo Directive method which is called by the Replication Framework classes with an argument specifying the directive string.

10.6   The Event Management Framework

The Event Management Framework provides support for registering interest in events and receiving notifications when an event occurs. It is similar to event handling in most windowing systems and other event managers (e.g., Teknekron, 1994). Using the event manager in SOMObjects involves registering interest in the event (by providing a callback specification to be invoked when the event occurs) and passing control to a central framework function that never returns. The program will invariantly remain in that function until one of the events takes place. At this time, the callback function will be invoked. When the callback function terminates, control is passed back to the main loop function; this is depicted in Fig. 10.10.

The Event Management Framework is extensively used by DSOM and by the Replication Framework. Any interactive applications

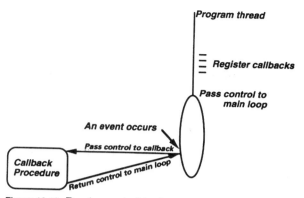

Figure 10.10 Passing control to the main loop and callbacks.

requiring event handling and using DSOM or the Replication Framework must therefore use the Event Management Framework (so that event handlers will not clash).

The Event Management Framework is especially used in single-threaded systems. In multithreaded systems, where it is possible to spawn multiple threads in any application process, event management becomes much simpler. If an application is required to respond to multiple events, for example, separate threads can be created, each with a responsibility toward a different event. This design relies on the possible usage of multiple threads; if only a single-thread model is supported, event management must be handled by a central component which reacts to all events and delegates the work to different callback functions. However, even in multithreaded systems, the Event Manager Framework is useful. Multithreaded environments must ensure thread safety. Scenarios in which multiple threads may require access to shared resources must be managed. The event manager itself in SOMObjects is guaranteed to be thread safe; its consistency is guaranteed even in the presence of concurrent operations. The event manager interactions are guaranteed to produce results identical to a serial ordering of all interactions. This is an important feature which can be used even when multiple threads are involved.

The Event Management Framework is defined in IDL, so that access can be provided for multiple programming languages as long as the IDL binding is available. Such bindings are easily created using the Emitter Framework.

10.7   The Emitter Framework

As is appropriate for a CORBA-compliant implementation, the heart of SOM is the IDL interface definitions. All interfaces are written in

IDL. The SOM compiler is then used to produce a translation of these interfaces to the native programming language or programming environment in which the implementation is actually done. SOM is intended to support many programming languages and to produce a common framework to be used by many programmers, using many programming languages, on many operating systems, running on many hardware platforms. For each such programming language that will be used with SOM, an IDL compiler must be produced; this will enable translating the IDL definitions to that programming language. To facilitate and ease the production of such translators, the SOMObjects toolkit includes the Emitter Framework.

The Emitter Framework is designed to allow developers to write extensions to the SOM compiler. Such extensions can be used to write any translator for the IDL specifications. These translators take the form of "emitters" which emit translated components derived from the IDL specifications and translation rules and formats. These emitters can then be embedded in the IDL compiler to allow for the new translation. This is mainly useful for programming language bindings for IDL, but it is also very useful for other purposes, such as generating automatic documentation from the interface definitions and deriving component information which can be used by CASE tools.

Figure 10.11 illustrates the function of the Emitter Framework components. The IDL interfaces and definitions are read by the IDL parser to produce an Abstract Syntax Graph (ASG). This graph repre-

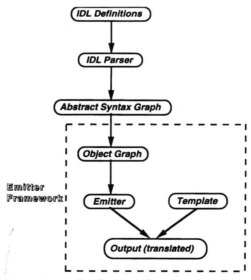

Figure 10.11 The Emitter Framework components.

sents the IDL constructs, such as operations, parameters, attributes, and interfaces. This part of the SOM compiler is identical for all translators and helps decouple the various translators from dependence on specific IDL syntax. All translators are based on the same IDL syntax, so this decoupling places no limitations on translators. It assures that if the IDL syntax were to be changed, only the IDL parser would be affected and the large base of translator code would not need modifications (so long as the new semantic constructs supported the semantic constructs used by developers).

Once the ASG has been created, it is used to form an object graph that represents each element in the ASG as an object. Each such object is an instance of one of the built-in SOMTXXXEntryC classes, where XXX is replaced by the various syntactic elements (e.g., SOMTParameterEntryC). The programmer may replace one of these built-in classes by a specialization allowing new object types to populate the object graph and allowing for an additional level of extensibility and flexibility.

Once the object graph has been created, the emitter begins the translation process from the object graph structures to the desired output format. This process uses a template for the output format which specifies the location and format of the various structural components. Since most of the formatting specifications are part of the template and not part of the emitter, it is very easy to modify the formatting rules of the translation.

The emitter is an instance of the built-in SOMTEmitC class or one of its (direct or indirect) subclasses. When a programmer extends the SOM compiler with a new translator, a new class in the SOMTEmitC hierarchy will typically be created. In addition, a template file will be created. The new emitter class will inherit most of its functionality from SOMTEmitC and override some of the translation generation methods. The template is used for defining location and formatting rules for the generated output.

10.7.1 Emitters, templates, and entries

The Emitter Framework includes three categories of entities which participate in the translation process. The emitter itself is the process manager, the template defines the output format, and the entity objects represent sections of the IDL specifications and are used as entry points with which translation behaviors can be associated. The emitter uses the information maintained in the entry objects, and uses the template for output creation. Each of these entities is implemented by a class in the Emitter Framework: the emitter class SOMTEmitC, the template class SOMTTemplateOutputC, and the class hierarchy rooted at SOMTEntryC.

TABLE 10.4   SOM Emitter Framework IDL Default Sections

prologS	Information that is emitted before any other.
attributeS	Class attribute information.
methodS	Class method information. Is invoked iteratively for every method in the class.
interfaceS	Information for the interface.
moduleS	Module information.
baseS	Information about the parent classes; used when a class inherits from others.
epilogS	Information emitted after all others.

Creating a new emitter typically involves two things: the emitter and the template. First a subclass of SOMTEmitC is created to provide specialized control of the translation process. The somtGenerate Sections is the method that is most commonly overridden to provide the customized specification determining what is emitted and in what order. This is done by attaching emitting methods for standard sections of the IDL. Some of the default sections are given in Table 10.4. Each of these sections has a method which is used to emit the section. By overriding the default definitions of these methods, customized emitter behavior can be defined.

Once the emitter class has been defined, the output is created by rendering the syntax graph on the template definition. The template defines the output format, locations, and symbols which will make up the resulting files. Template creation is a simple yet very powerful process. It is very easy to create emitters in a matter of minutes or hours for more complex translations, since much of the specification goes into the template definitions.

10.8   The Persistence Framework

The SOMObjects Persistence Framework provides persistence support for SOM objects. The Persistence Framework allows SOM objects to be stored in files, which allows the objects to exist after program termination. The objects can later be reconstructed to the internal representation. In many respects the Persistence Framework is really an externalization/internalization framework. However, the Persistence Framework is not limited to using external files; it can be

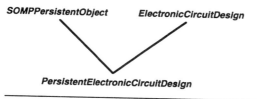

SOMPPersistentObject   *ElectronicCircuitDesign*

PersistentElectronicCircuitDesign

Figure 10.12 Creating a class for persistent objects

extended to use other storage strategies. The Persistence Framework provides both a base service that can be immediately used by developers as is to provide simple persistence and a complex framework that can be extended to support specialized persistence mechanisms. Customization can include customized object clustering, specialized persistence formats, and the use of specialized repositories. The basic service uses ASCII and binary files, simple object clustering, and externalization type formats.

To allow a SOM object to be saved using the Persistence Framework, the object's class must inherit from the SOMPPersistentObject class, (see, for example, Fig. 10.12). A persistent object must support the saving of its state to the persistent store. If the developer does not wish to provide extra code for making the object persistent, then the class must conform to the storing methods supplied by the default framework classes. The default classes provide generic facilities and do not handle special data elements. The storing operations provided by the default classes therefore handle only the CORBA-defined data types (e.g., short, long, array, union, double, etc.). Thus, any object that desires to be made persistent must be composed only of CORBA data types; otherwise specialized storing and retrieving methods must be provided. The default storing methods are similar in style to the write_* methods used in the Externalization Service discussed in Chap. 6. The default class used for storing object states comprising of CORBA data types only is SOMPAttrEncoderDecoder.

10.8.1 Persistent object ids and groups

Persistent objects are assigned persistent object IDs (OIDs). The persistent OID must be associated with an object before it can be externalized or internalized. This OID uniquely identifies a persistent object. The ID string value not only identifies the object but also embeds information about how the object should be stored and where. This string has the format of

<group manager class name>:<group name>:<group offset>

The group manager class name defines what class will be used to store the object. The group name defines where the object will be stored, and the offset specifies where precisely in the group the object will be stored, since multiple objects will typically be stored in a single group. For example, the default group manager class is SOMPAscii, so a possible persistent OID might be

SOMPAscii:myfilename:0

where myfilename is the name of a file. The SOMPAscii manager uses ASCII files for the persistence of objects; myfilename would therefore be the file in which the object would be stored at offset zero.

Persistent OIDs may be associated with an object in one of three ways:

1. An OID can be explicitly created (by creating and populating a SOMPPersistentId object) and associated with the object using sompInitGivenId.

2. A SOMPAssigner object can be used to create an OID (using sompInitNextAvail) and associate it with the object.

3. The developer may request that the object be placed near another object and the OID derived accordingly (a simple form of object clustering).

The last method is the one which is most commonly used. Typically only one object will be explicitly given an OID and the rest of the objects will be given OIDs by placing then near a previously identified object.

Groups are the unit of object storage and are collections of objects stored together in a single file (or some other persistent organization). Groups are represented in the Persistence Framework as instances of SOMPIOGroup and are associated with a group manager object (whose class derives from SOMIOGroupMgrAbstract). The group manager defines how the objects are stored, whereas the group specifies where the objects are stored.

The SOMObjects Persistence Framework supplies two built-in group managers: SOMPAscii and SOMPBinary. SOMPAscii is the default group manager; it stores each group as a single ASCII file. The SOMPBinary group manager is similar, but it stores the data in a binary format (e.g., the number 17 will not be stored as two characters "1" and "7" but as the binary representation of 17). Both the SOMPAscii and the SOMPBinary group managers have similar characteristics. The SOMPAscii group manager is usually used at the initial development stages, since it is easier to debug (since the storage can be viewed in a text editor), and is later replaced by the SOMPBinary group manager, since it is more efficient to use.

10.8.2 Storage formats

The file containing the persistent representation of a group of objects is a combination of persistent object information and group specification information. These are coupled together throughout the file; prior to the information for the actual object externalization, the object's grouping information is described. These sections have a format which is different from that of the sections holding the persistent object information. The format of the persistent object is called the Persistent Object Format (POF), whereas the format of the group information is called the I/O Group Format (IOGF).

Every persistent object is associated with an Encoder/Decoder object. The class of the Encoder/Decoder determines what POF will be used for storing the object. The Encoder/Decoder class is where the actual read and write methods are implemented and is responsible for the object externalization/internalization. The association of a persistent object with an Encoder/Decoder can dynamically change over the lifetime of the object. Clearly, when the object is restored, the same Encoder/Decoder class must be used as when it was stored. The association with the Encoder/Decoder is at the object level; therefore, different instances of the same class may still be associated with different Encoder/Decoder objects. It is also possible to associate a class with an Encoder/Decoder.

The SOMObject Persistence Framework provides a default Encoder/Decoder called `SOMPAttrEncoderDecoder`. `SOMPAttr EncoderDecoder` requires that every persistent element in the object be an attribute, that the accessor methods of `get` and `set` be defined, and that the attribute be declared with the `persistent` modifier in the IDL file. `SOMPAttrEncoderDecoder` uses a very simplistic POF that may be sufficient for many applications. For example, an object of type `Security` having attributes for the security's symbol, its name, the stock exchange name, and a price may be stored as

(4) (6) symbol (3) OBJ (4) name (14) Object Corp (14) stock exchange (4) NYSE (5) price (6) 43.125

The first number indicates how many attributes are stored. The remainder is a list of pairs, each pair comprising the number of characters in the string and the string. Each attribute is represented as two of these pairs; one specifying the attribute name and one specifying the value.

In many cases the default Encoder/Decoder will be sufficient, but in some cases the developer must create a customized Encoder/Decoder. The developer would do this by creating a subclass of `SOMPAttr EncoderDecoderAbstract` and overriding the `sompEDWrite` and `sompEDRead` methods. To associate the newly created Encoder/

Decoder, the developer would use the `sompSetEncoderDecoder Name` method to associate it with a single object or the `sompSet ClassLevelEncoderDecoderName` if the Encoder/Decoder is to be associated with a class of objects.

10.8.3 Saving and restoring

The saving and restoring process uses the framework components as described above. The steps performed when storing (externalizing) an object are:

- Create a Persistent Storage Manager (PSM) by using the `SOMPPersistentStorageMgrNew` method to instantiate the `SOMP PersistentStorageMgr` class. This initializes the Persistence Framework.
- Create the object to be stored.
- Assign a persistent OID to the object in one of the three ways described above.
- Use the `sompStoreObject` method to store the object based on the information in the persistent OID.

To restore the object, the following steps are followed:

- Initialize the Persistence Framework as above.
- Create a new persistent OID object using `SOMPPersistentIdNew`; this is not a persistent object but a persistent OID.
- Assign the actual OID to the persistent OID object using `somutSet IdString`.
- Use `sompRestoreObject` to restore the object.
- Use `somFree` to free the persistent OID object.

The saving and restoring process also incorporates a passivation/activation process. Just before storing the object, the Persistence Framework calls the object's `sompPassivate` methods, and just after restoring the object, the `sompActivate` method will be invoked for that object. These methods are defined in `SOMPPersistentObject` but should be overridden by objects which have to supply specialized activation or passivation behavior.

Once the object has been stored, the PSM provides various management capabilities. For example, the `sompObjectExists` method can be used to determine whether an object with a certain persistent OID exists. An object can be deleted from its persistent store using the `sompDeleteObject` method. The storage of the deleted object is not reclaimed unless one of the objects in the group is marked using `sompMarkForCompaction`. In this case, the next time the marked object is stored, a garbage collection process will compact the entire group (file).

DEC ObjectBroker
and Microsoft OLE2

ObjectBroker is a DEC CORBA 1.1-compliant technology for creating distributed heterogeneous systems. ObjectBroker [previously called Application Control Services (ACA Services)] provides platform-independent facilities for locating and invoking applications and for handling interapplication interaction and control in a multivendor environment. ObjectBroker is available on a surprisingly large number of platforms. These include Microsoft Windows and Windows NT (both on an Intel architecture and on an AXP architecture), Macintosh System 7.0 or 7.1, OSF/1, Ultrix, SunOS, HP-UX, IBM AIX, and Open VMS (both VAX and AXP architectures). ObjectBroker supports TCP/IP, DECnet/OSI, and Microsoft's WinSock API. In addition, ObjectBroker is unique in its interfaces to Microsoft technology. The Common Object Model (which will be discussed in this chapter) allows ObjectBroker objects to interoperate with Microsoft OLE2 objects. This interaction uses a DCE RPC-based protocol. ObjectBroker also provides integration with Visual Basic, allowing Visual Basic programs to make ObjectBroker calls.

ObjectBroker provides registration and invocation capabilities for applications running in a distributed heterogeneous environment. Registration includes tracking capabilities and application availability management, while invocation includes server startup within a user-defined context. Marshaling and translation are done both during invocation and within an active session. In addition, the OLE2 interfaces supported by the Common Object Model defined by DEC and Microsoft allow OLE and DDE messages to be mapped to and from ObjectBroker messages, thus allowing for desktop integration.

ObjectBroker is one of the more mature and advanced CORBA-compliant products available. A full implementation of ACA Services as a mature product was available as early as 1992 (see DEC, 1992a–1992c). The present version is ObjectBroker 2.5 (see DEC, 1994a–1994d), which is partially described in this chapter [since this product is a full implementation of CORBA, many of the details are omitted in this description and can be found in DEC (1994a–1994d)]. The maturity of the product is apparent in every facet of the software, from the multitude of platforms supported through the very comprehensive documentation set supplied by DEC. In fact, the documentation set details the process for constructing CORBA-based applications and is recommended even if not using ObjectBroker. The implementation language used in ObjectBroker (i.e., the programming language for which a binding exists) is the C programming language.

11.1 ObjectBroker

ObjectBroker (OBB) is DEC's implementation of a CORBA 1.1-compliant Object Request Broker. One of its main advantages is its availability on a very large number of platforms, as shown in Table 11.1. In a world where CORBA 2.0 has not yet been defined and implemented, and where ORBs of different vendors do not interoperate, OBB comes closest to providing cross-platform distribution. Apart from providing ORB functionality, OBB provides numerous software development and system management tools which are necessary for supporting real production systems. Many of these tools and tech-

TABLE 11.1 Platforms Supported by DEC ObjectBroker

Platform	Support for:
DEC OSF/1 AXP	Client and Server
DEC ULTRIX RISC	Client and Server
SunOS	Client and Server
IBM AIX	Client and Server
HP-UX	Client and Server
Microsoft Windows	Client
Microsoft Windows NT (AXP/Intel)	Client and Server
Apple Macintosh System 7	Client
DEC OpenVMS (AXP/VAX)	Client and Server

niques are derived from ACA Services, DEC's first-generation inter-operability product, and are thus fairly mature. Finally, OBB provides interfaces to popular PC environments, in hopes of tapping a huge market and providing a high-level communication channel between PCs and more powerful Unix workstations.

OBB follows the CORBA specification. Interfaces are written in IDL and stored both in IDL files and in the OBB Interface Repository. The Repository Manager provides sophisticated tools for browsing and inspecting IDL definitions. OBB commands and utilities are then used to generate stubs and skeletons to be used by clients and implementors of the objects. Other commands and utilities support capabilities for viewing and changing these definition files.

Operations defined in IDL are mapped to methods implemented by the object implementation. An OBB *implementation* is the collection of methods implementing an object; these implementations are described using the Implementation Mapping Language (IML) and are stored in the Implementation Repository and managed by the OBB Repository Manager. OBB also provides a Method Mapping Language (MML) which is used to specify options used when performing resolution of operations to methods. Using the MML, the developer may form a *method map* which is stored in the IR and is used by the ORB when performing method resolution.

Once the interfaces and maps have been written and installed, the client and the server may be implemented. Using the compiled client stubs or the Dynamic Invocation Interface, the client programs access the object implementation functionality. OBB provides support for the C programming language only in version 2.5 (as required by CORBA 1.1). These server skeletons are then used to implement the method implementations. The method implementations are linked with the skeletons and with the method dispatching routines. Finally, the different components are registered with the appropriate repositories and configuration maps.

OBB is made up of various components. The core components of OBB include the *Agent*, the ORB, and the Basic Object Adapter. The Agent is responsible for marshaling and unmarshaling requests sent by clients to implementations, and for locating the appropriate implementation servers. The ORB is a library implementing CORBA specifications, and the BOA is a library implementing a CORBA-compliant basic adapter. OBB maintains a number of repositories. These store IDL, IML, and MML definitions. An Interface Repository is used to store IDL interface information, and an Implementation Repository is used to store IML definitions for implementations. The OBB Repository Manager utility may be used for managing both of these repositories.

In addition to these components, the OBB Registry maintains configuration information necessary for deploying a system. The Registry maintains the following information categories:

- *Implementations.* A list of implementations available on each machine.

- *Configuration.* Platform-specific information necessary for interoperability.

- *Security.* Access Control Lists specifying authorization information.

- *Advertisement.* Information used for selecting an object implementation to service a certain request.

Other components in an OBB system include the Context Object and a collection of utilities and commands. The Context Object encapsulates information pertinent to the platform, environment, and user and is used by various components of OBB. Utilities may be used to change preferences by editing this Context Object. This Context Object is a central mechanism by which configurations and preference information may be stored and should not be confused with the context argument used in CORBA operation invocations.

OBB defines many commands and utilities that are necessary for developing and deploying distributed systems. The utilities include the Repository Manager, the Implementation Viewer, the Context Object Editor, a System Administration tool, a Network Tester, a DDE Listener, and an OLE Network Portal. A full command-line interface is supplied by OBB (mostly derived from ACA Services), allowing full application startup and management using a command-line interface and scripting mechanisms.

OBB provides a binding to Microsoft Visual Basic, thus providing an interface to a very popular PC development tool. Other PC-related interfaces include DDE and OLE capabilities, as will be detailed in following sections. This support is provided through both a set of API routines available for OBB applications and a more complete set of models and interfaces allowing full interoperability with OLE2; this is being developed in conjunction with Microsoft. These interfaces allow cooperative computing applications which make use of the popular PC platforms.

OBB places great emphasis on providing capabilities for integrating legacy applications so that they can be used in any environment. These capabilities are mostly derived from ACA Services capabilities, as will be described in the next section. Existing applications may be encapsulated using an OBB interface and then used as information servers. The OBB Script Server allows command-line invocation styles to be used for activating such applications, making the integration even easier (no actual APIs need be created).

11.2 ACA Services

OBB is not only an ORB implementation; it is also a rewrapping of functionality provided in ACA Services. This section describes some of these functionalities as well as how applications using ACA Services may be easily migrated to work within OBB. This section does not fully describe the entire option set of ACA Services; refer to DEC (1992a–1992c) for more information.

Although ACA Services provide functionality that is similar to an ORB-based environment, the terminology and strategy used in ACA Services often differ from those in OBB and other CORBA-compliant environments. This can often be confusing to developers performing evaluations of the product. In this respect, OBB is an important improvement on ACA Services; while maintaining the functionality expected from ACA Services, it completely follows CORBA.

Table 11.2 shows the ACA Services classes. These classes are divided into two groups: logical classes that represent an application abstraction, and physical classes that represent the implementation of the services provided by the abstractions. Methods implement oper-

TABLE 11.2   ACA Services Classes

Class Name	Abstraction Level	Inherits From	Description
ACAS_OBJECT			Root of hierarchy.
ACAS_CLASS	Logical	ACAS_OBJECT	Root of logical hierarchy.
ACAS_APPLICATION	Logical	ACAS_CLASS	An object providing services.
ACAS_DATA_OBJECT	Logical	ACAS_CLASS	An object which represents data used by an application.
ACAS_STORAGE_CLASS	Logical	ACAS_CLASS	A class used to integrate storage management.
ACAS_METHOD	Physical	ACAS_CLASS	An implementation for an operation.
ACAS_METHOD_SERVER	Physical	ACAS_CLASS	A collection of methods used for implementing a service.

ations (or messages) that are coupled with the applications. These methods are organized in method servers, which are similar to function tables in OLE2, as will be explained in a later section. This commonality makes it simpler to integrate the two object models.

After the domain has been analyzed and application design has been completed, information and meta-information about the applications are stored in the ACA Services class repository. The information is stored using the Class Repository Language (CRL), which is analogous to a combination of IDL and an implementation and context definition language. The class repository stores all information about the applications, including their attributes and the method maps. These maps define how each message is mapped to one or more methods which implement the requested functionality. These method maps are used during method resolution to determine which method gets called. This can be dependent on such things as platform and user. The normal service process is to initiate a service request, perform method resolution to determine the target, and service the request using a method implementation. During the method resolution process, both a server and the actual method are determined. The selection of the method uses the method maps, depending (among other things) on the signatures and on the user preferences stored in the context object. This information is encoded using the Context Object Language (COL) and created using a command-line interface or a programmatic interface.

The context object contains preference information that is used throughout ACA Services. It is basically a container of preference tables. Each table groups a set of related attributes (e.g., a name registry table contains information about named applications and dynamic libraries). Each attribute that is an entry in the table has a name, a type, and a value or a set of values. Context objects may be defined at the user, group, or system level. Each level overrides the next level if both contain a preference value; thus the user value will be used over the group value.

The server selection process includes verifying that the server can provide the required services and verifying that the server has available sessions. A session allows a client to have an extended interaction with the server. Once a server has been selected, the Control Server (a separate process) starts up a server process and manages the registration of method servers. Each new operation that is used will cause a method to be selected and possibly a method server to be registered with the Control Server.

Integrating an application using ACA Services can be performed using various techniques. If the application is being coded, the application can be tightly integrated by making direct calls to ACA

Services. If source code is not available but an API for the application is, then the API functions can be wrapped in stubs that can be used for ACA Services integration. If only a command-line interface for the application is available, then the command-line interface and the ACA Services scripting features may be used. ACA Services provides script application classes and script method servers, allowing methods to be interfaced as scripts. This is an important feature for integrating legacy applications where the source code may not be changed and no public API is available.

11.2.1 Migration from ACA Services to ObjectBroker

Systems which have been using ACA Services may be migrated to the ORB-based APIs and components. For this, DEC provides the *ObjectBroker Migration Guide* (DEC, 1994d). This document steps through the migration process, detailing what has to be changed and how to do it. This is an invaluable document for users of ACA Services that wish to use OBB.

In general, although ACA Services and OBB are based on similar concepts and methods, the detailed model, behavior, and functionalities provided by each product can differ substantially. The migration process is therefore not a simple one-to-one process, and the *Migration Guide* must be carefully read. The differences can be broadly categorized as API differences, syntactic differences, and differing commands and utilities.

The migration process involves three main stages. First, the ACA Services' Class Repository Language (CRL) definitions must be converted to IDL, IML, and MML. For this, OBB supplies the CONVERT utility. This utility accepts input in the form of CRL and produces IDL, IML, and MML files. Since IDL generation from CRL may require intervention and tweaking, the process will usually be

- Use CONVERT to generate IDL from CRL.

- Modify the IDL as needed.

- Use the COMPILE or GENERATE utility to generate the IML and MML from the IDL.

The *ObjectBroker Migration Guide* provides more details regarding the actual mapping between CRL and IDL, IML, and MML.

After the IDL, IML, and MML have been registered in the repositories, the client and server application may be migrated. This includes using the new stubs in the client and the new skeletons in the server, as well as other modifications which are specific to ACA Services versus OBB. These include changing the initialization procedures, the error handling, and other areas in which the ACA Services model differs from the OBB model. Finally the application-specific code must be modified to use the correct data types, the correct APIs, and so on.

11.3   Object Linking and Embedding 2 (OLE2)

OLE2 is a Microsoft Windows technology that is the basis for future Microsoft Windows operating systems and environments. It is an object-oriented enabling technology that packages and supports interfaces and frameworks. It is a programming paradigm that replaces API functions with interface constructs called *Windows Objects*. Each interface is a set of functions that are packaged together. These function groups do not limit or specify implementation details; they are pure interface specifications and may be used by applications using any programming language or paradigm. The actual implementation may be performed in any programming language without affecting the interfaces. The implementation is also not limited in terms of its form or its location. OLE2 is a very important and complex set of technologies. This chapter cannot even begin to describe all the features of OLE2; a separate book must be devoted to it (and in fact many are). The purpose of this section and the next is merely to outline what OLE2 is and how the Common Object Model is used to interface with ObjectBroker. For a full discussion of OLE2, the reader is referred to Brockschmidt (1994).

OLE2 is much more than an interface definition and manipulation technology. In fact, OLE2 is the central technology on which Microsoft will base most of future Windows offerings. OLE2 can be broadly classified into a core component and additional layers or frameworks. The core component defines the model used in OLE2, and the additional layers define specifications and concrete implementations for a variety of operating environment functionalities required by applications.

The core of OLE2 is the Component Object Model (COM). COM is both an abstract model and a concrete implementation. COM as a model is targeted to provide language-neutral, decoupled, binary interfacing between different components. The implementation of COM (provided as a DLL named COMPOBJ.DLL) implements a special Windows Object called a *Component Object*. Component Objects provide a client with access to tables of functions; these tables are interfaces as defined by the COM specification (see Fig. 11.1). An interface is a strongly typed "contract" between software components that is designed to provide a small but useful set of semantically related operations. The COM implementation supplies the standard lan-

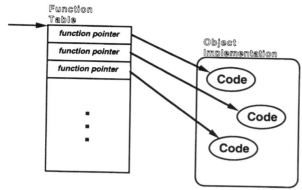

Figure 11.1 OLE2 function tables.

guage-neutral way of creating these objects. COM does not limit where the implementation of the functions is located. This is the key to the ObjectBroker link.

Function pointer tables represent interfaces. Actual interface objects wrap these function pointer tables in COM. Clients therefore do not directly access function pointers but use the interface abstraction for name-based access to functionality. Windows Objects encapsulate any number of interfaces and provide operations for navigating these interfaces. A client that is using one interface can use the QueryInterface operation to access the other interfaces supported by the object implementation. The QueryInterface operation is available in all OLE2 objects. New interfaces can be dynamically added and discovered safely and efficiently without disturbing current interface clients. This allows dynamic evolution of object interfaces and object systems in a safe and continuous manner.

The use of interface-based interaction is fast; this results from the simplicity of COM. When a client retrieves a handle to another object, method invocation using the interface is simply an indirect function call using two memory pointers. The performance overhead of an invocation of the object model therefore is only a small number of processor instructions, over a standard function call. Thus performance considerations place no limitations on the use of OLE2.

The COM implementation is also responsible for marshaling and unmarshaling of function arguments and return values. This is provided across address spaces and also potentially across machines. This additional capability is presently used for a single Windows architecture but has been designed to be easily extended to support distributed heterogeneous networks.

Based upon COM, OLE2 provides an extensive set of frameworks that are necessary for applications. These are defined as OLE2 interfaces and therefore use the capabilities provided by COM. The additional layers provided by OLE2 are

- Structured Storage
- Data Transfer
- Object Embedding
- Object Linking
- In-Place Activation
- Automation

OLE2 (COM and the above frameworks) can be separated into three levels as shown in Fig. 11.2. COM provides the lowest level, which is intended to form the common definitional infrastructure of OLE2. The next level includes Structured Storage (Compound Files) and Uniform Data Transfer. These are general services that are not targeted specifically for Compound Document support. The rest of OLE2 provides the Compound Document technology. Compound Document support is partitioned in OLE2 into Object Embedding, Object Linking, and In-Place Activation. In fact, historically OLE derives from Compound Documents (OLE1 provided Compound Document support only); hence the central position of Compound Documents in OLE2.

11.3.1 Structured Storage

OLE2 provides built-in interfaces defining the Structured Storage layer. These interfaces define how file systems should be structured and created. Structured Storage file systems are composed of *storage objects* and *stream objects*. Storage objects are similar to directories or folders, while stream objects are similar to files.

While the Structured Storage layer is an abstract specification, OLE2 provides a concrete implementation of this specification; the

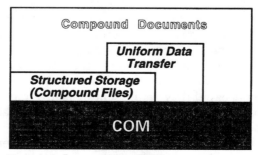

Figure 11.2 Layers within OLE2.

implementation is called *Compound Files*. Compound Files will be upward-compatible with the native file systems in future versions of Windows.

The Structured Storage specification and the Compound Files implementation are very powerful frameworks that may be customized and extended by developers. They are therefore not limited to a single file system strategy and can be enhanced by the programmer. Although the framework can be enhanced, Structured Storage and Compound Files standardize the information layout within a compound file. This is extremely important for facilitating consistent file management, since it allows the structure of the file system to be standardized for access from multiple applications (as it must be). Without this standardization, file managers and file browsers could not be built. Therefore, while the internal information of stream objects remains private to the creating application, the general structure of a compound file is standardized by OLE2.

As an example, consider Microsoft Excel files. Excel worksheets are stored using the Binary Interchange File Format (BIFF). Each BIFF file contains a collection of BIFF records. BIFF is a private format defined and used by Excel and users of the Excel SDK. In versions prior to Excel5 (BIFF2, BIFF3, BIFF4), the BIFF records were contained in the BIFF file as a simple data stream. It was thus possible to read the Excel file as a byte stream and interpret the BIFF records. In Excel5, the file is stored using OLE2 Structured Storage. It is therefore no longer possible to read the file as a byte stream. The file is now a "file system within a file" and may have a complex organization internally. To access the worksheets, charts, etc., it is necessary to use the OLE2 Structure Storage API set to get access to the various components in the Workbook. The internal streams are still composed of BIFF records, but, to access these, OLE2 calls must be made. Once such a stream is retrieved, normal BIFF5 interpretation may be performed.

11.3.2 Uniform Data Transfer

Uniform Data Transfer is the data transfer technology provided by OLE2. It is based on COM and on Compound Files and unifies all forms of data transfer, such as Dynamic Data Exchange (DDE), clipboard cut/copy/paste, and drag and drop.

Uniform Data Transfer is a COM-based framework. It defines the notion of a *Data Object* which is used for all forms of data transfer. Data transfer involves two steps. In the first, a pointer to the Data Object is passed from the data producer to the data consumer. Once this transfer is complete, the Data Object protocol is used to access the actual data. This is uniformly available for all data transfers, eliminating the necessity for different APIs for each transfer type. In addition, since all transfer mechanisms use Data Objects, an additional level of decoupling is achieved. An application can be written to use the clipboard for data transfer and later converted to use drag and drop. The Data Object definitions will remain intact, and only small segments of the data transfer procedure are changed.

Since OLE2 applications are Compound Document–oriented using object linking and embedding, Data Objects must allow Compound Documents to be transferred as easily as simple text is. This has to be supported for all transfer methods.

11.3.3 Object Embedding

A Compound Document is a container of objects. Each object has an application source (the application it was created by); for example, a spreadsheet object's source can be Microsoft Excel. Compound Document containers may be arbitrarily complex and recursively embed other objects. OLE2 maintains the embedding structures and the source applications, and most importantly, provides a uniform protocol to enable the different applications involved in the Compound Document to interact.

11.3.4 Object Linking

Containers can also include links to other objects. The OLE2 object linking facility for Compound Documents uses separate interfaces that must be implemented by the applications. These are fully specified in OLE2. Linking involves a new OLE2 concept called the *Link Source*. The Link Source allows Compound Documents to reference other objects (possibly other Compound Documents to an arbitrary complexity level) using a standardized and uniform paradigm. The Link Source for an object in a Compound Document can be accessed using OLE2 mechanisms.

The difference between linked and embedded compound document objects is in the real location of the object. A linked object continues to physically reside in its original location and only a link to the object is created in the compound object. Embedded objects are copies of the original objects that are physically stored within the compound object. These object types differ in the way they are copied, the way they are stored, and what limitations they place on access and activation.

OLE2 also introduces objects called *Monikers* that support object linking. A Moniker object encapsulates both the linked object and the code that is responsible for the correct bindings for that link. Bindings in the context of Monikers mean the responsibility for enforcing and maintaining the link, so that the Moniker is responsible for enabling the connection.

11.3.5 In-Place Activation

In-Place Activation (sometimes called Visual Editing) is the OLE2 capability that allows (among other things) a Compound Document to be intuitively used by users. For example, a Compound Document may be formed including a Microsoft Word document, an Excel spreadsheet, and a chart (e.g., Fig. 11.3). This Compound Document object embeds (or has links to) other OLE2 objects. When the user manipulates this Compound Document, each component behaves in accordance with its native application. Thus, when the user wishes to modify the text in the document, Word semantics are used. If spreadsheet data are to be changed, Excel is used. OLE2 permits each object to be supported in place by its own application.

11.3.6 Automation

Automation is an additional OLE2 technology that allows any OLE2 object to publish function sets that may be invoked by clients. Automation defines the protocol for describing these function sets to

This is an example of what a Compound Document might look like.

This text was created by Microsoft Word. The source is remembered so this text will always be edited using Word. The numbers below were created by Microsoft Excel and so will remain an Excel spreadsheet component. The chart will behave according to its source as well.

1	8
2	1 0
3	3
4	6
5	6
6	5
7	1 2
8	8
9	4
1 0	1 1

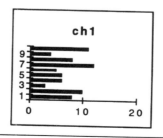

Figure 11.3 A Compound Document Example

be used by other programs. This can be used for building repositories, for dynamic invocation style mechanisms, for scripting, and for macro programming.

11.4   The Component Object Model (COM)

After the brief introduction to OLE2, this section provides a little more detail on the Component Object Model. COM is both a specification (a model) and an implementation (COMPOBJ.DLL). COM is the model defining the basis for what a Windows Object is as well as defining the basic ways in which it is created and used. It defines what interfaces are, how objects are created, and how marshaling is done. It implements the support for interfaces (as well as implementing some central interfaces), object creation, and cross-address space marshaling.

A Windows Object is any object that supports the IUnknown interface (recall that an interface is a group of functions). IUnknown supports two concepts that are central to OLE2: interface access and reference counting. The QueryInterface operation is used to retrieve a pointer to any interface supported by the object (assuming that a pointer to any of the object's interfaces is already held by the caller). This is the central mechanism by which functionality is accessed in OLE2. The AddRef and Release operations in the IUnknown interface support the notion of reference counting for any Windows Object.

COM addresses the central issue of the initial creation of a pointer to an object's interface (once one is acquired, a pointer to any of the object's interfaces can be acquired; the only question is how the first is acquired). The COM implementation defines the notion of a *Component Object*. A Component Object is a Windows Object that may be associated with a unique class identifier (CLSID). This identifier is used for mapping the object type to the implementation of the interface (e.g., a DLL file or an EXE file). The COM implementation supplies procedures that accept a CLSID and return a pointer to an instantiated and ready-to-use object.

CLSIDs are 128-bit data structures. For example, the hexadecimal representation of a CLSID may look like

00062205-0000-0000-0000-000000689200.

The CLSID of an object is returned by the GetClassID operation defined in the IPersist interface. This interface is a base interface in OLE2, and the GetClassId can be customized by the object implementor. IPersist also provides standard marshaling that can be used if no specialized requirements are necessary.

Once the CLSID is retrieved, the `CoCreateInterface` operation is used to create the object. This operation obtains an object implementing the `IClassFactory` interface for the class identified by the CLSID and uses the `IClassFactory::CreateInstance` operation to create the object.

Some CLSIDs will be returned by actual instances of that type. However, the process has to start somewhere; to instantiate the first object in any program, a CLSID must be accessed. The *registration database* is where CLSIDs are registered for the Component Object classes (using the `REGEDIT` program to create `REG` files). Registration can also be done programmatically so that dynamic type generation is supported.

11.5   DDE and OLE Interfaces

ObjectBroker provides interface routines for DDE as well as OLE. DDE allows applications to exchange information using a client/server relationship between two processes. ObjectBroker facilitates the creation of a DDE-aware server, thus utilizing this communication method. Support is provided for using DDE to communicate between Windows applications and applications interfacing with ObjectBroker on any platform. Tables 11.3 and 11.4 provide the interface routines used by the client and the server utilizing DDE. Tables 11.5 and 11.6 describe the interface routines used when the OLE protocol is used

TABLE 11.3   ObjectBroker DDE Client Interface

Routine	Description
DDESRV_Ack	Send an acknowledgment. The client acknowledgment is received by the server that has previously called OBB_DDE_SendData with AckRequired set to true.
DDESRV_Advise	Allows a client to request the creation of a warm or a hot data link. Allows for updated data to be supplied to clients.
DDESRV_Execute	Executes a request sent by a client. The server will call OBB_DDE_SendAck to specify positive or negative acknowledgment.
DDESRV_Initiate	Starts a DDE conversation between a client and a DDE server. Multiple initiate requests create multiple DDE conversation sessions.
DDESRV_Poke	Used by the client to send data to the server.
DDESRV_Request	Used by the client to request a data item from the server. If the item is available the server uses the OBB_DDE_SendData routine; otherwise, the OBB_DDE_SendAck routine is used with a negative acknowledgment.
DDESRV_Terminate	Used by the client to terminate a conversation.
DDESRV_Unadvise	Allows the client to request the deletion of a warm or hot link.

TABLE 11.4   ObjectBroker DDE-Aware Server Routines

Routine	Description
OBB_DDE_Register	Registers a DDE aware server
OBB_DDE_SendAck	Sends acknowledgments (positive and negative) from a DDE aware server to a DDE client.
OBB_DDE_SendData	Sends data from a DDE aware server to a DDE client.
OBB_DDE_SetServerAttributes	Allows a DDE aware server to change attributes at runtime after it has been registered.
OBB_DDE_SendTerminate	Used by the DDE aware server to notify clients that it is terminating a conversation.
OBB_DDE_Unregister	Unregisters a DDE aware server with ObjectBroker.

for interprocess communication. Once more, the server must be OLE-aware before such interaction can occur (using the OBB_ORB_OLE_Register() routine).

However, the real interfacing technology between ObjectBroker and OLE is the Common Object Model. The Common Object Model (although COM stands for Compound Object Model, some publications use COM as Common Object Model! This is very confusing since

TABLE 11.5   ObjectBroker OLE Interface Method Routines

Routine	Description
IClassFactory_CreateInstance	Requests the server to create an instance of a class. This is returned to the client for subsequent usage.
IClassFactory_AddRef	Add a reference to a data object.
IClassFactory_Release	Frees a reference to a data object.
IEnumFORMATETC_Next	Returns elements from an enumeration of the formats supported by the server.
IEnumFORMATETC_Reset	Resets the format enumeration sequence. This routine and the previous routine serve as an iterator over the supported formats.
IAdviseSink_OnClose	Called when the object has been closed.
IAdviseSink_OnDataChange	Called when a data object has changed.
IDataObject_GetData	Retrieves data from an object placing it in server storage.
IDataObject_QueryGetData	Used to test the availability of a data format.
IDataObject_DAdvise	Establishes a link between a data object and a sink through which the sink can be informed when the object changes.
IDataObject_DUnadvise	Deletes a link as created by IDataObject_DAdvise.
IEnumOLEVERB_Next	Returns elements from an enumeration of the verbs supported by the server.
IEnumOLEVERB_Reset	Rests the verb enumeration sequence. This routine and the previous routine serve as an iterator over the supported verbs.
IOleObject_Close	Used to close an object; notifies the server.
IOleObject_DoVerb	Notifies an object of a request to execute one of its verbs.

TABLE 11.6 ObjectBroker OLE Server Routines

Routine	Description
OBB_OLE_CreateDataAdviseHolder	Used by a server to delegate advisory tracking to the OLE server library.
OBB_OLE_Register	Registers an OLE aware server with ObjectBroker.
OBB_OLE_SendOnClose	Used to close an OLE client.
OBB_OLE_SetServerAttributes	Allows an OLE aware server to change attributes at runtime.
OBB_OLE_ReleaseDataObject	Release resources associated with a data object that are controlled by the OLE server library.
OBB_OLE_Unregister	Unregisters an OLE aware server.

the two models are so closely related) is a DEC/Microsoft joint technology intended to allow ObjectBroker and OLE2 to work together. It is intended to allow applications using DEC ObjectBroker to cooperate and communicate with OLE2 applications. This cooperation extends ObjectBroker platform interoperability by adding true Microsoft Windows access. The Common Object Model technology includes a communication protocol that is based on the DCE RPC.

The Common Object Model is the foundation for an architecture developed by DEC and Microsoft allowing interoperability between OLE2 objects and ObjectBroker objects. It is an extension to COM that is fully upward-compatible with OLE2. It uses a DCE RPC-based protocol to allow ObjectBroker objects to participate using a subset of core OLE2 functions. Using the Common Object Model, applications using OLE2 and ObjectBroker may interoperate across a variety of platforms, including Microsoft Windows, Microsoft Windows NT, OSF/1, SunOS, IBM AIX, HP-UX, Ultrix, and others.

DEC and Microsoft are proceeding with the Common Object Model as an open process for technology. This means that the Common Object Model specifications will be published for industry review and comment. Specifications will be provided to standards bodies and to the industry as a whole. The Common Object Model and its use of DCE RPC will be made freely available.

DCE-Based Interoperability

This appendix describes the joint submission to the CORBA 2.0 Interoperability and Initialization RFP by DEC, HP, Hyperdesk, IBM, NEC, and OSF based upon the specifications provided in Andreas et al. (1994). This proposal is a major contender for adoption by the ORB2.0 Task Force as the approach to be taken for providing ORB interoperability. The submission details how ORB interoperability can be achieved by providing both a high-level framework for interoperability and a low-level protocol using the interoperability characteristics of the OSF's Distributed Computing Environment (DCE). The approach taken by the submitters is one that strongly opposes interoperability based solely on gateways and translation; instead, a common low-level protocol must be agreed upon by the interoperating ORBs. Once this agreement has been achieved and the ORBs can communicate, the high-level interoperability framework is used for correct interoperable behavior. The submission therefore details both a high-level conceptual framework and a low-level protocol based on the DCE Application Environment Specification (AES) (see Lockhart, 1994). The submission does not state that the low-level protocol must be DCE/AES. However, since the proposal does require a common low-level protocol, and since DCE both is emerging as an industry standard and is targeted for heterogeneous interoperability, it was chosen by the submitters as the first and possibly most common low-level protocol that will be used. The choice of DCE is also motivated by the experience accumulated by the submitting companies over the last couple of years. In this (as well as in many other areas) the proposal is very mature and well designed.

To be based on DCE, the submission must map CORBA concepts to DCE; in particular, it must map CORBA IDL to DCE IDL. The mapping provided by the proposal leverages existing DCE features to implement CORBA constructs. The mapping stresses a natural mapping, especially in the IDL mapping. For cases where DCE does not have features that can be used to implement CORBA constructs, the submission does two things: It specifies a wire-level implementation that does not directly rely on DCE, and it suggests how DCE can be extended to support a natural mapping of CORBA. These extensions have been submitted as Requests for Changes (RFCs) and will be considered by the OSF.

The CORBA-to-DCE mapping includes many layers. The fundamental layer is the use of DCE Remote Procedure Calls (RPCs) for CORBA messaging of requests and responses. The next layer provides a full mapping of CORBA IDL to DCE. Higher layers (in terms of functionality) include implementation of ways in which objects are located and support for object migration (these are functionalities that are used by the ORBs). Since DCE itself is layered on top of DCE RPCs, the mapping to DCE RPCs is natural. The DCE RPC mechanism is inherently interoperable, so its use automatically allows requests to be serviced by object implementations in different ORBs. DCE transfer syntax handles the issue of different byte ordering and alignment across machine boundaries.

Locating services are defined in the interoperability protocol to use the DCE Cell Directory Service (CDS). Object adapters are registered in CDS and can therefore be consistently located to allow for object activation. Locating issues are resolved partially by the use of object references. The proposal details two different representations for object references, one of them a lightweight representation that stresses efficiency and the other supporting complex functionality by maintaining more information. Each representation can provide different information that can be used by the locating service. If lightweight object references are not of utmost importance, an object reference representation can be used that stores information necessary for locating the OA.

The submission also details a mechanism that supports object migration. This mechanism will forward a request from the location from which the object has migrated to the new location of the object (if it is known). The issue of object migration was not specifically requested by the RFP, yet the submitters provided a full solution to the problem.

Finally, the submission proposes the use of authenticated RPCs using the Shared Secret Authentication Protocol of Kerberos in order to provide the underlying security services that will be defined by the OSTF.

Because of the complexity of DCE (see Lockhart, 1994) and the high detail level of the DCE-based interoperability proposal, this appendix can provide only a high-level view of the submission. The interested reader is referred to Andreas et al. (1994).

A.1   High-Level Protocol

The submission stresses the fact that the client's view of the distributed heterogeneous environment does not transcend the local ORB. This is necessary if distribution transparency is to be maintained. All object references seem to be part of the local ORB. Although the object reference structure remains opaque to the client, it may encompass additional information as required by the interoperability mechanisms, including locating information. Object references are defined using an interoperable format so that they may be stringified by one ORB and destringified by another. Once a request has been issued by the client, the ORB assumes control. The object implementation may be residing within the local ORB environment; this case is trivially handled by the ORB. However, the locating mechanism may determine that the object adapter and the object implementation reside within a foreign ORB. In this case, the two ORBs communicate the request using some pre-agreed-upon common low-level interoperability protocol. The remote object implementation services the request and returns a value using the same low-level protocol. In the proposal, DCE RPCs are used for this low-level protocol (see Fig. A.1).

In CORBA 1.1 the client and the implementation skeleton both use the same IDL specifications. This allows the client and the implementation to consistently communicate using the same set of interfaces, types, operations, and exceptions. For different ORB environments to be able to interoperate, the consistency of IDL must be extended across different ORBs. To do this, the participating ORBs must agree on what uniquely identifies a type, an operation, an exception, and an interface. This may be supported in the future by a common federated Interface Repository framework, but at present the submission addresses the issue by providing DCE identifiers. The submission introduces *globally annotated IDL* (GA-IDL) to identify types, operations, exceptions, and interfaces in the requests that are transmitted between the ORBs. This has the effect of producing a "global IDL file" that is the basis for ORBs understanding one another. The DCE-

Figure A.1   DCE-based ORB interoperability.

based proposal then defines that IDL annotations use DCE UUIDs to uniquely represent such a component. Operations are identified by a 2-tuple, the first element being the UUID attached to the interface that the operation is a part of and the second element being an operation index number within the interface.

A.2 Low-Level Protocol

Andreas et al. (1994) details a low-level interoperability protocol based on DCE. This is an example of a low-level protocol that can be used by the high-level framework. It is more than an example, however, since the submitters view DCE as a strategic technology that will be extensively used by the industry. The submitters accept that there will be other concrete low-level protocols (and that not everyone will standardize on DCE), but they assert that there will be a relatively small number of such protocols, making this approach, which stresses a common low-level protocol, feasible. Given the growing popularity of DCE, it is reasonable to expect that the DCE-based protocol will be widely used.

The DCE-based low-level protocol described in the submission provides a detailed specification on how DCE is used to facilitate the high-level interoperability protocol, including

- *Object references.* A detailed definition of the proposed object reference constructs is provided in DCE IDL. Both the lightweight and the "implementation spreading" object reference formats are provided. (See Andreas et al., 1994, pp. 35–38.)

- *IDL.* A mapping of CORBA language constructs and especially CORBA IDL to DCE IDL is provided. The mapping uses DCE RPCs to implement requests and responses. CORBA IDL is mapped to DCE IDL in a natural way, since they have many common constructs, and the NDR transfer syntax is used. (See Andreas et al., 1994, pp. 42–54.)

- *CORBA constructs.* Some CORBA constructs cannot be directly mapped to DCE AES. In these cases, the submission details a wire-level protocol as well as proposing an extension to DCE. Examples of these topics are user-defined exceptions, support for the any type, support for the Dynamic Invocation Interface, and interface inheritance.

- *Locating object adapters.* The submission defines operations such as MapToOA, which is used by clients to identify the OA to be used. This is often performed by inspecting information stored in the object reference; appropriate operations are supplied. A detailed algorithm for selecting the OA is also provided.

- *Object migration.* The submission specifies the low-level support for object migration. A "bread crumbs" approach (in which migrating object leaves information regarding its new location at the previous site) is used at the low-level protocol. This will support automatic request forwarding to the new location or the raising of the `BAD_OPERATION` exception if the location is not known.

A.3 Optional Interfaces

Finally, the submission details a set of IDL interfaces that support the interoperability framework. This set of interfaces is optional; i.e., the proposal does not require a vendor to use them. The interfaces provide support for such issues as negotiating a common protocol, object and OA location, and request messaging. The supplied interfaces are

- `InteroperableObject`. This is similar to the `CORBA::Object` interface and provides operations such as determining whether an object reference is null and retrieving a protocol from the object reference. This interface is not used by client applications but rather by the ORB itself.

- `InteroperableORBInterface`. This is used for accessing interoperating ORBs. It provides operations for externalizing and internalizing interoperating objects.

- `Protocol`. This is used for representing protocol information.

- `LocationService`. This provides access to the locating service. It is used by the client ORB when attempting to connect to an object and by the server ORBs to advertise object availability. It provides a `locate` operation used to locate an interoperable object.

- `Connection`. This is returned by the `locate` operation and maintains the logical connection to the interoperable object.

For more information regarding these interfaces, see Andreas et al. (1994, pp. 24–28).

B

Gateway-Based
Interoperability

This section describes the submission made by IONA Technologies and SunSoft Inc. to the ORB2.0 RFP (see Chap. 3). This submission details SunSoft's strategy for ORB interoperability and is based on functionality that exists in Project DOE and in Iona's ORBIX. This functionality was demonstrated at Object World in January 1994. The submission is based upon the interoperability strategy that will be present in Project DOE. It should be noted that even if the interoperability proposal that will be chosen by the ORB2.0 TF is different from SunSoft's strategy, the gateway approach described in this section will still be applicable, and apart from some additions to make it conform to the chosen proposal (e.g., adding a low-level protocol mapping), it will most probably still be the basis for interoperability under Project DOE. In fact, the gateway approach is probably the most generic approach and can therefore be used in almost any scenario.

Clients use object references for issuing requests to object implementations. Figure B.1 shows two ORB-based environments. Environment A includes a client (Client_1) holding a reference to an object implementation (Impl_1), and environment B includes a client (Client_2) holding a reference to an object implementation (Impl_2). Finally, we would like to be able to invoke an object implemented by Impl_3 from Client_3. The client is in a different ORB environment from the implementation. Interoperability of the two ORBs would allow Client_3 to hold a reference to Impl_3 and use it as if it were completely within the ORB A environment. Note that this does not just mean that it must be possible to convey the request between the environments. The reference to Impl_3 held by Client_3 must be created in the first place. Also, this setup must be recursively enabled; the request sent from Client_3, for example, may include (as argu-

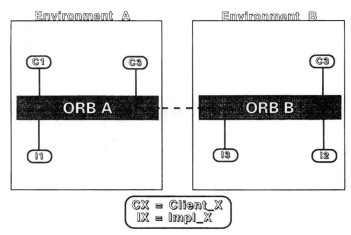

Figure B.1 Two ORB environments.

ments to the request) references to objects in the ORB A environment. Impl_3 may then invoke these objects' operations. Now Impl_3 becomes a client holding a reference to an object implementation in the external ORB environment.

SunSoft stresses interoperability without making any assumptions regarding ORB implementation. The approach does not make any assumptions regarding common protocol, implementation similarities, or any other restrictions. Instead, the solution uses a gateway approach that is built on ORB-independent interfaces. This is a central assumption in the SunSoft approach. It allows present ORBs (which will not agree on some common protocol, since they have already been implemented and deployed) to interoperate. It will also be more suitable for connecting ORBs that are used to solve different problems and that have extremely different characteristics. ORBs vary in request delivery time, security characteristics, scope, lifetime, and almost any other attribute. The ORB's role will grow tremendously in the future, as object systems will proliferate in the computing industry. The necessity for interoperability will also grow tremendously, not only because of the availability of ORBs from many different vendors with very different characteristics, but also because ORB boundaries will be purposely set up by organizations for security or management reasons. Therefore, SunSoft's view is that the interoperability approach must be as flexible as possible; hence the gateway approach.

B.1   Gateways

Figure B.2 shows the basic use of a gateway for interconnecting two ORBs. For every inter-ORB invocation, the gateway basically plays

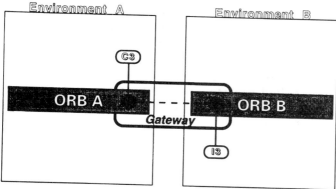

Figure B.2 Using a gateway to interconnect the environments.

the role of the object implementation in one ORB and the role of the client in the other ORB. When a request comes in to the proxy object in the ORB A environment, the gateway is responsible for performing the operation using the real object implementation in the ORB B environment. Note that the individual ORBs are totally unaware of gateways; ORBs are responsible for internal request management, whereas the gateways are solely responsible for connecting ORBs and forwarding requests. This implies that all performance-related issues, costs, and complexities are totally encapsulated within the gateway and do not affect intra-ORB functions.

The ability to have gateways connect arbitrary ORBs relies on three parts of the IONA/SunSoft approach. The first is the Dynamic Skeleton Interface, which provides a skeleton interface that will work on any object implementation (similar to the function played by the DII on the client's side). The second component is the Portable Request Translator (PORT), which actually performs the translation. Finally, higher-level agreement must be achieved so that requests in the different ORB environments will have identical semantic meaning. For example, the two IRs must have a common agreement as to the operations and interfaces.

B.2   The Dynamic Skeleton Interface

The Dynamic Skeleton Interface (DSI) is to the IDL skeleton what the DII is to the IDL stub. The DII is used when requests are to be issued for objects for which the interface was not known at compile time. The DSI is used to call methods for object implementations which were not known at compile time.

In standard CORBA methods, an object implementation is connected with a skeleton which activates the methods to service requests coming through the ORB and the Object Adapter. Each object type will have a different skeleton specially built to match the methods implemented. The DSI can replace the skeleton for any type. The DSI receives detailed specifications of the operation to be invoked as arguments. It includes only one routine, which gets called for any invocation [this routine is called the Dynamic Implementation Routine (DIR)]. This provides the capability of connecting a request to an object implementation without prior knowledge of the object type. In this respect it is similar to the use of the `perform:` messages in Smalltalk and Objective-C.

This information can then be propagated through the gateway to the other ORB environment. There the DII is used to call the object implementation, as shown in Fig. B.3. The DSI "processes" all incoming requests using the single DIR routine. The ServerRequest pseudo-object encapsulates the request invocation and is defined as

```
interface ServerRequest [
    readonly attribute Object target; // Typically a proxy object denot-
                                             ing the
                                      object in the foreign ORB.
    readonly attribute OperationSpec opspec; // This is a union which
                                      holds either the
                                      OperationDef or specific
                                      set or get
                                      defs to facilitate
                                      attribute access.
    readonly attribute Context ctx; // Context information for the oper-
                                      ation.
    readonly attribute NVList params; // The parameters named values
                                      list.
    readonly attribute NamedValue result; // The return value for the
                                      call.
```

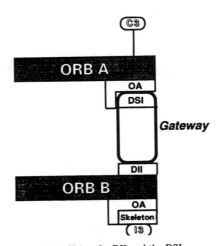

Figure B.3 Using the DII and the DSI.

The ServerRequest is analogous to the Request pseudo-object in the DII. After this invocation information is captured, a way to pass it to the DII in the other ORB environment must be defined; this is possible because of the PORT.

B.3 The Portable Request Translator

Having the DSI and the DII makes creating gateways possible. The major role to be played by the gateway then becomes the management of the translation process. This is handled in the IONA/SunSoft architecture by the Portable Request Translator. The PORT manages the creation of proxy state objects in two tables (shown in Fig. B.4). These entries serve as the implementation state and are used by the DSI. The proxies hold a reference to the "real" object implementation and forward incoming requests to that object using the DII in the foreign ORB.

Figure B.5 shows an example of a request sent by Client_1 to Impl_1 (on another ORB). The request has a parameter which is a reference to Impl_2 (which is in the same ORB environment as the client object). The invocation is propagated to the implementation in the ORB B environment using the DSI. The right half of the PORT causes the proxy to be created in the top right table. The invocation information is then forwarded to the DII, which creates the request in ORB B on the real object implementation. Since the request involves a reference to an object in the ORB A environment, a proxy state is created in the bottom left table in the left half of the PORT. When the DII invocation is being built, all references to objects in the ORB A

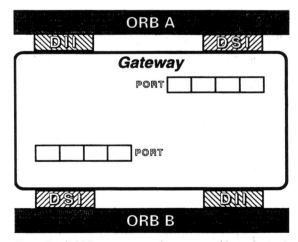

Figure B.4 PORT management of proxy state objects.

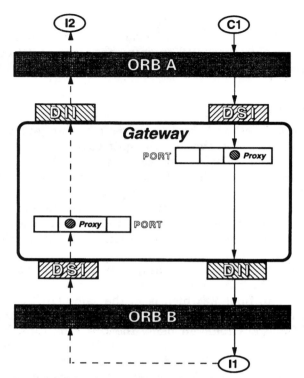

Figure B.5 Example request across ORB environments.

environment are replaced with such proxy objects in the ORB B environment. If the Impl_1 object now invokes a request using Object_2, it will be propagated using the proxy, the DSI, the PORT, and the DII, all in the opposite direction. The architecture is therefore completely symmetrical and consistent.

B.4   Interoperability Conventions

The gateway approach (or any other interoperability approach, for that matter) does not ensure interoperability. Interoperability can be achieved only through higher-level agreements and conventions that are adhered to by all components in the architecture. It is similar to the agreement needed regarding area codes in telephone numbers. Having a connection from London to any city in the United States will not enable communication if the person in London has no knowledge of U.S. area codes (assuming, for example, that the 7-digit number is available). Thus, for example, if the interfaces of the ORB B environment in Fig. B.1 are unknown to clients in the ORB A environment, no requests can ever be generated and no proxy objects created. The proposal therefore identifies a number of issues that must be addressed when contemplating interoperability. These include making the BOA interface consistent with regard to object binding and specification, completion of platform-specific details, security, simplification of the DII interfaces, and matching of the IRs in the different ORB environments.

References

Agha, G. H., *Actors: A Model of Concurrent Computation in Distributed Systems*, MIT Press, 1987.

Aho, A. V., E. Hopcroft, and J. D. Ullman, *Data Structures and Algorithm*, Addison-Wesley, 1985.

——— and J. D. Ullman, *Principles of Compiler Design*, Addison-Wesley, 1977.

Andleigh, P. K., and M. R. Gratzinger, *Distributed Object-Oriented Data-Systems Design*, Prentice-Hall, 1992.

Andreas, W. S., ed., *Object Services RFP 2*, The Object Management Group, OMG Technical Committee Document number 93-6-1, 1993a.

———, ed., *Revised IDL C++ Mapping (Hyperdesk)*, The Object Management Group, OMG Technical Committee Document number 93-11-5, 1993b.

———, ed., *Hyperdesk C++ Language Mapping: Example Code*, The Object Management Group, OMG Technical Committee Document number 93-12-25, 1993c.

———, F. Campagnoni, N. Jacobson, P. Pedersen, C. Soeder, and D. Vines, *ORB 2.0 RFP Submission: Interoperability and Initialization (DEC, HP, Hyperdesk, IBM, NEC, OSF)*, The Object Management Group, OMG Technical Committee Document number 94-3-5, 1994.

Barak, A., and R. Ben-Natan, "Bounded Contractions of Full Trees," *Journal of Parallel and Distributed Computing*, **17**, 1993.

Beeri, C., P. A. Bernstein, and N. Goodman, "A Model for Concurrency in Nested Transaction Systems," *Journal of the ACM*, **36**(2), 1989.

Ben-Natan, R., *Graph Contractions as a Model for Concurrency,* Hebrew University of Jerusalem, Ph.D. Thesis, 1992.

——— and A. Barak, "Parallel Contraction of Grids for Task Assignment to Processor Networks," *Networks*, **22**, 1992.

Black, A., N. Hutchinson, E. Jul, H. Levy, and L. Carter, "Distribution and Abstract Types in Emerald," *IEEE Transactions on Software Engineering*, **13**(1), 1987.

Borghoff, U. M., *Catalogue of Distributed File Operating Systems*, Springer-Verlag, 1992.

Borning, A., and D. Ingalls, "Multiple Inheritance in Smalltalk-80," National Conference on Artificial Intelligence AAAI-82, Miami, Florida, 1982.

Booch, G., *Object-Oriented Design with Applications*, Benjamin/Cummings, 1991.

Brockschmidt, K., *Inside OLE2*, Microsoft Press, 1994.

C Language Mapping, The Object Management Group, OMG Technical Committee Document number 93-6-4, 1993.

Cattell, R. G. G., *Object Data Management*, Addison-Wesley, 1992.

———, ed., *The Object Database Standard: ODMG93*. Morgan Kauffman, 1994.

Ceri, S., and G. Pellagotti, *Distributed Databases: Principles and Systems*, McGraw-Hill, 1984.

Chang, D., J. Eastman, T. Gorchs, and G. Lewis, *Relationship Service Submission (Bull, HP, Olivetti, IBM, SNI, SunSoft),* The Object Management Group, OMG Technical Committee Document number 94-5-5, 1994.

Cobb, E., ed., *Revised Transaction Submission*—Chapter 5, The Object Management Group, OMG Technical Committee Document number 94-8-7, 1994.

Codd, E. F., "Extending the Database Relational Model," *ACM Transactions on Database Systems*, **4**, 1979.

Cole, R., "A Model for Security in Distributed Systems," *Computers and Security*, **9**(4), 1990.

Conner, M., and S. Elliot, *A Brief Introduction to SOM: The System Object Model*, The Object Management Group, OMG Technical Committee Document number 91-5-13, 1991.

Coplien, J. O., *Advanced C++ Programming Styles and Idioms*, Addison-Wesley, 1991.

Curtis, D., *ORB 2.0 RFP Submission: Interoperability and Initialization (Expersoft)*, The Object Management Group, OMG Technical Committee Document number 94-3-6, 1994.

Digital Equipment Corporation, *DEC ACA Services: System Integrator and Programmer*, 1992a.

——, *DEC ACA Services: Reference Manual*, 1992b.

——, *DEC ACA Services: Using ACA Services on Microsoft Windows*, 1992c.

——, *ObjectBroker Overview and Glossary*, 1994a.

——, *ObjectBroker System Integrator's Guide*, 1994b.

——, *The Guide to CORBA*, 1994c.

——, *ObjectBroker Migration Guide*, 1994d.

Douglas, C. E., and D. L. Stevens, *Internetworking with TCP/IP, Vol. 3, Client Server Programming and Applications*, Prentice-Hall, 1993.

Eastman, J., "The HP Distributed Smalltalk IDL Language Binding," *The Smalltalk Report*, **3**(3), 1993.

Ege, R. K., *Programming in an Object-Oriented Environment*, AP Professional, 1992.

Ellis, M. A., and B. Stroustrup, *The Annotated C++ Reference Manual*, Addison-Wesley, 1990.

EXODUS Storage Manager Architectural Overview, University of Wisconsin—Madison, 1991.

Fairthorne, B., ed., *Security White Paper*, The Object Management Group, OMG Technical Committee Document number 94-4-16, 1994.

Goldberg, A., and B. Robson, *Smalltalk-80: The Language and Its Implementation*, Addison-Wesley, 1983.

Gorlen, K. E., S. M. Orlow, and P. S. Plexico, *Data Abstraction and Object-Oriented Programming in C++*, Wiley, 1990.

Gourhant, Y., and M. Shapiro, "FOG/C++: A Fragmented-Object Generator" *Proceedings of the C++ Conference*, San Francisco, April, 1990.

Gray, P. M., K. G. Kulkarni, and N. W. Paton, *Object-Oriented Databases*, Prentice-Hall, 1992.

Hewlett-Packard, *HP Distributed Smalltalk User's Guide*, 1993a.

——, *HP Distributed Smalltalk Reference Guide*, 1993b.

Holt, N., *ORB 2.0 RFP Submission: Interoperability and Initialization (ICL)*, The Object Management Group, OMG Technical Committee Document number 94-3-3, 1994.

Houston, I., ed., *Revised Object Transaction Service Proposal*, The Object Management Group, OMG Technical Committee Document number 94-8-4, 1994.

Hughes, J. G., *Object-Oriented Databases*, Prentice-Hall, 1991.

IBM, *SOMObjects Developer Toolkit User's Guide*, 1993a.

——, *SOMObjects Developer Toolkit Emitter Framework Guide and Reference*, 1993b.

Jacobson, N., ed., *ORB2.0 RFP Submission: Interface Repository (DEC, HP)*, The Object Management Group, OMG Technical Committee Document number 94-5-3, 21994.

Johnson, R. E., "Type Checking Smalltalk," *Proceedings of the Conference on Object-Oriented Programming Systems, Languages, and Applications*, 1986.

Joint Object Services Submission: Naming Service, The Object Management Group, OMG Technical Committee Document number 93-5-2, 1993a.

Joint Object Services Submission: Persistence Service, The Object Management Group, OMG Technical Committee Document number 93-5-5, 1993b.

Joint Object Services Submission: Overview, The Object Management Group, OMG Technical Committee Document number 93-7-1, 1993c.

Joint Object Services Submission: Event Service, The Object Management Group, OMG Technical Committee Document number 93-7-3, 1993d.

Joint Object Services Submission: Life Cycle Service, The Object Management Group, OMG Technical Committee Document number 93-7-4, 1993e.

Joint Object Service Specification: Compound Life Cycle Addendum, The Object Management Group, OMG Technical Committee Document number 94-5-6, 1994.

Jul, E., H. Levy, N. Hutchinson, and A. Black, "Fine-Grained Mobility in the Emerald System," *ACM Transactions on Computer Systems*, **6**(1), 1988.

Katin, N., ed., *Common Facilities RFP 1 Draft*, The Object Management Group, OMG Technical Committee Document number 94-8-6, 1994.

Kessler, P. B., *IDL C++ Mapping (Iona, NEC, SunSoft): Ease of Use Layering*, The Object Management Group, OMG Technical Committee Document number 93-12-2, 1993.

Khoshafian, S., *Object-Oriented Databases*, John Wiley and Sons, 1993.

Kim, W., *Introduction to Object-Oriented Databases*, MIT Press, 1991.

———, "Observations on the ODMG-93 Proposal for an Object-Oriented Database Language," *SIGMOD RECORD*, col. 23, no. 1, March 1994.

Kukura, B., ed., *ORB2.0 RFP Submission for the Interface Repository (DEC, HP, SunSoft)*, The Object Management Group, OMG Technical Committee Document number 94-8-3, 1994.

LaLonde, W. R., and J. R. Pugh, *Inside Smalltalk*, vols. 1 and 2, Prentice-Hall, 1991.

Lewis, G., ed., *Object Services Roadmap (Final Draft)*, The Object Management Group, OMG Technical Committee Document number 92-8-5, 1992.

———, ed., *Object Services RFP 1 (Final Draft)*, The Object Management Group, OMG Technical Committee Document number 93-8-6, 1993a.

———, ed., *Revised IDL C++ Mapping (Iona, NEC, SunSoft)*, The Object Management Group, OMG Technical Committee Document number 93-11-6, 1993b.

———, ed., *ORB 2.0 RFP Submission: Interoperability (IONA, SunSoft)*, The Object Management Group, OMG Technical Committee Document number 94-3-1, 1994a.

———, ed., *ORB 2.0 RFP Submission: Initialization (IONA, SunSoft)*, The Object Management Group, OMG Technical Committee Document number 94-3-2, 1994b.

———, ed., *Object Services RFP 4*, The Object Management Group, OMG Technical Committee Document number 94-4-18, 1994c.

———, ed., *ORB2.0 RFP Submission: Interface Repository (SunSoft)*, The Object Management Group, OMG Technical Committee Document number 94-5-2, 1994d.

Liskov, B., "Distributed Programming in Argus", *Communications of the ACM*, **31**(3), 1988.

———, L. Shira, and J. Wroclawski, "Efficient At-Most-Once Messages Based on Synchronous Clocks," *ACM Transactions on Computer Systems*, **9**(2), 1991.

Litwin, W., L. Mark, and N. Roussopoulos, "Interoperability of Multiple Autonomous Databases", *ACM Computing Surveys*, **22**(3), 1990.

Lockhart, H. W., Jr., *OSF DCE*, McGraw-Hill, 1994

Martin, B., ed., *Revised Externalization Service*, The Object Management Group, OMG Technical Committee Document number 94-6-21, 1994.

McCoy, K., ed., *Object Services RFP 3: Security and Time Synchronization*, The Object Management Group, OMG Technical Committee Document number 94-7-1, 1994.

Mischkinsky, J., ed., *ORB 2.0 Extensions RFI*, The Object Management Group, OMG Technical Committee Document number 92-12-10, 1992.

Moss, J. E. B., *Nested Transactions: An Approach to Reliable Distributed Computing*, MIT Press, 1985.

Mueller, P., ed., *Initial Smalltalk Mapping Submission (HP, IBM)*, The Object Management Group, OMG Technical Committee Document number 94-8-1, 1994a.

———, ed., *Issues Regarding the HP/IBM Initial Smalltalk Submission*, The Object Management Group, OMG Technical Committee Document number 94-8-5, 1994b.

NeXT Computer, *IDL Objective-C Language Mapping*, The Object Management Group, OMG Technical Committee Document number 93-6-4, 1993.

NeXTSTEP Object-Oriented Programming and the Objective-C Language, NeXTSTEP Developer's Library Release 3, NeXT Computer, Inc., Addison-Wesley, 1993.

Nichol, J., M. Howard, and T. Roberts, *ORB 2.0 RFP Submission: Interoperability and Initialization (BNR)*, The Object Management Group, OMG Technical Committee Document number 94-3-4, 1994.

Nitzberg, W., and V. Lo, "Distributed Shared Memory: A Survey of Issues and Algorithms," *Computer*, **24**(8), 1991.

Obin, R., *Issues for Object-Oriented COBOL IDL Mapping*, The Object Management Group, OMG Technical Committee Document number 94-4-3, 1994.

The Object Management Group, *Object Management Architecture Guide*, 1992a.

The Object Management Group, *The Common Object Request Broker: Architecture and Specification, Revision 1.2*, 1993.

The Object Management Group and X/Open, *The Common Object Request Broker: Architecture and Specification, Revision 1.1*, John Wiley and Sons, 1992b.

O'Neil, P. E., "The Escrow Transactional Method," *ACM Transactions on Database Systems*, **11**(4), 1986.

Ozsu, M. T., U. Dayal, and P. Valduries, eds., *Distributed Object Management*, Morgan Kauffman, 1994.

ParcPlace Systems, *ObjectWorks Smalltalk User's Guide*, 1992a.

ParcPlace Systems, *VisualWorks User's Guide*, 1992b.

Porter, H. H., III, "Separating the Subtype Hierarchy from the Inheritance of Implementation," *Journal of Object-Oriented Programming*, February 1992.

Powell, M. L., *IDL C++ Mapping (Iona, NEC, SunSoft): Rationale Supplement*, The Object Management Group, OMG Technical Committee Document number 93-12-1, 1993.

Rumbaugh, J., M. Blaha, W. Premerlani, F. Eddy, and W. Lorensen, *Object-Oriented Modeling and Design*, Prentice-Hall, 1991.

Sape, M., ed., *Distributed Systems*, Frontier Series, ACM Press, 1993.

Schelvis, M., and E. Bledoeg, "The Implementation of a Distributed Smalltalk," *European Conference on Object-Oriented Programming 1988*, Springer.

Shapiro, M., "Structure and Encapsulation in Distributed Systems: The Proxy Principle," *Proceedings of the 6th International Conference on Distributed Computer Systems*, 1986.

———, P. Gautron, and L. Mosseri, "Persistence and Migration for C++ Objects," *European Conference on Object-Oriented Programming 1989*, Springer.

Shlaer, S., *Object-Oriented Systems Analysis*, Yourdon Press, 1988.

Shriver, B., and P. Wegner, eds., *Research Directions in Object-Oriented Programming*, MIT Press, 1987.

Siegel, J., ed., *Common Object Service Specification, Volume 1*, The Object Management Group, John Wiley and Sons, 1994.

Soley, R., ed., *ORB 2.0 C++ Language Mapping RFP*, The Object Management Group, OMG Technical Committee Document number 92-12-11, 1992.

———, ed., *Policies and Procedures of the OMG TC*, The Object Management Group, OMG Technical Committee Document number 94-4-14, 1994.

Stankovic, J. A., "Software Communication Mechanisms: Procedure Calls versus Messages," *Computer*, **15**(4), 1982.

Stevens, W. R., *Unix Network Programming*, Prentice-Hall, 1990.

Teknekron Software Systems, *TIB API Programmer's Reference Manual*, 1994.

Thompson, C., ed., *Object Services Architecture (6.0)*, The Object Management Group, OMG Technical Committee Document number 92-8-4, 1992.

Ungar, D., and F. Jackson, "Tenuring Policies for Generation Based Storage Reclamation," *Proceedings of the Converence on Object-Oriented Programming Systems, Languages, and Applications*, 1988.

Vanderbilt, P., and LiWen Chen, *IDL C++ Mapping (Iona, NEC, SunSoft): Usage Examples*, The Object Management Group, OMG Technical Committee Document number 93-12-3, 1993.

Vinoski, S., *Comments on the Revised C++ Mapping Submissions*, The Object Management Group, OMG Technical Committee Document number 93-12-19, 1993.

———, ed., *IDL C++ Language Mapping Specification*, The Object Management Group, OMG Technical Committee Document number 94-8-2, 1994.

Watson, A., ed., *ORB 2.0 RFP for Interoperability and Initialization Extensions*, The Object Management Group, OMG Technical Committee Document number 93-9-15, 1993a.

———, ed., *ORB Architecture*, The Object Management Group, OMG Technical Committee Document number 93-7-2, 1993b.

———, ed., *ORB 2.0 Interface Repository RFP*, The Object Management Group, OMG Technical Committee Document number 93-9-16, 1993c.

———, ed., *Smalltalk RFP*, The Object Management Group, OMG Technical Committee Document number 93-12-21, 1993d.

———, ed., *ORB 2.0 RFP for the C++ Language Mapping*, The Object Management Group, OMG Technical Committee Document number 94-4-10, 1994.

Weber, B., ed., *ORB RFI*, The Object Management Group, OMG Technical Committee Document number 90-6-5, 1990.

Wilkinson, K., P. Lyngbaek, and W. Hasan, "The Iris Architecture and Implementation," *IEEE Transactions on Knowledge and Data Engineering* **2**(1), 1990.

Wilson, P. R., "Opportunistic Garbage Collection," *SIGPLAN Notices*, **23**(12), 1988.

Wirfs-Brock, R., B. Wilkerson, and L. Wiener, *Designing Object-Oriented Software*, Prentice-Hall, 1990.

Yonezawa, A., and M. Tokoro, *Object Oriented Concurrent Programming*, MIT Press, 1987.

Index

ABOUT THE AUTHOR

Ron Ben-Natan, Ph.D. is co-founder and Vice-President for Development at Entity, Inc. in Tel Aviv, Israel. He has extensive involvement in object-oriented technologies and distributed systems. He has served as a consultant to such companies as Merrill Lynch and J.P. Morgan in New York City.

ABOUT THE SERIES

The J. Ranade Workstation Series is McGraw-Hill's primary vehicle for providing workstation professionals with timely concepts, solutions, and applications. Jay Ranade is also Series Editor in Chief of more than 150 books in the J. Ranade IBM and DEC Series and Series Advisor to the McGraw-Hill Series on Computer Communications.

Jay Ranade, Series Editor in Chief and best-selling computer author, is a consultant and Assistant V.P. at Merrill Lynch.